IRAQ

its people its society its culture

George L. Harris

IN COLLABORATION WITH

Moukhtar Ani

Mildred C. Bigelow

John Cookson

Sheila C. Gillen

George A. Lipsky

Charles H. Royce

HRAF PRESS *New Haven*

Already Published in this Series

1 POLAND

2 JORDAN

LIBRARY OF CONGRESS CATALOG CARD NUMBER: 58–14179

MANUFACTURED IN THE UNITED STATES OF AMERICA

PREFACE

PERHAPS at no other time has so much been written about the different peoples of the world. While there remain critical areas of ignorance about motivation and behavior, the dynamics of society, culture and its power, there do exist quantities of recorded observations and information, and of highly detailed analyses of this or that aspect of life as it is lived by given groups. Observations, information, analysis—all usually are scattered, available but separate. The books of this series represent an endeavor to gather and interpret the separate pieces. The series itself proceeds from an earlier group of studies—the Country Series—issued experimentally in limited quantity to discover what needs they might fill and how they might be improved. The series will present works on representative societies in each major culture area of the world.

This, then, is a different kind of book in that it is concerned with the relationship of aspects usually studied separately. The focus of the book is a society as it functions, the interrelationship of its parts and of the parts to the whole. Emphasis is on the dynamics of that interplay, on constants of attitude and behavior, abiding values, the presence and impact of forces for change. Containing a great deal of information, and thus useful as a reference, it is not merely a collection of data. Covering the political, economic, and sociological aspects of a society, it presents no minute analysis of any element within these categories. It asserts as valid only what has stood up to the simultaneous and systematic challenge of the various social science disciplines represented by the authors. Most of the source materials will be found listed under Recommended Reading.

Much that has remained implicit in previous separate studies is here made explicit, and should generate controversy. In the course of challenging the available materials, and consequent selection, generalization, and implication, many gaps in knowledge have been exposed.

In some cases it has been possible to indicate the general outline and probable significance of such gaps, and this should be useful as a guide to further exploration. These are, in short, books out of which should come many questions. That there may also come some increased understanding of the seemingly endless and confusing diversity of ways by which men approach the experience of living with one another is the wish of all who have participated in the making of the series.

Thomas Fitzsimmons

Washington, D. C.

ACKNOWLEDGMENTS

PUBLICATION of this study, and of the series, is possible because many individuals gave unstintingly of time, talent, critical and creative energy. Review procedures designed to tap all the resources of the HRAF research staff as well as those of outside specialists were supervised by Dr. Herbert H. Vreeland, who read and commented upon each chapter as it was drafted. Mr. Percy Winner, of the senior staff, rendered especially valuable assistance to Dr. Vreeland and to the Editor.

The authors had the use of working papers prepared under contract at the School of Advanced International Studies of the Johns Hopkins University by Professor Majid Khadduri. Professor George L. Trager, University of Buffalo, provided basic linguistic materials and analysis. Miss Charlotte M. Morehouse, regional specialist, contributed valuable information and suggestions. The work also benefited from the criticisms of Dr. Doris G. Adams, College of Business Administration, Department of Economics, The Pennsylvania State University, who read most of the manuscript. Information on village life in southern Iraq was supplied by Mr. Malcolm H. Quint, currently engaged in field study in that area.

While these and many others contributed to the Iraq study, whatever shortcomings it may have are the sole responsibility of its authors and the Editor.

THE HUMAN RELATIONS AREA FILES

THE HUMAN RELATIONS AREA FILES is a nonprofit research corporation affiliated with Yale University and sponsored and supported by its sixteen member universities. HRAF was established in 1949 "to collect, organize, and distribute information of significance to the natural and social sciences and the humanities." It has concentrated upon furthering a fresh approach to the study of societies, culture, and social behavior.

The files themselves contain carefully selected sources analyzed according to G. P. Murdock's *Outline of Cultural Materials.* Located at each of the member universities, they are a new kind of reference library in which basic information about nearly two hundred peoples can be consulted with ease and speed. Preparation of the present study was facilitated by the use of the Middle East File and the Iraq File.

MEMBER UNIVERSITIES

University of Chicago
University of Colorado
Cornell University
Harvard University
University of Hawaii
Indiana University
State University of Iowa
University of Michigan
University of North Carolina
University of Oklahoma
University of Pennsylvania
Princeton University
University of Southern California
University of Utah
University of Washington
Yale University

AUTHORS' NOTE

ON July 14, 1958 a "free officers" group, led by Brigadier General Abdul el-Kassem, seized power in Baghdad, proclaiming the end of the monarchy and the establishment of a republic. King Faisal, Crown Prince Abdul Ilah, the former Regent, and Prime Minister Nuri as-Said were killed; in a brief outburst of anti-western rioting, the British Embassy was sacked and burned and an English officer and two Americans were killed.

The military group acted quickly, installing a council of state and a cabinet with General Kassem as Premier and Foreign Minister. The capacity of the new regime to organize and maintain control was quickly demonstrated. Among the first acts of the new leaders were recognition of the United Arab Republic, and withdrawal from the Arab Union, the barely launched federation of Iraq and neighboring Jordan. The coup was justified as the liberation of Iraq "from the domination of a corrupt group which was installed by imperialism to lull the people." In the weeks that followed, however, the regime seemed to desire continued friendly relations with the West, and indicated an intention to honor most existing international commitments.

It is too early to assess the struggles that might be in the making within the ranks of those now in power or to forecast the outcome of so recent a revolution, but some things are clear. The coup ended a political regime; it did not alter a scheme of society and culture which largely shaped the character of the old government—and contributed to the manner of its passing. The new regime, military in leadership and republican in form, can no more escape the imperatives of the human and cultural setting of which it is a part than could the monarchy. Iraq's new leaders have committed themselves to a sweeping program of social change, but the present significance and long-range prospects of that program can be evaluated only in terms of the needs, values, and goals of a society which, though changing, is the resistant product of long human experience in a particular region.

Iraq, new as a nation, is old as a center of civilization. The problem of what in the culture is specifically Iraqi and what broadly Arab is posed not only to the outside observer but to Iraqis themselves. The July coup brought to power a group of men, themselves of varied backgrounds, who clearly spoke for a large part of the country's small but growing middle class in declaring their friendship for President Nasser of Egypt and hence for a version of Pan-Arabism which deprecates any concept of nationality among Arabs other than that of a general Arab nationality. That outlook, however, is less attractive to many among Iraq's large Kurdish minority who cling with sensitive pride to their own ethnic tradition. The foreign policy of the monarchy, which allied Iraq with the western powers and the "Northern Tier," non-Arab states of the Baghdad Pact, represented a concern with specifically Iraqi national interest that contrasts with the Pan-Arab pronouncements of the present regime. This, too, reflects the viewpoint of vociferous elements in the new middle class whose anti-western sentiments perhaps stem not only from real or fancied injuries at the hands of the West, but from a frustrated sense that the bulk of material benefits derived from association with it have been the prerogative of a small ruling elite. On the other hand, Iraq's natural wealth in oil and water has enabled it to undertake a large-scale program of economic development that, as it proceeds, enlarges the vested interest of Iraqis in a future shaped, if not seen, in national rather than generalized Arab terms. The outcome of this intensified conflict between loyalty to this or that conception of the Arab world and to Iraq as a nation cannot be foretold, but that conflict is the central drama in Iraq today.

CONTENTS

Contents (*continued*)

LIST OF MAPS

LIST OF TABLES

IRAQ

1

THE CULTURE AND THE SOCIETY

THE BREAKUP OF THE OTTOMAN EMPIRE IN WORLD WAR I marked the end of a regime which for four hundred years had loosely governed most of the Arab lands from the Iranian border to North Africa. Such unity as the area knew was that of Arab culture, Arabic speech, and Moslem religion—elements which prevailed within a context of local and regional isolation, economic depression, and social stagnation. The several Turkish provinces which now constitute Iraq fully shared in that historical experience.

Iraq is in the third decade of independence. After World War I it had ten years of political tutelage as a British mandate. In these forty years—little more than a generation—the country has undergone processes of change less apparent, perhaps, on the surface of the people's lives than in what they signify for the future. Casual inspection reveals circumstances of life which, for the majority, seem not to have changed much during many centuries. Impoverished peasants working by traditional methods land they do not own; tribal pastoralists on the desert fringes; town dwellers divided by extremes of wealth and poverty and isolated by their urban concerns from the rural mass; a ruling elite not hesitating to apply repressive measures to perpetuate its power—this picture is very old. Some things are visibly new: great dams and barrages on the Tigris and Euphrates; motor roads, railways, oil pipelines, factories; many other indications of western influence in social behavior, political forms, technology, dress, and housing. The social innovations are most striking in the cities, but some have reached into the countryside and desert; all to one degree or another influence the people's lives. Most significant, however, are the changes which are not visible—changes in thought and feeling, especially as these concern the ways in which men relate to each other and their image of themselves in that relationship. The western impact in this century has not only presented Iraqis with new ideas and material techniques, it has set in motion internal forces which, however slowly and unevenly, are remaking the social order itself.

The Changing Political Order

The degree and direction of change in human affairs is easier to measure in some spheres than in others. Formal political changes in Iraq since establishment of the British Mandate stand in sharp contrast to any known before. The British introduced western models of political administration and a concept of the sovereign nation-state. In the nearly six thousand years of recorded history along the Tigris and Euphrates there had been tribes and tribal confederations, cities and leagues of cities; at times the region had been the seat of empire, as during the height of Arab power in the Middle Ages, or a portion of empire, as under the Ottomans; but there had never been the nation, Iraq.

Certain factors gave human existence on the Mesopotamian valley-plain a distinctiveness that made the area something more than a geographic expression and that provided a base for political and national identification. Among the rain-starved Arab lands, Iraq is set apart by the dependable water supply of its two great rivers. Mesopotamia, like the Nile valley, was one of the earliest centers of high civilization, and the agriculturally-based but urban-centered structure of power which developed there contrasts with the less articulated forms of the deserts, arid plains, and mountains of most of the rest of the Middle East. Foreign conquerors came and went and the people on the Tigris and Euphrates lost the conscious memory—revived in our time by archeological research—of their past, but they did not lose the basic imprint of a culture deriving some of its characteristic forms from the continuing effort to control and utilize the water of the rivers. While Iraq shares deeply in the generalized Arab tradition which spread over the Middle East after the Moslem conquest, it also has a distinct identity derived from the physical fact of the river system and a long continuity of history.

The British joined to this identity the forms and apparatus of a modern state—specifically a constitutional monarchy—and by 1932, the year of independence, a sizable minority of the people, including a ruling elite, had a vested interest in the new order. They had come to think of themselves not only as Arabs, Moslems, or members of some other traditional group, but as "Iraqis."

The nation has by no means affected all Iraqis alike. Constitutional franchise means little to the illiterate majority. Villagers, nomads, and the poor of the cities have had long experience of government as a tax-collecting agency and a punishing authority; they are more concerned to evade its notice than to deal with it as a representative institution. With the spread of modern education, however, more and more Iraqis are being involved in the workings of the government, either directly as members of the official apparatus or indirectly as persons with conscious political ideas about how and toward what ends government should operate.

New ideologies, ranging from the conservative nationalism of the elite to the communist predilections of some of the urban intelligentsia and industrial workers, compete for the allegiance of such people. But much as the points of view may differ, they have in common a secular orientation that contrasts with the religious cast of traditional Moslem thought. Historically in Islam the organization and management of human affairs were seen in the context of a divine dispensation that obscured any distinction between the secular and the religious. The social or political act was also a religious act; it was not for men to make their destiny but to recognize and accept it as preordained by God. Islam in Iraq, as elsewhere in the Middle East, still powerfully holds its followers, but for a growing number it is becoming less sufficient as an explanation and guide in the problems of social and political life.

This shift in focus is reflected in the search for new controlling ideas; because such formulations have social consequences, new loyalties and patterns of human organization also are developing. Nationalism, Pan-Arabism, democratic ideals, "anti-imperialism," "neutralism," socialist schemes, and communist dogma—all provide banners around which a younger generation, as in other Arab countries, is rallying today; it is this swirl of thought, feeling, and activity that constitutes the Middle Eastern "ferment" of our time.

There is tension, both regional and international, and although the important decisions in both foreign and domestic policy are made by a few men with little regard for popular opinion, the issues presented provide emotion-laden symbols for an increasing number of politically articulate citizens. Determined to enforce acquiescence but less concerned to attract public support, the government is widely, if cautiously, criticized as subservient to the West in the cold war, as soft on the question of Israel, as disloyal to the cause of Arab unity propounded by and given expression in the form of the United Arab Republic under the leadership of President Nasser of Egypt. The situation has its dangers for the Iraqi leadership and for the security of the state, but it also illustrates the way in which Iraqis are being drawn out of the narrowly local preoccupations of the past and propelled into a larger world.

For nearly two decades the hand of one man, General Nuri as-Said, has guided the affairs of the country. Committed to a program of long-range economic development, conscious of communism as a threat, and convinced that the national interest is best served by a policy of cooperation with the West and with Arab and non-Arab neighbors alike, he has been impatient of domestic criticism and has not hesitated to employ the police power of the state to enforce his policies. Whatever may be the ultimate outcome of those policies, they are giving a national and political cast to a society which a generation ago knew little more than the restricted politics of town, village, tribe, ethnic group, and religious sect.

The absence of a secure national consensus about the meaning and worth of the relatively new constitutional order, together with the traditional views of the ruling group, has permitted the government to interpret the guarantees of the Constitution so broadly as to prohibit political parties altogether and to make extensive use of police power to curb opposition activities of any kind. The consequence is a contradictory attitude toward what constitutes disloyalty to the state. On the one hand, almost any political opposition, including that of persons fully committed to the constitutional order, runs the risk of being treated as treasonable; on the other, the very breadth of the official definition of disloyalty tends to deprive the term of specific moral connotation in the community at large.

Economic and Technological Change

Economically Iraq continues to be an agricultural country. The work methods and tools of its peasant majority and the aspect of its villages, rural marketplaces, and nomadic camps reflect a mode of existence that has changed very little over the centuries. But change is occurring here too, perhaps the most significant resulting from technological and economic developments which seem remote from the poverty-stricken regimen of rural Iraqi life. Two things—oil wealth and modern engineering knowledge—have made possible a vast governmental program of dam and canal building that promises to revolutionize Iraqi agriculture and create the basis for the growth of industry. That promise has hardly begun to be realized, but as more water becomes available and more land is reclaimed the opportunity is created for converting the landless fellah into an independent farmer. The authorities have been slow to match their ambitious program of irrigation engineering with a related program of social rehabilitation, but something is beginning to be done in this direction. Such prospects, by rousing hopes, inevitably also create dissatisfaction with the present. Increasing numbers of peasants are drifting off the land to seek wage employment in the cities or on the great construction projects. Once there they may or may not better their economic circumstances, but they learn new skills and are exposed to social and political influences which decisively separate them from their village background.

The sharpest impact of technological change has been felt in the cities, where an educated segment of the population has been drawn into the specialized occupations and professions learned from the West. These individuals—doctors, lawyers, journalists, teachers, government administrators, business managers, engineers, and others—have by the nature of their training been brought to question or reject many of the traditional assumptions of the old social order. The ruling elite also has come under new influences in the course of exercising its power to command these new skills and to employ them for social and political purposes. The general urban population, for its part, provides the workers, who are developing wants and needs more nearly like those of their western counterparts than of the traditional Middle Eastern handicraftsmen.

Iraq participates in world commerce and finance as a producer of agricultural raw materials and oil and as a recipient of financial and technical aid from Great Britain and the United States. Other regional arrangements also give it economic ties with its Arab and non-Arab neighbors. These relationships imply a whole series of major changes: the introduction of a cash economy, modern banking and credit institutions, a national structure of taxation and public finance, commercial farming, new-scale business organizations, tariff policies, export-import regulations, and government partnership with foreign governments and private entrepreneurs in the development and exploitation of national resources. The subsistence production and barter patterns of the past still predominate in much of the countryside, and traditional Moslem attitudes toward money and the taking of interest have slowed the growth of credit institutions. The new sources and kinds of wealth, however, are remaking economic roles in the society: from old-fashioned merchant to modern wholesaler and retailer, from master craftsman to factory owner, from traditional landlord to commercial farmer, from peasant sharecropper to independent cultivator or wage laborer, from city artisan to industrial worker. This process is hardly more than a trend today, but it is slowly altering men's relationships to each other, their personal and social values.

The Remaking of Society

Change has taken place within a social environment that shares the main characteristics recognizable throughout the Middle East. In the past a small urban-dwelling elite held most of the agricultural land in absentee ownership and almost exclusively enjoyed the prerogatives of wealth, political power, and traditional education. Lower on the urban scale were the principal merchants and the wealthiest master craftsmen. Below all these were the urban poor and the peasantry of the countryside. On the margins of the cultivated area were the nomads, whose pastoral way of life, tribal identity, and warlike propensities set them apart from the settled sector of society.

Ethnic and religious diversity complicated these ecological divisions. In Iraq, non-Arabic speech and a particular cultural tradition divided Sunnite Kurd from Sunnite Arab. Religious sectarianism separated Sunnite and Shiite Moslems; Yezidis, Christians, and Jews stood apart in their own communities. Sons tended to follow in the footsteps of their fathers and a scheme of hereditary occupations developed in which a man's place was apt to be determined by birth. Kinship, too, in defining the circle of the individual's relatives, identified him as a person of noble or common extraction and as someone to be reckoned with as a member of a large and powerful group or to be dismissed as a nonentity from a poor and inconsequential family.

These cross-cutting lines of social, ethnic, religious, and kinship division marked a mosaic pattern on the Middle Eastern human scene which remains clear in Iraq today. The forces set in motion by the western impact in this century, however, are blurring some of the lines of the mosaic and, with a larger sweep, are drawing new ones. Ecologically, town, village, and nomadic tribe remain distinct, but urban influences are spreading into the countryside and a growing stream of the rural population is flowing into the towns. Economic factors and the extension of governmental authority are causing increasing numbers of nomads to leave their black tents for the houses of the agricultural villages. Ethnic difference is becoming less divisive as the minority languages give way to Arabic and the younger generations acquire a sense of common Iraqi nationality. The old religious antagonisms, too, tend to lose their force before the secular trend of contemporary thought.

In the capital and in the few other major cities the traditional gap still separates the elite from the rest of the population. It seems destined, however, to be closed by the emerging educated middle group on whose skills the country's effort to modernize itself ultimately depends. At its upper levels the middle group is brought into association with the elite by education and occupation; at its lower end it draws upon the general population, from which those fortunate enough to receive an education may rise into its ranks. The emergent group not only stands between the top and bottom segments of the society, it poses, as the ideals it articulates spread more widely in the society, a potential challenge to the prestige and power of the ruling elite.

2

HISTORICAL SETTING

UNLIKE ITS ARAB NEIGHBORS, IRAQ HAS A LONG HISTORY OF HIGH civilization and political power, an antiquity as great as or greater than that of its principal rival in the Arab world, Egypt. The Tigris and the Euphrates allowed the early development of a complex irrigated agriculture. With an increased food supply came population growth and the rise of the earliest cities. New forms of social and political organization succeeded the simpler patterns of the wandering bands of food gatherers and hunters and the small villages of dry farmers who inhabited the area in the earlier, Neolithic age. With the development of vocational specialization and the creation of leisure for a wealthy elite there were originated, or at least perfected, the basic ideas and techniques that marked man's emergence from his prehistoric past: the wheel, the plow, metallurgy, massive architecture, writing, mathematics, complex government, and written codes of law. Here, by the rivers, were developed the high civilizations of Sumer and of Babylon.

Similar developments were occurring almost simultaneously on the Nile and somewhat later on other great river systems of the Eurasian continent. Historically, however, what is important is the long continuity of civilized life on the Mesopotamian valley-plain. The magnificently engineered irrigation system constructed in ancient times functioned until the Mongol onslaught in the thirteenth century of our era. On the eve of that disaster the country was still pouring out the agricultural wealth on which the power of the Sumerian and Babylonian kings had been founded, and its cities were among the greatest of the Mediterranean world.

Islam came to overlay and rework all that had gone before, almost completely obliterating any conscious memory among the people of the ancient ways. Stultifying centuries of Turkish rule followed upon the destruction wrought by the Mongols. The past, nevertheless, ex-

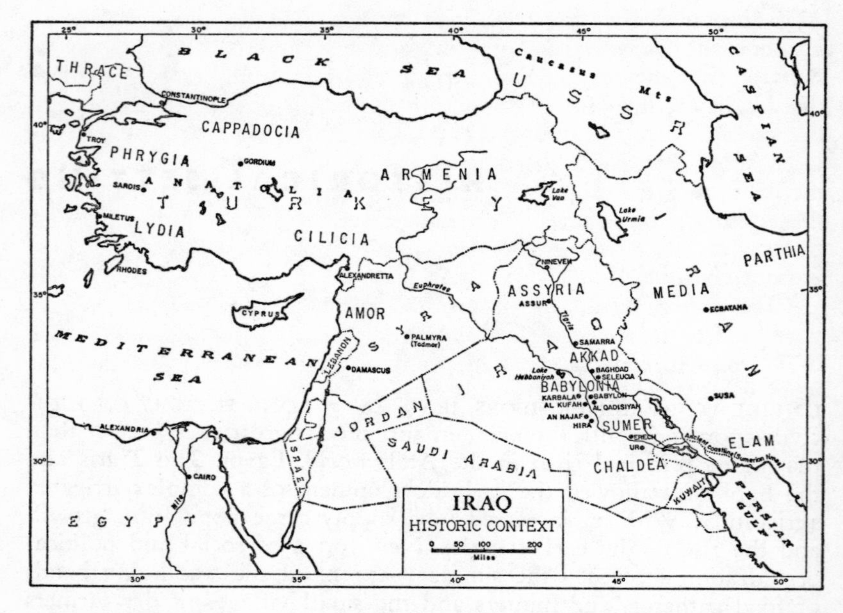

IRAQ
HISTORIC CONTEXT

pressed itself in subtle details of social life and outlook which still distinguish the Arabized Iraqi majority on the Mesopotamian plain from Arab populations elsewhere in the Middle East. These distinctions are not easy to identify, much less to demonstrate, but few observers would deny that there are aspects of community life in Iraq and a characteristic approach to the problems of government, technology, and economic organization which in degree or kind set off the country from its Arab neighbors despite common Moslem traditions and faith, and a shared language.

The essentials of Iraqi culture have endured despite incursions from all sides. The deserts to the south and west of the Mesopotamian plain constitute no barrier to mounted nomads, the passes in the mountains to the north and east provide entry corridors. Sumerians, Akkadians, Babylonians, Assyrians, Persians, Greeks, Romans, Arabs, Mongols, Turks have followed one another in the area, each contributing in greater or lesser degree to the physical mixture and cultural complexity of a civilization which three thousand years before Christ was already a composite one.

Thirteen centuries of participation in the Moslem Arab world, however, provide Iraq with ample reason to identify itself as both a bearer and shaper of the Arab tradition. There are important minorities in the country but most either are Moslem or count themselves

Arab insofar as they are concerned with such broad classifications at all. For the older, educated elite, not the grandeur of Sumer or Babylon, but the magnificence of the Abbasside Caliphate represents the zenith of the country's past achievement and a historical earnest that greatness is possible again in a revived Arab world. This outlook, more Pan-Arab than nationalist in its implications, is being modified toward a more specific sense of Iraqi identity in the course of the country's experience as an independent state and under the influence of the government's efforts to stress Iraq's inheritance of ancient civilization.

The pace of history has accelerated in Iraq, and the rush of changes witnessed by men not yet old constitute an unfinished chapter which in its immediacy is more compelling to Iraqis today than most of what went before. History, as an active component in human affairs, is perhaps less important as a record of what "really" happened than as a body of belief about that record. For most Iraqis with consciously held ideas about the nation's history—and this includes the illiterate villager with access to the coffeehouse radio as well as the educated townsman—Iraq's recent past is seen as a struggle for national independence: first against the Turks; later against the British; now against "western imperialism" (and what is regarded as its creature, Israel). The heroes vary with the ethnic and religious affiliation of the viewer, but the villains—official government policy notwithstanding—remain the same. History, then, is an active factor in the contemporary political scene and an instrument available to the principal contenders. The anti-western stereotype works to the disadvantage of the Iraqi Government in its competition with Egypt for Arab leadership and in its efforts to maintain an alignment with the western powers. Whether the government will succeed in changing the stereotype, while its opponents seek to reinforce and manipulate it, will be an important determinant of the future course of political events in the country.

Earliest History

The historical record in Iraq goes back almost three thousand years before Christ to Sumerian kings who were contemporary with the pharaohs of the First Egyptian Dynasty. Sumerian civilization was already far advanced, and archeological research gives glimpses of the incredibly long vistas of unrecorded history that lie still further back in time. It is not known what kind of culture the Sumerians brought with them when they first entered the area or, indeed, with any certainty where they came from; but it is clear that they were preceded by numerous other peoples who contributed to the social and political complexity that marked the region by the time the earliest Sumerian records were written.

In the oldest historic period small city-states faced each other across various artificial boundaries. Each possessed its own laws, customs, and government but recognizably shared in the larger Mesopotamian culture, which was remarkably advanced. Knowledge of reading and writing was no doubt the prerogative of the privileged few, but these few cultivated the science of the day and were concerned with its practical application. A major application of engineering skill were the irrigation and water-control systems created and maintained probably as early as 4000 B.C. So important were these irrigation works to general survival and prosperity that even in wartime contesting states took pains to avoid their destruction. Armed conflict between the numerous petty kings who ruled in the Tigris-Euphrates plain and delta seems to have been continuous, but in time the ranks of the contenders were thinned and a few victors began to assert control over larger territories.

When recorded history begins, the people of what is now Iraq were already known as Sumerians, although it is not clear whether the term was originally applied to a composite people or was a name brought in by a group of immigrants then applied to all the inhabitants of the area.

Sumer

With the Sumerian federations of city-states appear the first examples in history of government reaching beyond the local level. The records show a whole succession of dynasties, and although there is no extant account of actual political events in the early period, the reigns of some of the kings mentioned in chronicles have been dated by archeological discoveries. Some of the dynasties listed seem to have been contemporary with each other, indicating the persistence of political division among the Sumerians. A relatively detailed picture of the religious and domestic life of the period has been constructed from the remains of the ancient cities and indicates that a common Sumerian culture existed throughout Mesopotamia.

Akkad

The succession of Sumerian dynasties probably ended about 2800 B.C. with the conquest of the Sumerian federation by the Akkadians under Sargon, the first impressive historic figure to emerge out of the confused record. The Akkadians were a Semitic people from the west and northwest who had entered Iraq in numbers sufficient to give their name to the territory surrounding what is now Baghdad. Having consolidated their position in northern Iraq and southern Anatolia they moved under Sargon to conquer the southern cities of Sumer. They treated the religions of the conquered places with respect, collecting their gods into a kind of pantheon protected by a new and larger political order.

The Sumerians and Akkadians in effect combined their forces; and Sargon's military movements and conquests were extended to the Mediterranean and into Asia Minor. After Sargon's death the empire slowly fell before the onslaughts of Guti tribesmen from the north.

Gradually a revival of Sumerian and Akkadian power began under the leadership of the city of Erech, followed by that of Ur; there was established in Ur the capital of a new and prosperous Sumerian empire, which in its turn was gradually weakened by the attacks of Elamites, another Semitic-speaking people from the east. In the last days of the failing Sumerian power, about 2000 B.C., there swiftly rose to prominence a new state centering at Babylon, where western Semitic peoples (perhaps from Syria and Palestine) defied Sumer by asserting the power of Marduk, an Akkadian god. Babylonian authority was first asserted over southern Mesopotamia by the great Hammurabi (c. 1800–1760 B.C.), and the final submergence of the Sumerians under Hammurabi's son was symbolized by the destruction of the walls of Ur.

Babylon and Assyria

Babylon was both the center of political empire and a religious metropolis. It did not lose its latter status, which added to its luster as a center of wealth and power, until the time of Alexander the Great. Culturally, Babylon refined the basic Sumerian patterns. Hammurabi, sixth of his line of Amoritic rulers, is remembered not only as a conqueror but as a great lawgiver, and long after his time even the imperious Assyrian rulers of the region were always anxious to come to the city, a kind of more ancient Rome, in order to establish the legality and legitimacy of their rule. The code of laws collected by Hammurabi dealt with problems of living which are still pressing in the twentieth century: land tenure, rent, the position of women, marriage, divorce, inheritance, conditions and pay of labor, the functions of money and types of exchange, contracts, control of public order, and so on.

An invasion of Kassites, a people speaking Elamitic (one of a group of languages related to modern Georgian) around 1600 B.C. overthrew the Amoritic dynasty and established a new rule in Babylon. The city's predominant position was recognized but under the new regime it was no longer able to maintain control of the provinces. A new kingdom based on Assur in the north was expanding at this time and became the forerunner of the subsequent Assyrian empire, which was notable not only for its military innovations and ruthless proficiency in war but also for its contributions in the spheres of administration, architecture, sculpture, and literature (although the latter was largely in the form of renditions of earlier Babylonian works).

The first Assyrian sovereign of importance was Shalmaneser I, who elaborated the concept of a "Greater Assyria." Upon the failure of his dynasty another was established under the outstanding figure of Tiglath-pileser I, who succeeded in stabilizing the Assyrian empire as the greatest power in the Middle East.

The next ruler of note, Tiglath-pileser III (745–727 B.C.), created and elaborated an important political idea: the maintenance under the control of a permanent bureaucracy of a permanent military force, or standing army, which could consolidate conquests and subject defeated peoples to permanent occupation. Moving his capital to a new city, Nineveh, he organized the empire as an instrument of war into which was fed the trade and profits of captured territories. Ancient Babylon, completely absorbed about 1170 B.C., was raised to the status of a second capital. It was here in 729 B.C. that Tiglath-pileser III was crowned again. Although this ruler raised the Assyrian empire to its pinnacle of power—even Egypt was required to recognize Assyrian supremacy—the system he inaugurated eventually produced results opposite to those intended: enervation of the Assyrians themselves and increasing restiveness on the part of subject peoples, who were driven to hatred and desperation by the severity of Assyrian methods, the cruelest known to the ancient world. Revolt followed revolt; Egypt and Syria were lost; eventually in 606 B.C. Scythians destroyed Nineveh, and Assyrian power became a historic memory. Iraq's present-day Nestorian Christian minority calls itself Assyrian and claims ethnic descent from the dominant peoples of this ancient empire.

Babylon rose again as the center of a neo-Babylonian empire and produced in the second ruler of a new dynasty, Nebuchadnezzar, one of the most illustrious monarchs of the ancient world. Babylon was rebuilt with a great inner royal city, a sweeping main avenue, and new walls surrounding a much larger city than before—the whole presided over by the temple of Bel. Favored by its geographical position, the city became a center of trade where money was plentiful, pleasures numerous, the arts advanced, and life, for the times and the elect, magnificent. This glory, too, passed; Babylon fell to Cyrus, the ruler of the Achaemenian Persians, in 539 B.C.

Meeting of East and West

Iraq, so long a seat of Semitic power, now came under the control of an Indo-European-speaking people from the Persian highlands to the east. On their home ground the Persians under Cyrus had supplanted the native Scythian dynasty of a related people, the Medes, who had already conquered Nineveh, occupied Assyria, and by treaty reduced Babylonia to inferior status. From his capital at Susa, Cyrus proceeded to the conquest of Babylonia and the founding of a new empire, Persian in name but with its real center in Mesopotamia, whose ancient culture, agricultural wealth, and geographical position drew these latest conquerors as they had others. Cyrus' son, Cambyses, extended the empire from the Mediterranean, including Asia Minor, to the Oxus River, thus creating the last and greatest ancient Mesopotamian empire, renowned for its toleration under the religion of Zoroaster.

Meantime, the Greeks were evolving their own vigorous culture on the northern frontiers of the Persian empire. There ensued a long struggle between the Greeks and the Persians, studded with such events as the revolt of Miletus, the battles of Marathon and Salamis, the march, recorded by Xenophon, of the ten thousand Greek mercenaries, and, less spectacularly but more importantly, a cultural interaction which profoundly influenced both sides. Alexander the Great, having conquered Greece, continued until he finally brought the great Eastern empire, in which the Persian imperial idea had already been weakened by Greek influence, under Greek control. Alexander's ambition was to create a new empire combining Greek ideals with the political methods of the older political center. He died in Babylon in 323 B.C. The imperial political unity he had sought to create crumbled in the hands of his successors but the Greek and Asian cultural synthesis he initiated continued to evolve.

Greeks, Persians, Romans

Alexander's empire was divided among his principal followers. Seleucus, one of his generals, ruled Iraq and Persia from a new capital on the Tigris, Seleucia, just south of the subsequent site of Baghdad. The new ruler and his successors continued the spread of Greek civilization, but by 200 B.C. their power reached no further than the confines of Iraq and Syria. The Seleucid Greeks were beset by newly risen states to the north, by the Parthian Persians, by then in control of all Persia, and increasingly by a rapidly rising new power in the west, Rome. Not the Romans, however, but the Parthians conquered Iraq in 138 B.C.; they were to meet the Romans in a struggle that lasted nearly eight hundred years, until the coming of the Arabs. In this contest the

Romans supplanted the Greeks as the major protagonists of western influence; the effects, however, of the early Hellenic influence were never absolutely lost even after the coming of the Arabs and of Islam had reworked almost every aspect of life in the region.

In the course of the Persian-Roman conflict the Parthian Persians were pushed aside in A.D. 226 by a new Persian dynasty, the Sassanian, which developed a sounder political organization than had the Parthians and, by their hostility to Judaism and Christianity, gained the strong support of the powerful Zoroastrian priests. Under the Sassanians Iraq continued to be the principal scene of East-West conflict. In the fourth century, however, the transfer of the center of Roman power to Constantinople—in theory Roman, in language Greek, and in orientation Asian—importantly altered the character of the struggle. The Roman Empire had disintegrated and the West with which Persians had struggled was receding into the Dark Ages. Only in the twentieth century, was Mesopotamia (Iraq) again to meet a vigorous western influence—this time from two sources, the countries of the western alliance, and the Communist bloc, themselves locked in a larger contest. In the arena of that contest Iraq occupies a small but strategically important place.

The Age of Islam

The Arab conquest of Iraq in the year 637 brought not merely a new set of rulers but a language, religion, and certain of the patterns of life which have characterized the country ever since.

There had previously been small colonies of Arabs north of the Arabian peninsula, at Hira on the Euphrates, Nabataea in Transjordan, and notably at Palmyra (Tadmor) under the famed Queen Zenobia. Palmyra was a center of wealth, but Arabs in general at that time were despised as backward barbarians. For several centuries Arabia had been in a state of decline brought on when the shift of Roman power to Constantinople diverted the trade between the Mediterranean and the East, which had once passed through the peninsula, to the line of the Persian Gulf and the Tigris-Euphrates valley and to the Central Asian caravan routes farther north. The once dominant cities languished and the country fell into a confusion of civil strife and tribal warfare. The religion of Mohammed was in part a reformist response to these conditions.

The detachment of Iraq from declining Persian power was undertaken as the first major Moslem Arab conquest outside the peninsula during the brief reign (632–634) of Abu Bakr, first caliph (spiritual and temporal ruler) and successor to Mohammed. It began almost by accident when an expedition sent by the caliph to put down disturbances at Bahrein, offshore in the Persian Gulf, turned northward after accomplishing its mission and, unknown to Abu Bakr, invaded the delta of the Euphrates. The many Arabs, mostly Christian, living under Persian rule in lower Iraq at first supported their Persian masters against the Moslem invaders but gradually transferred their allegiance. Persian power was completely submerged once the Arabs decided to occupy the country thoroughly and to subdue the area west of the Euphrates. Final subjugation of Iraq was accomplished under the second caliph, Omar, in a decisive battle at Al Qadisiyah in 637.

The religion and, somewhat more slowly, the language of the conquerors were accepted by the majority of the population. The civilization of Iraq entered into a new phase with the advent of Islam but its essential continuity was not broken, and far from accepting the cultural elements brought by the victors it assimilated them so thoroughly that the Arab golden age that followed centered in Iraq, not Arabia. In this fusion it was the Arabs rather than the old population of Mesopotamia that were culturally absorbed.

Conquest and Division

As the Islamic empire grew and the center of power shifted from the Arabian peninsula northward to Syria and Iraq new kinds of division and conflict were added to the traditional Arab intertribal and interfactional strife. Long-standing regional conflicts reasserted themselves within the new empire. From the beginning an equalitarianism and intransigence characteristic of the Arab worked against consolidation of empire, of unity. The social apparatus for compromise existed on the local level, but neither then nor since has it proved adequate to the Arab ideal of political unity among all Arabic-speaking peoples. The centuries since have been marked by a continuous alternation between efforts at unity and retreat into division (see chap. 10).

Early conflicts in Moslem Iraq presaged major and lasting cleavages in the Islamic world. One of the most severe began when the Persians, having accepted Islam, began to transform it into a religion more suited to their own culture, traditions, and patterns of thought. The outcome was the division of Islam into rival Shiite and Sunnite sects, the former finding most of its adherents among Persians and Iraqi Arabs (see chap. 5). The Shiite holy cities of Karbala and Al Kufah in Iraq became centers of intrigue and tumult that promised conflict for the future.

Following the stabilization of Moslem power in the territories newly conquered by Abu Bakr and Omar (the latter was assassinated by a resident of Al Kufah), the problem of the succession, never dealt with by Mohammed, became pressing. Omar's successor, Othman, first cousin and one of the original companions of the Prophet, was selected by a committee of six in preference to Ali, son of the Prophet's paternal uncle and husband of his favorite daughter. Maladministration by Othman created widespread discontent and he was murdered in 656 by partisans of Ali. The line of cleavage between the latter and the followers of the Meccan nobles who claimed to be the proper guardians of rising Arab power had been drawn. Ali, after a battle against some dissidents, was recognized as caliph. But a rival, Moawiyah, the governor of Damascus, now refused to recognize the ascendancy of Ali unless he agreed to punish the assassins of Othman. This Ali would not do. Moawiyah was recognized as Commander of the Faithful in Syria and indecisively defeated Ali at the Battle of Siffin in 657. Four years later Ali was murdered in Al Kufah; his son Hasan was content to withdraw his claim to the caliphate in return for a grant of money. Moawiyah became the first of the Ommiad caliphs. The last flicker of armed resistance to the new dynasty was stamped out when Ali's other son, Husein, was killed at Karbala. Both Ali and Husein became Shiite martyrs; An Najaf, Ali's burial place, and Karbala, where Husein died, became holy places of pilgrimage almost as important to the Shiites as Mecca.

The Shiite doctrines attribute to Ali and his descendants a divine right to rule, a claim which accords with ancient Persian theories concerning the basis of kingly power. It contrasts with the Sunnite view, which emphasizes as the practical test of legitimacy the actual possession of power. The Shiites were strong enough to play an important part in overturning Ommiad power at Damascus in 750, and Iraq has remained the real area of struggle between Shiites and Sunnites in the Moslem world. Today the Shiites make up at least half of Iraq's Moslem majority; political power, however, is largely in Sunnite hands (see chap. 4; chap. 7) a fact that has accounted for much political controversy in modern Iraq.

The Moslem empire achieved its greatest political limits under the Ommiades in Damascus. From southern France, where it existed only fleetingly, its power extended to include the Iberian peninsula; the whole of North Africa including Egypt; Mediterranean islands; the Arabian peninsula; the Fertile Crescent; some of Asia Minor; Persia, with its boundaries pushed to the Oxus; Afghanistan; and, temporarily, some parts of India. But even as these conquests were being achieved, the age-old Arab tendencies toward feud and schism threatened the central authority itself. In addition to the Shiites other sectarians arose to question the political legitimacy of the Ommiad Caliphate.

These various groups were given effective cohesion by an ambitious and politically astute family descended from Abbas, the uncle of Mohammed, whose members had become Defenders of the Holy Places in Mecca. In aspiring to the caliphate they enjoyed an advantage in their claim through Abbas to eligibility, since under a frequently applied traditional Arab principle a man may be succeeded by his oldest paternal uncle. This principle also fitted the Shiite view that successors to the Prophet should be from the Prophet's family. The family of Abbas acquired additional influence through a claim to the imamate of a Shiite sect, whose imams descended from a son of Ali and whose religious secrets had been given to the head of the Abbasside family.

Ommiad power was on the wane toward the middle of the eighth century as the Persian Abu Muslim set about organizing the forces of revolt. He rallied the dissident Shiites, and other followers of Ali, by promising to reveal in due course a new imam; to their consternation the new imam proved to be head of the Abbasside family, but in the meantime sufficient force had been gathered to defeat the Ommiades. Stressing Ommiad tyranny and their own special right of succession, the Abbassides advanced their claim to leadership of the Sunnites as well as the Shiites.

In 750 the Abbassides triumphed and the center of empire was transferred from Damascus to Iraq. The move symbolized the new, more Persian foundation of the empire, and it inaugurated in Iraq an era of prosperity and magnificence that contrasted sharply with life under the Ommiades. The new location not only brought the Abbassides into close proximity with the Persians but also with the Turks, who some eight centuries later were to supplant them. Abbasside cosmopolitanism superseded the more purely Arab orientation of the earlier period, and the bedouin tide began to recede to the marginal lands and the desert from which it had come. The ideal of Arab unity had been briefly achieved, but the fragmentation of the empire already had begun.

The Abbassides

In the Abbasside capital at Baghdad there was kindled a blaze of philosophical, scientific, and literary glory remembered throughout the Arab world, and by Iraqis in particular, as the pinnacle of the Islamic past. The greatest caliphs of the period combined outstanding administrative and intellectual capacities with unrelenting cruelty. Their ruthlessness is significant as evidence of the substitution, perhaps under Persian influence, of the idea of the caliph as an absolute autocrat for the Arab notion of him as a leader chosen by a council of his peers and answerable to it. The Abbasside cultural renaissance spanned roughly the reigns of the first seven rulers of the dynasty (750–842). Of the seven, three achieved lasting fame: Mansur (754–775), Harun al-Rashid (786–809), and Mamun (813–833). These sovereigns had in common great administrative and political ability, both of which were vital in keeping under control the factional strife that was unremitting despite the excellences of the new order. The situation in Iraq—with its Sunnite dynasty and large Shiite population—was especially volatile and it required all the guile and sternness of the Abbassides to stay in power. No man's claim to Abbasside loyalty was sufficient to protect him from death if his survival seemed to threaten the prestige or status of the ruler.

Mansur, grandfather of Harun al-Rashid, had moved the capital to Baghdad in 762. The city, old and relatively prosperous, possessed the advantages of an adequate water supply, river communications, a generally equable climate, and freedom from malaria; the ruins of Ctesiphon, a nearby summer place of Persian kings, underscored the past. Although the early city was constructed entirely with the needs of political administration in mind, its population grew rapidly as it gained importance as a social and cultural center. Within thirty years it had become the second largest city in the Mediterranean world.

The high points of the Moslem renaissance in Iraq occurred during the reign of Harun, marked by its material splendor, and that of his son Mamun, which saw the greatest intellectual advances. In Mamun's time some of the greatest Islamic poetry was written and impressive advances were made in mathematics and the sciences. Historical and religious scholarship prospered and there began the editing and further creation of the fund of Arabic stories. Mamun encouraged and assisted all of these activities, and the liberality of his religious view strikingly contrasts with the binding orthodoxy that afterward so often restricted intellectual development in Islam.

Centuries of Decline

The Abbasside Caliphate did not end abruptly; it went into a long decline under the stresses of ethnic and religious division. A manifestation of the growing weakness of the caliphate was the separation of its religious from its political functions—heretofore combined in the person of the caliph. With increasing frequency regional and local forces rose and gained political autonomy, the strongest among them brushing aside the sovereign's political claims and sometimes forcing him to submit to extreme indignities. There was no desire, however, to dispense with the office of the caliphate, for the imprimatur of the incumbent continued to be important as a symbol for legitimizing claims to authority. Even the strong-handed Persian Buyid family, which for a time ruled in the capital, maintained the caliph as a shadowy symbol of spiritual authority.

The causes of decline were deeply rooted and longstanding. Sectarianism had weakened the effectiveness of Islam as a sanction for a single political authority in the empire. The various linguistic and cultural minorities complicated the human scene, and these complexities were nowhere more apparent than at the center of political power, Baghdad itself. Not only was there the cleavage between Arabs and Persians at this crossroads of empire, but the growing prominence of the Turks in Baghdad's political and military affairs gave cause for discontent. The Turks came as a stream of slaves brought in year by year to man the caliph's guard and fill the ranks of the regular military forces. Turkish military leaders began to supplant the Arabs around the seat of power. After the Caliph Mutasim (833–842) moved the political capital to Samarra, the Turks, no longer checked by their enemies in Baghdad, were able to bring the sovereign under their control. Alien influence in government heightened regional and provincial impatience with imperial control, accelerating the drive for autonomy. Sunnite orthodoxy became more and more rigid and the problem of religious division was met with a policy of harsh repression which instead of eliminating religious difference reinforced it, further weakening the unity of the empire.

Toward its end in the middle of the thirteenth century, the Abbasside Caliphate knew a brief revival under several strong rulers. The dynasty, however, was doomed; not least of the forces working for its destruction were the Crusades, which, though finally repelled, opened the way for invasion of the Mesopotamian empire from Asia.

The Mongols had in the first half of the thirteenth century reached the lower frontiers of what is now European Russia. Invited by the Caliph Nasir to assist in subduing the rebellious Persians, they entered the area south of the Black and Caspian seas and shortly revealed themselves aggressors rather than allies. In 1256 under Hulagu, grandson of Genghis Khan, they sacked the city of Baghdad. The material and artistic production of centuries was swept away. The commercial life of the city, so long a center of trade with the East, was crippled. Iraq itself was laid waste and—a tragedy from which the country has not yet recovered—the canal system, upon which the prosperity of the land depended, fell into ruin. With the passage of time the Mongol overlords began to yield to the Islamic culture of their subjects, but their rule remained alien to the end. Another wave of Mongols under Tamerlane conquered Iraq and occupied

Baghdad in 1393. Tamerlane was no more successful than his predecessors in stabilizing the vast Mongol empire, and new local regimes and additional Mongol groups rose and fell in quick succession.

The time was one of political chaos, economic depression, and social disintegration. As urban-based power waned, wandering Arab tribal confederations, such as the Shammar to the north of Baghdad and the Muntafiq to the south, more and more dominated the hinterland. The first outside force to take advantage of these conditions was the Persian Safawid dynasty; under Ismail Shah it turned upon Iraq early in the sixteenth century. Persian rule lasted for twenty-five years.

In the meantime a more formidable Middle Eastern power had come into being—the Ottoman Turks, who had supplanted the Seljuk Turks in Asia Minor. A scant two hundred years after the Mongol Hulagu captured Baghdad they had become the major political power in the area between Constantinople and Persia. With the Mongol conquest the Abbassides had fled to Cairo, where they continued to exercise the spiritual authority of the caliphate. In 1517 the ascendant Ottomans captured that city and the last Abbasside caliph consigned his office to the conquerors. The Turkish ruler was now both sultan and caliph, and he aspired to assert temporal power over the home territory of his Abbasside predecessors. This ambition was realized in 1534 when Baghdad was captured by Suleiman the Magnificent. Thereafter, except for an interlude of Persian control in the seventeenth century, Iraq remained under Turkish rule until the collapse of the Ottoman Empire at the end of World War I. The Ottomans, like those who had gone before, were afflicted with a progressive enfeeblement. In the latter days of their power in Iraq, certain Turkish governors, stimulated by western technology and thought, showed a renewed vigor and effectiveness; but by that time a larger world stage was being set on which events external to the Tigris-Euphrates region were to determine the course of history there.

The Ottoman Period

The inception of Ottoman rule in Iraq coincided with the rise of European sea power and the revival of western interest in Asia. By comparison with the abortive effort of the Crusades several centuries before, this expansive surge from the West was backed by the vastly greater power and the new motivations which had appeared with the commercial revolution. The wealth of India and Asia lay beyond the Tigris and Euphrates, whose valleys provided an attractive alternative to both the long sea route around Africa and to the shorter but insecure route across the Suez Isthmus and through the Red Sea. As Turkish power dimmed western involvement in Asia deepened and

Iraq took on additional importance as a strategic territory from which pressure might be brought to bear on a hostile Persia and from which India might be more easily penetrated.

In the seventeenth century competing western powers began to exert influence over warring Arab factions, particularly in the Arabian peninsula and North Africa; in so doing they inaugurated events which ultimately would lead to Arab nationalism in the modern sense and the re-emergence of the Arabs as an active force in the world scene. The western nations most directly and conflictingly involved in the region were Portugal and the Netherlands, then Britain, France, Russia, Germany, and the United States.

The Black Sea and the Caucasus gave Russia an avenue to the Middle East; prior to the 1907 Anglo-Russian entente its ambitions were clearly focused on that area. The Russian drive threatened the Ottoman government itself, as well as Iraq, Persia, and India. After 1907 the Germans and the British were the primary contenders for influence in Iraq. The most dramatic manifestation of German interest was the project for a railway from Berlin to Baghdad, with a connection to a port on the Persian Gulf. This scheme threatened to bring a potentially hostile German power into contact with vital British lines of communication, menacing British oil interests in Persia, and ultimately India itself.

The British-German struggle involved efforts by both sides to exploit the competition between the Rashid family, which held the Emirate of Hail, and the Saud family, which ruled in Nejd. The Rashids were pro-Turkish and pro-German; the Sauds were anti-Turkish and leaned to the British side. Other local forces were also exploited. German plans to make Kuwait the terminus of the Berlin-Baghdad railway were obstructed by British support of Sheikh Mubarak of Kuwait. On another occasion the British combined with the Sheikh of Kuwait, King Ibn Saud, and the Muntafiq Confederation in Iraq to prevent a reassertion of Turkish power in the lower delta area around Basra.

The internal history of Iraq through most of the nineteenth century was relatively uneventful. Ottoman authority, still nominally preserved, was at an ebb and the land was dominated by the great bedouin tribes. In the 1870's, however, a strong Turkish proconsul in Baghdad, Midhat Pasha, injected a new note into the affairs of the country: the vigor of his administration reflected a belated recognition of the land's potential wealth. From this time until World War I, change and reconstruction were in the air. For a time it seemed that the country might acquire importance in terms of its own internal developments rather than by virtue of its position on the East-West line of communication and as a point of contact between interests. This hope was ended, however, by World War I. Iraq reverted to its old, largely passive role as a pawn in the calculations of competing powers.

The Twentieth Century

War and Its Aftermath

German pressure in Turkey and Iraq was an item in the catalogue of grievances that led to war in 1914. Upon the outbreak of the conflict the importance assigned Iraq by the contestants was illustrated by the quick dispatch of British forces from India to Basra and by the immediate decision of the German-Turkish command to resist the British invasion from the Persian Gulf. The first British advance under General Townshend was stopped at Al Kut on the Tigris and the Anglo-Indian forces captured. Aroused, the British decided upon a major engagement in Iraq. New forces under the command of General Maude moved rapidly through the country and by 1917 had captured Baghdad and occupied the whole of Iraq north to the Anatolian highlands. The Allies had other successes in the Middle East, not the least being the defection to the Allied side of the Sherif of Mecca, Husein ibn Ali, whose Arab forces moved northward in conjunction with the British into Transjordan, Palestine, and Syria. For a time these successes seemed to be offset by the collapse of Russia, but by the end of the war British arms were supreme in Egypt, Arabia, Palestine, Syria, Iraq, and Persia—all lands formerly within the Ottoman Empire or threatened by the Central Powers during the course of the war.

Upon the capture of Baghdad, General Maude had proclaimed that Britain intended to return to Iraq some control of its own affairs. He had stressed that this would end the subjection to alien rulers which the country had known since the Mongol conquest in 1256. The proclamation was in keeping with the encouragement Britain had given Arab nationalist resistance to Turkish rule during the war. Now, however, the British were faced with the problem of reconciling their promises, explicit or implied, to the Arabs with their engagements with others. So far as Iraq itself was concerned, Britain was under no strong moral compulsion to pay any debt for the local population had been largely neutral in the struggle against the Turks and some elements had remained loyal to the enemy. Iraqi partisans of the Central Powers were perhaps not numerous but they reflected the developments of the immediate prewar period, when Turkish efforts at reconstruction and German educational influences were shaping attitudes—of the younger generation in particular. On the other hand,

Iraq had produced some notable proponents of the Allied cause—such as Nuri as-Said, Jafar al-Askari, and Jamil al-Midfai.

The British had followed the retreating Turks to the line where Arabic speech leaves off and Turkish speech begins. Free of its Turkish masters and of any sizable Turkish population, Iraq could be launched on its future without any serious problem of irredentism to confuse its relations with Turkey. This future was to be influenced in great measure by the family of Husein ibn Ali, Sherif of Mecca, who had refused to support the Sultan's demand for a holy war against the Allies. Husein had associated himself with the Arab nationalist movement largely through the agency of his son, Faisal, who was to become modern Iraq's first king. In October 1915, Husein obtained British assurances, transmitted through Sir Henry McMahon, High Commissioner for Egypt, of support for Arab independence in the future except in certain districts in which the population was not clearly Arab, and on the condition that Baghdad and Basra should have special administrative arrangements to safeguard mutual economic interests. These guarantees later proved to be in conflict with understandings reached among the Allies before the Arab revolt.

Anticipating the fulfillment of Allied pledges, the Emir Faisal arrived in Paris in January 1919 as leader of a Hejaz delegation to the peace conference. Iraq did not come under the control of the Occupied Enemy Territory Administration—as did Syria, Transjordan, Palestine, Lebanon, Alexandretta, and Cilicia—but was under the control of Arab leaders; the Shammar territory on the borders of Iraq for the time remained under Ibn Rashid. The peace conference proceeded to place the territories under mandatory regimes and refused to accept the action of a Syrian congress in Damascus which had proclaimed Faisal king of Syria and Transjordan. In April 1920 a conference at San Remo assigned the mandates of Palestine and Iraq to Great Britain and those of Syria and Lebanon to France. Faisal, confronting France in Syria, before long found himself and his government ejected from Damascus; the British then invited him to London as a token of their regard.

Nationalist sentiment had been mounting in Iraq and a British proposal to call into being an elected general assembly which would draw up a constitution for the country came too late to avert a revolt in July 1920. The initial preoccupation of those Iraqi elements holding any political awareness was with the establishment of effective government, under whatever auspices, in order to satisfy demands neglected during generations of Ottoman misrule; Arab nationalist sentiment had only begun to take shape among a few young persons. The early British administration had earned the inevitable resentments that are directed against any occupying force, but Iraqi leaders on the whole at first welcomed British measures to establish an apparatus of law and government.

By July 1920, however, Arab concepts of freedom, tribal tendencies toward schism, the conflicting ambitions of the sheikhs, the fears and recalcitrance of the Shiite mujtahids, resistance to taxation, and suspicion of government itself had exacerbated growing nationalist feeling and prepared the way for violence. For three months the country was in a state of revolution. The difficulty of bringing the situation under control was heightened by the weakness of the dispersed British military forces and by the poor coordination between them and the civil administration.

This revolt, known to Iraqis as the National War of Liberation, gave dramatic evidence of the immediacy of Arab discontent. Arab and Iraqi nationalism were gaining strength but had not yet become a coherent force in the country. At no time did the revolt show coordination or general direction; it consisted mainly of tribal disturbances, made possible by local opportunity and reflecting a diversity of local interests. Many outstanding sheikhs and urban figures remained aloof, and the police and security forces were notably loyal to the existing administration.

Nevertheless, the British accepted the revolt as an object lesson. They sought an arrangement that would permit an early end to the occupation while preserving essential British interests.

An Arab provisional government was established that could serve as a channel of communication between the British and the restive population and would provide opportunity for Iraqi leaders, such as Nuri as-Said and Jafar al-Askari, to come forward. In a canvass of various candidates to head the state, the Emir Faisal was finally decided upon. He was supported by a majority of those who voted and on August 23, 1921, was proclaimed King of Iraq. The country was now ready to embark on the path to constitutional government and full independence. Faisal, in the twelve years of his reign, pursued these ends with vigor and skill.

Independence

From a very early period Britain showed a disposition to terminate the Mandate. This was accomplished by stages. In the final stage a treaty of preferential alliance (June 1930) was drawn up. To be of twenty-five years duration, it was designed to replace the Mandate and was to become effective upon Iraq's entry into the League of Nations, which Britain agreed to sponsor. Membership in the League involved sovereign independence, and the country achieved both in 1932. By the terms of the treaty, which went into force on October 3, 1932, the two countries were to become automatic allies in case of war. Various external and internal problems remained. One—the problem of relations with King Ibn Saud—was ameliorated when, with the assistance of Britain, a treaty of friendship was concluded in 1936 between Iraq and Arabia. Iraq's rapidly growing oil revenues, which by 1932 already amounted to 25 percent of the entire national revenue, provided the means for solving many of the other problems faced by the new state. This circumstance was largely the result of the British decision to include the oil-rich Mosul region, to which Turkey laid claim, within the territory of Iraq.

During the years preceding independence, when the country was governed with the assistance of British advisers, there emerged many of the characteristics of Iraqi politics that persist today. One of these was the predominant position of the Sunnites, who had been the first to cooperate with the British. Another was the monopoly of political power by an elite whose wealth and social position enabled it to control elections, parties, representation, the police, and the military. The frequent overturning of cabinets was characteristic under the Mandate, as it has been since.

With the death of King Faisal in September 1933, Iraq lost a leader who had shown great strength and intelligence in balancing nationalist and British pressures within the framework of the Anglo-Iraqi alliance. He had been the main stabilizing personality in Iraqi politics and the one figure with sufficient prestige to draw the politicians together around a concept of national interest. The British withdrawal made the loss of Faisal all the more critical. The army in 1933 had some experience of political intervention in the suppression of the Assyrians. Later, in the suppression of the Euphrates tribes, further precedent was established for military involvement in domestic political affairs. During these years of bickering and struggle for personal advantage no figure emerged with enough strength to provide the leadership that had been given by Faisal. The new king, Ghazi, was not equipped to do so, and Nuri as-Said had not yet acquired national stature.

The military began to enter the political scene, and some army officers, stimulated by nationalist ideas and influenced by the Turkish pattern and by the totalitarian systems which were taking shape in Europe, began to call for military dictatorship. The civil politicians, seeking to lead the intelligentsia, responded with liberal and social democratic slogans and programs. In the confusion of these competing ideas and forces, military intervention in politics increased. In 1936 the country experienced the first of the seven military coups which were to take place in the next five years.

The climax came in April 1941 with the coup of Rashid Ali al-Gailani, leader of a violently anti-British and pro-Axis military group. Fearing for his life, the Regent (Ghazi had been killed in 1939 in an automobile accident) escaped to Egypt. Anglo-Iraqi hostilities occurred at Habbaniyah over the question of the transit of British forces in the country. The British, aided by Transjordan's Arab Legion, soon brought the situation under control and the Rashid Ali government fled. Succeeding Iraqi governments cooperated effectively with the Allies against the Axis.

After 1941, Nuri as-Said's strong leadership, whether in or out of the office of prime minister, basically stabilized the political situation, although cabinet crises continued to occur at fairly frequent intervals. By 1957, Nuri was still the central figure in the preservation of a strong-handed but constitutional political order. The problem of an ultimate successor to Nuri becomes a serious one when set against the pattern of Middle Eastern politics, in which the death or retirement of a leader is followed by a more or less protracted struggle among aspirants to his place. During that interval the greatest opportunity for military intervention exists, with the attendant possibility that the military itself may produce a strong man. Such developments have damaged the constitutional principle in other Middle Eastern countries and, in the past, have threatened it in Iraq. Whether an Iraqi military regime would be politically "left" or "right" is problematical and would depend importantly upon international conditions at the time. Any group coming to power from the present military establishment, however, would most likely be conservative and strongly nationalist, tending in the course of time under the pressure of the younger officers to move to the left while remaining nationalist.

Since World War II the following factors have stood out in Iraq's internal politics and external relations: (1) the treaty of friendship with Turkey, which became the core of the Baghdad Pact combining the "northern tier" states—Pakistan, Iran, Iraq, and Turkey—with Britain in a defensive arrangement against Soviet aggression; (2) the need to meet Egyptian claims to leadership of the Arab world, given expression in the federation of Jordan and Iraq in 1958 as a counter to the United Arab Republic; (3) the country's membership in the Arab League (the League was first proposed by Iraq); (4) the opposition to the existence of Israel, which Iraq and the other Arab states have publicly proclaimed; (5) the rising importance in Iraq's oil revenue, which has enabled the government to undertake large-scale projects of social and material improvement matched by few other Middle Eastern states.

Close to Russian power, accessible to western influence, immersed in the complexities of Arab politics, Iraq today is presented with a full measure of both dangers and opportunities. If external forces do not intrude, it is in a better position than many of its Arab neighbors to build a stable social order. Its advantages in this respect are not only its actual and potential wealth but the experience gained under British influence, which was important in producing the beginnings of an organic constitutional development. The government still faces, however, the danger of a combination of ultranationalists and leftists, now reinforced by the Palestinian Arabs in Jordan, all of whom, if for different motives, are pro-Nasser and pro-Syrian, and bitterly opposed to association with the West.

Iraq is in many respects unique in the Arab world. Its present boundaries are as arbitrary and of as recent origin as those of most other Arab states. Its population shows, if anything, an even more extreme development of the pattern of ethnic, religious, and occupational divisions which fragment loyalties throughout the Middle East. Yet, in the valley of the Tigris and Euphrates there is a historical and cultural unity, comparable to that of the Nile valley, which marks the people, despite their internal differences, as "Iraqi." That distinctiveness provides a foundation for the development of a sense of Iraqi nationality which may ultimately give a broader social reality to the political claims of the state.

3

GEOGRAPHY AND POPULATION

THE NAME "IRAQ," ADOPTED BY THE GOVERNMENT IN 1921, IS derived from *al-Iraq al-Arabi,* a term used in the area during the Middle Ages to distinguish the southern delta region of the Tigris-Euphrates river system from *al-Iraq al-Ajami,* the Persian mountain areas on the plain's northeastern and eastern boundaries. It corresponds roughly to the former Ottoman provinces of Baghdad, Basra, and Mosul. Before Iraq was established as a nation the area was known in a general way to Europeans as Mesopotamia ("the country between two rivers"), the name given to it by the ancient Greeks.

Iraq borders upon Iran to the east, Turkey and Syria to the north and northwest, Jordan, with which it was federated, to the west, Saudi Arabia and Kuwait to the south. It has religious ties with its non-Arab neighbors, Turkey and Iran; with Syria, Jordan, Saudi Arabia, and Kuwait it has close ethnic and linguistic links as well.

The census of 1947 placed Iraq's population at 4,816,185. Its 171,000 square miles—the country is as large as California—lie wholly within the desert belt that stretches from the Atlantic through North Africa and Iran into Central Asia. Although its oil riches may presage a more prosperous future, the country today shares with most of its neighbors the problems of a predominantly agricultural economy operating largely in terms of the subsistence patterns of the past.

Along four of Iraq's borders—those with Syria, Jordan, Saudi Arabia, and Kuwait—there are no inhabitants except occasional nomads, who think in terms of tribes and pasturage territories and to whom political boundaries mean little or nothing. The frontiers with Turkey and Iran are also of little significance to the majority of border-dwelling Kurds, the more so since many of their local politicians continue to speak of a Kurdistan which would embrace Kurds in all three countries. A counterinfluence, however, is exerted by the educated Kurds of Baghdad, some of whom are prominent in the gov-

ernment or the army. These, together with the small but growing number of educated Arabs, see the country's national boundaries as political realities—an awareness which is seeping down to the lower levels of Iraqi society.

Close ethnic and other ties with the rest of the Arab world make the ideal of Arab political unity attractive to many educated Iraqis. On the other hand, there is also a growing consciousness of Iraq as a national state responsible for its own political and economic destiny. The country's oil resources link its economy with those of the western democracies, but its Arab character and the ideal of Arab unity are producing, particularly among the younger generation, sympathy for a Pan-Arabism in which they see Iraq as the leader. That the tensions produced by the conflicts between political ideals and economic interests still operate largely below the surface is no doubt evidence of the firm hand of a government which has chosen to ally itself with the West.

Major Geographical Divisions

Topographically, Iraq can be divided from southwest to northeast into three main zones: the desert, the plain, and the highland. In the plain lies the river system along which the greater part of the country's population is concentrated and upon which the life of the country depends.

Desert and Highlands

Southwestern Iraq, the Badiyah ash Shamaliyah, is part of the Syrian Desert and the Arabian peninsula. Inhabited by bedouin nomads, it consists of a wide, stony plain, interspersed with rare sandy stretches, sloping down from the 3,000-foot altitude of Jabal Unayzah to the valley of the Euphrates. A widely ramified pattern of wadis—watercourses that are dry most of the year—runs from the border area across the plain to the Euphrates; some of them, of which the Hauran is the best known, are over 200 miles long and carry brief but torrential floods during the winter rains. There is a line of wells along the Hauran; notable among them is the one at Ar Rutbah, a pumping station on the oil pipeline which runs from Kirkuk to the Mediterranean.

In the Kurdish country of northeastern Iraq, high ground separated by broad undulating steppes gives way in the north to the ridges of Iran's Zagros Mountains. The highest crests are in Iran but within Iraq some of the peaks rise to between 8,000 and 10,000 feet. The highlands are roughly coextensive with the rainfall zone.

The Plain and the Rivers

The area between the edge of the Arabian plateau and the foothills of the Iranian mountains is the heartland of Iraq. Here are the foundations of the country's economy: oil, rich alluvial soil, the water of the Tigris and Euphrates. Sir William Willcocks, a British engineer whose studies of the Tigris–Euphrates system form the basis for the unified development of the central valley of Iraq, has contrasted the unpredictability and violence of the Tigris and Euphrates to the manageability of the Nile. These streams are being harnessed today but their rampages are a historic feature of the area.

The Euphrates, though longer, is the smaller and less complex of the two rivers. Streams from its two main sources in the mountains of eastern Turkey meet at Harput in central Anatolia; from there the river follows a winding course southeastward across Syria, where it is joined by the Khabur. After entering Iraq it is augmented only by the flow from the larger wadis during the winter months and by seepage from the Syrian plateau.

In northwestern Iraq the river winds through a gorge which varies from less than a mile to ten miles in width, flows out onto the plain at Ar Ramadi, and continues in one stream as far as the Hindiyah Barrage, completed in 1914. With the construction of this barrage the old Shatt al Hillah branch of the Euphrates was diverted into the Hindiyah channel, which carries the main stream. Below Al Kifl the river follows an unstable course, taking two channels and branching out into marshes which act as silt traps; at As Samawah the stream reappears in a single channel. The Euphrates falls only a few feet between As Samawah and An Nasiriyah and below that point the almost siltless water flows through extensive marshlands to join the Tigris at Qarmat Ali in a single channel, the Shatt al Arab.

Also rising in eastern Turkey, the Tigris continues, unlike the Euphrates, to receive water along much of its course in Iraq as a result of greater rainfall in the country's eastern highlands. Tributary to the Tigris between the Iraqi-Syrian border and the Jabal Hamrin range are the eastern Khabur, not to be confused with the Euphrates tributary; the Greater Zab and the Lesser Zab, which drain areas totaling some 30,000 square miles; and, just south of Jabal Hamrin in the old delta, the Uzaym. The Uzaym has a basin of 4,000 square miles and presents particular problems to the river-development planners since its floods, though normally not excessive, are subject to the widest fluctuations. It also carries an extremely fine silt which causes much trouble at the Baghdad waterworks just downstream from its confluence with the Tigris.

Twenty miles below Baghdad the Tigris receives its last major tributary, the Diyala. The Diyala's rise into flood is exceptionally rapid even for this region, but fortunately its flood usually precedes that of the Tigris and much of the excess is carried out of the stream before the main flood reaches its peak. At Al Kut (the scene of heavy fighting in World War I) is the Kut Barrage, completed by the Iraqi Government in 1939, where river water is diverted into the Gharraf Canal, one of the principal components of the Tigris irrigation system (see chap. 14). Below Al Kut the Tigris, like the Euphrates, breaks up into many channels and runs through marshes which, besides acting as silting basins, reduce the flow of the river by as much as 80 percent. At Al Qurnah, a short distance farther, the Tigris and the Euphrates come together to form the Shatt al Arab, flowing on as a single stream for 120 miles to the Persian Gulf. The Karun, coming out of Iran, empties into the Shatt al Arab, and it is largely its silt which, in slowly extending the delta into the Gulf, presents a continuous dredging problem for the navigation of ocean vessels into the Port of Basra. Tidal action on the river forces fresh water up the canals on either side of the Shatt al Arab to furnish irrigation for the region's famous date gardens.

The Tigris and the Euphrates are at their lowest level in September and October, at flood in March, April, and May, when crops are already at least half-grown. Both rivers, and especially the Tigris, have extremely steep gradients in their upper reaches and almost none in their lower; there they flow in channels above the level of the plain, itself sometimes flooded in the spring when the snows melt in the mountains of Anatolia. In spring the two rivers may carry forty times as much water as at low mark, and one season's flood may be ten times as great as that in another year. The Euphrates is more saline than the Tigris, and up to 60 percent of the land irrigated by its flow near the delta is affected by salinity, with as much as 20 percent of this estimated to be worthless for further agricultural use.

Efforts to control and utilize the waters of the Tigris and the Euphrates, calling for coordinated planning and centralized management, have had political implications for Iraq, and the adoption of modern techniques of dam building and large-scale irrigation is likely to reinforce the tendency toward strong central administration. Despite recent developments in the industrial sector, Iraq remains basically dependent on its agricultural production, and in any over-all plan for the future the use of the rivers must continue to play a crucial role.

Population

Population statistics for Iraq as for the Middle East generally are unreliable. The country's only official census was taken in 1947, and the impossibility of obtaining any trustworthy estimates for periods before and since that date places all figures given below in the category of informed but inconclusive estimates.

The 1947 census placed the sedentary population of the country at 4,566,185; to this must be added at least 250,000 nomads, though some authorities believe that the number of nomads and seminomads may be as high as 500,000. Other observers have pointed out that suspicion and lack of understanding by the people resulted in so much misinformation being supplied to the census takers that there may have been an underenumeration of as much as 20 percent in the census total. Writing in 1955, Iraq Development Board experts treated the population as upwards of 5,000,000. In any case, it is certain that Iraq does not have, nor is it likely to have in the near future, the population pressure which is bearing so hard on the economies of some other countries in the Middle East.

Also not included in the 1947 population totals were some 74,000 persons of nationality other than Iraqi. Of this number more than three fourths were Iranian; the remainder comprised small groups of Indians, Pakistanis, Saudi Arabs, British, and non-Iraqi (presumably stateless) Jews.

The rate of population increase in Iraq has been variously estimated from 1, to 1.5, to 2 percent, and the last figure corresponds with that of other Middle Eastern Arab countries. The effects of the large-scale public health programs undertaken since 1950 by the Iraq Development Board are not yet recorded.

Distribution

Population density ranges from 12 per square mile in Dulaym province (to the west of Baghdad) to 64 in Baghdad province, but these averages have little meaning since they include large desert areas having no sedentary population whatever. The density for the present cultivated area of Iraq is reported to be about 164 per square mile, but again there are wide local variations; the *qada* (district) of Baghdad has a population density of 300 per square mile of cultivated land and that of Basra 800 per square mile.

The largest area empty of sedentary population is the desert south and west of the Euphrates. Other large districts without settled inhabitants, such as the gypsum desert of Al Jazirah, lie west of a line running southward from Mosul. Another large uninhabited area lies east of the Tigris from Baghdad to the Iranian frontier.

The most densely settled region lies along the rivers. On the Euphrates the heaviest settlement is to the south, principally along the Husayniyah and Hillah systems. This region contains the large holy cities of Karbala, An Najaf, and Al Kufah. The region of closely settled land on the Tigris begins near Samarra and follows the river and its tributaries, notably the Gharraf and Dujaylah systems. To the south, in the Al Amarah district, rice supports a large population, and on the Shatt al Arab a narrow belt of close settlement follows the line of irrigated date palm gardens.

On the northern plain the rural population is fairly heavy between Mosul and Kirkuk. In the mountains settlement is confined to a series of valleys, and the chief mountain center, the Kurdish city of As Sulaymaniyah, is located in the largest of these valleys. Settlement thins out as the terrain becomes higher and more broken.

For administrative purposes Iraq is divided into 14 provinces (sing.: *liwa*), which in turn are divided into districts (sing.: *qada*) and subdistricts (sing.: *nahiyah*). (See Table 1.) The provinces account for about 82,000 square miles; the remaining area is under the Desert Administration (see chap. 8).

Composition

Of the estimated nomadic population of 250,000, about half are in Karbala province; 70,000 in Mosul province; 30,000 in Muntafiq province; and 25,000 in Dulaym province. The number of nomads is decreasing as the nomad turns from pastoralism to settled agriculture. This process is encouraged, for security reasons among others, by the Iraqi Government as it was by the Turks.

About two thirds of the population is found in rural villages, and 90 percent of these are cultivators. Even in centers of up to 20,000 inhabitants, a fair proportion of the population is employed as agricultural workers. There is an accelerating migration from the villages to towns; with the expansion of the oil industry and the development of trade the cities of Basra, Baghdad, Kirkuk, and An Najaf are growing rapidly. The shortage of housing for recent arrivals—in spite of some low-cost public projects, particularly in Baghdad—constitutes a serious social problem.

Of the total sedentary population recorded in 1947, 54 percent were females. In the Baghdad district, however, males were in the majority, comprising 51.6 percent of the population; recent estimates tend to show an even further increase. Some rural districts, however, such as Al Amarah, are losing large numbers of males by the exodus of young unmarried men to the cities and to the neighboring oil-producing Sheikhdom of Kuwait. Because of poor working and living conditions on the large plantations and the salination of the land, it is estimated that 50,000 persons have left Al Amarah in recent years; census figures for this province show a low relative number of males in the 20 to 25 age group and an excess of 30,000 females in the total population.

Age-group distribution in the settled population, as given in the *Statistical Abstract* of the Iraqi Government for 1955 indicates that over one third of the sedentary population is under 10 years of age; more than half is under 20—in Egypt, by comparison, persons under 10 years of age made up 26 percent of the population in 1947. In 1950 the birth rate was estimated at 27 per thousand, the death rate at 12 per thousand; the true figures are certainly higher: infant mortality is high, one leading authority putting the rate at 300 to 350 per thousand (and even higher than this in the malarial areas of the north). But if the high infant mortality rate is substantially reduced by the current health program and other increase factors remain relatively constant, Iraq will continue to have a youthful and fast-growing population for a long time. The figure for the 20 to 29 age group is low—less than 10 percent of the total—but this may be partially explained by the emigration of young male workers and by false census declarations for this age group made in the belief that censuses are taken to determine availability for military service.

Population Trends

The general population picture in Iraq, then, is one of a young and rapidly increasing population. Though the country is not immediately threatened by population pressure, the rapid rate of expansion presents the possibility that at some time in the future, unless agricultural and industrial development are maintained or accelerated, overpopulation may result.

Meanwhile, the Iraqi Government, through programs financed by oil revenues, is beginning to provide for the bulk of the population —rural and urban—the basis of a standard of living heretofore unknown. Federation with Jordan, however, increased the problem of extending and expanding social benefits. Improvements in living standards are not yet sufficiently tangible in the farming areas to lessen the drift to the towns, and Iraq's principal cities continue to grow rapidly as the new labor force moves in from the countryside. Under the industrialization program the majority of these arrivals are absorbed by the new enterprises. The few who return to their villages and the steady increment of bedouins turning to agriculture by no means replace the loss to the rural population.

Immigration and emigration are both very limited despite an increasing movement in recent years of young men from the depressed southern villages to the oilfields of Kuwait.

4

ETHNIC GROUPS AND LANGUAGES

WITH ITS HISTORY OF ADMIXTURE, THE SIGNIFICANT DIFFERENCES within Iraq's population are not those of race, for almost the whole range of the eastern Mediterranean physical types is represented in the various local communities, but rather those of religion, language, social and cultural tradition. As recognized by the people themselves, these set off Moslem and Yezidi from Christian and Kurd, or Armenian from Arab. Over all, however, there is the prevailing Arab identification, formed in the centuries of Arab domination and reflected in the supremacy of Arabic speech and an ideal image rooted in the historical recollection of Arab greatness.

The largest national minority, about 17 percent of the population, consists of the Kurds, whose native speech is Kurdish rather than Arabic. Other, smaller, minorities are the Armenians, Lurs, Jews, Sabaeans, and Turkomans, who altogether make up only 8 or 9 percent of the total population.

Arabic is the official language of Iraq and the only language spoken by at least four fifths of the population. As is the case everywhere in the Arabic-speaking world, the language shows much dialectal divergence. Almost every village and town has developed its slight variations of the language; the major dialectal variations, however, are between town, village, and tribe, although these differences are less striking in Iraq than, say, in Syria or Lebanon. All Iraqi dialects generally resemble each other, in contrast with the Arabic dialects of other regions, so that Arab speakers immediately recognize an Iraqi by his pronunciation, the vocabulary he uses, and the way he uses it. This is true even when the speaker is using the literary language, a locally influenced form of classical Arabic.

Arabic is a Semitic language related to Hebrew, Aramaic, ancient Phoenician, various languages of Ethiopia, and to the ancient Akkadian of Babylonia and Assyria. In classical Mesopotamia the first language known to history (from about 4000 B.C.) is Sumerian; as far as linguistic science can tell, Sumerian is not related to any other known language. The Akkadians used Sumerian as a religious language. Several dialects of Akkadian speech (two being the literary languages known in history as Babylonian and Assyrian) flourished for two thousand years and then were gradually overcome by the incursion of Aramaic from the west. Syriac, a language of the Aramaic subfamily, was the liturgical language of Eastern-rite Christians of the area. When the Arab expansion took place following the introduction of Islam, this area was conquered and colonized by speakers of Arabic from farther south in Arabia. As time went on the various Aramaic dialects died out, being replaced by Arabic, and at the present time there are only a few isolated villages where Aramaic is still spoken (the so-called Syriac of the groups known as Assyrians).

The spread of Arabic is also to be observed among the peripheral ethnic minorities. Thus among the Yezidis, whose language is the Kermanji dialect of Kurdish, the younger people now for the most part speak Arabic as well and some are beginning to accept Arabic as a first language. The Armenians who when they arrived in the country at the end of World War I spoke only Armenian and Turkish today speak Armenian in the home and Arabic in outside contacts. The Aramaic dialect of the Assyrians has almost completely given way to Arabic. Classical Syriac continues to be used only by some Eastern-rite Christians of the area as a liturgical language. The Turkish of the Turkomans, the Kurdish dialects of the Sarliya and Shabak minorities, and the Persian-related language of the Lurs are now spoken mainly by the older generations of these groups.

English, introduced by the mandatory authorities and British business firms in Iraq, is used to some degree in the cities. It is also taught in the high schools and the university. It is, however, held in less esteem than formerly and is in any case generally limited to the middle and upper classes.

If the idea of Iraqi nationality continues to take hold among the minorities, it will become obvious to them that progress in most walks of life will depend upon the mastery of Arabic; the non-Arabic languages spoken in Iraq, therefore, are likely to disappear in time. Kurdish, however, will certainly last for years, and should there be any weakening of the unity of the Iraqi state it may even revive and expand.

Arabs

Between three fourths and four fifths of Iraq's total population is Arab, speaks the Arabic language, and, with the exception of a small

Christian minority, shares the Islamic religion. Internally, this majority is divided by differing ecological and cultural patterns, by a wide range of economic pursuits, by differences of political status (determined, though to a lessening degree, by religious affiliation), and by a sectarian split between Shiite and Sunnite Moslems which continues to be the source of tensions that pose a basic obstacle to the social unification of the country.

In the northern part of the country the Arabs are found mainly along the rivers above Al Fallujah and Baghdad, on the Mosul plain, and on the Tigris tributaries up to the Kurdish–Turkoman foothills. Overwhelmingly Sunnite, the population of these areas shows a higher rate of literacy and enjoys a somewhat higher standard of living than does that of the Arab areas farther to the south, where the population consists largely of Shiite agriculturalists concentrated along the banks of the Tigris south of Baghdad and on the Euphrates south of Al Fallujah. Most of these fellahin (cultivators) are not distinguishable from the Arabs of Khuzistan province in Iran; ties between them are reinforced by the presence in Iraq of such important Shiite holy places as An Najaf, Kadhimain (Al Kazimiyah), Karbala, and Samarra.

In the southern marshes of Iraq are the marsh Arabs (the Madans), remnants of conquered peoples who have found refuge there. Although those living on the peripheries of the marshes blend physically and culturally with the peasantry and have absorbed some bedouin groups, those living in the permanently flooded areas in the heart of the marshes are quite distinct, practicing little or no agriculture and living on fish and on milk products from their water buffaloes.

Sunnites, Shiites, Christians

Overriding all other distinctions is the Shiite-Sunnite division, originally exclusively a religious one but today having equally if not more important economic and political concomitants. The Sunnite Arabs, though predominant in the north, are less geographically concentrated than the Shiites. Throughout the generally Shiite south a sizable proportion of the big Arab landowners are Sunnites. About 20 percent of the population of Basra is estimated to be Sunnite; there are large populations of Sunnites in the southern towns of An Nasiriyah, Suq ash Shuyukh, and Al Khamisiyah. The nomadic Arab tribes are also mainly Sunnite.

Although the economic activities of the Sunnite Arabs range from the top to the bottom of the occupational scale, the group as a whole feels a sense of superiority to the rest of the community. In Ottoman times Sunnite Arabs furnished most of the native officials, and the royal family today is Sunnite, as have been most of the ministers and senior government officials. Sunnite influence is also reflected in the output of the press and radio and other media of mass communications, which are taking on increased importance in the formation of Iraqi public opinion. Although its monopoly of power is lessening, the Sunnite group will continue to play a major role in the country's affairs for some time to come.

Generally less literate and less often possessing modern technical skills than the Sunnites, the Shiite Arabs tend to be found in occupations regarded as menial. This circumstance is the source of growing resentment, and the predominantly Shiite provinces of Al Muntafiq and Ad Diwaniyah have been centers of unrest during periods of political or economic crisis.

Less than 3 percent of Iraq's Arabs are Christians. More than half of this number live in Mosul province, traditionally a Christian center in the Middle East. There are also sizable concentrations in the cities of Kirkuk, Irbil, Basra, Baghdad and in Ad Dulaym province.

Two tendencies are apparent in the Christian community. In the first place, the Christians have taken more readily to westernization than any other element of the population. They have been first to learn European languages; first to discard traditional dress; first to accept new occupational roles for women; first to grasp modern technological training. Secondly, their religion and their readiness to accept innovation have not stood in the way of an increasing identification in the secular sphere with the Arab Moslem majority, whose language, manners, and political outlook they share.

Wealthy Christians, like well-to-do Moslems, have long had educational and social access to western material and intellectual culture; significantly, however, on the lower economic levels Christians more than Moslems have been brought into direct contact with Europeans by the occupations they have pursued. There is a high percentage of Christians among house servants and among clerks in business establishments. They are also to be found as hotel owners, waiters and bartenders, dealers in antiques, assistants to archeological expeditions, in all activities connected with European influence. Christians further up the economic scale are prominent in the professions and in banking and finance.

Although this close association with Westerners has been a source of Moslem resentment in the past, the fact that the Arab Christians have never been politically wedded to any particular western country but have been strong proponents of Iraqi nationalism has minimized intergroup hostility. The loyalty of politically articulate members of the Christian group evidently reflects the better treatment given native Christians in Iraq by the Moslem ruling group than in such neighboring countries as Iran and Turkey. Moreover, the receptivity to western ideas and technical skills, which might have isolated the Christians from the Moslems, is spreading among the latter under a government concerned with maintaining friendly and cooperative relations with the West. Friction between the two communities is by no means absent but the present trend seems to be toward acceptance by both groups of widening areas of common interest.

Kurds

Iraq's 800,000 Kurds are overwhelmingly Sunnite Moslem; a small number are Shiites. Speaking various dialects of Kurdish, an Indo-European language distantly related to Persian, the Kurds, apart from the few who have drifted to the cities, live in isolated villages in the mountain valleys of the Turkish and Iranian border areas. The provinces of Mosul, Irbil, Kirkuk and Ad Diyala are heavily Kurdish and As Sulaymaniyah province is almost exclusively so.

The common stereotype of the Kurd is the hardy mountain warrior, taller and more strongly built than the Arab fellah, devoted to his upland farm and alpine pastures, fiercely resentful of his political subordination to the Arab ruling groups. The majority have been for some time settled cereal agriculturalists and transhumant stockbreeders. A few tribes are still pastoral nomads. Three general groups of Iraqi Kurds are recognized, conforming to tribal affiliation, linguistic differences, and geographical location. The first group, the Badinan, an extension of the Turkish Kurds, lives in villages which range from Lake Van in Anatolia to the Greater Zab River in Iraq. They speak Kermanji, or "literary" Kurdish. The second group, the Suran, lives between the Greater and Lesser Zab. The third, the Baban, inhabits the region from the Lesser Zab to the Diyala River. The Suran and the Baban speak a single dialect of Kurdish, found also among the Iranian Kurds. Each of these groups contains nomadic herdsmen organized in tribes, freehold farmers who retain their tribal affiliation and whose land is usually in the area of the former tribal domain, and tenant farmers and laborers who are largely detribalized.

In these predominantly Kurdish areas the spread of Arabic is seen as a threat to the survival of Kurdish as a first language. Kurdish is the language of instruction in primary schools in the Kurdish area and is insisted upon in the home. In spite of this, young Kurds, particularly those whose aspirations take them to the cities, are turning to Arabic; the Kurdish origin of many city Kurds is today revealed only in their names.

Despite their reputation for clannishness and rigid adherence to traditional ways, some of the Kurds are beginning to enter more actively into the main currents of Iraqi life. This trend is made easier by their Sunni Moslem faith and is no doubt hastened by the tendency of leading Kurdish families to adopt the attitudes and aspirations of the Arab elite. Thus, paradoxically, an insistently separatist minority is showing signs of allying itself with Iraqi nationalism.

Kurdish irredentism, however, remains strong in many quarters. Dreams of a Kurdish state, carved out of parts of Turkey, Iraq, and Iran, are nurtured among Kurdish elements in the countryside. Such groups are isolated from realities of the regional political situation; they are encouraged, moreover, by propaganda emanating from the Soviet Union, which also has a Kurdish minority, and from exiled Kurdish nationalist sources in western Europe. The Kurds are far from having articulated a unified pattern of loyalty to a Kurdish nation, and their primary allegiance, except as it may be shifting to the countries in which they reside, remains focused on kin group and village.

Shabaks and Sarliyas

The 10,000 to 12,000 Moslem Shabaks, who speak a Kurdish dialect, may be distinguished from the main body of the Kurds by their religious beliefs and observances, which resemble those of the Ali ilahi Shiite sect but which are peculiar in respect to certain secret rites. The Shabaks live in agricultural villages on the Tigris south of Mosul and in the Sinjar district, maintaining close relationships with the neighboring Yezidis. They are gradually being absorbed linguistically and culturally into the general Arab population.

A very small Kurdish-speaking people, also Shiite, the Sarliyas occupy a few villages on both banks of the Greater Zab just above its junction with the Tigris.

Yezidis

The last national census in Iraq, taken in 1947, counted 32,437 Yezidis. The official use of the term "Yezidi" is indicative of their status, for the word has a pejorative connotation; the name employed by the group itself is "Dasnayi." More concentrated geographically than any other Iraqi minority, all but 27 of those listed in the census were residents of Mosul province.

The only district in which Yezidis form the majority is Sinjar, west of Mosul, where they are a rural population. They form about one third of the population of the Shaykhan district, north of Mosul. Here are located their principal shrine, Sheikh Adi, and the residence of their emir, Ba Advi. It is believed by several observers that they now form a considerably smaller proportion of the population than they did some hundred years ago. They were subjected to several decimating excursions by the Turkish authorities and their Kurdish neighbors in Ottoman times. They speak Kermanji, a Kurdish dialect, but commonly know Arabic as well.

The Yezidis have traditionally been set apart from the mainstream of Iraqi life. They are execrated as "devil worshippers" by the major Moslem sects, and individual articles of faith make it difficult for them even to send their children to public schools. They were not a millet (semiautonomous non-Moslem community) under the Ottoman Empire, as were many minorities, and so were deprived of many benefits of legal status. Their emir, head of the strictly graded religious political hierarchy, exercises full control over his followers. Grave charges have been made in the past (some by Yezidis) against the cruelty and capriciousness of these hereditary leaders.

Despised by the majority and at the bottom of the economic scale in Iraq, the Yezidis have so far participated less than any other group in the benefits of the country's drive for development.

Other Minorities

Assyrians

The Assyrians, adherents of the ancient Nestorian "Church of the East" which flourished in Mesopotamia and carried on vigorous missionary activity from central Asia to China until the Mongol conquests in the thirteenth century, are scattered throughout the Middle East. Their Syriac dialect is giving way to Arabic and seems likely to be relegated to the place of a liturgical language. They have a long history of difficulties with the authorities in Iraq and other countries and their communities have moved so often during the last fifty years that it is difficult to make more than a guess at how many are now in Iraq. The number in 1931 was estimated to be about 40,000; in 1933, however, after operations against them by the Iraqi army during which hundreds of Assyrians were killed, several thousand left Iraq for the settlement project sponsored by the League of Nations on the Khabur River in Syria.

In 1936 there were many Assyrians in central Iraq, the majority of whom were members of the "Iraq Levies" organized by the British as a protective force for their military bases and composed almost exclusively of Assyrians. The Levies were dissolved when the British turned over their bases to the Iraqi authorities following World War II, and many Assyrians have since moved to a new settlement at Dawrah, south of Baghdad, where they are employed in the new oil-refinery installations. Others reside near Kirkuk, where they work in the British-leased oilfields. There are also Assyrian settlements at Mosul and in the villages of the surrounding area.

The titular head of the Assyrians is the Patriarch of the East, now living in the United States, who was expelled from Iraq by the government in 1932 because of his pretensions to secular as well as religious authority.

The Assyrians enjoy a reputation in the area for bravery, resourcefulness, and capacity to learn technological skills. Politically, their insistence that they constitute a "nation" and the frequency with which they have petitioned foreign and international organizations for protection or redress of grievances have made them a constant problem for the authorities. Assyrian particularism seems to be breaking down and today for many Assyrians the sense of being Iraqi has transcended the concept of Assyrian nationhood.

Armenians

The Armenians, probably numbering upwards of 4,000, are relatively recent arrivals in Iraq, most of the older generation having entered the country from Anatolia following the Turkish violence against them there in 1915. Their relations with the larger community have on the whole been good but certain problems of assimilation do exist. Most of the group now speak Arabic as well as Armenian and often speak Turkish. A popular phrase of derogation in Iraq, however, is to say of someone, "He speaks Arabic like an Armenian." The Armenians are Christians, mainly Armenian Orthodox or Armenian Catholic. Quick to acquire modern skills, they have made a place for themselves in Iraq's larger cities as professionals, artisans, and, particularly, mechanics.

Lurs

The Lurs, of whom there are thought to be about 60,000 in Iraq, are settled in the eastern part of the country, which they entered generations ago over the Pusht i Kuh Mountains. Shiites who speak a dialect of Persian, they form a large part of the population of Badrah and Mandali, and are numerous at Ali al Gharbi and Qalat Sukkar and Ar Rifai on the Gharraf Canal system. More often town or village laborers than agriculturalists, they are found as porters of heavy loads in Baghdad and Basra. Nationalist Kurds refer to the Lurs as the "Fayliya" Kurds and claim them and the Persian Lurs for the proposed Kurdish state, but no such concept seems to have been accepted by Lurs themselves, who have not been a politically conscious group.

Jews

The 1947 census figure for Iraqi Jews was 118,000, but the number was unofficially estimated at about 150,000. They were concentrated in Baghdad province (77,542) and in Mosul and Basra (over 10,000 in each), but there were also communities in most of the large towns, notably in Al Hillah, as well as in some villages in the north. In 1950–51 almost the entire Jewish population left the country for Israel. Israeli figures show that more than 120,000 Iraqi Jews have entered Israel since the establishment of the state in 1948. A few thousand went to India, Lebanon, Europe, and the United States. The Grand Rabbi of Baghdad in 1955 estimated the Iraqi Jewish community at 5,000 persons, but most other observers put the number at 8,000 to 10,000. Those who are left in Iraq abjure Zionism completely and declare their undivided attachment to the state; the official attitude is that a loyal Jew is on the same footing as any other loyal citizen.

Jews formerly constituted almost the entire body of moneychangers and were also prominent in commerce and banking. Some of the younger Iraqi Jews were established in the fields of medicine and law.

Sabaeans

The Sabaeans, or Mandaeans, were in 1947 an urban-dwelling group of 6,597 persons, scattered among the towns along the rivers south of Baghdad. Even in the town of Suq ash Shuyukh, their principal place of settlement, they form less than 10 percent of the population. They are generally thought to be diminishing in numbers—the popular explanation being the reputed beauty of their women, who are much sought as wives by men of other groups. They are peaceable and industrious. Since they must live near running water in order to perform the numerous ablutions required by their religion, one of their principal traditional occupations has been boatbuilding. They also enjoy a high local reputation as silversmiths, specializing in Amarah-work of antimony designs on silver.

Physically, the Sabaeans stand out from among their neighbors; the women for their beauty, the men for their extreme hirsuteness.

Turkomans

The Turkomans are a Turkish-speaking Sunni Moslem group settled in northern Iraq in the areas of Qarah Tappah, Kirkuk, Irbil, and Tall Afar. Their numbers were put at 38,652 in 1919, and some estimates for today run as high as 75,000. Their Turkish dialect is considerably different from standard Turkish. While the Jarjariyah Turkomans around Tall Afar west of Mosul retain a tribal organization, the group as a whole, and particularly the younger generation, is being assimilated in language and social patterns into the larger Arab population. The Turkomans today, as in Ottoman times, furnish a much larger percentage of government functionaries than might be expected from their small numbers.

Aliens

In 1947 there were 73,828 persons, or about 1.5 percent of the total population, who claimed nationality other than Iraqi. This group is to be found largely in the cities: 63,886 lived in three urban centers —29,204 in Baghdad, 21,670 in Karbala, and 13,012 in Basra. More than three fourths of these—52,430—were Iranians.

The next largest group, the Indo-Pakistanis, called "Indians" in the census of 1947 but now probably Pakistani in majority, numbered 4,790 in 1947. Approximately half of these lived near the Shiite shrines, and most of the rest in the Basra district, where traditional connections with India have been close. To replace Jewish emigrants, additional numbers of Pakistanis were brought into the country in 1950–51 to work in the telegraph and railroad administrations; the exact number is not available.

Of the 3,400 Saudi Arabs, nearly 3,000 live in Az Zubayr in the Basra district, a trading center of long standing for the desert to the south. There is a Syrian-Lebanese community—most of whose members are engaged in the professions—of about 2,800, and about 1,000 Shiite Afghans live in the two holy cities of Kadhimain (Al Kazimiyah) and An Najaf. They are closely identified with the Iranian community in language and religion.

The British community of somewhat less than 3,000 persons is not entirely European in its geographical origin. A few hundred British subjects living in the holy cities have British citizenship but are of Middle Eastern origin. Half the remainder live in Baghdad and Basra. There are some 300 British residents in Kirkuk, center of the oil-producing installations.

An insignificant category in the 1947 census was that of Palestinian Arabs, but in 1948 about 5,000 such refugees came to Iraq, almost all to the Baghdad area. They are at the present time politically suspect, and 47 of them were deported early in 1956 for "subversive" acts, that is, anti-Baghdad Pact and pro-Egyptian activity.

Amalgamation

Iraq's various ethnic and religious communities all are being affected to one degree or another by the western influences that have been bearing on the country since the last century. The agents of that influence are not only Westerners who come into contact with Iraqis but more importantly the growing number of Iraqis who, having acquired new skills, ideas, and behavior patterns, transmit them to their fellows. Whatever the outcome of this process, the trend is clearly toward the disappearance of the visible signs which once identified people with a particular group.

The drift of the nomads to the villages, of villagers to the towns, and the pull of the towns on all segments of the population is altering the character of Iraqi society. It is slowly breaking down the isolation which traditionally has helped to preserve the barrier between one rural community and another. In the cities it is reducing the differences between ethnic groups; the Baghdadi Kurd today is likely to have more in common with his Arab neighbor than he is with his Kurdish compatriots in his home village. The Chaldean Christian hotel owner is far removed in his daily preoccupations from his cousins in Tall Kayf but close to his Moslem patrons. The newly sedentarized nomad becomes absorbed within a generation or two into the settled existence of the agricultural village, more and more villagers, including many of recent nomad origin, continue to leave for the towns. The political control of a central government and the influence of a growing system of public education are creating a widening area of shared experience and contributing to a sense of national identity which may in time come to transcend the still primarily local focus of Iraqi life.

Nevertheless, if the old ways are giving ground, they persist and it is still possible to identify the ethnic, religious, or occupational backgrounds of many Iraqis by their dress. The bedouin wears his headcloth fastened down with a plaited camel's-hair rope (decorated according to his wealth), a long straight gown under a camel's-hair cloak, and sandals. The tribal Kurd still wears baggy pantaloons, girded at the waist with a cummerbund in which he keeps his valuables and, more likely than not, a dagger or two; he wears peaked leather slippers, and, during the inclement mountain winter, a quilted jacket and a long cloak of bright colors which contrast with the sober black, brown, and white of the bedouin.

Women of conservative Moslem households still wear out-of-doors the shapeless cloak which covers them from head to foot; underneath they wear a straight gown and pantaloons, and, if well-to-do, some gold or silver head ornaments. Many city Arabs still wear the long tunic with a divided skirt, and a turban. The Christian men of Tall Kayf often wear conical hats of silver or other metals, reminiscent of figures from the ancient Babylonian and Assyrian bas-reliefs; their women, especially the older ones, may wear gaudy orange kerchiefs and voluminous red dresses. The black-bearded Yezidis wear Kurdish pantaloons; the Sabaeans also wear beards but use Arab headdress and white robes.

In all of these groups, however, the young men who have visited the cities usually possess one suit of western clothes and a pair of factory-made shoes. Western dress is now worn by some townswomen, but the veil is only slowly being discarded; even in the case of some of the more westernized families a compromise is still sought in the combination of a western dress, silk stockings, high heels, and a veil.

The social significance of physical traits is also changing. Among the upper classes blue eyes, supposedly a sign of Turkish-Circassian origin, stamped one as a member of the ruling aristocracy. To be grossly fat was evidence of material prosperity and a matter for congratulation; obesity is still common among the prosperous townsmen, but the younger generation, exposed to physical education courses at school, is popularizing a new ideal of physical fitness.

Until recently in the cities one lived within one's own group in a well-defined quarter. Under influences emanating from the towns, villages, if they were not occupied by members of a single group, were also divided into quarters. Today the rigid association patterns of the past are breaking down. The old ways persist strongly in the countryside but they are changing; differences between various communities are visibly narrowing and the process of westernization, with Arabization, is superimposing a homogeneous pattern on the Iraqi community as a whole.

The Arabic Language

In Iraq as elsewhere in the Arab world, Arabic exists as a literary form and as various local spoken dialects. The literary language, used in all serious writing and for all official purposes, is essentially the classical Arabic of the Koran as pronounced with a more or less Iraqi dialect accent and with a modernized vocabulary adapted to the necessities of present-day life.

As Arabic followed the spread of Islam it developed local variations. But the number of literate persons in the Arab world was so small and the prestige of the traditional written language so great by virtue of its religious sanction in the Koran that the local variants which developed never came to be used as independent literary languages. Devout Moslems believe that the Koran is God's word in form and substance: with only certain sectarian differences as to detail, the words of the Koran are believed to be the very words of

God's revelation to Mohammed through the angel Gabriel. Obviously, God chose Arabic over all other languages for its perfection; consequently, the language of the Koran represents an a priori standard, and deviation from it can only fall short of the pinnacle of linguistic beauty. The continuing effect of classical prose and poetry has also done much to keep the classical form alive and valued. In western Europe, Latin was held in great esteem and was a liturgical language, but an entirely different attitude toward the local developments of Latin grew up, and from the ninth century there are written documents in the local forms of Latin—French, Spanish, etc. In the Arab world this did not happen, and even though Iraqi, Syrian, Egyptian, and other forms of Arabic differ from each other to a considerable degree, they are hardly ever written and are nowhere used as teaching or official languages. When they are written at all, they appear in comic strips, jokes, plays, and folk songs.

All this means that in Iraq, as in all Arabic-speaking countries, educated persons tend to be bilingual—in the local dialect and in classical Arabic, although their classical Arabic may be somewhat weak. Even the completely uneducated have acquired some smattering of the classical language and the problems this presents for education are serious (see chap. 19).

Usage

In everyday usage Iraqis speak their local dialect, and people do not consciously change their dialect when they move, as from a village to a large city, though in time everybody adapts more or less to the language spoken by those about him.

Educated persons use in their spoken language varying numbers of words and expressions from the literary language. On all formal occasions, on the radio, in parliament, in schools, and in government offices, the language ideally used is the standard literary form. The pronunciation remains essentially local, though sometimes sounds are used that never occur in the colloquial form. The grammatical constructions are those of the classical language, with some tendency toward the colloquial depending on the speaker's education; the vocabulary, especially for special subjects, will often be very different from the colloquial. Classical and colloquial proverbs and religious quotations of various sorts are popular literary devices and the ability to quote them appropriately is a social asset.

On all formal occasions, educated Arabs in Iraq as elsewhere are sure that they are using pure, classical Arabic. But deviations from the ideal are extensive. More and more there is being used on formal occasions a language that in essence is a consciously archaized form of colloquial, with elegant turns of syntax, special grammatical forms here and there, occasional learned pronunciations, and many special words and expressions.

Poorly understood by the vast majority, classical Arabic is nevertheless regarded with reverence by all Arabs, whether or not they are able to use it. Even the illiterate refer to it as "our language," and most Arabs will declare that colloquial Arabic should be abandoned and classical used everywhere; as noted, the actual trend is toward a wider use of colloquial. Nevertheless, colloquial Arabic is looked upon, not as a separate language in itself, but as a corruption of classical Arabic. Classical Arabic is "correct"; colloquial Arabic is "incorrect"—and anyone who openly advocated the use of colloquial rather than classical would be considered at best an eccentric and at worst an enemy of religious and Arab unity.

Writing

Iraq is an area in which one of the world's few independently elaborated writing systems had its origin. The cuneiform system of writing was invented by the Sumerians, and it is not improbable that it evolved spontaneously—even though the Sumerians may have heard of the general idea of writing from Egypt, where writing was invented earlier, or possibly even from the Indus valley region, where there seem to have been earlier writing systems.

The Sumerian writing system is called "cuneiform" because its symbols are composed of wedge-shaped (Latin *cuneus,* "wedge") strokes made by pressing the end of a stylus into soft clay. The clay tablets were then baked into bricks, many of which still exist. The early form of this system was much like that of Egyptian hieroglyphics or modern Chinese writing. There were arbitrary symbols, some of which originated as pictures, denoting words. Some of the symbols occasionally were used to denote whole syllables simply as sounds, regardless of the original or imagined pictured meaning.

Use of the cuneiform writing system persisted despite changes of dominant language in Mesopotamia, but it was destined to be supplanted. Sometime around 4000 B.C., probably in the Sinai peninsula area, someone who was a speaker of a Semitic language had invented, on the basis of Egyptian hieroglyphics, a simple alphabet of twenty-two letters to represent the consonant sounds. From this alphabet came the known forms of Phoenician writing from which Greek writing and, eventually, all the writing systems of the western world, as well as Hebrew and Aramaic script, were derived. In Mesopotamia, Aramaic writing was used from before 1000 B.C., and it spread eastward into India, giving rise to the writing systems there.

The original Semitic alphabet spread to Arabia, and there the Arabic alphabet, an extremely cursive form, developed. When Arabic speakers came to Mesopotamia they brought this system with them. In Iraq today all normal writing of Arabic, and of Kurdish, is in the Arabic alphabet.

European languages used in Iraq are written in their usual alphabets—Latin, Greek, Cyrillic, Armenian. There is no movement to write Arabic in the Latin alphabet, nor is there yet much attempt to adapt Arabic writing to the colloquial language.

The Arabic alphabet is complicated, in some ways ill adapted even to the language for which it was developed, and poorly suited to any other language. In Iraq it is known to only a portion of the population. The illiteracy rate is high, and the language problem is such that the rate of literacy is not likely to rise rapidly. The failure of Arabic script to indicate vowels (except in certain cases such as the Koran, special literary publications, and primary school books) adds to the difficulties of education, especially of learning to read and write classical Arabic correctly. An Iraqi school child must learn not only a complex set of visual and motor skills but what is in many respects a language different from the one he usually speaks, one represented in writing mainly by consonant signs.

5

RELIGIONS

ISLAM REACHED IRAQ WITHIN A FEW YEARS OF THE DEATH, IN 632, of its founder, Mohammed, and has remained the dominant faith. Like other great religions it has been much affected by sectarian schisms. The most important of these, the Sunnite-Shiite division, is almost as old as Islam itself. Of the 350 million Moslems in the world, all but about 30 million are Sunnites; in Iraq, however, the Shiites comprise about half the Moslem population. The rivalry between the two groups has given special character to the country's history, and the division continues to complicate the social, economic, and political life of the nation. The religious roots of the schism have receded and the active frictions are those that come from competition for economic and political advantage. Religious difference and the recollection of injuries inflicted in the name of doctrinal rectitude remain a reservoir of symbols to be invoked in anger, but the disposition to employ them is being tempered, however slowly, by emergent Iraqi unity.

Iraq's religious minorities—a mere 3 percent of the population—are Christians, Yezidis, Mandaeans (Sabaeans), Jews, and small numbers of Bahai. Never numerous since the mass conversions to Islam in the seventh century, the minorities at times have been subjected to discrimination and even persecution, but for the most part have been free to follow their faiths without interference. Iraq's Christians comprise adherents of the native Chaldean Church, the Assyrian (the ancient Church of the East, Nestorian), Greek, Syrian, and Armenian Orthodox churches, and the Syrian and Armenian Catholic churches. The formerly large and prosperous Jewish colony (estimated at 150,000 at the outbreak of the Arab-Israeli war in 1947) has been reduced to 10,000 by mass emigration to Israel.

Islam is the state religion of Iraq, and though adaptations of western legal codes are now in use almost everywhere in the Moslem world, questions of personal status (marriage, divorce, inheritance, orphans, endowments) are still adjudicated in Iraq, as in all Moslem countries except Egypt, Turkey, and Tunisia, in the sharia courts applying Islamic law.

Islam

Islam ("submission"), the predominant religion of the Middle East, was first preached by the Prophet Mohammed, who was born in the Arabian town of Mecca in A.D. 570. According to tradition, Mohammed received a call from God while engaged in solitary contemplation at the mountain of Hira. The calls continued and Mohammed's preaching in Mecca against prevailing beliefs and practices earned the hostility of important personalities, who forced him to flee with his closest followers to Medina. This flight (hegira) in A.D. 622 marks the first year of the Moslem calendar. Ultimately Mohammed, gathering followers, was able to defeat his Meccan enemies and bring the entire Arabian subcontinent under his control. Mecca became the holy city; its principal shrine, the Kaaba, became the rallying point of Islam and the object of the greatest of Moslem pilgrimages.

In the theocratic order established during Mohammed's lifetime, he was judge, lawgiver, and social arbiter. The words he uttered while inspired were regarded as from God and were compiled into the Moslem holy book, the Koran; his noninspirational statements and the example of his personal conduct provided the basis for a code of behavior which, with local variations and sectarian differences, was to apply throughout Islam.

Building upon the precepts of Mohammed, devout Moslems held—and still hold—that religion, law, commerce, and social policies are inseparable. To deny this is to deny Islam in its totality, and herein lies one of the many great problems facing the Moslem world today, for the religion of Mohammed is feeling the impact of modern secular forces, and these are working to separate the components of the Islamic synthesis.

Islam continues to hold millions of adherents. It is, however, being tested in new ways, and, in the testing, both gaining and losing significance for its followers. In Iraq the strains on Islam are likely to become especially strong as the country's economic development program gives, as it seems likely to do, an increasingly secular focus to popular interest.

The Tenets of Islam

The fundamental article of faith of Islam is the testimony (*shahada*): "There is no God but God [Allah] and Mohammed is his Prophet."

The recital of the *shahada* in full and unquestioning belief is all that is required to become a Moslem.

Other Islamic dogmas involve belief in a general resurrection, in the final judgment of all mankind, in the preordainment of a man's every act and of his ultimate fate. Four books of scriptural revelation are recognized: the Koran (disclosed to Mohammed by God through the angel Gabriel), the Pentateuch and the Psalms from the Old Testament, and the Christian Gospels.

The Koran ("the bountiful, the beneficial") is the compilation of the inspired statements of Mohammed; it sets forth all man needs to attain salvation. The teachings of the four Gospels are accepted, though Moslems claim that the present texts have been corrupted by Christian translators and are not as God revealed them. The first five books of the Old Testament and the Psalms are also revered, but the charge is made that they have been falsified by the Jews. Also regarded by Moslems as scriptural but not divinely inspired are the Hadith: traditions based on the noninspirational sayings and the deeds of Mohammed. Koran and Hadith together provided a basis for the adaptation of existing customs into a comprehensive Moslem code of behavior, the Sunnah. Sunnites and Shiites each have their own Sunnah.

Islam teaches that God has given mankind a succession of revelations of divine truth through his prophets and that each time the human race falls into error God sends new prophets to lead it back into the ways of truth and righteousness. Altogether, according to Islamic traditionalists, there have been over two thousand prophets since the Creation; the foremost of these are Adam, Noah, Abraham, Moses, Jesus, and the last and greatest, Mohammed.

The Five Pillars

The basic teachings of Islam, called the "Five Pillars," declare the oneness of God, the spiritual value of prayer, and the duties of fasting, almsgiving, and pilgrimage. These positive injunctions parallel those of antecedent Judaism and Christianity as do the Moslem prohibitions against adultery, gambling, usury, and the consumption of carrion, blood, pork, and alcohol.

THE CREED. The testimony of the faith, "There is no God but God and Mohammed is his Prophet," must be repeated at least once in a lifetime, aloud, correctly, and with full understanding of its significance and fervent belief in its truth. To this declaration Shiites add "and Ali is the vicegerent of God."

PRAYER. Every Moslem is required to pray, in a prescribed manner, five times a day. The formalized prayer consists of a series of obeisances made first from a standing and then from a kneeling position. Men should, whenever possible, make their prayers in a mosque, but they are free to pray by themselves; women usually pray in the seclusion of the home, though many attend the mosque, omitting the ritual movements of prayer. On Friday large numbers of Moslems attend the mosque for communal prayer—the form advocated by the Prophet as being most beneficial—and hear the weekly sermon. Friday, however, is in no way to be considered the equivalent of the Sabbath; the Koran enjoins the faithful to return to their business after hearing the sermon.

FASTING. The severest formal test of a Moslem's ability to practice his faith is met in Ramadan, the ninth month of the Moslem calendar. During this period all are required to fast from daybreak (reckoned from the moment a black thread can be distinguished from a white one) until the last rays of light have disappeared from the sky. The fast involves abstention from all food, drink, tobacco, and all indulgence in worldly pleasures, though exceptions are made in the case of the sick, the weak, soldiers in front lines or on patrol, and travelers. Today, Ramadan is not observed widely in rural areas or among the urban poor. It is not unusual for members of the working class, both rural and urban, when asked if they are fasting, to reply "No, I must work." Relatively few Baghdad slum families, which include many of recent rural origin, keep the fast. The majority of fasters are tradition minded upper- and middle-class people, such as merchants and civil servants, plus some established urban people of the lower class.

Since the Moslem year consists of twelve lunar months and is shorter by eleven or twelve days than the astronomical year, Ramadan periodically falls during the midsummer heat and its observance imposes very real hardship. The psychological effect of Ramadan is marked; as the month progresses people's tempers become shorter, personal violence and divorces increase sharply, riots are frequent. The firing of a cannon at nightfall is the signal for all to repair home to break the fast, and, as the days pass, it is common for those who can afford it to rest all day and to banquet far into the night. The nights of Ramadan are the time for shadow plays and other public entertainments.

ALMSGIVING. The Koran lays great stress on the giving of alms. In early times it was customary to give one fortieth of one's annual income—either in money or in kind to "the poor, the needy, those employed in the collection of alms, those who are to be conciliated, slaves and prisoners, debtors and to mosques for the 'Way of God'." The religious obligation of almsgiving is everywhere still recognized, but with the general slackening of rigid observance only a minority of Moslems make their contributions today in strict accordance with Koranic stipulations.

PILGRIMAGE. The pilgrimage to Mecca—the hadj—is regarded as the ideal culmination of every Moslem's religious experience. The Koran refers to Mecca as the "Station of Abraham," and according to tradition the foundation of the Kaaba, the central shrine of Islam, was laid by Abraham and his son Ishmael. Adam is said to be buried in Mecca, and according to some the tomb of Mohammed is there, though consensus of belief places the resting place of the Prophet in Medina. The Kaaba, the shrine of shrines, is regarded not only as the center of the earth but as the center of the universe; it is the place where earth and heaven join, where God is to be met face to face. The uncompromising insistence of the Koran on the true holiness of Mecca has from the beginning made the pilgrimage something to be achieved at least once in a lifetime if humanly possible. Those who are too poor to travel, however, are tacitly exempted, since authorities disapprove of a pilgrim's begging his way, as many do. In the case of Shiites, pilgrimage to Mecca may be undertaken by hired substitutes or replaced by visits to one of the great Shiite holy places, usually An Najaf (where Ali is buried) or Karbala in Iraq, or Meshed in Iran, where Shiite saints are buried.

Jihad

In theory jihad (literally: exertion) is a permanent struggle to make the word of God supreme among all men. In Moslem teaching it is presented as part of the collective duty of the faithful to Allah and sometimes referred to as the sixth Pillar of Islam. Mohammed urged the feuding Arab tribes to compose their differences and divert their energies to the task of converting the world. The notion of many non-Moslems that jihad means "holy war" is erroneous, and, with specific reference to Christians and Jews, the Koran makes it clear that as "People of the Book" they are not to be Islamized by force.

The secular temper of Iraqi political leadership today makes unlikely any call to jihad in the old proselytizing sense, although in other parts of the Arab world jihad has been invoked quite recently by Moslem leaders to add a religious incentive to political motives in waging war against other states.

The Institutions of Islam

The Moslem's relationship with God is seen as personal and direct; orthodox Islam acknowledges no communion of saints to intercede for sinners; there is no ordained priesthood or other sacramentary institution. The Prophet Mohammed was born an ordinary man; the divine revelations did not change his nature. He died and was buried, and no resurrection is claimed for him—"Mohammed is dead," said his successor, Abu Bakr. Among the Shiites, however, the cult of saints—which grew along with the teachings of the Sufis, the Moslem mystics—has a wide following. Some Shiites even attribute quasi-divine power to Mohammed; all hold that the special powers of Mohammed were handed down to his descendants through Ali, enabling them to interpret the Divine Will.

The Arabs, who within a few years of the Prophet's death spread Islam throughout the Middle East and North Africa, brought to those regions a system in which the religious and secular were knit together. Mohammed's spiritual and temporal successors, the caliphs, reminded Moslems that the religion of the Prophet was an infallible guide in all aspects of human conduct. The Word as revealed in the Koran was taught to the faithful by imams (prayer leaders and preachers); on a higher level of religious learning were the ulemas, expounders and interpreters of theology and law. The faithful were called to prayer five times a day by the muezzin. Today these functionaries continue to discharge their duties—somewhat narrowed by the secular developments of the modern period—as they have done down the centuries, and a strong doctrinal and ritual continuity has been maintained.

The only appointed officials are the imam and the muezzin; some of the imams are highly educated scholars, well paid and influential; others, in the poorer urban districts and in the villages, may be barely literate and so badly paid that they have to make ends meet through part-time employment, often manual labor. Other religious functionaries are the mullah, the religious teacher in Shiite villages, and the aga of the Kurds, who exercises some religious authority and may claim descent from the Prophet.

Islam takes no account of those elements which in other religions make for the ritual observance of a liturgical calendar. It has few of the holy days which characterize Catholic and Orthodox Christianity. Its mosques, however ornate and carefully tended, are not consecrated; they are simply halls set aside for congregational prayer and the delivery of the weekly sermon.

Of the institutional religious observances, Ramadan and the pilgrimage to Mecca have been discussed above. Part of the pilgrimage period is celebrated as Aid al-Kabir, the Great Feast, a four-day commemoration of Abraham's willingness to sacrifice his son (Isaac in the Bible version, Ishmael according to the Koran) at God's command. The end of Ramadan is marked by three days of festivities (Aid as-Saghir). Mouled, the birthday of the Prophet is a one-day festival, as is Ashura, the tenth day of Muharram (the first month of the Moslem year), on which the death of Husein, the son of Ali, is remembered. The Shiites, holding that Husein was the rightful caliph, commemorate his death in battle for the first ten days of Muharram; except among the traditionalists the observance now has more of a festive air than in the past, when physical self-punishment as a penitential act was a common practice.

Islamic Law

Islamic law, while giving wide latitude to local law and custom, embraces the whole range of personal and social life. It tells the believer how to live righteously and the community at large how to conduct its affairs, spiritual and temporal. Of the several schools of law, four—the Hanafi, the Hanbalite, the Shafiite, and the Maliki—have been preserved as equally orthodox. Named after their founders, they differ not in principles but in the degree of emphasis laid on the four recognized sources of law—the Koran, tradition, consensus, and analogy. All schools agree that the Koran and tradition are the two basic sources, but the Hanafi school, adopted by the Ottoman sultans and widely followed in their Empire, is regarded as the most liberal and makes proportionately more use of analogical deduction. The Shafiite, which maintains a balance between the liberal and conservative schools, and the liberal Hanafi are the most widely followed in Iraq.

In the days before western civil and criminal codes began to supplant Islamic law, the mufti, who interpreted the law, and the cadi, who handed it down, were persons of considerable importance. Litigants were anxious to obtain the help of a mufti known for his compelling interpretations, and the controversies between certain learned muftis are famous. Much sought after, many muftis became rich and influential. Western-based secular law has reduced their influence, but the specialists in traditional law still function in the limited competence of the sharia courts and are consulted on the adaptation of western law to the Islamic tradition.

The Great Schism

The development of Islam has been marked by numerous sectarian divisions; the earliest and most important had its beginning in A.D.

657, only twenty-five years after the death of Mohammed. The occasion was the Battle of Siffin, when, following his defeat by Moawiyah (who later became caliph), Ali, Mohammed's son-in-law and the fourth caliph, was compelled to submit to arbitration his claims to the caliphate. A number of Ali's followers thereupon claimed that arbitration was inadmissible where a clear mandate was to be found in the Koran. From this point stemmed the Sunnite-Shiite schism, and though the Shiites have since experienced further division it is usual today to classify all Moslems as either Sunnite or Shiite.

Sunnites

The Sunnis hold that the caliphate is an elective office and must be held by a member of the Koreish (Mohammed's tribe). They derive their name from the Sunnah. Generally referred to as orthodox—in the sense that in their great numerical superiority they may be said to represent the Islamic community as a whole—Sunnites have developed their faith and practice more strictly in accordance with prophetic tradition and precept than have the schismatics, and have been less willing to accept innovation, particularly in regard to practices which might be imported from other religions.

Shiites

Although they are the second largest group in Islam, the Shiites, the "party of Ali," had by 1950 shrunk in numbers to about 30 million, of whom 19 million were in Iran. After the defeat of Ali by Moawiyah and, later, Ali's assassination, the political center of the faith was moved to Syria and away from the House of Ali. Ali's followers formed a "legitimist" group to restore the caliphate to what they claimed were its rightful holders; gradually this political issue took on a doctrinal color which involved the reputation of Abu Bakr, Omar, and Othman—the first three caliphs and closest companions of Mohammed—and this act serves to the present time to condemn the Shiites in the eyes of the orthodox.

From the beginning, Shiism began to adapt old beliefs (Babylonian, Persian, Indian) as well as some of the current beliefs of the countries which succumbed to the Arab conquest. Shiism thus grew under conditions favorable to sectarian splits within Shiism itself. There promptly arose differences on the nature of the imamate. Only the Zeidis of Yemen permit the election of their imam from among all the descendants of Ali; all other Shiites restrict the succession to the direct line of Ali. There are, however, two subdivisions, the "Twelvers" and "Seveners," resulting from a dissension which arose after the death of the sixth imam, Jafar as-Sadiq (d. 765).

The Twelvers, also called Jafaris, acknowledged the younger son of Jafar, Musa al-Khazim. The Seveners (Ismailis) supported the claim of the elder brother, Ismail. The majority of Shiites are Jafaris; the Ismailis, of whom the Agha Khan is the supreme leader, are concentrated mainly in Pakistan, along the Persian Gulf, and in East Africa.

Islam in Iraq

Sunnism and Shiism in Iraq have been about equal in number of adherents; they have not been equal in economic and political power, for Iraq's rulers from the early caliphs and the Turkish sultans down to the contemporary ruling house have been Sunnites. Sunnite power bore heavily on the Shiites and these keep alive the memory of historic injuries. Today the Shiite position is improving but Shiites are resentfully conscious of being at a disadvantage. Sunnite leaders, on the other hand, have not forgotten that during the times of Ottoman persecution the Shiites sought Persian support, and the mistrust of Shiite political reliability engendered then has not yet disappeared.

Religious factionalism seems to be declining as a direct source of political instability and strife. The traditional theocrats have been giving ground to the proponents of western ideas and technology; Islamic law, apart from questions of personal status, has been superseded by western codes; religious certitude is having to contend with doubt; the growing body of educated Moslems tend to neglect the mosque and pay less attention to the dietary laws. Industrial growth and the necessity of adapting trade patterns to the imperatives of the international market have led to major changes in the social as well as the economic life of the country. Such developments seem to indicate less a weakening of the hold of Islam on the population at large than a process which, in altering the lives of the people, is changing the meaning and social uses of their religion. Meanwhile, the public manifestations of piety go on. Prominent personalities perform their religious duties, whether out of political expediency, deep religious conviction, or both. Their appearances at the mosques contribute to the prestige of Islam as the state religion and reinforce political ends and means with religious sanctions.

The conscious tendency to criticize or depart from Islam as a faith and guide to life has been largely confined to those urban elements most exposed to western influences. In the smaller towns and the countryside, tradition is still strong: the Kurds in the northeastern mountains and the Arabs of the northern plain remain staunchly Sunnite; the riverine peoples to the south of Baghdad are no less staunchly Shiite. The bedouin of the southern and western desert areas may be either Sunnite or Shiite; though casual about ritual observance, he questions his faith as little as his ancestors did. With economic change and the spread of education, however, religion in the countryside and the desert inevitably will meet the secular challenge it now confronts in the cities.

The Religion of the Bedouins

Religious activities among the bedouins are presided over by the sayyids, who claim descent from the Prophet. The sayyids are not members of the tribes with which they live but are supported by them for their services in giving sanction to weddings, circumcisions, funerals, and other celebrations. As the only literate man in most groups, the sayyid also generally serves as physician, scribe, and a link with the outside world (see chap. 6).

Compared with the devotion of much of the settled population to formal religious observance, the attitude of the bedouins, both Shiite and Sunnite, seems casual, if not indifferent. The ritual practices which mark Moslem life in the towns are largely absent in the desert. Of the Five Pillars of Islam, only the set declaration of faith seems to be of much concern to the bedouin, and although this is often on his lips its meaning for him is diluted by his belief in spirits, demons, and other manifestations of the supernatural. As for the other four Pillars, there is little pretense even of formal compliance; few nomads pray five times a day, keep Ramadan, offer alms, or make the pilgrimage to Mecca—and the time is not long past when the bedouins regarded pilgrims as a source of tribute or loot.

The religion of the bedouin retains a core of customary beliefs and practices that long antedate Islam. Transmitted orally from generation to generation, this indigenous tradition gives sanction to many aspects of bedouin life. God in the nomad's world is strong, arbitrary, unchanging, and immovable, but this belief does not lessen the fear of cruel and capricious spirits, jinns, and afreets. The man who has lost God's blessing by violating such bedouin moral canons as those pertaining to courage, truthfulness, loyalty to kin, and hospitality is at the mercy of these malignant spirits, who have power to bring sickness and misfortune. They are propitiated with charms, amulets, and prayers.

The jinns may also be propitiated by partaking of the *baraka,* the mystical power of someone who has *wajh khayr,* a good or lucky face. The *baraka* of these lucky ones, male or female, may be obtained by eating with them, being given some of their property, or receiving their good wishes. Most old people are assumed to be possessed of a lucky face, both because they have succeeded in living a long time and because their approach to the grave in old age is thought to bring them nearer to the supernatural.

Folk Belief and Superstition

Popular customs among uneducated townsmen and villagers also involve the use of magic to control nature and destiny. The jinns are here too and are held at bay with magical formulas, amulets, and other devices which may be obtained from wandering sayyids. The "evil eye," a mysterious and hateful power carried by the glance of certain persons, is much feared in both the village and nomad groups. Objects of a sky-blue color or sky-blue decorations around the windows or doors of dwellings are thought to be efficacious in warding off the "evil eye."

Local cults of saints are numerous, especially in Shiite areas. The difficulty of finding theological justification for saints in Islam has been overcome, not without opposition in orthodox circles, by declaring the saint to be the possessor of transcendental knowledge; closer to God than his fellow Moslems, he is able to perform miracles by the grace of Allah. Practically every Shiite village has a grave shrine to some man or woman locally esteemed as a saint. The cults which have grown up around these saints give the villager a sense of security against the omnipresent evil spirits. Disease and childlessness are perhaps the two most frequent misfortunes against which the help of the saints is invoked. A saint's popularity is compounded of stories and legends about his life, miracles, and ascetism, and his reputation for granting supernatural help to his followers. The shrines of the more renowned saints attract pilgrims throughout the year; the greatest ones in the Shiite cities are visited by the Shiites in much the same manner as Sunnites make the pilgrimage to Mecca.

Religious Minorities

Christians

There are some 150,000 Christians in Iraq; half of them are in Mosul province, long a Christian center; sizable groups live in the larger cities; and some villages are mixed Christian and Moslem, while in the Mosul area a few villages are entirely Christian.

Throughout the Arab world religion has been an important determinant of social status. Under the Ottoman Empire, Christians and other non-Moslems found themselves in a position of inferiority, tolerated and sometimes oppressed by the authorities. Today the Iraqi Government, in an effort to unite the population of the country in a sense of common Iraqi nationality, is emphasizing equality and Christians are beginning to play a larger part in the affairs of state than they have at any time since the rise of Islam.

There is only a small number of Roman Catholics but almost all Iraq's Christians belong to churches in communion with the Holy See and therefore accept the same articles of faith as do the Roman Catholics. These Uniate churches are of the Eastern rite, however, and employ liturgical languages other than Latin; generally speaking, feasts and fasts occupy a larger place in the lives of their members than is the case among Catholics in the West. Parish priests—but not monks or bishops—of these churches may marry. The monasteries are the centers of the hierarchial life of the churches and many of them are connected with shrines that are reputed to have miraculous virtues.

In Ottoman times, when the several religious communities were largely self-governing, the bishops had great power over their adherents. With Iraq's emergence as a secular national state this power has largely disappeared and is preserved only in such matters as marriage, divorce, and some aspects of inheritance.

The largest Christian group in Iraq, claiming a membership of almost 100,000, is the Chaldean. Headed by the Patriarch of Babylon, whose seat is at Mosul, this indigenous community was formerly Nestorian (see Assyrians) but became Uniate largely as the result of successful missions sent out by Roman Catholic monastic orders during the nineteenth century.

Jacobites, like the Egyptian Copts, believe in Monophysitism, the doctrine that there was but a single nature in Christ—that the human and divine constituted but one composite nature. They are one of the poorest and least westernized of the Christian groups. Named after Jacob, Bishop of Edessa (d. 578), and headed by Mar Ignatius (the hereditary title "Mar" may be translated as "lord"), many members of this church have in recent years been received into one or other of the Uniate bodies.

Of all the Christian churches in Iraq the one which has held most tenaciously to its concept of also being a "nation" is the Assyrian, or Nestorian, Church. Formerly called "The Church of the East" and in the thirteenth century extending into India and through Central Asia to China, this church today represents a small remnant of what it once was. It has a scattering of adherents over the Middle East, and, in recent years, a few have come to the Americas. Its head, Mar Shimun, the "Patriarch of the East," now lives in the United States and is on bad terms with the Iraqi authorities. His position, to which he acceded at the age of ten, is hereditary, having been transmitted in his family line from paternal uncle to nephew for several hundred years.

In the last century this church fell upon such hard times that some of its bishops could not read and were quite ignorant of the formal articles of their faith. Since then the Church of England has maintained a mission to the Assyrians with the principal purpose of educating the priesthood and the hierarchy in their liturgical language and in the precepts of their faith. As a result the Assyrians have become closely identified with the Anglican communion and also politically with Great Britain. Those now left in Iraq tend to divide their loyalties, some remaining faithful to Mar Shimun, others identifying themselves with the Chaldeans, and still others beginning to extend their allegiance beyond the confines of the secular state.

Of the remaining Christians, the Syrian Catholics (about 25,-000) are Uniates who broke away from the Jacobites; the Roman Catholic and the Orthodox Armenians, originally refugees, number altogether about 4,000.

Other Religious Groups

All other religious groups in Iraq number only a few thousand and, since the exodus of the Jews after the Arab-Israeli war, none of them plays any important role in the life of the country.

The Yezidis constitute the largest of these groups. Their religious beliefs and practices are highly esoteric. Basically, however, their religion apparently involves not only worship of God but propitiation of Satan (Shaitan), which has led them to be reviled as devil worshippers. They do not in fact worship the devil, but, since they posit God in a passive as well as an active aspect, it is thought that they believe Satan is more active in this world than the forces of good and therefore is to be appeased. Yezidis even avoid words containing the letter *shin*, holding that they invoke Saton's attention and malevolence. The "good" divinity symbolized by a metal peacock—Malik Taus, the "Peacock Angel"—is carried in religious processions and is asserted to have miraculous powers. Long defamed and persecuted as heretics by Moslems, the Yezidis in present-day Iraq enjoy religious toleration by the authorities, who also tacitly exempt them from participation in national politics (see chap. 4).

Another noteworthy group is the Mandaeans or Sabaeans. Although they are often called Christians of St. John, and have also claimed to be the descendants of the ancient Sabaeans (since they could then be counted as "People of the Book" and not classified as infidels by their Islamic rulers), their faith seems to contain elements of several creeds. Their books are written in Mandaean script; access to them is a prerogative of the priesthood. The principal external characteristic of their faith is the frequency of baptismal rites; baptism is seen, as in Christianity, as a ritual ablution of guilt, but among the Mandaeans it is performed after any act which brings defilement. Thus the Mandaeans are always to be found near water, and this has localized them on the banks of the rivers to the south of Baghdad (see chap. 4). Both the Yezidis and Mandaeans have been decreasing in numbers for many years and the continued defection of their young people points to the ultimate disappearance of both groups.

There is a small group of members of the Bahai faith in Baghdad. Since many converts to this new faith had renounced Islam, Bahais were subjected to some ill-treatment as recently as the 1920's and 1930's, but feeling against them seems to have subsided.

Iraq's religious minority groups are rarely heard from today. In the past, persecution was more often political than religious in its motivation. The Assyrians in particular in the years before the British withdrawal invited action against themselves by strongly identifying themselves with the British, appealing for their "national rights" to international organizations, and rejecting the notion of Iraqi nationality.

Growing conscious acceptance of Iraqi nationhood is gradually leading to mutual acceptance and some social amalgamation between the majority and minority elements; differing religious beliefs now have only a contingent and decreasing importance as a divisive factor in the country.

6

SOCIAL ORGANIZATION

IN ITS MAJOR OUTLINES IRAQI SOCIETY CONFORMS TO THE generalized traditional social pattern found throughout the Middle East. Town, village, and nomad camp have long defined very different ways of life in the area; and, although larger identities within the framework of the modern Iraqi state are taking shape, contempt and prejudice still color the relations between these three fundamental divisions. There exist, however, wide spheres of interdependence. The townsman and the bedouin depend on the food production of the village; and the town supplies commodities such as cloth, sugar, salt, and metal goods which the limited economies of the villager and of the bedouin cannot produce.

Less sophisticated than the townsman and less aggressive than the bedouin, the villager has been exploited by both. The townsman tends to regard the villager as an unlettered oaf. The villager sees the townsman as an instrument of governmental authority, a hard-dealing merchant or moneylender, a tax collector, or a neglectful absentee landlord. Though the villager knows the bedouin to be a customer for produce, he remembers him only too well as a warlike plunderer and imposer of tribute. Townsman and bedouin, sharing contempt for the villager, have been no less contemptuous of each other. In times of weakness even the largest Middle Eastern cities have suffered from bedouin raids, and the fringes of the sown area have many times reverted to nomadic pasture. Only during periods of urban ascendancy have the bedouins been contained within their desert grazing lands and restrained from pillaging the village agricultural produce on which the towns depend.

Divided like the Arabs into nomads, villagers, and townsmen, the kinship patterns of the Kurds basically resemble those of the Arabs. There are, however, significant differences. Persistence of the Kurdish language as mother tongue of the Kurdish minority and of a highly specific sense of Kurdish identity have already been discussed (see chap. 4). The Arab preoccupation with lineage and kinship is qualified among the Kurds by the relatively independent role of the small family and by a less rigid insistence upon hereditary right in the assignment of chieftainship. Both Kurds and Arabs follow the traditional Moslem ordering of the status of the sexes, but the Kurdish woman has enjoyed somewhat greater latitude in community life. The value assigned bravery and skill in arms, which among the Arabs rests chiefly with the bedouins, runs throughout Kurdish society. Both Arabs and Kurds are bound to their kin and local groups by strong ties, but among the Kurds there is a somewhat more individualistic outlook.

Economic and social changes in Iraq are lessening the differences between the Kurdish and Arab social patterns. Indeed, throughout Iraq, new sources of wealth and political power have combined with the decline of bedouin strength to alter traditional intergroup relationships. The family-based patterns of urban and village life are themselves being modified. But the nomadic minority, though dwindling, still adheres to its traditional social scheme.

The Bedouins

The bedouins of Iraq inhabit the Desert Administration areas west of the Euphrates and, across the river, the Jazirah region adjacent to Mosul province. Officially estimated at about 250,000 (some authorities go much higher), they belong for the most part to tribes of the great camel- and sheep-breeding Shammar confederation, which has member tribes in north-central Saudi Arabi and the Syrian Jazirah. The territory of the Iraqi Shammar is traditionally the Jazirah of Iraq, which lies between the rivers well to the north of Baghdad, but Shammar incursions into the territories of other tribes resulted in permanent encroachments which have given rise to hostility not yet completely quieted.

Immediately to the south of the Iraqi Shammar's grazing territories lie those of their traditional enemies, the sheep-raising Dulaym (who also have much cultivated ground in the Euphrates valley), while the desert south from Al Fallujah to Basra is the home of the Muntafiq and Dharfir tribes; the latter, formerly notorious as pillagers of pilgrimage caravans, are also traditional enemies of the Shammar.

Very few, if any of Iraq's bedouins are today exclusively camel breeders, though in the areas more remote from the river system—where only the camel is able to survive for long periods—some subsist mainly in this way. In the zones abutting the area of settled cultivation the camel gives way to sheep and goats. Those bedouins closest to the cultivated areas supplement the breeding of sheep and goats with farming, and in a progressive process of sedentarization many have turned to village life and full-time farming.

The bedouins classify themselves and the sedentary population in several ways. Villagers and townsmen constitute the despised *hadar.* The nomads refer to themselves as *ruhhal,* claiming that they alone have the right to be called Arabs—a term which they reserve for tent dwellers of noble blood. Among themselves they further distinguish between those groups whose herds consist exclusively or mainly of camels and those whose flocks are predominantly made up of other animals. The rich and powerful camel-breeding tribes reserve the term bedouin (desert dweller) to themselves; they refer to the others, even though true desert nomads and calling themselves bedouins, either as *shawayah* (sheep herders) or *maazah* (goat herders).

Traditionally, the great camel-breeding tribes, well armed and able to command tribute from others, have held the pinnacle of the desert aristocracy. Government control has brought an end to the levying of tribute, and the shrinking of the camel-based economy is drawing the nomads closer to the river system and turning increasing numbers of them into *raiyyah,* shepherds who during the spring and summer live in the sown area and cultivate crops and during the more moist winter season move into the desert with their flocks and tents.

Lowest in the nomad social scale are the base-born groups of indeterminate origin called *solubah.* (Originally the name of an individual tribe, the term has come to indicate despised status.) The *solubah* wander the desert, temporarily attaching themselves to noble tribes for which they work as smiths, tinkers, carpenters, and cattle surgeons. Their women provide entertainment as dancers, singers, and prostitutes. In return the *solubah,* as nonfighters, enjoy the protection of the patron tribe, and in any case their noncombatant status has always been recognized by enemy raiding parties.

A final broad classification used by both nomads and the settled population is based on the notion of northern or southern ancestry. The entire Arab population claims descent either from the north Arabian (or Quaysi) tribes or from the south Arabian (or Yemeni) tribes. This dichotomy, originating in pre-Islamic times, has today lost practically all significance, though in the past rivalry was sometimes intense and much feuding was caused by it.

Tribal Structure

The Iraqi tribes vary in structure and size, as do nomadic tribes throughout the Arab world. A tribe may consist of only a few families or, like the Shammar tribes, it may have hundreds or even thousands of tents. Origins, too, are hard to pinpoint, for though most tribes have strong traditions concerning their founding ancestor, a complex process of amalgamation, division, reamalgamation and re-division has been going on for a long time.

The tribe (*qabilah*) is usually subdivided into two or more sub-tribes (*ashirah*); each subtribe, in turn, is commonly divided into two or more subdivisions (*firqah*). The *firqah* comprises two or more further divisions (*fakhdh*); the *fakhdh* is divided into two or more *hamulah,* and finally the *hamulah* into two or more related extended families. Kinship is reckoned through the male line. As a rule each tribe claims that it comprises descendants of a single an-cestor whose name it often bears. It is not unusual, however, for this ancestor to be a fictitious figure whose existence is affirmed to give prestige to the tribe.

It is doubtful that the ideal six-level tribal structure can be found in any Iraqi tribes today; even the largest and most com-plex groups probably do not show more than four levels—extended family, lineage (*hamulah*), subtribe, and tribe. Furthermore, two or more subdivisions of the same level in any particular tribe are rarely symmetrical; of several related subtribes, for example, one may be built on two levels while others will contain three or four.

Lineage and Family

The *hamulah,* or lineage, consists of several related extended fami-lies with a common ancestor. Next to the extended family the *hamulah* is the group with which the individual identifies himself most closely and which functions as a unit in grazing its flocks and camping and in protecting its members.

The extended family, the nucleus of all Arab tribal organization, consists of three generations of parents and children who reckon de-scent in the male line. Such a family comprises paternal grandparents, married sons and their wives, the sons' married and unmarried sons, and unmarried daughters. The group may also include widowed or orphaned female relatives of the senior male. Formally, authority is vested in the senior male; he may, however, delegate his powers in old age or may even be superseded by a more aggressive son. Tradi-tionally, marriage is confined to the lineage, but this is by no means exclusively the case.

Khamsah

An important social unit among the nomads, and to a lesser extent in the settled population, is the *khamsah,* the group of five. A man's *khamsah* ideally embraces all his patrilineal relatives who are within five degrees of relationship. The actual definition of the *khamsah* varies from tribe to tribe, but an idea of its extent may be gained from the fact that it would normally include relatives as distant as a grandfather's brother's grandson. The *khamsah* is the traditional vengeance group which functions in cases of conflict, notably the blood feuds to which bedouin society is so addicted. Governmental pressures are beginning to break down the vengeance group concept but formerly if a tribesman had been murdered his relatives within the *khamsah* were required to avenge his death, and all members of the murderer's *khamsah* were considered as sharing responsibility and thus as legitimate targets for reprisal.

Leadership

Leadership in nomadic tribal society is vested in the heads of successively larger kinship aggregates. Every competent male can count on becoming in due course head of his own extended family. For example, when the head of an extended family dies, each of his sons becomes the head of a family consisting of his own sons, his grandsons (if any), and their womenfolk. As a rule, among the extended families comprising a lineage, one family has the hereditary right to leadership of the lineage, and one of that family's senior males—not necessarily the most senior—heads the lineage. The headship of the next higher group in the tribe is vested in one of the lineage-head families, and so on up to the leadership of the tribe itself. In this hierarchy each leader exercises authority on the level to which family position and personal ability may have brought him. The traditional title of all these chieftains is "sheikh."

Although the position of sheikh is usually filled from particular families who enjoy that hereditary privilege, no strict rule of inheritance governs the selection within the family. If, for example, the sheikh is ill or old and infirm the tribe will be preoccupied with the matter of succession and out of the deliberations of the elder men a decision will be reached on which of the sheikh's sons or close male relations is most suited to fill his place. A sheikh who prefers one of his sons or kin may entrust him with the conduct of tribal affairs in order to give him a chance to prove himself, but with the death of the sheikh the relative who has the support of the tribal elders—and through them of tribal opinion—is chosen regardless of the former sheikh's preference. Should two or more members of a sheikh's family aspire to leadership, and should all have a large number of adherents, the tribe may split into independent units.

The sheikh of the tribe is assisted by the *majlis,* the tribal council. Composed of the heads of the various subdivisions of the tribe, the *majlis* meets every day in the guest tent of the sheikh when the tribe is encamped. All adult males of the tribe may attend the *majlis,* but when more serious matters are brought up for discussion it is usual for the young men, including the younger members of the sheikh's family, to leave the tent.

At the sessions of the *majlis,* which last until about midday, such matters are discussed as when to break camp, where to find grass, relations with other tribes, and cases of litigation. Today government backing and the transformation of many tribal sheikhs into big landowners has rendered sheikhly authority more arbitrary; traditionally the sheikh could not make any decision to which the elders were opposed, though he was frequently able to carry a decision by force of personality, understanding, and good judgment.

The duties of the sheikh are to represent his tribe, to rule on water rights, to act as arbiter and judge in litigation, to give consent to marriages and divorces, and to work generally for his tribe's welfare. The sheikh also has the onerous responsibility for collecting taxes within the tribe or for assisting the government tax collector. Today, with the necessity for increased contacts between the tribes and the central authorities, some sheikhs are employing business advisers (generally not tribesmen—most of whom are illiterate—but persons brought in from outside). In many cases the tribal sheikhs, and often the sheikhs of the larger subtribes, have become town or city dwellers; some have compromised their traditional status as opponents of the central authority to the extent of becoming members of the Iraqi parliament.

The Sayyids

With each bedouin *hamulah* is usually to be found a sayyid and his family. Claiming descent from Mohammed and marrying only among themselves, the sayyids are not full members of the tribe and participate in lineage activities only in the religious sphere. They are supported by the lineage and in return provide religious sanction for weddings, circumcisions, funerals, and other celebrations, besides serving as a contact with the world of the supernatural. The sayyid's prayers in times of drought, sickness, or any other crisis are looked upon as the collective prayers of the tribesmen though the latter participate in them only irregularly.

Most sayyids are believed, by virtue of their descent from the Prophet, to possess various saintly qualities which may be exercised to cure the sick and obtain grace for the dying. The sayyid, usually the only educated person in the lineage, also serves as a scribe on those occasions when written communications are called for; when a newspaper is received in the lineage the sayyid reads and interprets it to the tribesmen. These practical abilities to read and write, coupled with the elements of piety and descent from the Prophet, set the sayyid in a position of such respect in the lineage that the tribesmen willingly contribute to his support. It is not at all unusual for a sayyid to change from one lineage to another, or even from one tribe to another.

The normal method by which a sayyid joins a lineage is for the lineage to inform the tribal sheikh of its need. The sheikh then selects and appoints a suitable candidate. The sayyid may also be removed by the sheikh. He thus owes some measure of allegiance to the sheikh of the *qabilah* and quite often serves him as a political agent, keeping him informed of what is going on within the lineage. Theoretically, the ultimate loyalty of the sayyid is to the lineage, but in practice it is often to the tribal sheikh.

The male children of sayyids are usually sent off to towns or cities to acquire a religious education; when this is completed they present themselves to the tribal sheikh for appointment with a lineage.

The Decline of Nomadism

The influences of the twentieth century are drawing the bedouin into the world of the villager and the townsman. Sedentarization has been going on for centuries, but in the past there were times when villagers of nomadic descent reverted to the life of the desert. In the modern period this cycle has been arrested and sedentarization hastened by changing economic and social conditions. The process first affects the poorest nomads, but at the other end of the economic scale the wealthier nomads are attracted by the enticements of life in the towns and by the prestige and relative certainty of an income derived from the ownership of agricultural land.

Motorized transport has reduced and promises to eliminate the need for camels; nomadic raiding and levying of tribute have been stopped by vigilant government forces; the extension of cultivation has taken away much of the best grazing territory. Economic circumstances are forcing the bedouin to turn to farming, for at least some of the year, the arable parts of his grazing territory and once he has done this, complete sedentarization usually follows sooner or later. The former nomad may, like many an Iraqi peasant, practice a shifting agriculture, but he gives up the tent for the hut or house and pastoralism for cultivation. The newcomers find themselves in a changed relationship with the peasantry their fathers despised. Economic cooperation with the villagers leads to increasing social interaction and results in intermarriage. The romantic past is left behind, though not forgotten; bedouin values continue to be prized but the bedouin himself has in fact become a fellah.

The Village

With two thirds of its people living in rural areas, Iraq, like other countries in the Middle East, is a land of villages. Ranging in population from 200 to 2,000 or more, they are almost entirely agricultural. Crops and methods of cultivation differ from region to region, but social structure and ways of life resemble each other in broad outline.

The Iraqi villager likes to consider himself a settled nomad and will usually claim descent from a formerly nomadic tribe. In the smaller settlements, he believes himself related to nearly everyone else in his village, just as the bedouin believes he is kin to all members of his tribe. The notion of blood ties between all members of a community is at once powerfully integrative in holding the group together and divisive in keeping different groups apart.

Class and Status

The Iraqi villager has a complex system of social ranking in which the prestige attaching to certain occupations may be more important than economic circumstances. In ascending order of prestige there are the landless sharecroppers and tenant farmers, the craftsmen and tradesmen, the small landowners and local religious dignitaries, and, at the top, the large landowners—who are often absentees. The larger villages may have an assortment of resident government officials, but these remain essentially outsiders.

The landless peasant is not only the poorest man in the village, he is the least respected. Although most fellahin in the northern areas own a small plot of land, they earn the greater part of their livelihood as tenant farmers or sharecroppers and sometimes as day laborers; they consequently fall into the lowest group. In the Shiite areas of the south most peasants, desperately poor and entirely landless, occupy a still more depressed position in the social scheme.

The independent farmers are found mainly in the Sunnite Arab and Kurdish areas, rarely in the Shiite south. They own enough land to support themselves and their families but cannot afford to hire labor; they are often extremely poor, but by virtue of their status as independent landowners they are held in higher esteem than their tenant or sharecropping neighbors.

The few craftsmen and merchants found in the villages usually are more prosperous than the small independent farmers. Handicrafts and trade, although not generally esteemed as highly as landownership, are economically rewarding enough to enable craftsmen and merchants to buy the symbols of power and wealth: veils, hair coverings and jewelry for their womenfolk; impressive ceremonies at circumcisions and weddings; horses; and nowadays, more often than not, education for their sons. Thus equipped, the village craftsman and merchant may bypass the prestige requirement of land ownership and be accorded a higher place than the small independent farmer.

The small landowner who is able to employ tenants and sharecroppers is on a higher social plane than the craftsman-trader group, though economically he may be less well off. On much the same level as the small landowner group are the representatives or general managers for the extremely rich landowners. Landowners themselves very often live in the cities; they are considered townsmen by the villagers.

The Moslem mullah, Christian priest, or other religious figure in the village is held in special reverence by the villagers despite the fact that financially he may be little better off than the lowest peasant. His prestige, therefore, hinges not upon his financial circumstances or the possession of land but upon his piety and learning. The religious leader, as the authority on tradition and custom, as the leader in prayer, and as the village teacher, deals with important matters in the community and he enjoys a consequent deference. Many of the larger and more prosperous villages or towns are able to support more than one religious functionary; in these places there is frequently a division of labor between the divines; one or more may be imams of the mosques or priests in the Christian churches; others will be religious teachers.

Living in the villages, but only participating in a minimal way in village life, are the representatives of the government in Baghdad. The large villages will usually have a mudir (director) who is the administrative liaison with the central authority, a police official, government clerks, a doctor, and at least one schoolteacher. These "alien" elements, dressed in military uniforms or western clothing and often regarded with suspicion by the villagers, never enter fully into the life of the village and rarely if ever intermarry with the villagers. Such social contacts as they maintain are usually with the landlords, with whom, educationally and economically, they are likely to have something in common. At times they may also be of a different religious or ethnic group from the villagers, although the government, whenever possible, sends Kurds to Kurdish villages, Shiites to Shiite villages, etc.

Political status within the village lies with those families who through wealth, numbers, or the capacity of their leaders acquire a prestige which is in one degree or another reflected on all members of the family. The most powerful family in the community normally is able to put into office the village headman (mukhtar), who is frequently not the real head of the leading family but more often a lesser kinsman through whom the power group chooses to work. In larger villages with more than one lineage, there often develops a struggle for political power; in such cases the mukhtar is normally the appointee of the most powerful lineage. As the mudir is oriented upward from the village to the central authority, so the mukhtar is oriented downward to the lowest village level—registering marriages, births, and deaths, mediating disputes, and acting as the village spokesman before the local representatives of governmental authority. The successful ordering of village affairs depends to a large degree on effective cooperation between the mudir and the mukhtar.

Although the heads of the more prosperous village lineages, as important landowners, have extensive economic powers over the village families, traditional reciprocal relationships operate to modify their control. Kinship ties, real or fictitious, impose certain responsibilities on the local landowners which they are traditionally bound to observe. The resident landowner, like the bedouin sheikh, holds regular meetings to which all male villagers working the landowner's estate are invited and which they attend whenever possible. At these sessions village politics and matters of public interest are discussed, quarrels are mediated, and petitions made.

Economic status among the villagers is difficult to determine by external appearances. Clothing styles of all classes are similiar; the wealthier are distinguished by the better quality of the material used and, among the women, by the wearing of fine jewelry. European-style dress is being widely adopted by those who have spent some time in the towns, a trend particularly noticeable, and especially among Christians, in the north, where a comparatively large number of people have visited or worked in the towns.

Among Moslem villagers, only the more prosperous can afford to avail themselves of the Koranic permission to take more than one wife. For such men, several wives are a prestige symbol and a practical advantage in providing a widened circle of kinsmen whose combined efforts and pooled resources are helpful in acquiring wealth and power. The man with more than one wife is in a position to call upon a larger number of kin for political and economic purposes; his alliance with more than one family increases the economic interdependence within the family groups and at times leads to the consolidation of landholdings or the pooling of wealth for the purchase of additional land.

The Kinship System

The basic principles of kinship organization among the bedouins are also found in the villages: male descent, paternal residence and authority, the extended family, and the lineage are all present. Save for recently settled nomads, however, the village, as a local entity, replaces the kinship-based tribe as the largest immediate social unit with which the individual identifies himself.

A small village may have only one lineage, all of its members tracing their descent back through the male line to a common ancestor, but in larger villages two or more lineages are common. Marriages are preferably within the lineage, ideally between first cousins, but intermarriage between lineages is becoming more and more common.

The individual is bound to his kinsmen by a network of mutual obligations which is strongest within the extended family but which can also draw the whole lineage together in instances of any external threat. Where there are several lineages within a village, for example, rivalry is common and not infrequently leads to feuds; but in dealing with the outside world the village usually proves itself capable of acting as a unit.

The extended family, uniting a group of closely related males and their wives and children, has long been a more important unit of work and residence in the Iraqi village than the nuclear family composed of a married couple and their children. The bonds of the nuclear family are strong but they exist within the extended family, the interests of which are expected to come first. Western influence and economic change are, however, breaking down the unity of the extended family, reducing more and more Iraqi families to their basic components of husband, wife, and children. This process, most apparent in the cities and larger towns, is now beginning to affect segments of the rural population.

Village Association

The non-kinship patterns of association found in the villages are perhaps more reliable than any other indicator in determining village class structure. The only formally organized groups found in Iraqi villages are the religious *tariqahs* (associations). Males of all classes may join a *tariqah,* and, theoretically at least, class lines are wiped out by membership; this is not true in fact, however, since the *tariqahs* are almost invariably controlled by men who are village leaders for other reasons. There is little evidence, moreover, that contacts initiated within the *tariqah* carry over into other aspects of life.

In all villages the coffeehouse is the gathering place for males. It is a clearing house for both local and outside news, a political forum, a chamber of commerce, and the place where such family matters as marriage contracts are arranged. Theoretically informal and open to all, the relationships developed within the coffeehouse show a definite and rather rigid pattern. The fellah is excluded by poverty; the regular customers gravitate into groups delineated by wealth, age, and the other attributes of social status. The oldest and most valued customers assume the function of arbiters in debates and disputes; the newcomers, younger men, quickly become aware of their position as onlookers. In villages where there are two or more coffeehouses there is a tendency for rivalry—usually concerning local politics—to be reflected, and members of one group will shun association with habitués of a rival coffeehouse.

The marketplace, the sook, is another gathering place for men; here lines of class also appear and associations follow the coffeehouse pattern of respect for prestige and deference to station.

The main association patterns of women revolve around visiting. Women visit each other frequently but restrict their visits to the homes of social equals who, more often than not, are also close relatives. They may also gather to gossip at the river or well (while drawing water) or at the sook. During these meetings activities important to the families are discussed, marriages are arranged, domestic problems aired, and disputes eased. These matters are generally not settled by the women themselves. Other, more formal, mechanisms such as arbitration, councils, or official action are often required. But the women's visits and meetings do serve to strengthen the bonds between kin groups, pave the way for agreement, and remove possible sources of friction before these develop into grave quarrels.

Mobility

Village class structure, as such, operates almost entirely to the advantage of the richer and more influential groups. Burdened with debt, the members of the lower and largest stratum of the peasantry have little hope of acquiring the land which would enable them to rise on the social scale. Neither does the educational system help the fellah, who, unable to dispense with their services as field laborers, can allow his children only a short time in school. The new government schools are as yet rarely found outside the urban centers and the largest villages; the traditional village religious school (the kuttab) offers little beyond some reading and memorization of the Koran—or other sacred writings in non-Moslem villages and many peasants cannot afford even the small fee charged for this instruction.

The small independent farmer is in much the same position as the landless fellah. He lives at subsistence level and finds it almost impossible to better himself. Like the peasant, he is perpetually in debt; he faces a lifelong struggle to retain his landholdings. Many slip back into the landless fellah group. Even if the smallholder manages during his lifetime to cling to his farm, the Moslem practice of dividing the inheritance among the heirs tends to leave sons and grandsons with holdings so small that many in time become landless peasants. The towns and the new industrial projects are drawing increasing numbers of this poorest group away from the villages and into wage work, but relatively few of these accumulate enough savings to return to their home places and become independent landowners.

On the upper levels of village life a sizable percentage of the younger generation today is involved in a process of social climbing which takes them from the countryside to the city. The sons of the village landowners and more well-to-do shopkeepers and artisans —having been educated in the towns—are unable to find either intellectual stimulation in the village or the material amenities they have been educated to want, and for them the city itself becomes a symbol of social status. The educated villager, like the born townsman, sees only ignorance and squalor in the village; this attitude poses a social problem in the general reluctance of educated Iraqis to accept even high-status employment as doctors, teachers, mudirs, etc., in the rural areas.

Change in the Village

Village life in Iraq, as throughout the Middle East generally, has been marked by the devotion of the people to the land, the immersion of the individual in the kinship group, deep religious attachment, and community cohesiveness. These characteristics, though still dominant, are being weakened and changed.

The strongest forces for change are the western ideas and techniques learned from close contact with the towns. The villager becomes aware of his low subsistence standards; he sees his life of toil as unrewarding and is attracted by urban life. The cohesion of the extended kin group tends to weaken as more individuals, either from choice or through force of economic circumstance, strike out on their own. Such a move generally takes them to the cities; here, the erstwhile peasant may or may not much improve himself economically, but, distant from home and dependent on his own efforts in the complex urban setting, he begins to leave behind him the values and the respect for the sanctions which were central to the village scheme.

The force of religion remains strong but the secular influences of the town also are reaching into the villages. Education is bringing the countryman to question those religious ties which helped bind him to his place in village society. Political currents, too, are being felt in the countryside: Pan-Arab sentiment, nationalist aspirations, the competition of political ideologies, and the growing influence and authority of the central government present the individual with more inclusive definitions of personal and group loyalty than those which have endured for so long within the boundaries of the village.

The Town

If the contrast between village and nomadic tribal patterns in Iraq is marked, the difference between either of these and the life of the town is even greater. The great heights attained by Islamic culture was the work of the town; the Baghdad of Harun al-Rashid represented the pinnacle of Islamic achievement. Although the cities depended on the villages for tax revenues, food, and some raw materials, intercourse was limited to ensuring their procurement; the townsman of Baghdad in the Islamic middle ages was likely to have more in common with his counterpart in Cairo or Damascus than with the inhabitants of villages only a few miles away. The gap between city and country persisted until well into the modern period and still is a major cleavage in Middle Eastern society.

Class and Status

The Iraqi urban population presents a more complex social picture than does either the village or nomadic sector. The inhabitants of the towns and cities are divided and subdivided into dozens of occupational specializations, each differentially important and differently rewarded in terms of economic advantage and social prestige.

The topmost socioeconomic stratum of Iraqi urban society comprises the royal family, the ministers and former ministers, the urbanized tribal sheikhs, and the wealthiest landlords. Altogether the accepted members of these groups are estimated to number less than 2 percent of the total population.

Below this elite is the growing and highly stratified middle class within which the greatest changes are taking place. The vast majority of the urban population—the unskilled workers and small shopkeepers who abound in the working-class districts—comprise the lower classes.

At the very upper limit of the middle class are the middling landowners (500 to 1,400 acres), the wealthy merchants (who may also be landowners), and government officials just below the highest ranks. Next come the moderately well-to-do, middle-level merchants, government officials, teachers, and an assortment of professional and technical people. At the bottom of the middle class are the small shopkeepers, some clerks, and the skilled workmen. Some skilled workers may, in fact, be economically better off than certain members of the groups which stand near the top of the middle class but prestige factors keep them at the bottom of the category.

The ranks of the middle class are constantly being swollen by recruits from the urban lower classes. In this process, education seems to be the main factor. A secondary school certificate fits a man for a job as a government clerk, a normal school certificate for a position as a primary schoolteacher, a university degree for the lower rungs of the government and professional ladder, a graduate degree for the more responsible posts in government and the learned professions. The diploma is the key to increased social status in this class; without it a man is almost certainly destined to remain at the lower levels.

Kinship

The social organization of the Iraqi city shows a basic resemblance to those of the nomadic tribe and village; among the poorer classes the likeness is reinforced by the villagers who have drifted to town bringing their rural patterns with them.

Within the town extended families are grouped into lineages. Paternal descent and authority, family loyalty, and cooperation within the lineage are characteristic, although the cohesiveness of the extended kin group varies from the traditional closeness to the looser ties of the western-influenced family.

Traditionally town lineages have tended to congregate in certain quarters, and these quarters have functioned much as a series of independent villages. The inhabitants of a quarter may range on the economic scale from rich to poor, but they have tended to concentrate on a number of particular occupations. Given common occupation as well as kinship ties, they have been set off from other sectors of the population, and jealousies, hatreds, and blood feuds between the lineages have been a prominent feature of town life.

Since World War II there has been a gradual disintegration of the traditional residence pattern. The new suburbs of the rapidly growing towns are attracting the well-to-do away from the old sections. Modern technology is reducing the importance of the craft specializations which were once clustered in particular districts. In this rearrangement the old lineage quarters increasingly are being left to the very poor.

Mobility

The quest for success and prestige under contemporary conditions is another factor forcing changes upon urban society in Iraq. The patriarchal order—with its required obedience to authority in the person of the head of the household, adherence to tradition both Islamic and customary, and kinship solidarity—is a deterrent to the social mobility of the individual. Only a small proportion of the traditionalist families are able to provide more than a rudimentary education for all their members; these families can hardly ever move up the social scale *en bloc.* The higher education bestowed upon the favored few means a loosening of the bonds between these persons and their kin groups. The new members of the middle class, acquiring fresh sets of needs and new patterns of social behavior are prone to look down upon their illiterate relatives and the environment from which they sprang.

No longer satisfied with traditional family surroundings, educated sons leave home and develop their social relations within the higher class of which they become members; loyalties to the old patterns are replaced by a middle-class orientation—education, western dress, certain consumption patterns, the accumulation of wealth—these are the touchstones. The young man may reject the prospect of marriage to his cousin; he casts around for an educated woman with social antecedents as good as, preferably better, than his own who can help him attain the goals he has set for himself in a changing society.

The ruling elite, solidly entrenched and anxious to preserve its status and wealth, remains closely knit, with most of its families interconnected in a network of economic, political, and marriage ties. Proud of its place and sensitive to its prerogatives, this elite does not readily admit newcomers to its ranks; only on rare occasion is a member of the middle class elevated by an upper-class patron to a high-status position for which an upper-class candidate is available.

Association

The association patterns of the top elite are also strictly class-oriented. Upper-middle-class guests may be invited to an upper-class club but aspirations to membership are likely to be fruitless. Probably the only examples of upper-class associational patterns extending downward are provided by some learned societies and such service organizations as the Red Crescent Society (the Moslem counterpart of the Red Cross), which have upper-class patrons and middle-class membership.

One society that in some degree crosses class and rural-urban lines is the Kurdish Program Club, dedicated to Kurdish interests. Controlled by the upper-class Kurdish agas its membership is open to all Kurds.

The occupational and intellectual interests of the middle class have produced various professional groups. Societies exist for doctors, lawyers, engineers, writers, and other professional persons, and these help to further the aspirations of younger men by bringing them into contact with the older and more influential members of their professions. A number of these groups have taken on political overtones, which among other things reveals the desire of the struggling middle group for higher social status.

The city coffeehouse fills much the same function as that in the village. But the middle-class person is beginning to seek more formalized, western-style clubs and associations, leaving the coffeehouse more and more to the lower class.

Change in the Town

The larger towns of Iraq, like those everywhere throughout the Middle East, are undergoing a transition involving both things and ideas. Modern buildings and avenues exist alongside tumbledown quarters with unpaved streets and primitive sanitary arrangements; the white-collar employee and the factory worker mingle in the streets with the small merchant and craftsman whose ways of work have changed little in two thousand years; the western-educated student trained in science confronts the Koranic scholar for whom all important truth is contained in the tenets of Islam.

Among the numerically predominant poor and depressed groups, the old ways are dying hard, as they are at the other end of the economic scale among the landlords and the old-fashioned merchants. The growing middle class, with ideas and skills developed in the West, finds it difficult to apply its knowledge in the changing social scene.

The town is also the proving ground of the political changes which are having telling effects on social organization. The political ideals of the Arab nationalists have materialized in some sense through the appearance of the Arab states. A concept of nationality is arising which is transcending the bonds hitherto based on kinship. The educated townsman sees the focus of his society shifting from family and lineage and the state becoming the major center of authority. The trend is unmistakable but it will be many years before the new values and ways have taken clear shape in the Iraqi setting and reached throughout the whole population.

7

DYNAMICS OF POLITICAL BEHAVIOR

IN ITS FORMAL ASPECT IRAQ'S POLITICAL SYSTEM, LIKE THAT OF Jordan and other Arab states is borrowed from the West. The traditional system of social and religious controls, although changing, still has a greater immediacy for most of the population. What the interplay of tradition and western elements will produce in the way of a distinctive political system rooted in the culture remains to be seen.

Despite the conflict between traditional ways and borrowed ways and borrowed forms, and despite the heterogeneity of the society, the basic nature of the Iraqi Government has remained essentially unaltered since the promulgation of the Constitution in 1925. Perhaps the most important factor contributing to political stability is the tendency of the major political interests to counterbalance one another. Still another is the characteristically Middle Eastern domination of politics by personalities rather than by issues. With no firm base in popular political organization centered on principles and programs, the opportunity given to personal leadership has contributed to the continuing power of such figures as Nuri as-Said, for more than a generation the strongest political personality in the country. Moreover, in this environment of religious, social, ethnic, and local diversity, compromise has acquired a high value and the individual competitors for power generally have been able to establish workable relations among themselves. Compromise failing, political crises have ensued, but in the more than a generation of Iraq's existence as an independent state, the political order and the original holders of political power have survived, in part by continuing the traditional pattern of authoritarianism in government.

The other side of the coin of stability is repression. The Iraqi Government tends to react to all opposition as western governments react to subversion. All political parties, for example, have been banned since 1954. From time to time anti-Hashemites, ardent Arab nationalists, recalcitrant Kurdish tribesmen, and persistent critics of the group in power as well as genuine revolutionaries have been treated as subversive. Despite the official attitude, it is, however, possible to distinguish between those forces merely opposed to the government in power and those forces and groups which aim to subvert the political and social order as a whole.

In Iraq, as in other Middle Eastern countries, antigovernment movements—in contrast with western movements, which most often are the culmination of a long, gradual, evolutionary process—usually develop clandestinely and unobtrusively, suddenly breaking out with little warning, often in combinations of seemingly disparate forces. While the conditions which generate opposition to the government may be known, the time and place of the impending crises are not always foreseeable. This has been the situation in instances such as the Assyrian movement in the early 1930's, the military coups from 1936 to 1941, the various Kurdish uprisings, and the more general popular outbursts.

Various cabinets—particularly since World War II—have adopted strong measures to suppress political opposition. Stringently applied martial law has usually involved military censorship of the press and the use of troops to reinforce the police. Schools have been closed, the parliament suspended, and individuals and organizations prosecuted on weak evidence. Those who have spoken out in protest against such actions have often been taken into preventive custody.

Vigorous suppression of even mild opposition as well as subversive efforts has kept the present political elite firmly in power, maintaining a relatively stable government since 1954. In the long run, however, it probably will have the effect of creating strong public sentiment against the government and of forcing many young, educated potential leaders who earnestly desire political, social, and economic reform to associate—if only temporarily—with clandestine groups of both the right and left. All opposition groups want change of one kind or another, but they generally are vague about how these reforms should be accomplished. While the lists of grievances vary, most groups are impatient with the rate of progress of the Development Board, resentful of alleged graft among high officials, and opposed to Iraq's isolation from much of the Arab world (caused by the western orientation of the ruling clique). Young professional men are bitter about lack of political freedom and the regime's indifference to popular demands. Communist and other radical programs, often cloaked with the slogans of Arab nationalism have a growing appeal to such persons as well as to all those, the urban poor, for example, who feel their needs have been ignored. While poverty has prevailed in Iraq for thousands of years, the problem has taken on new importance in recent years as the differences in wealth have become more visible as more of the wealthy acquire such conspicuous modern luxuries as automobiles. The repressed and frustrated groups also are ripe for exploitation by a strongman such as Nasser. They represent what is probably the greatest contemporary threat to stability in Iraq. The Palestinian segment of Jordan's population, strongly oriented toward Nasser, may intensify this problem. An authoritarian government such as Iraq's, once infiltrated, provides a starting point for swift transition to dictatorship, whether Communist or other.

Political Participation

Universal male suffrage is established in Iraq's electoral laws, but actual participation in the national political process remains minimal. Just as a few men control the central government, in the local communities and tribal groups a relatively small number of individuals and families wield authority by virtue of hereditary position, religious status, or wealth. In this setting the right of all legally competent males to vote has only a contingent bearing on political events. Of those who are not oblivious to the voting process and its ends, many cast their ballots according to the wishes of persons whose authority they accept—father, employer, tribal chief, village head, religious or political leaders. In any case, the government, through the electoral laws and the actions of local officials, is in a position to control the outcome of elections and in practice the opportunity to achieve important civil or military office is practically, although not formally, restricted to an elite.

The major fact about the great majority is that they are for the most part illiterate, tied to kin group and locality, and too preoccupied with the difficulties of day-to-day existence to know or be much concerned about large political issues. Talk in the small-town coffeehouse and nomadic camp alike turns on the topics of family relationship and obligation, male authority, sex, and local or group economic pursuits. Conversation about politics is not lacking but it generally has to do with the utilization of family or social relationships to obtain favor, gain an appointment, or bring about a desired official decision. Among the people at large, then, politics are not approached directly through an apprehension of broad issues and participation in the formal political processes contemplated in the Constitution, but indirectly through the local and social concerns and devices of a still largely tradition-bound rural society. For those at the top the majority remains a passive but excitable mass to be led, controlled, used (sometimes, and if need be, in riots and disturbances), and occasionally appeased.

Aside from the distinction between the elite and the ruled, various segments of the Iraqi population differ in the degree and character of their accessibility to political manipulation. The ordinary bedouin is farther removed from the formal superstructure of national politics than is the fellah, who, for all his isolation, as a settled villager is closer to the seat of provincial government and more aware of its existence. The larger bedouin tribes, however, as cohesive political units whose members give a positive loyalty to their sheikhs, play a larger role in influencing national political decisions than do the villages. The absentee landlord, living in Baghdad and receiving the income of many villages, may be a power in the government, but his authority is that of wealth and he lacks the ability of the great tribal sheikh to command his people. The result is continual complaint about disproportionate bedouin influence in national affairs.

In the towns and cities differences also exist in the relative political roles of unskilled workers, artisans, and skilled workers. Unskilled workers, many of whom are drawn from depressed areas, bring their rural outlook with them and in the first generation at least —except as they may be drawn into demonstrations and riots in times of stress—show little political initiative. The artisan, as the inheritor of a traditional skill, is also likely to preserve the attitudes of an earlier day when the dominant connections in the life of the community were social, occupational, and religious rather than formally political. The skilled worker in the new industries, although still sharing much in outlook with these two groups, is being changed by the nature of his work and the way in which it is organized; the trade union, the ballot box, and the new political forms have become somewhat more relevant for him than for the others.

As elsewhere in the Middle East, government in Iraq has long been regarded as oppressive by its very nature. The official, if not a relative or personal friend, is to be feared and suspected, avoided or placated. Independence and a constitution have by no means dispelled these feelings and elections remain for many an essentially meaningless innovation: political power is an attribute of wealth and family, and the vote of a poor man is not thought likely to change the fact. In recent years this skeptical passivity has on occasion given way to violent outbursts of public emotion in demonstrations and riots. Such disturbances may be spontaneous but they are more often organized. Riots and public demonstrations have become important devices for expressing popular political feelings. They have been employed both by opponents of the government and by the government itself when a particularly vigorous manifestation of public sentiment has been desired. The danger to civil order is evident. Frequently such a disturbance begins as an innocuous affair among, say, college students, spreads to other elements, and ends in killing, looting, and arson.

Iraq's first electoral law was enacted by the Constituent Assembly in 1924. Derived mainly from the old Ottoman law, it provides only for the election of the deputies who make up the lower chamber of the Iraqi parliament; senators are appointed by the king (see chap. 8). Suffrage is extended to all male Iraqi subjects who have reached the age of 20, are mentally competent, are not undischarged bankrupts, and have not lost their civil rights or been convicted of a crime. Soldiers and policemen serving under arms do not usually participate in elections but may do so if they are on leave in their home localities. By this law all Iraqis not disqualified were "primary electors" and could vote for the "secondary electors," of whom there was one for every 250 primary electors. It was the function of the "secondary electors" to elect the members of the Chamber of Deputies, with one deputy representing 20,000 male inhabitants.

A new electoral law was enacted in 1946 in response to criticism that the old one had permitted too rigid control of the elections by the government and did not allow for adequate representation of the people. The principal changes in the new law (1) require that elections and candidatures be announced a fixed period in advance and (2) substitute one- or two-member constituencies for the old provincial constituencies, which had between two and fifteen members. Previously the government often sent the lists of nominees to voting districts only the night before an election. Candidates either lobbied the Minister of Interior or simply waited, hoping that their social status would suffice to get their names on the list of government approved candidates. The reduction in the size of constituencies was intended to make it more difficult for the government in power to nominate out-of-district candidates to an electoral district.

The 1947 and 1948 elections were held under the new electoral law. The first, organized by Nuri as-Said, who sponsored the preparation of the revised law, was an improvement upon former elections in the cities, but in the rural and tribal areas elections were probably as rigidly controlled as before.

The Political Spectrum

The dominant political group is composed of persons who may be described as Arab nationalists of the traditional type. The age, wealth, and aristocratic lineage of these persons bolster their claim to authority. Original goals having largely been accomplished, they accommodate themselves—more easily than the younger aspirants—to western relationships and institutions. They fought against Turkish rule and later against the British Mandate. Despite the repressive measures they employ to maintain themselves in power they are vaguely liberal in a nineteenth-century sense. Their rather secular outlook contrasts with that of some of their younger competitors, whose hostility to the West is expressed in a self-conscious assertion of Moslem identity. Their rather static concept of Arab unity is reflected in the basic program of the Arab League, of which they were the principal creators. Mainly Pan-Arabic in outlook before Iraq achieved independence they have since become more exclusive Iraqi nationalists. The Arab-Israeli war of 1948 revealed their unwillingness to pursue an Arab League cause further than they believed consonant with Iraq's national interest; federation with Jordan also was dictated by national interest. With respect to Israel, they do not so much lead as follow public opinion.

The winning of independence in a sense complicated the position of Iraq's political leaders, for with this paramount issue gone there remained the less popular task of preserving the agrarian, commercial, or industrial interests with which they were associated. Oil revenues have permitted them to engage, without sacrificing their own interests, in a large-scale economic development program, which, while it promises much for the future betterment of the country as a whole, has been conducted in a way little calculated to solve such basic social problems as absentee landlordism and tenantry.

The opposition, labeled leftist or rightist as expediency dictates, sometimes both simultaneously, is mainly recruited from the growing middle class. Ranging from the unemployed middle school graduate, or the low-paid junior civil servant or clerk, to the successful doctor, lawyer, engineer, or journalist, the members of this middle group in one degree or another share with the top elite the advantages of modern education though they differ from it in being dependent on salary or wage income. Frustrated in their expectations—derived from the West and the example of the elite—and fearful of a return to poverty, they demand tax equality, civil service opportunities, social security programs, opportunities to own and control land, and a whole gamut of other changes. Lacking power to enforce these demands, the middle class has supplied allies to both right- and left-wing critics of the government at home and abroad. In fighting the authoritarian control of the elite, they frequently subscribe in the name of democracy to doctrines that would involve the establishment of authoritarianism of another sort.

In external affairs the typical middle-group Iraqi is emotionally preoccupied with what he regards as the threat of "western imperialism." Some may also describe the Soviet Union as imperialist and aggressive, but the focus of criticism is on the West. The inventory of grievances includes the colonies, mandates, former spheres of influence, and present policies, especially as they concern Israel. As between the Communist and non-Communist powers the tendency is to favor a "neutralist" position.

A number of specific points of view can be identified in the middle group. There are the Communists, who although outlawed continue a clandestine existence and appear to be gaining strength among students and industrial workers. There is also a gradualist Marxist socialism, which contrasts with Communist revolutionary doctrine. Not particularly strong, this group has nevertheless acquired importance since the war with Israel. It supports a strict neutralism and identifies Israel with the designs and aggressions of imperialism. Appealing to schoolteachers and students especially, it charges its followers to stand with firm discipline against the ruling circles. Its members claim to be the exponents of a sound nationalism but rarely participate in any coalition government—presumably out of a fear of responsibility and a belief that the old elite will eventually bring about its own collapse.

Sharing some of the Marxist outlook of the socialists, a less easily identified but larger and more active segment of the urban population is moved by the powerful persuasions of President Nasser of Egypt. The Nasser position, eclectic and pragmatic, comprises an array of reformist ideals, conservative values, and Arab nationalist designs. Always anti-Israeli, often anti-Western, and critical of any Arab leadership which does not accord with Egyptian policy, Nasser's pronouncements employ some of the main symbols of popular discontent in Iraq and elsewhere in the Arab world. Nasser's reputation for standing up to the West and winning arms and economic benefits from the Soviets bring him the admiration of many who would object to certain aspects of his claim to regional leadership.

Still another sector of political opinion in Iraq is a mild form of the Moslem Brotherhood. Like other political groups in the country, it is without legal status, but claims adherents from many walks of life and represents a significant focus of opinion. The mildness of its position no doubt proceeds from respect for Shiite feelings. Anti-Communist but neutralist, its members have been willing to cooperate with the Communists on occasion; at other times they have taken to the streets against them. Opposition to western ties springs from its view that Israel is a western creation.

Persons participate in politics in Iraq not merely as individuals but as members of the tightly knit family groups which for most Middle Easterners mark the boundaries of the strongest personal loyalties. At the top are such families as the Umari and the Ayyubi, from which for many years have been drawn prime ministers and important leaders, and the Said family, which has achieved importance through the outstanding success of Nuri as-Said. The kinsmen of an official, high or low, expect that within the limits of his opportunities he will serve family interests through the procurement of appointments and other benefits. In the common assumption that it is the obligation of relatives to assist one another people take it as a matter of course that family connections are a legitimate road to political protection and favor. Thus the family, through its extended role, intrudes into politics, and the families of chief importance are joined in a web of interrelationship and intermarriage that almost amounts to a structure of invisible government behind the formal, constitutional façade.

Former Political Parties

Although banned since 1954, political parties in Iraq have played a part in the modern evolution of national political life, and in one degree or another the important ones maintain a shadow existence through the continued allegiance of their partisans to their erstwhile leaders.

According to the Iraqi Constitution, any legally organized group with definite political objectives which it is willing to pursue peacefully is a "political" party. Before 1954, membership was open to all citizens except government officials and members of the armed forces. Students were denied membership by the internal regulations of their schools, although college and high school students regularly took active part in the parades and riots.

Before they could operate political parties were required to obtain a license from the Ministry of the Interior and submit their programs and the names of the organizations' executive committees for approval. If the party program was held to be contrary to the Constitution or to law, or if any of the organizing members were suspected of subversive activities, permission to organize could be denied. Even after a party had been allowed to organize a central headquarters in the capital, permission to establish branch offices had to be obtained from generally reluctant provincial authorities who saw in party activity only a source of trouble.

These obstacles—together with the opposition of landlords and religious and tribal leaders in the countryside and the general lack of awareness in the rural population—restricted party activity to the larger cities. Lack of funds constituted another problem, since the major sources of party income were almost always membership fees and small donations from a few wealthy supporters.

Each party was headed by an elected leader and executive committee; several other committees dealt with such matters as propaganda and publications, and the more successful parties maintained one or several newspapers or journals. The personal control of the party chief and of his closest followers in the executive committee was always strong. The typical party suffered from a form of organization which made it little more than the poorly coordinated following of the party leader—a figure who generally walked a narrow line between popularity based on a reputation for personal strength and unpopularity created by the arbitrary exercise of his authority. Lack of effective organization was particularly manifest during political campaigns, when it was common for party demonstrations, irrespective of what had been planned, to get out of hand and degenerate into riots.

Party Activity

The nucleus of the party system which developed after World War I was provided by two political groups which under the Ottoman regime had worked to defend Arab rights against the Turks. After the accession of King Faisal I in 1921, three new political parties were formed. Two of these were opposition parties in the sense that they were critical of the moderate party in power, which had agreed to cooperate with the British mandatory authorities. The three parties agreed on basic social and economic issues; they shared the objective of terminating the Mandate and winning independence, differing only as to means. Each displayed the characteristic dependence on the personality of its leader; when, in 1929, the head of the moderate Sadun Party committed suicide, that party was dissolved.

A regrouping of parties took place after the conclusion of the Anglo-Iraqi treaty of 1930. General Nuri as-Said, who had negotiated the treaty, in order to carry it into effect formed a party called al-Ahd. Membership was drawn from the dissolved Sadun Party and from other groups supporting the treaty. The two opposition parties formed a new opposition bloc called al-Ikha al-Watani (National Brotherhood) led by Yasin al-Hashimi. With the coming of independence in 1932 and the resignation of Nuri's government, al-Ahd was dissolved. The other two parties survived only two or three years longer.

Shortly after Iraq became independent, King Faisal invited the leading politicians to discuss the possibility of forming new parties on the basis of domestic issues, but the King's death intervened. Leadership devolved upon the politicians who formed his entourage and the need for active parties became even more pressing, but the removal of Faisal's restraining hand upon rival politicians, made their formation exceedingly difficult. From 1934 to 1945, except perhaps for the Ahli group, no formal political parties were in evidence although informal groupings existed.

This was the decade of coups and countercoups. Much political opinion deplored the increasingly authoritarian tendencies in the government. After the Constitution was amended (1942–43) to restrict the powers of the executive—an effort which in fact strengthened the Palace rather than the Parliament—it was keenly felt that the time had come to revive political parties. In December 1945 the Regent promised the formation of political parties and freedom for their activities. In the following year a new government formed by Tawfiq as-Suwaydi granted permission for the formation of new political parties. Five were founded in April 1946. All but one—that organized by as-Suwaydi himself—were recruited from opposition elements, the majority of the elder politicians holding aloof. Suwaydi recruited his followers from the younger generation in forming al-Ahrar (the Liberal Party). The party was urban based and advocated moderate social reforms. After the fall of the government, Suwaydi, then out of office, also resigned from the party. None of the other four opposition parties was on good terms with either the Palace or the elder politicians.

Al-Hizb al-Istiqlal (Independence Party) advocated a strong nationalist right-wing policy of moderate social reform. Most of its members were extreme nationalists and had been in sympathy with the Rashid Ali coup. The party was supported mainly by Sunni Moslems, although its leader, Mohammed Mahdi Kubba, was a Shiite. Strongest in the cities of Baghdad, Mosul, and Basra, it had little influence in the rural and tribal areas. Representing the outlook of adherents of the party were Fariq as-Samarrai and Siddiq Shanshal: leaders suspicious of all foreign influence and both anti-Western and anti-Russian. They advocated a policy of neutralism and a strong pro-Arab bloc policy.

Al-Hizb al-Watani ad-Dimuqrati (National Democratic Party) comprised mainly a group claiming to be reformist along socialist lines. It was led by Kamil Chadirchi, recently in prison on charges of leftist activities, and the membership of the party at its top levels and the character of its program suggested that it may have become infiltrated and controlled by Communists. Prominent in the group were Mohammed Hadid, a member of a wealthy and conservative family from Mosul, and Husein Jamil, from a well-to-do family. Both have been anti-Western, sympathetic toward the Soviet Union, and "neutralist." The party drew its principal support from the new generation in the big cities and towns and has had very little direct influence in the countryside.

Al-Ittihad al-Watani (National Union Party) was led by Abd al-Fattah Ibrahim. Although more avowedly socialist in its doctrine than the National Democratic Party, it placed more emphasis on parliamentary democracy. The neutralism of this group in foreign affairs was compounded of hostility to the West and sympathy for the Soviet Union.

The Shab (People's Party), led by Aziz Sharif, was frankly nearer to the Communist position than either the National Union or National Democratic parties. It was the most outspoken in attacking the West and in advocating a pro-Soviet foreign policy. The party did not survive long in the open. Its newspaper was suppressed by the government in 1947 and soon afterward its leader disappeared. His subversive activities during the initial stages of the Arab-Israeli war were well known. He later lost his citizenship because of his failure to return to Iraq and his "assistance in the interest of a foreign country." The People's Party attracted a considerable following in the cities, and its principles undoubtedly still appeal to the many who regard the government as oppressive at home and subservient to the West abroad.

The initial response to the formation of these parties alarmed both the elder politicians and other conservative elements. Every new government since 1946, while paying lip service to the value of political parties, has in fact tightened its control of their activities. The five parties represented in the main a new generation out of sympathy with many of the values of the elite and restive under its monopoly of power. Seeing in the new parties a potential, when not an actual, subversive threat, the elder politicians continued to influence every government to limit party activity. Martial law, established during the Arab-Israeli war, provided an opportunity for further restrictions. The People's and the National Union parties were suppressed in 1948 because of their socialist activities. In the same year the Liberal and National Democratic parties, recognizing the futility of attempting to carry on, agreed to suspend their activities until conditions were more favorable.

Only the Independence Party continued in open existence in Baghdad and the larger towns; while it claimed to represent the feelings of all nationalists in the country, in fact only a small section of the people supported it. In 1950, with the abolition of martial law and press censorship, the National Democratic Party resumed its activities. The two opposition parties renewed their attacks on the government. The elder politicians continued to align themselves behind one or another leading personality within their own ranks.

In order to keep a balance between leftist and rightist parties and, perhaps, to induce other elder politicians to enter the political arena, General Nuri announced in 1949 the formation of a new political party called al-Ittihad ad-Dasturi (Constitutional Union Party), recruited from members of the old and the new generations. With pronounced pro-western sympathies, it advocated reform measures no less liberal than the other parties. It was supported overwhelmingly by conservative elements and moderate nationalists, and included some nomadic tribal chiefs.

Prompted by Nuri's action, Salih Jabr, a former supporter of Nuri but later his greatest rival, formed al-Umma al-Ishtiraki (Nation's Socialist Party). Its principles were avowedly democratic and nationalist but its members were in fact recruited from tribal and feudal elements. A Shiite, Salih Jabr drew his main support from the middle Euphrates area and other sections of the Shiite community. The party advocated pro-western and pro-Arab policies.

Another group of elder politicians, despite intense rivalry among themselves, formed a National Bloc, composed of two or three subgroups. The Nasrat-Shabibi faction, a small group in the Chamber of Deputies, joined with General Taha al-Hashimi (a former prime minister), who had a following of younger men. Under General Taha's leadership, the combination advocated a strongly nationalist and neutralist policy until it broke up in disagreement.

Four parties survived: two opposition parties advocating anti-western and neutralist policies, and two representing a moderate pro-western policy. The latter two were no less antagonistic to one another than to the "opposition" parties themselves. The bitter competition among the parties taxed the patience of General Nuri (who like others of his generation and social group had never been a firm believer in the party system) and when he formed a government in 1954 he announced the dissolution of all parties, including his own, on the ground that they had resorted to violence and street riots during the elections of that year.

The formal dissolution of the party system, however, did not mean that unofficial groupings ceased to exist. At present the leaders of the former Independence Party and the National Democratic Party form an opposition group. Nuri as-Said—supported by Ali

Jawdat, Suwaydi, and several other elder politicians—leads a group which advocates moderate reforms and a pro-western policy. Salih Jabr, representing another group of elder politicians, was until his recent death a contender for General Nuri's leadership, although he generally supported the latter's foreign policy.

There is also a small group of elders known in Baghdad as the "Palace politicians." Most prominent among them are Ahmad Muhktar Baban, Nasrat al-Farisi, Fadil Jamali, and Ali Mumtaz. These are often consulted by Crown Prince Emir Abdul Ilah, the former Regent, on matters pertaining to Palace policies. Nuri, although a strong and consistent supporter of the ruling dynasty, has often found it difficult to carry out certain domestic policies if they are opposed by the Palace entourage. In 1955 he agreed to remain in office only if there were no Palace interference in the affairs of his cabinet.

The Military

Since achieving independence Iraq, like most Middle Eastern states, has experienced several military *coups d'etat.* Beginning in 1936 and ending with the Rashid Ali coup of the "Golden Square" in 1941, there were seven changes of government brought about by military intervention. Opposition leaders, already long excluded from office, precipitated the first coup by convincing some senior military leaders that military control of the state was better than the maintenance in power of the existing regime. A number of factors caused alienation of the loyalty of leading army officers from the cabinet. Some officers felt that only a strong government modeled after that of Mustafa Kemal in Turkey, which they greatly admired, could provide the strength and stability for reform.

The military participants in the first coup had declared that after a new regime was established the army would leave the administration of the government in the hands of civilians. Once the military had intervened in politics, however, the involvement became difficult to halt. Six more military coups followed. The last military intervention ended in 1941, when numerically inferior British forces defeated elements of the Iraqi Army and brought the Rashid Ali regime to collapse. The army in its various interventions was unsuccessful in accomplishing any of its planned reforms. After its defeat by the British many Iraqi soldiers deserted; army morale and prestige were practically nonexistent.

Since that time the Iraqi Army has appeared to avoid any political ambitions or intrigues. This has been due primarily to the control Nuri as-Said has exercised over it and a memory of past failures.

In 1952, because of widespread unrest and a threat of violence, General Nuri ad-Din Mahmud, Chief of the General Staff (CGS), was asked to form a government and maintain order. It has been reported that after the failure of his cabinet Mahmud requested reassignment as CGS, but the Regent refused even to restore his commission in the army.

The present regime has done much to improve conditions in the armed forces by increasing pay, making faster promotions, erecting new housing, and issuing better equipment. A continuing effort is made by the government to represent the military as loyal supporters of monarchy and country. Moreover, many of the senior commanders appear strongly in favor of the Baghdad Pact. The present Chief and the Deputy Chief of the General Staff (fall 1957) are professional soldiers, reportedly loyal to the state, and respected and admired by the army. Even so, there is some discontent, especially among the junior officers, because of rumors of graft and the isolation of Iraq from such Arab nations as Egypt and Syria.

Should the material conditions of the military deteriorate, or general poverty increase, or the middle class—enlarged each year by often unemployed or underemployed college graduates—continue to be frustrated in its attempt to have a voice in the government, a military leader could appear who would be able to gain sufficient army and popular support to overthrow the regime. The pull of the United Arab Republic will undoubtedly complicate loyalties.

The Shiites

The Shiites resent discrimination against them in the civil service, the army, and in educational and other fields. The educational level of the Shiites is generally lower than that of the Sunnites, and they traditionally have been looked down upon by the latter.

In the Shiite hierarchy, particularly in the middle Euphrates region around the holy cities of An Najaf and Karbala, there has been an apparatus of leadership which was able to stimulate and direct opposition to government projects and policy during the Mandate period and after. Such opposition has inevitably been suspected by a predominantly Sunnite government as finding some support across the frontier in Shiite Iran.

For decades the great pilgrimages from Persia to An Najaf, Karbala, Kadhimain (Al Kazimiyah), and Samarra have provided occasions for Sunnite authorities to harass Shiites in ways ranging from extortion to obstructionism in visa and quarantine requirements. Along the roads and in the cities Shiite pilgrims have been subject to the private oppression of innkeepers, porters, and operators around the shrines. These public and private oppressions have left their imprint of resentment and bitterness.

In the middle Euphrates region in the past fifty years, towns and the adjacent countryside inhabited by Shiites have suffered heavily from floods and damage to the irrigation system. In this prospective and active scene of discontent the teachers of the Shiite law, the *mujtahids,* have been a power to be reckoned with. The government, particularly since the achievement of independence, has had to court their support or face their opposition. In this region learning and law have been practically synonymous with religion. Intellectual life and the practical affairs of the community have been dominated by the Shiite teacher-leaders, dogmatically disposed to take adamant stands on political as well as religious issues.

Shiite representatives, often at the price of weakening their position in their own communities, have from time to time participated in the Iraqi Government—on occasion as prime minister, but most often in the Ministry of Education and other technical ministries (in contrast with the more important political ministries of Interior, Finance, Defense, or Foreign Affairs). The complaint can still be heard that Shiites are not given positions of power in proportion to their numbers and importance.

Shiite grievances have been exploited not only by Shiite but by Sunnite politicians, some of whom have made opportunistic use of Shiite dissidence to further their own political ends. The army's disgust with these tactics in part accounts for the stern military measures used, under Bakr Sidqi's direction, to repress restive Shiite tribal groups in the middle Euphrates in the 1930's. Since the Arab-Israeli war and the emigration of the Jews from Iraq, many Shiites have come to occupy a position in trade and business similar to that formerly held by the Jews (see chap. 16). The Sunnites deny that they pursue a policy of discrimination against the Shiites, and though religious, economic, and political tensions persist between the two groups, they are diminishing. It is now very doubtful that the Shiite community would attempt to better its position by other than constitutional means.

The Kurds

The Kurds have never felt any particular loyalty to the government. External strains upon their loyalty have come from Kurdish groups in neighboring Iran, Turkey, and Syria as well as from a Kurdish community in the USSR, which contains a number of exiled Iraqi

Kurds. To the voices of the Russian Kurds urging their fellows in Iraq to defect or to support Soviet interests was added the appeal of the scheme for a Kurdish Republic of Mahabad in Iranian Kurdistan, initiated by the USSR during its invasion in 1946 of Azerbaijan province in Iran as a lure to Middle Eastern Kurds generally.

The presence of the large Kurdish minority in northern Iraq gave Turkey after World War I an ethnic argument against the loss of Mosul province in the postwar settlement. The Turkish Government did not renounce its claim to the province until June 1926 in a treaty with the United Kingdom and Iraq. During World War I the Allies encouraged Iraqi Kurds to seek autonomy by helping to defeat the Turks, and their hopes for independence had been raised by President Wilson's Point 12, affirming the right of national self-determination. Moreover, the Treaty of Sèvres in 1920 declared the Kurdish right to an independent Kurdistan which would include Mosul vilayet. Again in World War II the autonomy theme was carried in German propaganda, which promised help in creating a Kurdish national state. By this time, however, it was difficult to arouse Kurdish confidence in any promises of independence.

The Communist Party, however, continues to exploit Kurdish nationalism in its own interest. Appeals are directed at two fairly distinct Kurdish sectors—the tribes and the settled Kurds of the towns and larger villages. These two social divisions are often mutually hostile although alliances may be formed on specific questions. Neither is unified and no leader commands more than a limited local following. Some tribal chiefs (agas), to whom the peasants and tribesmen owe a kind of feudal loyalty, resent the government, claiming oppression in the form of economic restrictions and unwarranted arrest of tribal leaders. Fear of losing authority over their tribes seems to be the real factor underlying their resentment. Such loss of authority takes place as the new resettlement program places tribesmen on their own land, thus destroying their feudal obligations to the agas—especially that requiring them to give part of their crop to the agas. Most resettled peasants have little economic reason for supporting complaints by the agas.

Another source of Kurdish discontent may arise from the building of the great dams at Dokan on the Lesser Zab and at Derbendi Khan on the Diyala for they will back up waters that will submerge many Kurdish villages and many acres of agricultural land. Failure to relocate these farmers and villagers adequately may become a source of Kurdish unrest and possibly increase their subversive potential.

Most Kurds living in the towns and larger villages have almost completely broken their tribal ties. These people are the tangible evidence of the development program's benefits in the form of schools, hospitals, bridges, and roads. The Kurdish city As Sulaymaniyah is a boom town; its population has doubled since 1950. These urban dwellers are gradually drawing closer to Iraqi Arab society and communism makes little appeal to them.

With one possible exception, Kurdish uprisings in the past were caused by specific local resentments such as the arrest of an aga, economic restrictions, or other provocations on the part of provincial or central government authorities. The exception was the Barzani uprising in 1945, which was accompanied by the formation of a Kurdish Democratic Party with the announced aim of setting up a Kurdish federal state. The revolt was put down. The leader of the revolt, Mulla Mustafa Barzani, fled to Iran where, with the blessing of Soviet officials, he assisted in the formation of the abortive Kurdish Peoples' Government. Now in Russia, Barzani is reported to be a general in the Soviet Army and to head a Kurdish training unit in Soviet Azerbaijan. While Barzani has lost prestige among the Kurds he continues to make Communist propaganda broadcasts in Kurdish over Radio Azerbaijan.

Educated and informed Kurdish leaders realize that it would be impossible to obtain the independence of Kurdish areas in Iraq, Iran, Turkey, and Russia in order to form a Kurdish state. The Kurdish peasant, as long as he is employed and his standard of living is rising, is generally indifferent to the idea. Religious and economic ties tend further to unite Iraqi Kurds with the Arab majority. Kurds hold high positions in both government and army. Kurds and Arabs now more frequently intermarry. Many Kurds are entering industry and there is a growing respect among them for the power of the central government and the benefits to be derived from it. Most Kurds realize, moreover, that, although in the past they have often been more than a match for the Iraqi Army, their rifles alone would be inadequate today against modern arms, especially aircraft and tanks. Any revolt would have little chance of success unless quickly reinforced from outside. It is therefore unlikely that the diverse and often discordant Kurdish groups will achieve the degree of cooperation necessary to organize a successful drive for independence unless they are united by an unusually strong and gifted leader, moved by some extreme provocation on the part of the government, or aided directly by Moscow. While the possibility that Communists will successfully incite tribal insurrection in Iraqi Kurdistan is remote, a potential threat does exist.

Politically conscious Kurds complain that the Kurdish areas are ignored in provisions for social services, education, irrigation projects, and road building and charge that official emphasis has been upon police control rather than upon needed services. When the Arab Iraqis counter the charge that the Kurds have been politically neglected by pointing to the number of Kurds who have held cabinet and other high governmental posts, the reply is made that the Kurds in question represent expatriated families or those which have identified themselves with Arab interests. It is no doubt true that such individuals have, in effect, made a transition from one community to another and from a narrower to a wider set of loyalties. In so doing they provide a possibility of an increasing Arab-Kurdish identification of interests.

The Communist Party

History

Although authorities differ on the date, the Communist Party of Iraq (CPI) is believed to have been first organized under its own central executive committee in 1927. Except for a short period in 1936–1937, it was of little importance until World War II. Following the Bakr Sidqi coup of 1936, Communist sympathizers were able to infiltrate the government to some extent, but they were soon forced to relinquish their posts and were subjected to persecution by a government under conservative influence. Some of the leaders, having fled the country, were tried *in absentia* for crimes of subversion and deprived of their citizenship.

The present CPI may be regarded as a reorganization of what was in 1942 a rather loose alliance of several separate or splinter groups of the original party. The party seems to have split over questions involving local political ties, personal rivalries, and matters of procedure. Little information is available concerning the ways in which the reorganization of these groups was accomplished.

After World War II in 1945, when the Iraqi Government licensed and permitted the reorganization of five parties, the Communists asked permission to organize the Hizb at-Taharrur al-Watani (National Liberation Party). Their request was refused on the grounds that it was contrary to Iraqi legislation. The CPI, outlawed since its inception, has continued to resort to clandestine activities: it has circulated unlicensed literature and has been particularly active in organizing demonstrations inciting workers to strike and students to agitate against the government. A noticeable spread of communism among students in the cities and big towns was the direct result of the Communists' close contacts with student organizations. Probably the most important events in which the Communists have taken active part, especially in their initial stages, were the Kirkuk strike of July 1946 against the Iraq Petroleum Company; the uprising of January 1948 in protest against the provisions of the revised Anglo-Iraqi treaty; and the Baghdad riots of November 1952 caused by agitation for free elections.

During this postwar period the Iraqi Government, faced with increasing discontent and public outbursts, was greatly alarmed and sought to blame such troubles as a whole upon Communist activities; there were other contributing factors. As early as 1946, the government accordingly instructed the Police Department to give special attention to clandestine Communist activities, and the principal leaders were arrested in a surprise police raid in January 1947. Yusuf Salman Yusuf (known as Comrade "Fahad the Leopard"), secretary-general of the underground CPI, and others (including Daud Sayigh, leader of a Communist group dissident from the main party) were brought to trial and given severe sentences that were later commuted.

Further investigations in 1948 and 1949 resulted in the arrest and trial of a few other Communist activists, chief among whom was Husein Shabibi. The four principal leaders—Fahad, Shabibi, Haqqi Muhammad Basim, and Yahuda Ibrahim Siddiq—were again brought to trial, charged with secretly corresponding with outside Communist organizations from prison, and sentenced to death. On February 14, 1949, they were hanged.

These measures undoubtedly rid Iraq of a handful of active Communist leaders but the fundamental causes stimulating the growth of communism remained in the absence of sufficient social and economic reforms to mitigate the widespread frustration and discontent and inspire confidence in the existing regime.

As of late the chief response to Communist appeals seem to come from college and high school students, lawyers, some schoolteachers, and workers in the cities and big towns. The urban poor and the Iraqi peasant have generally been politically indifferent, but their condition of economic depression could eventually make them susceptible to Communist propaganda.

Appeals, Aims, and Techniques

It is the general western belief that the mode of Arab society is fundamentally in conflict with communism and that Islam offers an antithesis to communist ideology. Iraq and the other Arab states, however, have not had the experience with Russian occupation forces that almost all of them have had with those of western powers. The USSR gives verbal support to the aims of the Arabs, voting with them in the United Nations against the West, and Iraqis do not generally regard the USSR as imperialistic. Furthermore, communist ideology aside, Russia is thought of as an example of a hitherto undeveloped society that has made rapid economic advances benefiting the majority of the people. Even for many educated Iraqis, the compatibility of communism with Islam is not an issue. The educated tend to be religiously indifferent or believe their culture to be so deeply rooted that it cannot be changed without their approval. The question of religious conflict becomes for them largely irrelevant; the uneducated, on the other hand, are either ignorant of or indifferent to the question. Communist propaganda can thus appeal to many groups: to workers, small shopkeepers, and farmers by promising material benefits; to intellectuals by releasing their frustrations; to Arab nationalists of various types by attacking the regimes of Nuri as-Said, as well as those of others, and the royal family for their western orientation as expressed in the Baghdad Pact.

The CPI has generally de-emphasized communist doctrine in making its appeals. Its technique has been rather to identify itself with popular causes. Around these causes, Communist leaders working through front organizations—such as the Partisans of Peace, the Students Union, and the Committee for Aiding Justice (a front group within the Iraqi Lawyers Association)—have attempted to organize movements to attack economic injustice and corruption in the government, have helped to incite or prolong civil disorders, and have exploited Kurdish nationalist aspirations and the Sunnite-Shiite schism. The present aims of the CPI are to rebuild party strength and to infiltrate government, army, schools, and trade unions.

Because of government action against the Communists and Communist-front organizations, there is little internal Communist propaganda—most of it is carried in a few clandestine newspapers and pamphlets of small circulation. *Az-Zaidah,* the official organ of the CPI, is the largest; it publishes about 2,000 or 3,000 copies monthly.

Strength

In late 1957 the strength of the Communist Party in Iraq was estimated to be about 2,000, of whom approximately 600 were card-carrying members. Communist sympathizers may total 7,500 to 10,000, with centers of strength in Baghdad, Basra, and As Sulaymaniyah. The main support comes from the educated, urban, and westernized groups—young intellectuals, minor civil servants, lawyers, teachers, and members of religious and ethnic minorities.

Party membership is believed to consist of professional men and workers in about equal proportion. It is poorly organized and undisciplined; party leaders, generally from the intelligentsia, struggle among themselves for power and prestige and are given to forming splinter movements. Many, after arrest and imprisonment, have agreed to testify against the party and its members and have signed pledges not to engage further in Communist activities. The number of Communists whose membership dates back to 1948 and 1949 has been greatly reduced by executions then and the frequent arrest of others in the years that followed. Although operating underground and poorly organized, the hard-core leadership, either from prison or adjoining countries, has been able to maintain contact with discontented groups in the country and would be able to rebuild the party should repressive measures be relaxed.

Propaganda emanating from abroad aids the CPI. Radio Damascus and the "Voice of the Arabs" in Cairo very often reflect the line of Moscow's International Radio Broadcasts in attacks on the Iraqi Government. Radio Damascus has usually been the most effective and sharpest in its attacks. Among the illiterate masses in Iraq, radio is the primary means of disseminating information; the extravagant stories heard over loud-speakers in the coffeehouses and bazaars lose nothing in detail as they are passed from person to person.

The CPI has no known direct connection with Moscow. In 1955 the main channel of communication was Khalid Bakdash in Syria, via Syro-Lebanese Communist Party members; a reserve channel was the illegal Tudeh Party in Iran.

Outlook

The greatest potential threats to stability of government in Iraq appear to come from people of the middle class and from the educated youth of the country. They have become frustrated and resentful of the repressive nature of the government. Many have had their traditional way of life dislocated and find few answers to the new problems presented to them. As groups, these elements are not presently subversive, but the danger lies in the appeal communism may make to them. This danger is enhanced by the lack of communication between the two thousand or so of the ruling clique and the mass of the population. Communism, which promises progress by doing away with many obstacles to reform which now appear insurmountable, has considerable appeal to many persons opposed to the regime.

The Syrian crisis in the fall of 1957 widened the gulf between the Iraqi Government and the Iraqi people. Some of the leaders became alarmed by growing Communist influence in Syria. The man in the street, on the other hand, shared the popular view of many in the Middle East that Russia was the Arab's friend and that Syria was not going Communist. Conditions in Syria were ascribed to a United States "plot." The Syrian chief of staff and his followers, along with Nasser of Egypt, were viewed as men of action who would provide a chance of real accomplishment in the Arab world for the first time.

The young King Faisal II—under the sway of his uncle, the Crown Prince Abdul Ilah—has only limited ability to provide constructive leadership. For years the Crown Prince has been involved with politicians in jousting for political influence. All this has lowered the prestige of the palace and has reduced its ability to act as a unifying force in the country.

It is apparent that internal political conditions in Iraq offer many opportunities for active and potentially subversive forces within the country to work against the regime. These conditions may create a movement that in its beginning would not be subversive. Aided by pressure from Egypt and Syria and the belief that the West is losing the cold war, such a movement could, however, acquire sufficient support to undermine the present government and establish one not committed to the West, one more subject to the traditional Arab tendency to move toward the side which appears to be in the ascendancy.

8

THEORY AND STRUCTURE OF GOVERNMENT

SINCE 1925 IRAQ HAS HAD ONE CONSTITUTION, WHICH HAS BEEN twice amended but never formally suspended or superseded by any other official instrument. The Constitution is, on the whole, flexible enough to permit constitutional growth. Many are dissatisfied with the manner in which this or that provision is implemented, but the politically aware as a whole do not ascribe bad effects to the terms of the Constitution itself. In some this merely reveals indifference to the instrument; in others it seems to signify an awareness of the distinction between politics as such and the Constitution as a framework of political action.

Although it has not been formally suspended since Iraq gained its independence in 1932, the Constitution has in practice frequently been violated in spirit if not in the letter. The executive—particularly the cabinet—has dominated the parliament, and when the military has intervened in politics, as it did between 1936 and 1941, neither king nor parliament has been able to exercise much authority in government.

Such violation has been resented, especially by politically articulate educated groups. It seems clear that there is growing public sentiment to support and protect the Constitution; increasing evidence for this is shown by views revealed in the press and by the attitudes expressed in political circles of the larger towns. The government, in justifying many of its actions, has on more than one occasion felt it necessary to declare that it had adopted severe measures against certain individuals out of respect for the existing constitutional system. Opposition political parties have also appealed to the sanctions of the Constitution in contesting such government measures as press censorship, prohibition of formal meetings, and the arrest of political leaders. Group interest, traditional outlook, expediency, and sometimes necessity have often made for a wide gap between constitutional prescription and actual practice; but the constitutional ideal has survived difficult tests and seems to be gaining strength.

That a borrowed organic constitutional law could come to reflect, even to the limited extent that it has, the realities of governmental practice can be attributed to a fortunate conjunction of circumstances in Iraq. British tutelage and experience, for example, were vital during the formative years of the kingdom as well as during the previous period of declining Ottoman power. The fact that Iraq was not subjected to the kind of direct British control exercised in Egypt during the nineteenth and twentieth centuries, however, made possible the acceptance in Iraq of new political devices without the degree of nationalist resistance shown in Egypt. Iraq was fortunate, moreover, in the high caliber of the British representatives who came to the country after World War I and in the policy context within which they worked. Iraq was not so clearly as Egypt an area of importance to the Empire, and the group of British administrators could concentrate on problems of internal reconstruction rather than on the preservation of authority for imperial strategic reasons. The British electorate at home, resenting the cost of administering an area not directly a part of the Empire, exerted pressure upon the government for early withdrawal, which meant that the task of preparing Iraq to take full responsibility for its own affairs had to be accomplished quickly.

Long experience with ineffective Turkish government conditioned much of the Iraqi elite to the acceptance of a new order, and in the modern period the contact of the Iraqi intelligentsia with French and German culture introduced them to western constitutional law and to the social and political values which make its concepts meaningful. The leaders of the Sunnite Moslem upper stratum in and around Baghdad were the natural successors of the Sunnite Turks. Strongly influenced by the new ideas, they felt the need, as it became obvious that the British intended eventually to withdraw, to develop a framework of legitimate authority which would permit the new state to contain and control such diverse groups within it as the Shiites, Kurds, Christians, Jews, Armenians, various bedouin tribes, and others. Among the minorities, however, were many who were concerned about the risk that separate community values and interests might be lost with the establishment of an independent state whose claims on the individual might override the traditional claims of his group. To the leaders of certain of these minorities direct British mandatory control appeared preferable; if the British departure was inevitable, these leaders wanted a constitution containing adequate safeguards for the minorities. Such concerns account in part for the large amount of controversy about constitutional provisions and amendments which has occurred in the kingdom since its establishment. The attention focused on the subject contributed to the importance assigned by politically articulate Iraqis to constitutional principles, however much these may from time to time have been ignored in practice.

Through all of the difficulties following King Faisal's death the constitutional ideal was preserved, and in this there is apparent a quality of political aptitude and realism among Iraq's leaders which has enabled them to work through consensus and compromise and often at critical junctures to see beyond immediate expediency to long-range objectives.

Creating the Constitution

When it became apparent that the British intended to give up the Mandate earlier than had been anticipated, while attempting to preserve their dominant position in the country, constitutional issues became important since they would have considerable bearing upon the relative advantages to be enjoyed by various groups and interests, including the British. The Provisional Government, set up in October 1920 after the suppression of the Arab revolt, had as its main function preparing for the accession of Faisal. Faisal was proclaimed king on August 23, 1921 in the presence of civil and military officials, tribal sheikhs, the religious leaders of all sects (including Christians and Jews), and notables representing most of the various provinces. The ceremony marked the beginning of the national government of Iraq.

The League of Nations Mandate document for Iraq had provided (Article I) that the country would have a constitutional system, a provision to which the British had subscribed in an official statement in June 1920. The Provisional Government on the accession of Faisal asserted that his government would be "constitutional, representative, . . . democratic, [and] . . . limited by law," and the King announced at the time that he would proclaim a constitution. These assurances were followed by the Anglo-Iraqi treaty of 1922, which, containing many provisions taken from the Mandate document, defined the position of Iraq under the Mandate and stipulated that an organic law (constitution) would be drawn up for the country. The treaty outlined the fundamental principles of the projected government. Article III of the treaty stipulated that:

> His Majesty, the King of Iraq, agrees to frame an Organic Law for presentation to the Constituent Assembly of Iraq and to give effect to

> the said Law, which shall contain nothing contrary to the provisions of the present Treaty and shall take account of the rights, wishes, and interests of all the population inhabiting Iraq. This Organic Law shall ensure to all complete freedom of conscience and free exercise of all forms of worship, subject only to the maintenance of public order and morals. It shall provide that no discrimination of any kind shall be made between the inhabitants of Iraq on the ground of race, religion or language, and shall secure that the right of each community to maintain its own schools for the education of its own members in its own language, while conforming to such educational requirements of a general nature as the Government of Iraq may impose, shall not be denied or impaired. It shall prescribe the constitutional procedure, whether legislative or executive, by which decisions will be taken on all matters of importance, including those involving questions of fiscal, financial, and military policy.

This treaty, which was opposed by the Shiites and the nationalists was not only an important landmark in the constitutional development of Iraq, it was for its duration a source of superior law for the country, not least of all in its provision of a bill of rights.

In addition to the 1922 treaty, the Organic Law as it was finally promulgated on March 21, 1925, and the Mandate document, there were certain other sources which, for their duration, must also be considered components of Iraq's constitutional law: Article 22 of the League Covenant, which provided for the establishment of a Permanent Mandates Commission by the League Council; Articles 30 to 36 of the Treaty of Lausanne, dealing with Iraqi nationality; Articles 1, 3, 4, and 5 of the Anglo-Iraqi treaty of June 30, 1930 (see chap. 10); the seven guarantees by which Iraq was declared bound by the League of Nations as a condition of release from the status of a mandated territory; and, finally, the separate electoral laws governing candidacies for office and voting.

After at least six drafts, a proposed organic law was submitted to the Constituent Assembly on June 14, 1924. Much of the difficulty of drafting came from the fact that the British participants had to work in English and their Iraqi counterparts in Arabic, but a great deal of it can be ascribed to British determination to hold up promulgation until the oil concession they sought had been granted. The British participants also were concerned to draft a constitution consistent with British policy. Their original view was that the power of the King, and indirectly that of the High Commissioner, must be improved so as to avoid potential obstruction by an elected legislative body. They sought to include within the Constitution as many details as possible having to do with arrangements they desired to preserve, and to safeguard them further by making the amending procedure difficult. On the other hand, they showed some disposition to allow administrative procedures to remain flexible and subject to ordinary law. Finally, they were determined that decisions taken by the High Commissioner, the King, and his ministers prior to promulgation should not be called into question and that an article to this effect should be included.

The Iraqi drafters, however, by resisting such limitations and by their reluctance to support a difficult amending procedure, appeared to want previous arrangements and understandings brought into question. Realizing that enlarged royal authority was a defense of British interests and points of view, they consistently tried to limit this authority, usually on the grounds that a constituent assembly would not accept proposals for a strong kingship.

Many other constitutions served as models and sources, including those of Australia, New Zealand, Japan, the Ottoman Empire, and Egypt (that of 1923, which came to Iraqi notice during last-minute drafting). The actual work of preparation was done by preliminary committees rather than by the Constituent Assembly, which discussed and gave formal approval to the final document.

When the time came to create a constituent assembly to ratify the 1922 treaty and approve the draft organic law, the nationalists and the Shiite ulema, who had been most vigorous in calling for a constituent assembly, united in opposition to it, fearing that the government to be established would weaken their control over their followers. Among the people in general, reaction to their rights as electors ran the gamut from indifference to fear that the registry rolls might be used for purposes of conscription. Following important efforts at compromise by King Faisal, the elections were finally held, and the Assembly began its work in March 1924. The Assembly was quite representative of the local leadership of the various sections of the population: dignitaries from the various towns, tribal sheikhs, middle-class representatives, and dignitaries representing the Kurds and other minorities. The Assembly devoted most of its time to a discussion of the Anglo-Iraqi treaty of 1922 and was not disposed to ratify it. But a warning from the British High Commissioner that this matter, falling under the terms of the Mandate, would be referred to the League of Nations finally prompted approval.

Assembly discussion of the Organic Law lasted less than a month —from June 14 to July 10, 1924. No essential or significant modifications were made. Advance preparation had been so careful and exact that there was no need nor any disposition on the part of the government to make changes. The Organic Law was approved and signed by the King on March 21, 1925, whereupon it came into force.

Finally, the Assembly passed an electoral law to govern election to the new parliament.

The reaction of the Iraqi people to the promulgation of the Organic Law was not strong. The uneducated majority knew little of its existence, much less its meaning. Educated and intellectual circles, more concerned with ending the Mandate and gaining independence than with a particular form of government, tended to be cynical. With the achievement of independence in 1932, however, there was growing interest in the significance of the Constitution and heightened concern about the working of the constitutional system.

The Organic Law

The written Organic Law of Iraq establishes a constitutional, limited monarchy within a unitary—as opposed to a federal—state, "sovereign, independent, and free." In theory, if not in practice, the executive policymaking and administrative powers in the state are responsible to the legislature and in turn to the people in their several communities acting through an electorate. The generally limited nature of the royal authority is qualified by the king's power to issue decree laws when the parliament is not in session and to dismiss the prime minister "if the public interest renders it necessary so to do." The "Introduction" describes the state as indivisible, no portion of it may be surrendered.

The Constitution is relatively long, divided into 10 parts and 125 articles. It may be accounted rigid rather than flexible, since it cannot easily be amended by the ordinary process of legislation. In consequence the internal laws of the country may be conveniently divided into ordinary and constitutional laws. The latter in theory always predominate, and subordinate legislative enactments conform to them. Actual practice does not always conform, however, and the real political forces in the country are not fully revealed by the Constitution.

Civil, Religious, and Political Rights

The provisions of Part I of the Constitution, "The Rights of the People," may be divided into four categories: (1) absolute general rights, not qualified by the provisions of any law; (2) conditional general rights, defined and limited by law; (3) absolute specific rights; (4) and conditional specific rights, defined by law. This part of the Constitution represents a rather lofty standard which, if met in spirit as well as word, would make the Constitution a significant definition of the government's powers to deal with individuals and groups in large and important areas.

The absolute general rights inhere in persons of Iraqi nationality, defined by Article 5. They include equality before the law without regard to "language, race, or creed" (Article 6); freedom from torture or deportation (Article 7); freedom of conscience, viewed especially in a religious context (Article 13); and equal right to the enjoyment of civil and political rights and to the performance of public duties and obligations (Article 18)—no doubt a political provision meant to stress equality among the various communities and religious sects.

The conditional general rights inhering in Iraqi nationals are those that must be limited by law in terms of the needs of the social and political order (but, in theory, no more than those needs demand). These include liberty of person (Article 7); the inviolability of one's residence (Article 8); the right of access to the courts of law (Article 9); the right of ownership of property and freedom from the expropriation thereof unless for a public purpose and for just compensation (Article 10); the right to equality of taxation according to law (Article 11); freedom of speech, press, and association (Article 12); freedom of religion (Article 13); freedom from the censorship of postal, telegraphic, and telephonic communication (Article 15); and the right of the various communities to run schools in their own languages, provided public programs are fulfilled (Article 16).

The absolute specific rights establish Islam as the official religion of the state and guarantee freedom to practice the various forms of worship of the sects of Islam as they are known in Iraq (Article 13).

The conditional specific rights make Arabic the official language of the state (Article 17) and extend the right of petitioning and memorializing all public authorities concerning personal or public matters (Article 14). Finally, only Iraqis may be employed by the government "except in accordance with law, treaties, or special agreements" (Article 18).

Social Philosophy

The Iraqi Constitution neither charges the government with the accomplishment of social and economic purposes nor prohibits it from seeking such goals. Except for Part I, which deals with rights, it is largely procedural rather than substantive in its provisions concerning the powers of government in general and the organs for exercising these powers. Various provisions assert standards of official action and establish the theoretical hierarchy of official power, but none sets forth any philosophy of governmental control, planning, and ownership except insofar as the bill of rights provisions having to do with property may be interpreted to limit government action in these spheres. The main limitation upon direct government manipulation of the society and the economy is clearly meant to be public opinion and the consensus of the elite in power at any given time—an approach which is in accordance with the British tradition of leaving to the responsible policymaking organs wide discretion in the formulation of economic and social policy.

Amendments

The Constitution was intended to be a rather inflexible organization of certain governmental procedures. The actual political processes in the country may in fact be extremely flexible, but the "façade" of the Constitution gives an appearance of stability, permanence, and order. Part IX, having to do with constitutional amendments, provides that:

> Parliament may, within one year from the coming into force of the Organic Law, amend any of the matters of secondary importance contained therein or add to them . . . provided that Parliament shall agree by a two thirds majority of votes in both Chambers (Article 118).
>
> Subject to the provisions of the preceding Article, no amendment whatsoever may be made in the Constitution for a period of five years from the date of the coming into force thereof, nor after the expiration of that period, except in the following manner (Article 119):
>
> Every amendment must be approved by a two thirds majority of both the Chamber of Deputies and the Senate. After such amendment has been approved, the Chamber of Deputies shall be dissolved and a new Chamber elected. An amendment which has been approved by the former Chamber shall be submitted again to the new Chamber and Senate. If approved by a two thirds majority of each assembly the amendment shall be submitted to the King for confirmation and promulgation.

The First Amendment Law was passed in keeping with the above provisions on July 29, 1925. It dealt mainly with providing a representative for the king during his absence from the country and prescribed a maximum of four months' absence unless parliament decided otherwise.

From 1930 to 1942 no amendment was passed. Until the death of King Faisal in 1933 no need was felt for amendment; after his death (and particularly after the military interventions in politics in the 1930's) it became difficult to pass an amendment provision. The need to do so, however, was becoming increasingly apparent, particularly in connection with the parliament's inability to end the life of a cabinet harmful to the country—a dilemma which became acute during the prime ministership of Rashid Ali in 1941.

After the fall of the Rashid Ali regime, the government appointed a committee, in December 1941, under the chairmanship of Jamil Midfai (an elder, moderate politician), to prepare certain proposals for amendment. The committee worked for several months, and its proposals were communicated to the cabinet in March 1942 and then to the parliament. The fundamental proposals were as follows: (1) to give parliament the power, in an emergency, to meet outside the capital; such a need actually arose in 1941 when the Regent fled to Basra; (2) to prevent parliament from passing acts of amnesty on behalf of individuals who had taken part in violent action against the state; (3) to limit membership in the Senate to former ministers, deputies, and senior military and civil servants; (4) to replace the special religious courts by civil courts.

Parliament began its discussion of these proposals on March 23, 1942. A joint committee of senators and deputies met and prepared additional recommendations: (1) a provision empowering the king to dismiss his prime minister; (2) a provision dealing with the nomination of an heir apparent in order that there should be no interruption in the succession to the throne; (3) a provision making the number of senators indefinite, but not to exceed one fourth the number of deputies (before this amendment the number of senators was established as not more than twenty); and, (4) a general provision by virtue of which any constitutional practice might be adopted from foreign countries by a joint resolution in the Chamber of Deputies and the Senate, on the condition that it not be contrary to Article 124 of the Organic Law.

Parliament quickly adopted all but three of the proposals, those (1) empowering the king to dismiss his prime minister; (2) pertaining to qualifications for membership in the Senate, and (3) concerning the abolition of religious courts. In accordance with Article 119, the Chamber of Deputies was dissolved and new elections were held in September 1942. Parliament met after the elections and approved the Second Amendment Law.

The general public paid little attention to the new amendment law; in the educated community, however, there developed considerable opposition both to the new power given the king and to the provision depriving the parliament of the right to pass an act of amnesty. It was wartime, however, and the press could not freely express opinions on these matters.

The amendment empowering the king to dismiss the prime minister has not yet been used. Its value is perhaps largely psychological since no prime minister would be likely to refuse, even though he enjoyed the confidence of the parliament, if he knew the king wanted him to resign.

The Executive

The King

Iraq's first king was of the Sherifian Hashemite family, which traces its descent from Mohammed and looks back to ancestors who held political authority around the Holy Cities of Arabia. There could be invoked for its establishment as the royal house of Iraq, therefore, the sanction of political legitimacy traditional in the Arab world. The constitutional provision (Article 20) that, failing issue in the direct line through the eldest son of Faisal, the descent of authority should be through the ablest Iraqi among the sons of Ali ibn Husein, Faisal's elder brother, also followed an important Arab tradition of passing authority through a paternal uncle and his descendants.

The terms of the Constitution designating the king as chief of state represent a modification of the British pattern. In the theory of the Constitution, "sovereignty belongs to the nation, and is entrusted . . ." to the king and his heirs (Article 19). This does not mean, even in theory, that the king exercises sovereignty in the every-day direction of the activities of the government. In this sphere, the Constitution gives larger authority to the cabinet and the prime minister, although various provisions make it clear that the king is meant to exercise more decision-making power than the chief of state in the United Kingdom. Moreover, he is in a position as the final guardian of sovereignty to step into the breach in a national crisis and to employ measures which, if not sanctioned by the letter of the Constitution can be justified in the name of defending it.

The king achieves his majority on the completion of his eighteenth year (Article 22). Before that time his prerogatives are exercised by a regent designated by the previous king with the approval of the parliament; failing designation by the previous king, the regent is named by the parliament itself. Both the king and a regent are required to take an oath of loyalty to the Constitution, nation, and fatherland, and to swear that they will support the independence of the country. During any interval between the rise of an occasion for the appointment of a regent and his assumption of office, the royal prerogatives are exercised by the cabinet.

The king is "safeguarded and not responsible" (Article 26)

That is to say, he is safeguarded against any responsibility for or consequences of constitutional action taken in his name over the countersignature of a member of the cabinet, as well as against responsibility for or consequences of the exercise of any prerogative —such as the right to dismiss a prime minister in case of necessity— not requiring the countersignature of a minister. This provision is seen as a logical and necessary part of a parliamentary system in which the chief of state is supposed in most cases to act only upon advice, and in others to preserve the constitutional system itself.

The king as chief of state is commander in chief of the armed forces and has the power to declare martial law and states of emergency in keeping with the Constitution (Article 26). He confirms laws passed by the legislature, orders their promulgation, and oversees their execution. Under his supervision ordinances are issued within the terms of the various laws for their implementation. He issues orders for the holding of general elections and for the convoking of parliament, which he also opens, adjourns, prorogues, or dissolves as occasion demands and in conformity with the Constitution. Should parliament not be in session and the necessity arise for special measures for the maintenance of public order, for the expenditure of funds not otherwise authorized, or for actions in order to carry out a treaty provision, the king, upon the advice of the cabinet, may issue ordinances directing such steps as may be required by the circumstances. These ordinances must be countersigned by the ministers; they have the force of law if they are in conformity with the Constitution and are submitted to the parliament at its first subsequent session. If they are not approved by the parliament, they are regarded as repealed from the date of parliament's failure to approve. The consequences of their previous application, however, remain valid following their repeal (Article 26).

The king selects the prime minister and, upon the recommendation of the latter, appoints the other cabinet ministers (Article 26). In practice, the appointment of the prime minister is made after consultation by the king with former prime ministers and ministers. The king also may dismiss the prime minister if the public interest makes it necessary (Article 26), a provision incorporated in the Constitution by the Second Amendment Law of 1943. The king also appoints members of the Senate (Article 26), upon the recommendation of the prime minister or the cabinet, although the latter procedure is not specified in the Constitution.

The royal authority is exercised by the king on the advice of the minister(s) concerned, with the concurrence of the prime minister, by means of royal decrees countersigned by the minister(s) (Article

27). This provision in effect transfers the royal responsibility and exercise of authority to the ministers, subject only to the approval of the king. The right to dismiss the prime minister under circumstances of necessity is the only exception specified.

Iraq's foreign relations are carried on in the king's name (Article 26). He appoints and dismisses diplomatic representatives and declares war with the consent of the Council of Ministers. He concludes treaties by delegation of authority to his diplomatic representatives. Treaties, but not declarations of war, must be approved by the parliament, and treaties of peace require parliamentary approval prior to ratification. The king may issue with the consent of parliament any ordinances required to fulfill treaty obligations already accepted by parliament. Agreements of a minor nature may be reached with other states without the approval of parliament.

Since the inception of the kingdom, three kings of the Hashemite dynasty have reigned: Faisal I (August 23, 1921, to September 8, 1933); Ghazi (September 8, 1933, to April 4, 1939); and Faisal II (April 4, 1939–). These three reigns have demonstrated the importance of personality, background, and training in the fulfillment of the royal role. Faisal I unquestionably exercised more powe in the Iraqi Government than the letter and logic of the Constitutio envisaged. Ghazi, although possessing strong nationalist views and desire to fulfill them, lacked Faisal's experience and political judg ment; he was unable to contain the divisive forces in the country, a his father had done, or to make his will effectively felt. The presen king, Faisal II, is youthful and much under the influence of hi uncle, the Emir Abdul Ilah, who acted as regent during his minorit from 1939 to 1953. Abdul Ilah has been able to exercise a stron influence upon policymaking in the country, although he was i frequent collision with nationalist groups during his regency. Th experience of the three reigns has shown, however, that the king ca play a strong part if he has the personal force and the disposition t do so.

The Council of Ministers

The working executive, the Council of Ministers or cabinet, und the direction of the prime minister (the chief of government) is i theory responsible to the parliament, and its members also hold sea in one or the other of the two chambers of the parliament. In theor the ministers exercise the royal authority with the concurrence of majority in the Chamber of Deputies and participate in the makin of laws through their leadership of that majority. In practice, t executive, particularly the Council of Ministers, dominates the legi lative branch, which has little real power or opportunity to call executive policy into serious question. In a real sense the government of Iraq has been government by the ministers, themselves usually under the domination of a strong figure such as Nuri as-Said. On the other hand, the parliament, with its roots in the most influential sectors of social and political life, is by no means without capacity to influence the executive.

The size and composition of the Council of Ministers varies with the time and the political situation, but it must have a minimum of seven members, including the prime minister (Article 64). It may contain a number of deputy ministers, provided they are members of the parliament, and of ministers without portfolio. In mid-1956 the Council was made up of the Prime Minister, Minister of the Interior, Minister for Foreign Affairs, Minister of Finance, Minister of Defense, Minister of Justice, Minister of Communications and Works, Minister of Education, Minister of Social Affairs, Minister of Economics, Minister of Agriculture, Minister of Health, and Minister of Development. A person who is not a member of parliament may be appointed a member of the Council of Ministers, but he cannot retain such a position unless within six months he is appointed a senator or elected to the Chamber of Deputies.

Responsible for the direction of all affairs of the state (Article 65), the Council of Ministers meets once or twice a week under the presidency of the prime minister to consider all matters of joint concern and all matters of importance to each of the ministries. Its decisions are referred by the prime minister to the king for the latter's approval. The ministers are jointly responsible to the Chamber of Deputies for all decisions of the Council of Ministers and individually for acts of their own ministries (Article 66). The Council must resign in the event the Chamber passes by a majority a vote of nonconfidence in the Council as a whole; should the vote apply to one minister, he must resign. The prime minister may request the postponement of such a vote for a period not to exceed eight days, during which time the Chamber may not be dissolved. The Chamber has never passed a vote of nonconfidence in any Council of Ministers or any minister since the establishment of the Constitution, although ministers are frequently asked questions in parliament (Article 54)—a fact which both contributes to and stems from critical public discussion of their conduct of public affairs.

Although the British model was used in constructing the Iraqi cabinet system, in its functioning it is closer to the French pattern. From 1921 until 1956 there were more than fifty Councils of Ministers in Iraq—an average of a new one every seven and a half months. Even under the Mandate the country had fourteen Councils, or a new one almost every year, and the rate of turnover caused the Permanent Mandates Commission of the League to question the country's readiness for self-government. The British representative, charged with ending Britain's mandatory responsibility as soon as possible, admitted the difficulties indicated by the poor functioning of the system but pointed out that parliamentary experience was thus being spread more widely. Actually there was less instability than the short tenure of cabinets suggested, for many of the same individuals appeared in government after government, sometimes representing one political grouping, sometimes another. Something of the flavor of the political situation is revealed in Nuri as-Said's observation that "with a small pack of cards, you must shuffle them often."

The membership of the first 50 cabinets was drawn largely from the same group of 150 men. Since the overthrow of the Rashid Ali regime in 1941, however, other and younger men have more often been found in ministerial positions. This development has sharpened competition among ambitious candidates, and it has also been accompanied by heightened maneuvering and intrigue, often with the Palace, for a place in the Council of Ministers.

The Administration

The highly centralized bureaucracy operating under the supervisio of Iraq's collective executive is a focus of political and social am bition and prestige. Members of the bureaucracy are often more in terested in preserving the bureaucratic apparatus and their place in i than in advancing public policy. An aspect of this attitude is th common reluctance to accept responsibility or to take any actio which might conceivably bring criticism from above. One consequenc is that decisions which should be made and executed on lower level of the government frequently are pushed all the way to the top, wit the inevitable slowing down of the administrative process and th congestion of problems at the higher levels. The various department are subject to frequent reorganizations undertaken for political rea sons, such as conflict between Shiite and Sunnite officials and interest —once again contributing to inefficiency and instability. Nepotis and peculation remain constant factors in the governmental spher they reveal the popular attitude that official position is an appropria means to personal advantage and reflect the continued dominance o kin loyalties over the new ideal of public service.

Prior to the civil service law of 1931 there had been no statuto policy governing the appointment, transfer, or dismissal of gover ment personnel; tenure was entirely in the hands of a departme head acting in concurrence with his British adviser. Frequently amended, the civil service law of 1931 was superseded by a new one in 1939 that incorporated many of its provisions. None but Iraqis by birth or persons who have been naturalized for at least five years may be employed in the government service (a special law excepts aliens employed for technical purposes for a specified time). The minimum age of employment is eighteen (sixteen for female school teachers), and there is a general requirement of good reputation and good health. The general provisions of this law apply to all categories of other than political office, but special laws differing only in details relevant to the particular agency apply to the departments of Education, Justice, and Defense.

Appointment to the administrative services is made from among those passing an entrance examination, from which, however, graduates of Iraqi and foreign institutions of higher learning are exempted. Appointments to lower positions are made by heads of divisions when positions are created or vacancies occur, those to higher levels are made by the minister or political head through formal letters of appointment authorized by royal decree. Promotions and transfers are similarly handled, the theory being that the requirement of royal authorization for personnel actions on the higher levels should protect senior administrators from arbitrary political decisions. Retirement on pension is permitted after twenty-five years' service or at the age of sixty.

Behind all these formal provisions of the civil service laws, there is, of course, a reality of practice which is at points widely separated from the legally defined ideal. In addition to nepotism, personal connections and sectarian influences operate powerfully in the selection of public officials. Well-connected but otherwise unqualified men not infrequently appear in posts of considerable responsibility where they may have discretionary powers over more devoted and able subordinates; under these circumstances the capable official is at a grave disadvantage. The effect on the efficiency and morale of the service is obvious. Civil service positions are much sought after in Iraq, but in the population at large the prestige of official place is apt to invoke more envy, mingled with fear or contempt, than respect. A frequent consequence is that the civil servant retaliates with a kind of obstructiveness of action and attitude toward the people in general.

A few years ago a committee made up of respected former members of the judiciary, and other persons of high standing, was appointed to investigate corruption and irregularities in public administration, and in such major economic organizations as banks. The committee reportedly did its work thoroughly and with an unusual disregard of the pressures brought to bear on it. As a result of its findings a number of officials, especially at the provincial level, and including governors, were found guilty of malfeasance in the performance of their duties and dismissed. Members of the committee were later integrated into the regular government structure as a kind of civil service commission and were given authority to pass on appointments and promotions in the government administration.

The National Legislature

In theory, the members of Iraq's Council of Ministers are responsible to, as well as members of, the majority in the parliament; in practice, the king selects the prime minister after consultation with important political figures and the prime minister dominates the parliament mainly by controlling the elections. Thus the initiative in government is effectively confined to the executive arm, and a gauge of the real success of the parliamentary system in the country will be in the capacity of the legislature to begin to enforce some kind of reciprocal relationship with the Council of Ministers.

A clear-cut conception of legislation, as opposed to executive ordinance, is set forth in the Constitution: Article 28 vests legislative power in the parliament and the king. Made up of two houses, the Chamber of Deputies and the Senate, the parliament has met regularly since 1925. Under particular conditions the king may issue ordinances having the force of law (Article 26), and he performs certain functions in the electing, opening, adjourning, proroguing, and dissolving of the Chamber, and in the appointment of members of the Senate. The parliament enacts legislation; and it must confirm ordinances issued by the executive or these are deemed repealed.

The Senate

Members of the Senate, which is limited to one fourth the size of the Chamber of Deputies, are appointed by the king, on the recommendation of the Council of Ministers, from among men who are prominent in public life and have attained the age of forty (relatives of the king are not eligible). Senators are appointed for a term of eight years and are eligible for reappointment. They may with the approval of the Senate accept a call to undertake "important duties in the service of the state" at home or abroad for a period not exceeding two years (Article 31). The Senate meets and adjourns at the same time as the Chamber of Deputies. A president and two vice-presidents of the Senate are elected by the body from among its members, subject to confirmation by the king. These officers serve from the beginning of one ordinary session until the beginning of the next, or in the case of a dissolution of the Chamber until the assembling of a new parliament so that they may be available to sit as members of the High Court (Article 33 as amended in 1943).

Since 1933 half the senators have retired every four years. Before that time the original senators nominated in July 1925 remained in office until June 1929, when lots were drawn for the retirement of half their number, as provided by Article 32 before its amendment. Five of the retired members were reappointed, and four new members were added. In 1933 the remaining original senators retired, having completed their term of eight years. The Senate, although selected by the king upon the recommendation of the Council of Ministers, has for the most part included leading political figures such as former prime ministers and ministers. With such a composition, the Senate has been far more critical of the government than has the Chamber of Deputies, and, although it is without power to express its disapproval in a vote of nonconfidence (as can the lower chamber), it has acquired something of the character of a controlling house.

The Chamber of Deputies

The Chamber of Deputies is elected directly by secret ballot. (Before a modification of the electoral law in 1952, elections were held in two steps, with the voting public choosing electors who finally selected the deputies.) Each deputy represents 20,000 male inhabitants. A deputy must have reached a minimum of thirty years of age; he serves for four ordinary sessions of six months beginning on December 1st. The sessions may be extended if there is need for additional legislative action. Members of the Chamber may also be called to undertake "important duties in the service of the state" for a period not exceeding two years. Each year at its first sitting the Chamber elects from its membership, subject to royal confirmation, a president, two vice-presidents, and two secretaries.

By 1956 there had been fifteen different Chambers elected, of which only two had completed their terms. The others were dissolved by the government either because they were critical of it or because the government wished to increase the number of its supporters in the Chamber. At the first election there was general reluctance to stand for office, but thereafter candidacies were much more numerous and competition for seats more determined. Both urban and rural populations—including tribal elements—have been represented. There have been general complaints that the tribes have been over-represented in the rural districts and the landlords and middle classes exclusively represented in the cities; this situation has been a source of bitterness among opposition elements. Criticism of the government's rigid control of elections—principally, but not exclusively, in rural areas—is often voiced, and it is evident that official manipulation of elections is an important factor in keeping the parliament weak in relation to the executive.

The Legislative Process

Legislation may be initiated by the government in the Chamber of Deputies or the Senate, and deputies may themselves initiate legislation on any but financial matters. Senators may not initiate legislation. If a deputy proposes legislation acceptable to the Chamber, it is sent to the Council of Ministers so that a formal draft may be prepared. If rejected by the Chamber, it may not be reintroduced during the same session.

The draft of a law introduced in one of the chambers is ordinarily referred for examination and report after the first reading to one of the standing committees that exist in both chambers: petitions, administrative, military, finance, foreign affairs, economic matters, legal matters, education. Any changes or suggestions are usually made and accepted on the second reading of a bill. Any draft law prepared by the government, if passed by one house, must be submitted to the other. A budget law must be presented by the Minister of Finance to the Chamber of Deputies. A draft law twice rejected by one chamber but insisted upon by the other must go before a joint meeting of the two chambers, where it may be passed by a two thirds majority. Draft laws are usually passed article by article by each chamber and then passed again as a whole, although either chamber may consider a draft initially as a whole if the need is urgent. After passage by both chambers, a law becomes valid after confirmation by the king. The king must ordinarily confirm or reject a measure within three months; if he rejects a measure it is returned with his reasons for doing so. If one of the chambers considers the legislation urgent the king must act within fifteen days (Article 54).

Members of the parliament may question ministers and ask for explanations of policy eight days after giving notice of intention to do so. The constitution guarantees them complete freedom of speech subject to the regulations of the respective chamber, and theoretically they enjoy immunity from any consequences of having expressed opinions or cast votes in a particular manner in their respective chambers. They are not liable to arrest—nor can they be brought to trial while parliament is in session—unless they have been arrested while committing a crime or unless the chamber of which they are members has passed a resolution permitting their arrest.

The Judiciary

The principle of a separation of powers, with an independent judiciary free from interference by the government, is in theory applied in Iraq. Four types of courts are provided for: civil, tribal, religious, and special. The king appoints judges upon the proposal of the Minister of Justice, and (Article 68) they are not removable except in conformity with the special law establishing their qualifications and the terms of their appointment, dismissal, and grade. It is further provided by the Constitution that all trials should be public except those in which there exists a legally prescribed basis for secret actions. Decisions are rendered by judges either singly or sitting in panels. Trial proceedings and court judgments may be published unless they relate to secret sessions (Article 72).

The Civil Courts

The jurisdiction of the civil courts covers cases of civil, commercial, and criminal nature, as well as actions brought against or for the government; exception is made for certain categories of cases which are under the jurisdiction of the religious courts. This court system in the main follows the French pattern and is based upon Articles 68 and 74 of the Constitution, supplemented by various legislative enactments.

The courts of the first instance and the peace courts are the courts of original jurisdiction in civil cases. The courts of first instance are in turn divided into those with limited and those with general jurisdiction; each court is presided over by a single judge. Those of limited jurisdiction may hear cases not involving more than ID 500 (1 dinar = $2.80); they are established at all *liwa* (provincial) and *qada* (district) and in important *nahiyah* (subdistrict) headquarters. Courts of general jurisdiction sit at provincial headquarters and in the principal districts. The area of jurisdiction of a court of first instance may comprise more than one district or subdistrict. Peace courts operate wherever there is a court of first instance and at other places determined by the Minister of Justice. In some cases more than one such court may be established at the same place. The peace courts, each with a single judge, have jurisdiction in cases involving not more than ID 100 and in suits over water rights, the partitioning of property, and eviction, regardless of the sum involved.

Magistrates' courts are courts of original but limited jurisdiction in criminal cases. Presided over by a single judge, magistrate's courts are divided into three classes on the basis of the extent of their jurisdiction. Third-class courts may only try minor offenses, known as contraventions. Second-class courts may also try misdemeanors, and first-class courts may try all offenses except crimes for which a penalty greater than imprisonment for seven years is stipulated.

Courts of sessions have both unlimited original jurisdiction in criminal cases and appellate jurisdiction in cases decided by courts of first instance. Presided over by a bench of three judges, a court of sessions is located in each of Iraq's six judicial districts, with headquarters in the principal cities of the provinces of Baghdad, Kirkuk, Mosul, Al Hillah, Ad Diyala, and Basra.

Eliminated for a time during the period of the Mandate, intermediate appellate courts have been re-established at Baghdad, Mosul, Basra, and Kirkuk to hear appeals from the courts of first instance and the peace courts. They consist of a president, vice-president, and two members, with three members constituting a court. The highest court of appeal is the Court of Cassation in Baghdad, composed of ten judges including a president and two vice-presidents. It is divided into two benches, civil and criminal, each made up of three members and presided over by a vice-president or a senior judge. Certain occasions require a full bench of seven judges presided over by the president or a vice-president. Criminal cases involving the death penalty must be heard by at least five judges.

All original judgments of a court of sessions must be submitted to the Court of Cassation for confirmation. This court may confirm, reduce, remit, or suspend sentences of the lower courts, or it may refuse to confirm the findings and order a retrial.

Juries are not employed in Iraqi criminal procedure. All phases of investigation and trial are in general the responsibility of the public prosecutors and magistrates, although in some localities police officers may fulfill the function of public prosecutors.

During the Mandate the courts earned a reputation for fairness and efficiency. They continued to be subject to British influence to some extent through the retention of British magistrates until 1951, when the last British judge left the country. In recent years the independence of the courts from executive interference, specified in the Constitution, has not been maintained. The Minister of Justice in practice exercises considerable indirect influence over the judiciary through pressure on judges and by delegation of judicial powers to administrative officials.

The Tribal Courts

The Tribal Criminal and Civil Disputes Regulation, issued in 1918 and subsequently amended, provides for the operation of customary law among tribesmen. Tribunals range from tribal councils (*majalis*) or similar bodies appointed by the government to individual chiefs, sheikhs, or other arbiters. The result has been the maintenance of a traditional law system working under the supervision of new local officials and the central government. Provincial governors are charged with the broad administration of tribal law in their jurisdictions and may request civil courts to surrender cases involving tribesmen. The provincial governor may exercise the widest possible discretion in making final determination in penal cases. He may, moveover, delegate the handling of such cases to district officials, but if he does so he is responsible for reviewing the decisions. Decisions of provincial governors may be appealed to the Ministry of the Interior. A tribal court of cassation was established in 1950.

Attempts to codify tribal customary law have generally been criticized for their failure to reflect the actual tribal system. Another objection has been that frequently persons with but vague tribal connections are enabled to escape regular judicial processes when the latter would be disadvantageous to them. It is also often contended that the system perpetuates an outmoded and unjust law. On the other hand, recognition of tribal jusisdiction in tribal legal affairs reduces tension in the government's relations with this segment of the society and regularizes practices which otherwise would persist to one degree or another despite the wishes of the authorities.

The Religious Courts

All cases involving the personal status of Moslems, either Shiite or Sunnite, are dealt with in the sharia courts. Each sect has its own system of courts. The courts also have jurisdiction in disputes arising from administration of the wakfs (pious, charitable, or family foundations). The personal status of Christians, Jews, and other sects (such as the Sabaeans) is dealt with by the Spiritual Councils of the separate communities. These religious courts administer justice according to the sharia (Islamic law or canon law) of the particular community. The sharia courts apply the law appropriate to the Sunnite or Shiite tradition, and it is provided that the judge (cadi) should be a member of the sect to which the majority of the inhabitants of the district to which he is appointed belong. Both Sunnite and Shiite (or Jafari) cadis are assigned to the cities of Baghdad and Basra.

The Special Courts

The High Court is composed of eight members, in addition to its president (who is the president of the Senate or his deputy). The eight members are elected by the Senate and confirmed by the king; four come from the Senate and four are senior judges either from the

Court of Cassation or other courts. The Council of Ministers and the king make the selection if the parliament is not in session. The function of the High Court, as defined in the Constitution, is to try ministers, deputies, and senators for political offenses related to their conduct of public office; to try judges of the Court of Cassation; to render interpretations of the law; and to pass on the constitutionality of laws (Article 81). Unlike the Supreme Court of the United States, of course, this court is an *ad hoc* body called into being by the government.

The Special Court (Diwan Khass) is established at the request of a minister, its membership in each case being determined by special legislation. It is composed of three judges from the court of Cassation and three chief administrative officials, with three senior military officials if the army is concerned. Its purpose is to render interpretations of laws other than those under the jurisdiction of the High Court. Its decisions become operative if they are agreed upon by two thirds of the judges.

Other special courts are established *ad hoc* to deal with military offenses, disputes between officials of the government and the government, and disputes relating to the possession or boundaries of land. In keeping with the Constitution, courts-martial may also be established as special courts in areas where a state of emergency has been proclaimed.

The Legal System

The legal system of the state is based partly upon western secular models and partly upon religious models, Islamic and others. The predominant Sunnite schools of jurisprudence are Hanafite (see chap. 5) in the south and Shafiite among the Kurds of the north. The Shiite school is that of Jafari. The Christians and Jews apply their own religious laws.

The secular law of Iraq has been extensively codified on the continental European pattern. The precedents for this process are historical—under the Ottoman regime (in the course of its westernization in the nineteenth century) codified French models had been used in criminal law, the law of criminal procedure, and commercial law. The Islamic law of the Hanafite school had been codified into the *Majallah,* covering in the main the law of contracts, evidence, and procedure. As such it was meant to be a guide to new secular courts established in the Ottoman Empire.

The British occupation under the Mandate and the period of independence saw a continuous process of adaptation of the law to meet new conditions. The British military occupation in its earliest period replaced the Ottoman criminal code and code of criminal procedure with the "Baghdad Penal Code," which followed the Egyptian Penal Code (in turn based on French models), and the "Baghdad Criminal Procedure Regulations," which followed closely the Sudan Criminal Procedure Code. Since the time of the occupation these codes have been greatly amended, but they have not been entirely superseded. A new commercial code, replacing its Ottoman predecessor, was enacted in May 1943. A new civil code was completed in 1947, by a commission which began its work in 1936, and was enacted into law. Other laws have been passed replacing portions of the Ottoman legislation; certain difficulties have arisen from the attempt to adapt western principles to a non-western society.

By and large, there is scant popular respect for or understanding of the borrowed alien codes or the agencies for law enforcement. Attitudes toward individual and group violence differ substantially from those in the West. Secular criminal law may even be regarded as sacrilegious by conservative Moslems, who respect only the law derived from the Koran and the sayings of Mohammed. Basic distrust of government is reflected in attitudes toward the national police. Traditionally—especially in nomadic and other rural areas—they have been regarded as intrusive agents of an arbitrary and external authority rather than as a force to protect life and property. Moreover, much of what under the law codes falls in the province of court decision and police action remains for the villager or tribesman purely a matter for family or community concern. Murder or insult call for revenge. Theft outside one's local group is not a crime but an obvious means of enriching oneself at the expense of an outsider. Taxes are an onerous burden to be evaded if possible. Accusations, convictions, and imprisonment are to the average Iraqi not the workings of a reasonable system of justice but serious affronts to dignity and, as such, ample justification for retaliation.

Law Enforcement

The Police System

One of the most heavily policed countries in the world, Iraq maintains a highly centralized police system with administrative control divided between a Director-General of Police and a Director-General of Security, each directly responsible to the Minister of the Interior except during periods of martial law, when the police are under the jurisdiction of the Minister of Defense.

Totaling about 29,000, the police forces are organized into: the police proper, including both rural and urban police and night guards;

desert police and mobile police; special police including railway, customs, forest, petroleum, and port police; and police under the Directorate of Security.

The regular police stationed in a province are commanded by a police commandant but are actually under the control of the provincial governor, who is ultimately responsible for the maintenance of internal security within his province.

The desert police force consists of three units: the Northern, the Southern, and the Al Jazirah forces. Under the direct supervision of the Minister of the Interior, this force patrols bedouin areas, maintaining order and customs control. Since the three desert administrations are not part of any province, the police commandant in each of these regions exercises very wide powers.

The mobile police, functioning as a tactical force, is organized along military lines into three brigades and one cavalry regiment, with a total strength of about four thousand. Partly motorized, it has the mission of reinforcing local police wherever serious disturbances occur. Although considered a paramilitary force, the mobile police reportedly would require considerable additional training in order to be effective as an auxiliary military unit.

The municipalities of Iraq provide night guards for the maintenance of order and the protection of property. Although not directly connected with the police organization, the night guards function under the supervision of police officers and in many respects act as a supplementary instrument of the police by calling serious incidents to the attention of the authorities. No special training is given night guards, but many of them are retired policemen or former soldiers and thus have some qualifications for their jobs.

The petroleum police, paid by the oil companies, guard oil wells, pipelines, and refineries. The other special police forces are financed by the ministries concerned, but are trained and administered by the Directorate of Police.

Formerly a division of the Directorate of Police, the Directorate of Security is primarily an intelligence agency. Its Department of Criminal Investigation is not concerned with ordinary crime detection but with political intelligence, counterespionage, and the penetration of subversive organizations. The Directorate also includes a Department of Residents charged with supervision over the movements and activities of foreigners and a Department of Nationality which is concerned with information on Iraqi subjects both at home and abroad.

During the period of Ottoman rule the police in Iraq were notoriously corrupt and ineffective. The Mandate administration reorganized the police system along British colonial lines and considerably improved its efficiency. British methods and types of training still prevail in the police college at Baghdad. In the past, senior police officers were generally sent to the United Kingdom for advanced training, but increasing numbers are now going to the United States.

The use of the police to quell disturbances—by both the Mandate authorities and Iraq's independent government—has tended to perpetuate popular fear and distrust of them as a repressive force. This attitude is reinforced by the police's reputation for shooting while suppressing disorders. The army, on the other hand, has earned popular respect through its ability to restore order without recourse to violence.

The lower ranks of the police force are generally drawn from majority elements of the areas concerned—Sunnite Moslem Arabs, Kurds, or Shiite Moslems—depending on which group predominates. Despite these ethnic ties, mutual distrust tends to prevail between the police and the general population. Police power as provided by law is subject to numerous abuses: charges of bribery, illegal arrest, and torture of suspects under investigation are frequently made, often in the parliament. The lower police ranks in particular are said to be brutal and overbearing in their dealings with the poor while showing favoritism toward persons of influence. There is undoubtedly some graft in the higher ranks—particularly in outlying districts. Police officers tend to prefer these remote posts to duty in the cities or the mobile force, where there is less opportunity for graft. Although frowned upon by the higher police administration, the acceptance of bribes is somewhat taken for granted by the general public, which tends to regard such opportunities as natural perquisites of office.

The morale of the police tends to be low for a number of reasons: discipline is harsh; police pay is lower than that for comparable ranks in the army and, except for officers, those with families do not receive a living wage; the widespread use of influence in promotion and assignment is resented, as are the superior attitude of the officers and their indifference to the welfare of the ordinary policemen. Police morale and effectiveness are further undermined by inadequate transport and communications equipment.

In the past a certain amount of jealousy has existed between the army and the police. In particular, the army has resented the mobile force, claiming that it served no useful purpose since it was unable to maintain internal security without assistance from the armed forces. The recent appointment of a high-ranking officer on leave from the army as Director-General of Police was expected to increase the prestige of the police and to make for better cooperation between the two forces.

The government is attempting to raise the morale and efficiency of the police through modernization of equipment and techniques, better training, and the recruitment of personnel of higher caliber. The Development Board has allocated ID 3.5 million for construction to replace the present police posts and barracks. At the present time a U. S. mission is helping to train police personnel in modern police procedures and the use of American equipment. In view of the widespread unpopularity of the police, this program, unless handled carefully, might give the government's opposition an occasion to claim that efforts to improve and strengthen the police force have the sole purpose of keeping the present regime in power.

The Prison System

The jails of Iraq are the administrative responsibility of the Director-General of Jails in the Ministry of Social Affairs. Central jails are in Baghdad, Basra, Mosul, and Al Hillah; and provincial jails are in Kirkuk, Al Amarah, Al Kut, An Nasiriyah, Ar Ramadi, Baqubah, and As Sulaymaniyah. There are also desert camps for political prisoners and a reformatory for juvenile delinquents.

Prisoners are treated differently depending on whether they are serving a court sentence, awaiting trial, or detained for political reasons. By law, political prisoners and prisoners awaiting trial must be held separately from ordinary prisoners. Because of overcrowding in the jails, however, this is not always done. Political prisoners and prisoners detained for trial are not forced to work and are granted certain other privileges.

Although greatly improved since the days of Turkish administration, prison conditions are unsatisfactory by western standards. Jails remain dirty, airless, and vermin infested notwithstanding the provisions of prison health regulations.

Detention camps, established for political prisoners, have been a highly criticized part of the Iraqi prison system. In recent years, particularly in periods of martial law, the government has been severe on those suspected of Communist or other activities it might deem "subversive"; detention camps, originally set up on a temporary basis, seem to be becoming a permanent feature of the penal system. A certain amount of "re-educational" effort has been directed at these political detainees, and in recent months many have been released upon their promise to desist from further subversive activities. The fact that many still remain in camps, however, has recently become a source of popular resentment. In August 1957 a deputation to the Prime Minister demanded the release of persons imprisoned under the provisions of martial law (December 1956–May 1957)—particularly the well-known political leader, Kamil Chadirchi, head of the former National Democratic Party. Pressure was also put on the government for reinstatement of the more than three hundred students expelled for demonstrations during the Suez crisis. The Ministry of Education has since announced that these students have been permitted to resume their studies.

Provincial and Local Government

Under Turkish administration the territory of Iraq was divided into three provinces (vilayets), each administered by a governor (wali) directly responsible to the government in Constantinople. The three provinces, Mosul, Baghdad, and Basra, were in turn divided into districts (sanjaks), each administered under an official responsible to the respective governors.

Following the establishment of Iraqi independence, the country was divided into 14 *liwas* (provinces) each governed by a *mutasarrif* (governor). This appointed official, who represents the central government in the province and represents provincial interests to the central government, is immediately responsible to the Minister of the Interior but is also the agent of other ministers. He is assisted by two councils made up of both ex officio and elected members; one council assists in the conduct of administration, the other devotes itself to public finance. Recently there has been a tendency to increase the authority and discretion of the provincial governors, particularly with respect to finances and to education; and competition among the provinces is being encouraged in the holding of industrial and trade fairs. Where there is an acute problem of public order or the province is on a difficult national frontier, the governor may be a military official. In any event, he, along with his subordinates at the lower levels, is empowered to call on the military for assistance in case of emergency or necessity.

Each *liwa* is divided into a number of *qadas* (districts), each administered by a *qaimmaqam* (deputy governor), who acts on behalf of the governor of the province and represents local interests in the district before higher authority. He likewise is assisted by an administrative council. Each district is divided into a number of *nahiyahs* (subdistricts or counties), each administered by a *mudir* (director of the subdistrict or county). The country's desert areas are divided into three separate administrations directly under the Minister of the Interior, acting through a director in each area (see

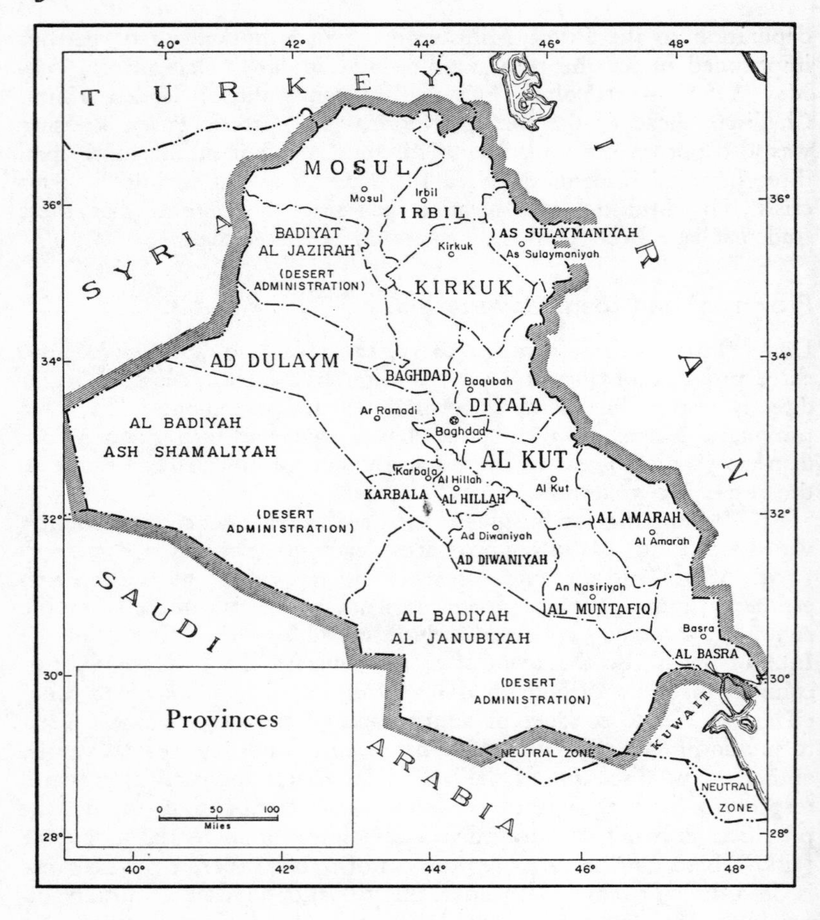

Provinces

Map, Provinces of Iraq). The main administrative problems in these areas are connected with tribal matters and with frontier relationships. Police posts distributed through the desert areas maintain order and enforce the decisions of the authorities.

Every major city or town (*baladiyah*) is administered under a municipal council elected by the people and presided over by a mayor (*rais al-baladiyah*). The council considers all matters of importance at the municipal level, but the mayor is appointed by the Minister of the Interior and is responsible to him for the conduct of municipal affairs. The municipality of Baghdad, as the capital, has a unique position, yet also serves as a model for the others. It is called *amanat al-asimah* (governorate of the capital), and its mayor is called *amin al-asimah* (guardian of the capital).

The lowest level of government, other than the extended kinship groupings of the bedouin tribes, is found in the agricultural villages, where the village officials and notables and a few local representatives of higher governmental authority come into direct contact with the peasantry. At this level the power of government is not only most surely felt but is perhaps also most often in collision with the resistant attitudes and institutions of the countryside.

9

DIFFUSION AND CONTROL OF INFORMATION

AN ENORMOUS DIFFERENCE IN ACCESSIBILITY TO PUBLIC information exists between Iraq's small, educated elite and the illiterate majority of the population. Moreover, attention to the press, radio, and films also varies with occupational group, economic position, and urban or rural residence. Ethnic, linguistic, and religious divisions further limit the extent of their effectiveness. Radio broadcasts of interest to upper-class urban dwellers may not attract industrial workers; programs which appeal to townsmen may be considered sacrilegious by the more devout villagers and may have little relevance to the interests of nomads.

The direct influence of the press is severely limited by Iraq's low literacy rate (estimated at 10 to 15 percent). It is further curtailed by the fact that a large percentage of the reading public is not fully equipped to deal with the complexities of classical or modern classical Arabic, the language of the press. Similar difficulties of comprehension limit the effectiveness of the radio. Newcasts and most other programs are in the classical language and contain many words unfamiliar to illiterate Iraqis, who get the general sense but rarely a precise understanding of such broadcasts. The bulk of the population continues to rely on the informal word-of-mouth communications which are the traditional news channels of the Middle East. The coffeehouse provides a center where news is read aloud and broadcasts are interpreted and discussed, later to reappear in distorted form as gossip in the marketplace or rumors in the public bath or in the courtyard of the mosque. The bedouin obtains news during infrequent visits to towns and villages and from wayfarers and merchants. On the rare occasions when a newspaper finds its way into a tribal area a sayyid (person claiming descent from the

Prophet Mohammed who often functions as a religious leader) may read and interpret it, but the average bedouin's zest for information traditionally has been limited to news concerning family and tribal matters. With the exercise of increasing control over tribal affairs by the government, it is likely that the bedouin's interest in events outside his own home is being whetted by access to the radio sets which are being acquired by more and more bedouin (and Kurdish) tribal leaders.

The rumor and gossip circulated by informal channels are not subjected to critical scrutiny or any process of verification. The significance of reports is magnified or minimized indiscriminately; consequently the factual and emotional content of public opinion varies widely from place to place and is inevitably based upon a mixture of truths, half-truths, and falsehoods.

The output of formal information media in Iraq, as elsewhere in the Middle East, bears the imprint of this background of hearsay communication. Exciting and intriguing presentation tends to take precedence over accuracy, and there is a general tendency toward extreme statement. Issues are presented in black and white without intermediate shading, and any kind of verbal communication tends normally to be louder, more forceful, and more emotionally charged than in the West.

The public information activities of the Iraqi Government have so far not been large-scale—except during the Arab-Israeli war in 1948—nor systematic. The Directorate of Guidance and Broadcasting does not conduct anything resembling a modern propaganda campaign: official policy in this sphere has been negative rather than positive. By and large, reliance has been placed on censorship as opposed to political indoctrination, and on restrictive measures in preference to persuasion; however, covert propaganda techniques may be used to some extent. Official broadcasts dealing with controversial matters have tended to be defensive. Criticism results more often in attempts to refute it than in the launching of counterpropaganda.

The Iraq Development Board, established in 1950, has emphasized flood control, irrigation, and road building, involving many projects remote from heavily populated areas. In the priority given long-term development objectives, the Board clearly has not been interested in catching the popular imagination or in silencing critics. Until recently Iraqis were largely unaware of the progress being made in development schemes, or of their import for the country as a whole. Meanwhile, the officials in charge of the program were subjected to widespread criticism at home and abroad for "slowness," "extravagance," and "exploitation of the poor" in their expenditures of oil revenues. In the last year or two (1956–57), the Board has noticeably increased its propaganda activities, as shown, for example, in the publicity given the opening of the Wadi ath Tharthar and Habbaniyah projects.

The government's past disinterest in a vigorous domestic information campaign stems in large part from the attitudes of the small group of key leaders who have dominated Iraqi politics for the past thirty years. Nuri as-Said in particular—thirteen times prime minister—has ruled with seeming indifference to public opinion. Intimately acquainted with the focal centers of power in his country and experienced in dealing with them, he evidently has seen little point in striving for popular approval of his policies through explanation or persuasion. Some observers have suggested, however, that the frequent failure of high Iraqi officials to prepare the ground for popular acceptance of new policies has often played into the hands of extremist opposition elements by providing them with opportunities to agitate against the government.

Through its control of the educational system, censorship of the press, and monopoly of radio broadcasting, the government has access to numerous channels for the dissemination of propaganda. In the use of these channels, there are indications of the development of a more positive approach aimed primarily at instilling in the population as a whole loyalty to Iraq as a national entity and support for official policies.

Organization of Government Propaganda

Government information activities are largely the responsibility of the Directorate of Guidance and Broadcasting (until recently the Directorate of Propaganda) of the Ministry of the Interior. In addition other ministries and agencies—for example, the Development Board and the Ministry of Education—operate their own information programs on a small scale and publish pamphlets and leaflets, generally of an educational nature. The principal functions of the Directorate are the licensing of newspapers and implementation of censorship provisions, the supplying of official news to the press, and the supervision of both the programing and operational aspects of broadcasting. Little information is available about the administrative details of the propaganda agency or the precise content or effectiveness of its output. Staffed by career civil servants and a few political appointees, the Directorate lacks specialists in public relations and propaganda.

The general public tends to distrust the government's information activities. Official censorship is also unpopular. Although its scope has not changed materially in the last twenty years, the recently more rigorous application of censorship regulations has reinforced the widespread view that the Directorate of Guidance and Broadcasting is a repressive agency.

Through its tight control of the curricula of both private and public schools, the Ministry of Education is attempting to instill a shared sense of national loyalty in all segments of the population (see chap. 19). Iraq is depicted as the "cradle of civilization" in efforts to make the younger generation, in particular, proudly conscious of the country's long history. The effectiveness of political indoctrination through the school system, however, is somewhat undermined by the fact that students are the primary target of Communist propaganda and have been among the most vociferous critics of the government.

The accession of King Faisal II to the throne in 1953 provided an opportunity for exploiting the appeals of history and the monarchy as unifying symbols. This was done through elaborate pageantry and colorful historical tableaux which extolled the reigning Hashemite family as the descendants of the Abbasside caliphs, rulers during Iraq's "golden age" (see chap. 2).

The achievements of the Development Board also are beginning to be made occasions for ceremony and display affording favorable publicity for the government's policies. In the spring of 1957, special week-long celebrations were held to mark the progress made by the development program. The King's ceremonious inauguration of bridges, factories, housing developments, and other projects was filmed for broadcast by the new television station.

Covert propaganda techniques such as subsidies to editors of newspapers in return for support of government policy, grants of holidays with pay when "popular" demonstrations are wanted, and subsidies to public speakers and rumor spreaders have long been familiar in the Middle East; presumably they are employed to one degree or another by the Iraqi Government.

The Press

There was little development of journalism in Iraq before World War I. With the establishment of the British Mandate came a rapid growth in nationalist newspapers. The attainment of nominal independence in 1930 gave rise to a new group of newspapers operating as the personal organs of politicians, each of whom sponsored his own following of journalists. When politicians fell from office their newspapers tended to be replaced by others supported by new leaders. The highly political focus of these newspapers and their tendency to represent persons rather than issues are characteristic of the press throughout the Arab world. In recent years the newspaper which functions as the personal vehicle of its editor—often a well-known author, poet, or politician—has been the most common type.

In the early days of Iraqi journalism when the cities were smaller, the literacy rate was even lower than today, advertising had not developed extensively, and no paper could hope to support itself. If not independently wealthy, owner-editors frequently solicited funds from politicians and others, many times offering in return secret commitments of editorial and other support for the donor's personal or local interests—a practice which helps to explain the frequent shifts in editorial policy to which Iraqi newspapers have been subject.

There is no strong tradition of objective reporting of the news, and editors seem to believe that their opinions, rather than the adequacy of their news coverage, sell their papers. Editorials, generally placed on the front page, are usually signed by the editor and composed in a different style and print from news stories. They are often highly literary and are discussed as much for stylistic merit as for political content. Quotations from the Koran, classical poetry, and proverbs are frequently used to clinch an argument or to begin or end an editorial.

Censorship

Freedom of the press was guaranteed by the Constitution (1925), only to be limited subsequently by law. A press law of 1950 provides for the licensing of newspapers and formal censorship. Before 1954, however, the government did not often or rigorously invoke legal means to stifle criticism except in periods of martial law or in the case of highly inflammatory material. Roughly half the dailies in Baghdad were opposition papers which thrived on attacks on official policies. One Iraqi editor has been quoted as saying: "The press law is so strict that there could be no papers if it were rigidly enforced."

The present system of strict censorship arose out of the near collapse of the central government in November 1952. The return to the premiership of Nuri as-Said in 1954 brought about the dissolution of all political parties and the suspension of all party organs. Eighteen newspapers were closed, and the remainder continue to be faced with the threat of suspension for any criticism which might be deemed improper by the authorities. Newspapers today are not supposed to comment adversely on the Baghdad Pact or attack powers with which Iraq has friendly relations. They are permitted to criticize the Soviet Union, French policies in Algeria, and the policies of the United States toward Israel. Many Iraqi newsmen, particularly those of anti-western or neutralist leanings, bitterly resent these restrictions and spread their discontent to other politically articulate elements in the community. The government has not so far relaxed its controls, but in practice—since the attack on Egypt in 1956 by Britain, France, and Israel—a considerable amount of anti-western material has been permitted.

In addition to its censorship activities, the Directorate of Guidance and Broadcasting supplies the press with official news. Factual reports from the various ministries are readily accepted by newspapers, but press releases designed to project or justify the official line tend to meet with unfavorable reception. Occasionally the Directorate publishes material designed for overseas consumption. Such publications tend to emphasize current progress in education, economic development, and social reform set against the backdrop of a long and illustrious past.

The Current Press

Like other Arab countries, Iraq has tended to have a comparatively large number of newspapers with no single one occupying a commanding position in the press. In late 1957 there were thirty dailies in the country as a whole—most of them in Arabic—with an estimated total circulation of 100,000. There is a small Kurdish press, about which detailed information is lacking, and an English-language newspaper, the *Iraq Times,* which is published at Baghdad and Basra. Table 3 lists the major daily newspapers, including some suspended papers.

Circulation figures are not available for many of the newspapers. By and large, those enjoying a reputation for relatively accurate news reporting, notably *az-Zaman,* have the larger circulations. The number of newspapers distributed is no index to their actual circulation or influence, since a single copy may be read by a dozen or more people and read aloud to still others. The printed word is held in great respect, and much of the information contained in newspapers is heatedly discussed and passed along by word of mouth.

Because of a shortage of newsprint the size of papers is limited by informal agreement among publishers to about four standard eight-column pages. Relatively less space is devoted to advertising than in typical small American papers and proportionately more to foreign, national, and local news. The inadequacy of news coverage in Iraqi papers stems in part from the general tendency to slant it:

stories are frequently colored for political purposes, and news coverage as a whole tends to be slanted by selection; slanting now tends to mirror the official line.

Apart from three political weeklies with a circulation of about 7,000, periodicals published locally are for the most part technical journals or official organs of government ministries. The most important of these are the following. *Majallat Ghurfat Tijjarat Baghdad* (sponsored by the Baghdad Chamber of Commerce) contains articles on economic and commercial subjects; editorial writers: Mir Basri and others. *Al-Muallim al-Jadid* (sponsored by the Ministry of Education) contains articles on educational problems and literary subjects; chief editor: Jabir Umar. *Al-Qada* (sponsored by the Ministry of Justice) is a legal review; editor: Hasan Zakariyyah. *Sumer* (sponsored by the Department of Antiquities) contains articles in Arabic, French, and English on archeology.

Until recently the demand for popular magazines was met largely by a few Lebanese and many Egyptian illustrated periodicals, in particular *al-Musawwar, al-Ithnayn,* and the satirical, leftist *Rose al-Yusuf.* (It is not known whether these Egyptian publications are still allowed into the country.) In addition many British and American newspapers and periodicals are read in the larger cities, English being by far the most widely known foreign language. Such publications as the *Times, The Economist,* the *New York Herald Tribune* and *Time* (International Edition) are more influential than their limited circulation would indicate, since they tend to reach the people who figure most prominently in the political and intellectual life of the country.

Despite the fact that censorship restrictions prohibit the dissemination of Communist literature, a considerable number of clandestine Communist publications reach the Iraqi public. Their readers are for the most part students, teachers, minor government officials, industrial workers, and professionals. Replete with slogans designed to exploit the outlook and concerns of these groups, Communist leaflets emphasize the contrast between the "imperialistic" policy of the West and the "peace" policy of the Soviet Union. After the Suez crisis of late 1956 a concentrated attack was made on all pro-western elements. Characterized an "imperialist and Zionist," Nuri as-Said was a favorite target of this propaganda offensive.

Radio

Radio broadcasting is a monopoly of the government, operating under the direct supervision of the Director-General of Guidance and Broadcasting. Radio Baghdad, the country's only station, broadcasts in Arabic ten hours a day on medium wave and sixteen hours a day on short wave. It also broadcasts daily transmissions in Kurdish and English on short wave. Table 4 gives the power, wave lengths, and frequencies of the transmitters.

The number of persons in Iraq owning radio sets is small but increasing. It has been estimated that at the end of 1954 there were only 66,000 licensed radio receivers in the country—roughly 1 for every 75 people. The importance of the radio, however, cannot be reckoned on the number of receiving sets per capita. Loudspeakers in the coffeehouses of the towns reach everyone within earshot, and word-of-mouth carries to remote parts of the country more or less distorted versions of what has been heard on the radio. Moreover, each private set usually serves not only its owner but his neighbors, since it is regarded as inhospitable to keep one's radio to oneself. It is thus probable that radio has the largest audience of the mass-communications media. The effectiveness of Radio Baghdad is somewhat undermined, however, by a widespread tendency to suspect much of its program content as government "progaganda." Educated listeners in particular tend to distrust broadcasts which are too obviously designed to disseminate official views.

Radio Baghdad makes general use of nationalist and patriotic themes, but, like other government media, it tends to be negative rather than positive in its handling of political material. Newscasts and political commentaries consist largely in the denial of rumors, the refutation of charges made by critics at home and abroad, and the discrediting of unfriendly propaganda, particularly that emanating from the Soviet Union. In recent months the Iraqi radio station has also been constantly on the defensive against the "medacious propaganda" and "fabricated accusations" broadcast from Egypt and Syria. Broadcasts on the subject of Israel, on the other hand, are more aggressive in tone, being devoted to violent attacks on the Israelis and making use of a variety of emotional and religious appeals.

The major portion of broadcast time is devoted to recorded, mainly vocal, music. Newscasts based on official and agency reports may be heard five times a day. A short religious feature including a reading from the Koran is broadcast daily, and during Ramadan and other Moslem holidays a considerable amount of time is given to religious programs. Poetry also occupies an important place in programing, as do lectures on cultural and political matters.

Television

The first television station in the Arab world was opened in Baghdad in 1956. Operating in the evening hours, it has a range of about eighteen miles in the vicinity of the capital. The few hundred television receivers in the country are owned for the most part by well-to-do families but some sets are on view in public places. Television programs include children's features, music, and drama as well as newscasts.

Films

There are 137 cinemas in Iraq, mostly in the towns, with an estimated total seating capacity of 70,000. The time-consuming demands of agriculture, the cost of theater tickets, and the distance to cinemas are factors which seriously limit movie attendance by the rural majority of Iraq's population.

One local production company has made several feature films in the past few years (see chap. 20). Of the nearly 400 feature films imported annually (by 1956), 69 percent were supplied by the United States and 17 percent by Egypt, the film-producing center of the Middle East. The remainder were from Italy, Germany, Turkey, India, and the United Kingdom. The United States Information Service and the British Council also show films in connection with their programs.

Foreign films, with the exception of those from Egypt, are shown with captions in classical Arabic and are understood only by the few who are literate or who know the language of the movie. In Egyptain films, on the other hand, the dialogue combines Egyptian colloquial phrases with those common to other Arab countries and are readily comprehensible to the large illiterate segment of the Iraqi public.

Foreign Information Activities

Since becoming a signatory to the Baghdad Pact, Iraq, somewhat drawn apart from the other Arab states, has been subjected to an increasing amount of propaganda from all sides.

Material entering Iraq from abroad is subjected to close scrutiny. Any literature orginating behind the Iron Curtain is automatically banned (Iraq suspended diplomatic relations with the USSR in 1955), and in the recent period of strained relations with Egypt, Egyptian publications also have been highly suspect.

The principal foreign information programs operating in Iraq are those of Britain and the United States. Stressing cultural exchange, the British effort is directed largely through the British Council, a paragovernmental agency which sponsors lectures, films, and exhibitions of scholarly or literary interest.

United States information activities in general are regarded by Iraqis as a more obvious attempt to influence opinion than those of the British. Nevertheless, the United States Information Service films are usually well received and the USIS libraries have been welcomed by the reading public.

Foreign Broadcasts

Probably the most widely listened to of all foreign broadcasts are those emanating from Cairo's violently anti-western "Voice of the Arabs." In part this receptivity to Egyptian programs is due to the tendency of many Iraqis to look up to Egypt as the intellectual center of the Arab world. In part it reflects the recent political climate, in which Egypt has been regarded by many Iraqis—particularly the younger educated groups—as the best defender of Arab interests against the encroachments of western "imperialism." The reception accorded Egyptian broadcasts is also explained by the tremendous popularity of certain performers. Singers such as Umm Kulthum and Abd al-Wahhab enjoy large personal followings among urban listeners in Iraq.

Broadcasts from Syria are also widely heard. In 1956 and early 1957 Radio Damascus was echoing the Cairo station's propaganda line in its denunciation of Nuri as-Said as a "traitor to the Arabs" and "imperialist dictator," and in its virulent attack on his regime's policies. The Iraqi Government jammed these broadcasts during the first half of 1957 but in July it was reported that Ali Jawdat, the new premier, had ordered a cessation of the jamming in a move aimed at improving relations with Syria and Egypt.

The British Broadcasting Corporation and its affiliated station on Cyprus enjoy a reputation gained during World War II for objective reporting of the news. The Cyprus station in particular has appealed to many Iaqis through its support of a strong Arab stand against Israel.

Viewed by many as "propaganda" and as having little relevance to Arab interests, Voice of America broadcasts are less popular. VOA's audience is further limited by poor reception in comparison with that of other major foreign stations and the fact that many radio listeners are not familiar with the times or wave lengths of the programs.

Soviet broadcasts in Arabic have been in much the same vein as those from Cairo and Damascus. Capitalizing on popular "anti-imperialist" slogans, they have attempted to discredit Iraq's pro-western policies in every possible way. Broadcasts in Kurdish from Yerevan in Soviet Armenia also attack the West and contrast the "radiant life" led by the Kurds in the USSR with their "persecution" in Iraq. Listening to Soviet programs is prohibited by the Iraqi Government, but how effective the ban may be is not known.

10

FOREIGN RELATIONS

GEOGRAPHICAL LOCATION, NATURAL WEALTH, AND POSITION AS a major Arab state leave Iraq no alternative to an active foreign policy. Geographically, the country is at a confluence of power from three continents, and its valley-plain has long figured as a strategic corridor in the passage of men and goods between the lands to the north and west and the Persian Gulf. The agricultural wealth of the Tigris and Euphrates, which has at times made the country an active center of power in the region, as under the Abbasside dynasty during the Arab middle ages, at other times a resource to be exploited by conquerors, as under the Turks for six centuries before World War I, now is augmented by petroleum income. As a claimant to Arab leadership, Iraq is matched only by the other great riverine country of the area, Egypt, and the historic competition between the two has been intensified in modern times. The force of this rivalry was demonstrated in early 1958 when two competing Arab groupings were formed. The competition is more than strategic, institutional, or a matter of prestige; it also involves awareness on both sides of historical conflict between the two areas as sources of civilization which go back as far as the Egyptian pharaohs and the Sumerian kings.

Although Iraq and the other Arab states conduct their foreign relations within the modern framework of international politics, they do so against a background of historical experience and traditional attitudes which continue to influence in varying degrees both their people and their leaders. In this situation, the patterns of the past help to explain some of the developments of the present.

The historic Moslem empire—extending at its height from Persia across North Africa to Spain—claimed universality under the banner of the Islamic religion. The ultimate aim of Islam was the proselytization of the whole of mankind. Non-Moslems within the empire were tolerated if they accepted the order of things as laid down by the faithful, but there could be no question of permanent dealings with non-Moslem powers on terms of equality. There was only one right dispensation, and that had been conveyed to man by and through the Prophet. The Moslem ruler might make war on the unbeliever or live with him in peace, but the decision was seen as a unilateral one for there could be no binding reciprocity of relationship between the justice of Islam and the error of the infidel.

Since the divine mission of Islam ultimately was to encompass all mankind for Moslems the world was divided into *dar al-islam* (Islamic territory) and *dar al-harb* (enemy territory). *Dar al-harb* consisted of all countries outside the territory of Islam. In theory, *dar al-islam* was always in conflict with *dar al-harb*. The Moslem offensive, called jihad, was always "just" because waged against infidels and enemies of the faith. But jihad did not always mean actual combat; peaceful as well as violent means were used. Thus jihad took the form of a continuous process of warfare that was as much psychological and political as it was military. It did not preclude the possibility of initiating negotiations and concluding treaties, for such actions were justifiable temporary expedients to be employed in the service of the faith when stronger measures were not possible. Permanent peace and the end of jihad would be achieved only when the *dar al-harb* was absorbed by *dar al-islam*.

In practice, the concept of jihad was adapted to suit the changing circumstances of life. Islam often made peace with the enemy, and not always on its own terms. Moslem jurists began to interpret jihad to mean merely the preparation for war; then it was allowed that jihad could go into a dormant state, from which the ruler might revive it when he deemed it necessary. In recent times, the so-called modernist theorists argue that the jihad has become merely a defensive instrument against aggression by the enemies of Islam.

No important Moslem figure today is attempting to lead in terms of jihad, but the word probably has not lost its potential power as a mass rallying cry in the event of a development which might be regarded as a threat to all Islam. The traditional zeal against *dar al-harb* has had its modern reflection in Moslem invective, mass risings against colonial powers, and agitation against local forces regarded disloyal to Arab and Moslem national interests.

It has been only in the last generation that Iraq and its Arab neighbors as sovereign states have been able to develop national governments. Differences of interest among them and in the outlook of their leaders divide them on important issues, but the appeal of Pan-Arab unity is strong; and the ideal is reinforced by a tradition which was shaped during centuries when religion and secular rule were combined in a single Islamic world order. The Pan-Arab ideal, in conveying a sense of common problems and shared goals, has been a unifying force among the Arab states; but it has also provided a weapon which one Arab government can use against another in denouncing it to its own people as a betrayer of general Arab interests. Such criticisms have been leveled against both Iraq and Jordan by Egypt and Syria and the new federation of Jordan and Iraq continued to be so attacked by Nasser's United Arab Republic and vilified by Communist propaganda as Iraq had in the past been criticized for its alignment with the West. As an assertion of Arab loyalty transcending and conflicting with that owed to the national state, this particular manipulation of Pan-Arabism carries a subversive threat not only to Iraq and Jordan but potentially to the other Arab states as well.

The basic strategic orientation of Iraq's foreign policy has been maintained with increasing difficulty during a period of mounting international crisis which has seen some of its Arab neighbors take a different course. Iraq's alliance with the West through the Baghdad Pact and its refusal to have dealings with the Communist bloc are condemned by those Arabs who are disposed to a "neutralist" position or hold that the Arab world must make common front against a western threat. Various factors, however, have moved Iraq's leaders to pursue an independent policy and at points to collaborate with such non-Arab neighbors as Turkey and Iran without regard to Arab opinion elsewhere. Shiite ties with Iran provide a basis for similarity of interest with that country. Both countries have had generations of experience with invading forces coming out of present-day Russia. Many of the elder Iraqi elite were schooled in Turkey and, despite the recollection of Turkish domination and some continuing issues, they do not find much difficulty in joining with the Turks in the Baghdad Pact. Any serious conflict between Turkey and another Arab state, however, such as threatened Syria in 1957, would severely strain the Pact and might make it impossible for Iraq to remain a member.

A major factor in the continuity of Iraq's foreign policy is implicit in the fact that internal political power has from the beginning been in the hands of a small oligarchy whose members through compromise and common interest have been able to collaborate on matters of foreign policy. Uninhibited by an active national electorate or an informed public opinion, they can act positively, often in ways which may be opposed by many of the people. They have to contend with occasional popular emotional outbursts and increasingly with the challenge of the growing urban middle class, but their control of the instruments of military and civil power has enabled them to repress any overt threats to their monopoly of decision in the foreign affairs of the country.

It is perhaps characteristic, not only of the complexity of this setting but of a way of thought it has produced, that Iraq's foreign policy has attempted to balance the demands of local nationalism against Pan-Arab nationalism, and obligations under the western-oriented Baghdad Pact against those within the "neutralist" if not anti-western Arab League. In this outlook, practical compromise and expediency are more highly valued than logical consistency. Power carries prestige and it is to be recognized through its demonstration. Iraq and the rest of the Arab world are acutely sensitive to any apparent alterations in the relative prestige of other nations. The visit of Iraq's Prime Minister Ali Jawdat al-Ayyubi to Syria in 1957 when that country, strongly supported by the USSR, seemed on the verge of hostilities with Iraq's ally, Turkey, was not only a gesture of Arab solidarity but an acknowledgment of Russian advances in the development of missiles. A strong Iraqi leader such as Nuri as-Said can construct ties with the West, but in the long run his ability to maintain them will hinge importantly on the preservation of the prestige of western power.

Major Aspects Since 1918

Although there were groups of nationalists in Iraq at the close of World War I, groups which provided much of the stimulus to the revolt in 1920, they were in the main supporters of Iraq's independence from the United Kingdom rather than Pan-Arab nationalists. Aside from a relatively few then young men such as Nuri as-Said, most of the Iraqi elite was indifferent, attached to a conception of specifically Iraqi interests, disapproved of the separation from Turkey and the destruction of the caliphal authority, or, in the case of representatives of religious or ethnic minorities, feared the possible consequences of a new dispensation. Iraqi nationalism grew and took shape in the struggle to gain independence from the Mandate—a goal which was achieved in little more than a decade. The outcome, in the case of the ruling elite at least, was a nationalism which tempered Pan-Arabism with specifically Iraqi premises and which was less belligerently defensive in relation to the West. Thus, although Iraq itself originally proposed the establishment of an Arab League it has been able to pursue a foreign policy in alliance with the western powers. There has been less aggravated inflation of the peril of "western imperialism" in Iraq than in other Arab countries. Iraq's leaders seem better able to think in terms of constructing for the future rather than fighting the ghosts of the past.

Anglo-Iraqi Relations

Recent Iraqi foreign policy can be understood only against the background of Anglo-Iraqi relations. Iraq owes to Great Britain not only much of its governmental structure but also the early shaping of its foreign policy.

In September 1929, Great Britain moved to put an end to the Mandate, an act probably precipitated by the coming to power of a Labor Government. The change of government in Britain was followed by the emergence of a liberal nationalist government in Iraq which the British authorities believed was capable of leading the country to independence. The Iraqi leaders for their part were confident that the Labor Government in England would pursue a policy favorable to nationalist aspirations.

A treaty was signed, on June 30, 1930, providing for the establishment, after the termination of the Mandate, of a "close alliance" between Great Britain and Iraq and for "full and frank consultation between them in all matters of foreign policy which . . . [might] affect their common interests." In the event of an imminent threat of war, the two parties would concert as to the necessary measures of defense. Iraq recognized that the maintenance and protection of essential British communications were in the common interest of both parties. For these purposes Iraq granted to Britain the full use of two sites for air bases at Basra and Habbaniyah. The treaty was to come into force after Iraq's admission to membership in the League of Nations and was to be of twenty-five years duration.

The opposition parties were far from satisfied with the new treaty, and the Iraqi press, except for progovernment organs, condemned it as inconsistent with the sovereignty of an independent state. Specific criticisms related to the aid which Iraq was required to give in case Great Britain became engaged in war and the grant of air bases at Shuaybah near Basra and at Habbaniyah. Some went so far as to argue that the treaty would make Iraq virtually a British protectorate. While King Faisal I had shrewdly made use of the opposition to obtain better terms during the negotiation of the treaty, he was impatient with the extremists whom he regarded as obstructing Iraq's advancement to independence.

In England, too, the treaty was received with some misgiving and suspicion. The supporters of empire warned the government that British air communications across an independent Iraq might become insecure; that Britain had surrendered an important area admirably suited to air training; and that Britain might be involved in war or complications arising from Iraq's relations with its neighbors.

The treaty was approved by the Iraqi parliament on November 16, 1931 (after a four-hour debate in the Chamber of Deputies), by a majority of 69 out of 82 present, and by a vote of 11 out of 16 in the Senate. The Anglo-Iraqi treaty remained in force until 1955, when Britain and Iraq entered into the Baghdad Pact.

THE FORMULATION OF FOREIGN POLICY. Iraq's foreign policy during the Mandate period was controlled by Great Britain, as the mandatory power, on behalf of the League of Nations. Britain undertook to establish friendly relations between Iraq and its neighbors and sought to settle the frontier disputes that the country had inherited from the Ottoman Empire. Treaties were concluded between Iraq and France (the mandatory power for Syria), between Iraq and Saudi Arabia, and between Iraq and Turkey. These agreements delimited the frontiers of Iraq with the three countries; the boundary between Iraq and Iran, however, was not settled until 1936, after Iraq had become independent.

During the Mandate period Iraq sought to cultivate friendly relations with European as well as Middle Eastern countries. Its relationships with Arab countries, however, were not as close as many Iraqis desired them to be; even after Iraq was released from the Mandate in 1932 it did not at once join the other Arab countries in a larger union. Before Faisal I's death certain weaknesses became apparent in the positions of the two Iraqi schools of nationalist thought: the Pan-Arabs, who advocated an unqualified pro-Arab policy of helping other Arab states to gain their independence and forming a union with them; and the Iraqi nationalists, who advocated an independent foreign policy reflecting Iraq's peculiar internal circumstances (such as the existence of the strong Kurdish minority) and favored the special treaty arrangement with Britain. King Faisal freely expressed his own views on foreign policy to his leading ministers. In the compromise of the extreme positions they set forth was reflected Faisal's mediating role in the early history of the independent kingdom—a role carried out in the face of vociferous opposition which included large segments of the educated class, particularly the younger generation, and officers of the Iraqi army. Faisal sympathized with the Pan-Arab school and hoped for the independence and unity of all the Arab countries, but he hesitated to follow a foreign policy which might expose Iraq to unnecessary danger.

The foreign policy advocated by Faisal may be summed up in

three fundamental principles. First, the King, feeling that British and Arab interests were not irreconcilable, believed in and worked for Anglo-Arab friendship; he regarded the treaty of 1930 as a bulwark safeguarding Iraq's independence and the basis of Anglo-Arab friendship. Second, Faisal advocated a "good neighbor" policy toward all Middle Eastern countries; he visited Turkey and Iran to bring about a settlement of the boundary disputes with those countries and met King ibn Saud of Saudi Arabia in an effort to end the dynastic rivalry between the latter's house and his own. Third, he worked for a *rapprochment* between Iraq and Syria; this move was resisted by France, then mandatory power over Syria, but it was popular in Iraq (except among the Kurds) and was pursued by Faisal's successors as the "Fertile Crescent Scheme" for unity.

A few of the King's leading ministers shared his belief about the importance of cooperation with Britain and continued to advocate such a policy. Among those still alive, Nuri as-Said may be regarded as the chief champion of Anglo-Arab friendship. The independent politicians, Midfai, Ali Jawdat, and Tawfiq as-Suwaydi also belong to this school of thought. Salih Jabr, leader of the Nation's Socialist Party, until his death in 1957 supported a policy of cooperation with Britain and the West, but his support was qualified by his Pan-Arab views. General Nuri remains by far the strongest leader in Iraq and he has been able to impose his viewpoint on his followers, but there has been an increasing trend toward acceptance of the Pan-Arab position of Salih Jabr.

After Faisal's death, Iraqi leaders, although they often made contradictory statements, in practice followed the King's main ideas about foreign policy. The frontier dispute with Iran was settled and Faisal's "good neighbor" policy with Turkey and Iran bore fruit in the signing of the Sadabad Pact, later replaced by the Baghdad Pact. The principle of close cooperation with the other Arab countries, to the satisfaction of the Iraqi Pan-Arab nationalists, was also maintained; it found expression in the signing of the treaty of Arab brotherhood and alliance with Saudi Arabia and Yemen and also in the establishment of the Arab League in 1945.

When World War II broke out, army officers unfriendly to Great Britain began to make their attitude felt in Iraq's foreign policy. The British landing at Basra was dictated by the need to keep the country out of German hands, but many Iraqis, still in the flush of their recently won independence, regarded the move as an attempt to restore British rule. As a result they rallied to the support of the army. Rashid Ali, at the head of the government, found himself leading a movement which took on the proportions of a national upheaval against "western domination." In its origins this development reflected the frustrations of the more extreme Arab nationalists not only in Iraq but also in the other Arab countries.

Rashid Ali was overthrown by the British forces in 1941 and a government friendly to Great Britain was established, first under Midfai and later under Nuri as-Said. The treaty of 1930 was applied for the duration of the war, but its increasing unpopularity made the question of its modification more and more pressing.

THE BAGHDAD PACT. Following World War II, Anglo-Iraqi relations entered a phase of deep involvement in international as well as Middle Eastern regional politics. It was against the background of this evolution from an earlier period when Anglo-Iraqi relationships had had a largely bilateral significance that new formulas had to be found that might be embodied in treaty form. The pressures in this direction were notably those generated by the global cold war between the Soviet bloc and the western alliance and by the continuing development of nationalist sentiment in the Arab world. Behind the new treaty relationships which emerged, however, was a long line of antecedent agreements which provided positive precedents for the arrangements that became known as the Baghdad Pact. These precedents include not only agreements with the United Kingdom, but also agreements with members of the "Northern Tier" states, Turkey and Iran, and collaterally with the United States. The latter was, in fact, the major proponent of a defensive structure against the Soviet bloc.

An attempt was made in 1948 to change the treaty of 1930, but the substitute Treaty of Portsmouth was met by a clamor of protest from opposition elements and did not go into effect. In 1946 a treaty of mutual security was signed between Iraq and Turkey providing for mutual consultation in foreign affairs, but it too was never implemented. In 1955 the Baghdad Pact, a more elaborate agreement for mutual defense, was signed between Turkey and Iraq. The Pact, held open to other powers, was joined by Great Britain, which replaced its treaty with Iraq by an agreement in which it gave up its air bases (with the proviso that it could use them for defense purposes in time of war) and promised to assist Iraq in creating and maintaining an effective Iraqi air force. This was to be done by means of joint training and exercises in the Middle East, and the efficient maintenance and operation of such airfields and other installations as might from time to time be agreed to be necessary. Britain also promised to join with the Government of Iraq in establishing an efficient system of warning against air attack (ensuring that equipment for the defense of Iraq be kept there in a state of readiness), in training and equipping Iraqi defense forces, and in providing the British technical personnel needed for these purposes. Another stipulation provided for the use of air space and air services by each partner in the other's territory. A direct British commitment for Iraq's defense was made in Article 8:

> In the event of an armed attack against Iraq or threat of an armed attack which, in the opinion of the two Contracting Governments, endangers the security of Iraq, the Government of the United Kingdom at the request of the Government of Iraq, shall make available assistance, including if necessary armed forces to help defend Iraq. The Government of Iraq, shall provide all facilities and assistance to enable such aid to be rapid and effective.

The term of the agreement was five years, subject to renewal by mutual consent.

Although there was no serious criticism of the Baghdad Pact at the time of its signing, increasing hostility to it in the other Arab countries aroused some of General Nuri's opponents to initiate opposition in the Senate. Such opposition has many proponents in Iraq among nationalist elements, especially intellectuals and middle-class groups, opposed to any agreement with Britain at the alleged expense of relations between Iraq and Arab countries.

Regional Relations

The idea of a Middle East security pact, bringing together several Middle Eastern countries for defense against outside aggression, was proposed by Turkey before World War II. As a result a pact was signed by Turkey, Iraq, Iran, and Afghanistan in July 1937 at Sadabad which sought to provide a basis for consultation among the four powers in matters of common concern on foreign policy. In the absence of any strongly felt solidarity among the signatories, the Sadabad Pact became a dead letter when war broke out in 1939, and efforts to revive it in 1946 were unsuccessful.

The initiative to create a similar pact in the postwar period again came from Turkey. General Nuri, in his turn, tried to enlist the cooperation of Syria and Egypt; but failing in this he signed an agreement with Turkey in 1946. Jordan followed Iraq by signing a separate agreement with Turkey in 1947, and the Turko-Iraqi pact remained a bilateral and unimplemented agreement to which no other Middle Eastern power adhered.

Prompted by the Soviet threat in the Middle East, the United States, seeking to assure the defense of the area ever since the proclamation of the Truman Doctrine in 1947, urged Great Britain to come to an understanding with Egypt in order to enlist the Arab countries in a comprehensive Middle East security pact. A four-power Middle East pact, including Turkey, Britain, and the United States, was proposed to Egypt, with a view to replacing the Anglo-Egyptian treaty of 1936. Upon its rejection in 1950, the idea of a Middle East pact was for the time discarded. In 1954, Turkey—which had joined the West through NATO—took the initiative and proposed to Egypt and Iraq a mutual security Middle East pact. Egypt postponed action, suspecting the pact to be a substitute for another alliance with Britain, but Turkey and Iraq concluded a Pact of Mutual Cooperation on February 24, 1955, indicating their intention to invite other Middle Eastern countries to join later. Although it sponsored the plan at the beginning, the United States up to 1957 had not adhered to the Pact except for membership in some of the committees established under its terms. Great Britain, Pakistan, and Iran in 1955 and 1956 joined and ratified the Pact, which came to be known as the Baghdad Pact. In accordance with Article 51 of the United Nations Charter, the signatories pledged themselves to "cooperate for their security and defense." A permanent council was set up to carry out the purposes of the Pact and the measures agreed upon for mutual security and defense. The duration of the Pact is five years, and it is subject to renewal.

Although the Pact was denounced by Egypt as conflicting with the Arab Collective Security Pact signed by the Arab League states in 1950, the Iraqi Government took the position that there was nothing inconsistent in its adherence to both agreements. Continuous agitation by Egypt and Saudi Arabia, however, culminated in an Egyptian-sponsored counterpart pact with Saudi Arabia, Yemen, and Syria, which virtually ostracized Iraq from Arab affairs. This brought criticism by certain Iraqi politicians who questioned the wisdom of their government in linking the fate of Iraq with Turkey and Great Britain at the expense of Arab solidarity.

In practice, the Baghdad Pact completely failed to win the cooperation of other Arab countries. The violent propaganda against it appears as an important aspect of the steps that led to the formation of a solid Arab counterbloc willing to accept Soviet aid in order to frustrate the purpose of the Pact. On the surface, opposition elements are quiet at present, but it is entirely conceivable that a change in circumstances could lead to a sudden popular eruption which might—as it did in Jordan in 1956–57—result in rejection of the Pact. This would have serious consequences for the government, which in the eyes of many Iraqis is still *al-Wad ash Shadh* ("the unnatural political order").

THE ARAB LEAGUE. The movement to cultivate cordial relations with other Arab states began immediately after Iraq won its independence. For the proponents of Arab nationalism the ultimate goal of this movement was to link Iraq in a type of a federal union with all other Arab countries. Iraq began by signing treaties of cooperation and alliance with Saudi Arabia and Yemen (1936) and later with Jordan (1946); but the principal move was the establishment of the Arab League in 1945 and the signing of the Arab Collective Security Pact in 1950, both projects in which Iraq took an active part.

Nuri as-Said took the lead in formulating a plan of unity which he submitted to the British Government in 1943. This proposal was advanced in response to Anthony Eden's statement, made in May 1941, that the British Government would support any plan for unity acceptable to the Arabs. Soon Egypt showed interest in the plan and consultations among Arab leaders took place during 1943 and 1944. A conference was held at Alexandria in which seven Arab countries (Egypt, Syria, Jordan, Iraq, Lebanon, Saudi Arabia, and Yemen) pledged themselves to cooperate in a loose framework of Arab unity. In March 1945 the delegates of the seven Arab states met and signed a pact which formally led to the establishment of the Arab League in 1945. In 1950 the Arab Collective Security Pact was signed to implement the pact of the Arab League.

The establishment of the Arab League was favorably received in almost all Iraqi political circles, where it was regarded as a step toward further Arab cooperation. As it turned out, the League did not extend much further the trend toward unity, and it lost credit with extreme nationalist elements. The majority of the Arab nationalists, however, continue to have hopes for the League and to favor cooperation with the other Arab countries through that medium.

RELATIONS WITH JORDAN. Before 1941 relations between the two Hashemite kingdoms were confined to the personal affairs of the two dynasties; but thereafter the two countries began to consult with each other about foreign affairs. The representatives of Iraq and Jordan often consulted one another at meetings of the Arab League and other international conferences. Jordan's Arab Legion also took part in putting down the Rashid Ali revolt in 1941.

King Abdullah of Jordan—then Transjordan—negotiated with

Iraq regarding the possibility of Iraqi-Jordanian union, but, owing to opposition in both Iraq and Transjordan as well as Lebanon and Syria, a treaty of alliance was signed in 1947 instead which helped to coordinate the foreign policy of the two states. This situation continued even after the assassination of King Abdullah although it underwent various vicissitudes owing to certain concerns within the two countries and the indirect influence of Saudi Arabia, Syria, and Egypt. The termination of the services of Sir John Bagot Glubb, British head of the Arab Legion, represented a gain for Saudi-Egyptian influence in Jordan and a weakening of the Iraqi-Jordanian alliance. The Soviet-supported threat by Egypt and Syria to Jordan's independence in early 1957, however, brought Jordan and Iraq closer together again and resulted in their federation in 1958.

RELATIONS WITH EGYPT AND SYRIA. Egypt and Iraq maintained friendly relations until the establishment of the Arab League in 1945. From that time onward there have been constant rivalry and jealousy over their relative position in the Arab League and Arab world as well as basic differences in their evaluations of world affairs in general. The Egyptian leadership has seen itself at the forefront of an Arab resurgence and has been extremely sensitive to any moves by Iraq to take an independent position. Thus Egypt opposed the Baghdad Pact not only because it did not want to enter into an alliance with the western powers, but also because Iraq took the initiative without the active participation of Egypt. Arab solidarity had not been lacking at the initial stages of the Palestine conflict. Iraq took an active part in the plans of the Arab League to oppose partition and entered the war of 1948 to prevent the establishment of Israel. But on the grounds that it had no borders touching Israel, Iraq refused to sign an armistice agreement with the latter. Ever since, the rivalry between Iraq and Egypt has been intense, with Nasser coming to represent an "anti-imperialist" cause and Nuri as-Said in a position of accommodation with the West.

Iraq's relations with Syria have generally been friendly since the establishment of the Iraqi Government in 1921. After Iraq won its independence in 1932, nationalists in both Iraq and Syria (especially during the 1940's) sought to unify the two countries, but France, then the mandatory government for Syria, stood in the way. General Nuri during World War II pursued plans to create a Greater Syria, which would have included Syria, Iraq, and Transjordan under a single Hashemite monarchy. This plan was also strongly supported by King Abdullah of Transjordan, who aspired to the enlarged kingship. Many Syrian leaders, identifying their own power with an independent Syria, have been opposed to such projects. Others, especially young radical elements and some moderate politicians, have supported the idea of a Greater Syria although often rejecting Hashemite dynastic ambitions. Egypt and Saudi Arabia have consistently and for obvious reasons been opposed, especially to an enlarged Hashemite monarchy. For various Syrian politicians, the price of Egyptian support has been to give up projects of unity in the Fertile Crescent—a further illustration of Egypt and Iraq's polar positions, which set the two riverine powers off against each other in the Arab world. Britain for a long period during World War II and after supported the Greater Syria idea. Iraq showed signs of supporting Syria when the latter, with Egyptian and Soviet backing, charged that it was threatened by a western-abetted attack by Turkey; in this, aside from the pull of Arab ties, there can also be seen Iraq's concern for its vital oil pipelines across Syria.

RELATIONS WITH SAUDI ARABIA. Relations between Iraq and Saudi Arabia have generally not been friendly from the time of the establishment of the Iraqi Government. This has been due mainly to periodic transfrontier raids and the rivalry between the Hashemite and Saudi dynasties. The nomadic raids have been gradually brought under control by the cooperation of the two governments, and attempts have been made to reconcile the differences between the two dynasties. The meeting of King Faisal I and King Ibn Saud in 1930 was followed by the signing of several agreements, the most important of which was that of 1936 regulating relations between the two countries. But dynastic jealousies persisted and became heightened after the death of Ibn Saud in 1953. The worsening situation after July 1956 involving the Suez crisis and the troubles in Jordan in early 1957 drew the two governments closer together again. King Saud made a state visit to Baghdad. It began to appear that common monarchical and other interests might transcend dynastic rivalries. With the penetration of Soviet influence into Syria occasioning strong Turkish and western reactions, Iraqi Prime Minister Ali Jawdat visited Damascus when King Saud was also there, a circumstance evidently intended to symbolize Arab solidarity. Various issues, not least the quarrel between their royal families, have stood between Iraq and Saudi Arabia; but the two countries also have shared interests, the most important of which is the uninterrupted operation of the pipelines which carry their oil across Syria to the Mediterranean.

RELATIONS WITH LEBANON. Relations with Lebanon have generally been friendly. Lebanon, influenced by its proportionally large Christian population, has consistently opposed such schemes as that for a Greater Syria, insisting upon the full sovereignty of Arab League members and the maintenance of friendly ties with the West to counter complete absorption in the Moslem world. The bipolarization of the Arab world around Cairo and Baghdad in early 1958 made this position increasingly untenable.

Iraq in World Affairs

The Iraqi Government has always shown keen interest in international organizations. From 1932, when it became a member of the League of Nations, to the present Iraq seems to have accepted the principle of international cooperation, has shown regard for international law, and has preferred to use peaceful methods of resolving differences with other states, as demonstrated in its willingness to make concessions in the frontier dispute with Iran.

Iraq declared war on Germany in 1943, participated in the San Francisco Conference in 1945, and was one of the original members of the United Nations, taking an active part in its activities. Although Iraqi delegates dissented from the West's stand on the Palestine question in the United Nations, Iraq has almost always stood with the western powers on other issues. When Arab affairs are in question Iraq tries to maintain solidarity with the other Arab countries.

The Iraqi Government has taken a stiffer attitude toward the Soviet Union—with which it has had no diplomatic relations—than have other Arab countries as it demonstrated at the Bandung Conference of Afro-Asian nations in 1955. This attitude is by no means shared in all political quarters within Iraq.

Iraq has cooperated with the United States, entering into a number of agreements relating to commercial, cultural, and technical matters. Iraq received United States lend-lease assistance during World War II and technical assistance in the postwar period. In 1954 an agreement was signed between the two countries providing for American aid under the Military Defense Assistance Program. Finally, Iraq took its place in the "Northern Tier" system, which was initiated by the United States, by signing the Baghdad Pact.

Much opinion on the upper levels of Iraqi political and economic life, although still critical of American policy toward Israel, is confident that the interests of the country lie with the West; but probably even larger numbers of educated persons in the lower ranks of the ruling elite and the emerging middle class can see no reconciliation with the West save by a change of American policy toward Israel, and they are disposed to use the Soviet threat as a means of exacting advantages from the West. Only the Communists and their sympathizers seem to be permanently hostile to the United States and willing to accept no argument other than that the West is planning to wage war against the Soviet bloc.

11

BASIC FEATURES OF THE ECONOMY

UNTIL ALMOST A DECADE AGO IRAQ'S ECONOMIC SITUATION WAS similar to that of other underdeveloped Middle Eastern countries. Since then, however, oil wealth has provided the basis for a plan of economic evolution that has promised to make Iraq's position unique in the Middle East. The new revenue has been used by the government to carry out an ambitious policy of developing the nation's idle resources. Few countries in the modern world provide a more dramatic combination of financial resources and development plans and opportunities than modern Iraq.

Iraq's economy is based on oil and agriculture. Oil is the major export, accounting for some two thirds of foreign exchange receipts; it pays for most of the country's imports and is the largest single source (60 percent) of national income. Agriculture directly supports about 75 percent of the total population, but produces only a subsistence income, largely in kind, for the peasant majority. Despite its long-range importance, it is today a less dynamic force in the Iraqi economy than is oil, providing about 25 percent of the total national income. In the long run, however, the agricultural sector, the productivity of which can be greatly increased, will no doubt prove the more important. Relative to its size, Iraq may well become one of the great food-producing areas of the world. It has not had the population problems that plague many another Middle Eastern country, and for the indefinite future there is likely to be demand for Iraq's surplus agricultural production. By contrast, oil reserves are exhaustible and it seems unlikely that industry will ever dominate the economic picture.

Certain obstacles to economic progress are obscured by the general picture of natural and financial wealth in Iraq. Many resources remain unexploited; private capital is limited; production methods in most fields are inefficient; the great mass of the people is poverty stricken, uneducated, unskilled. While the country has great oil deposits, it is unfavorably situated in relation to the main world trade routes; only inadequate port facilities exist on the Persian Gulf, although improvements are planned, and access to Mediterranean ports is complicated by problems of transshipment across Syria and Lebanon. Iraq's control and utilization of the Tigris and Euphrates rivers could be disturbed by actions of the upstream countries, Turkey and Syria.

Even the boon of petroleum is somewhat qualified by dependence on the oil companies, themselves vulnerable to any external crisis which might halt the flow of oil through the pipelines to the Mediterranean or by way of the Persian Gulf. Oil revenues have made it possible to keep down the burden of taxes and to reduce the necessity of government borrowing. Iraq's trade balance would show a dangerous deficit without oil exports since its consumer requirements, except for most food items, fuel, tobacco, and some building materials, must be imported. The loss of almost three fourths of government oil revenues for several months following the Suez crisis suggests the serious political and economic consequences which would follow any lengthy disruption.

Contrasts between actuality and aspiration, between old and new, are evident in almost every sector of the economy. The traditional, almost static, economic life of the countryside, still largely a mosaic of many small, self-sufficient local units, stands in striking contrast with the more modern mercantile and financial arrangements found in the city. Baghdad now is not only the largest single market but also the financial and industrial heart of the country. Banking and trading operations are concentrated there, and from it radiate all those influences which are causing the barter system of the past to be replaced by a money economy. Village economic patterns are gradually changing and the countryside is moving, however slowly, into greater dependence on the economic leadership and facilities of the towns and into closer relation with the general needs of national development.

Agriculture

Land and water are the country's most important resources, with the conservation and management of water the most critical factor. Only the northern and northeastern mountain zones of the country receive enough rainfall to support cultivation; the major crops produced elsewhere depend on irrigation based primarily on the waters of the Tigris and the Euphrates. These great rivers are being harnessed by massive projects for flood control, storage, and irrigation which recall and sometimes even restore some of the great irrigation works constructed thousands of years ago.

The steps being taken to revive Iraq's agriculture come after centuries of abuse and neglect during which much land was allowed to deteriorate to the point of no longer being cultivable. In spite of the relative abundance of land and water, most crops in Iraq—such as barley, wheat, rice, and cotton—show lower yields per capita of rural population than do those in neighboring countries. Responsible are the use of rudimentary implements, ignorance of efficient farming methods, and a system of land tenure which leaves the majority of cultivators in a state of poverty with little incentive to increase productivity. With absentee landlordism and sharecropping dominating the agricultural scene, major reforms are indicated, but they will by no means be easy to accomplish. The landed interests remain politically strong and the peasants have only begun to acquire knowledge and the consciousness of need which could move them to take an active role in their own betterment.

Industry and Commerce

The importance of industry is limited by lack of capital, managerial skills, adequate market, and high-quality raw materials. Some of these deficiencies can no doubt be removed in the course of time, but at least one, the lack of raw materials, constitutes a difficult kind of problem. Iraq at present exports practically no manufactured or industrial goods and, except for processed agricultural goods and the products of a developing petrochemical industry, is unlikely to expand its industrial exports in the future. Up to now the government has not used development funds to create non-self-sustaining industries which would bring prestige but little economic advantage; in those industries that are developed, however, there is a tendency to overmechanize methods of production.

There is a shortage of private capital for Iraqi industrial enterprise. Contributing factors are the tendencies of people with money to invest in land and to seek out quick-return, high-profit ventures, or enterprises receiving government assistance or subsidies. The small investor is particularly handicapped by the difficulty of obtaining credit from the banks, which operate on a traditional, personalized, and deeply conservative basis. Incentives in the form of tax relief, and the enlargement of the market through improved communications and transportation are helping overcome these problems.

Old methods persist in the small family enterprises which constitute the great majority of Iraqi manufacturing establishments, but artisan and small craft production is losing ground in competition with products of modern concerns, domestic and foreign, and artisans are being absorbed by the industries in and around the cities.

In trade and commerce contrasts between old and new also reveal the transitional nature of the present period. The major characteristics remain those of the old order: bargaining, especially in retail trade, concentration on small turnover, on selling few goods at high profit rather than on volume sales, the absence of uniform grading and packaging standards, and the persistence of a distribution system that places a number of intermediaries between the producer and consumer. New mercantile methods, derived mainly from the West, are emerging, but change is centered in the city. The countryside, with its peasant majority living on a subsistence level and largely excluded from the cash sector of the economy, is being only slowly affected.

The Development Board

The main agency working for the balanced exploitation of Iraq's immense potential wealth is the Iraq Development Board which has been directed to develop the country's productive resources to raise the standard of living. On the premise that mined petroleum is a limited and diminishing asset, 70 percent of the government's income from this source has been entrusted to the Board. Great increases in Iraq's petroleum revenue since 1950 have given the Board huge sums with which to work; the Suez crisis, however, forced some curtailment of the Board's activities in 1957.

The Board has been able to secure the advisory services of outstanding experts from other countries, and the International Bank for Reconstruction and Development in 1952 assisted it in drawing up an initial five-year plan. In 1955 the British economist Lord Salter was engaged to prepare a master plan appraising present activities and future possibilities, with special attention to the coordination of the various sectors. Foreign firms and experts administer the new projects and carry out large-scale construction work like the building of dams. Recognizing the paucity of technical skills in Iraq the government does not hesitate to use foreigners in responsible positions. Their advice is generally accepted and implemented; two members of the Development Board are foreigners.

Almost since its establishment in 1950 the Development Board has been subjected to criticism of its organizational structure, its role in internal politics, and the priority and timing of its programs. Not the least of its problems derives from the fact that it must, for efficiency, coordinate its activities with those of the regular departments and agencies of the central administration, thereby curtailing its own freedom of action.

Originally, the Board was to have a majority of members whose tenure would be independent of changing governments; this goal has not been realized. Popular dissatisfaction and impatience—combined with the protests of politicians and members of parliament who from the beginning resented the autonomous powers of the Board or who simply wished to discredit the government in power—led to a reorganization in 1953. The head of the newly created Ministry of Development became the third cabinet representative, with the Prime Minister and the Minister of Finance, on the Board and, significantly, the Board's technical and administrative staff was placed under his Ministry. The immediate result was a general lowering of salaries for the Board's Iraqi employees, who now became part of the civil service, the resignation of several leading staff members and increased opportunity for political interference in planning. The ministerial members of the Board may be outvoted but the Minister of Development nevertheless has to defend the Board's policies before parliament; as an important political figure he is both vulnerable to and the agent of political pressure. Placing the Board's staff under his supervision increased the power of the ministerial members and contributed to a dualism between political and professional considerations in planning. The Board is a policymaking agency but is no longer in control—except through its ministerial members—either of the staff that provides it with data upon which policy is based or of the operating sections that implement its decisions. There is no section or individual within the Board with exclusive advisory and evaluative functions.

Despite these difficulties, the operation of the Board has been relatively smooth. Indecision, changing personnel, and the neglect of technical reports have caused problems but have not prevented development of continuity in both policy and operations. Much has depended on the efforts and political acumen of Nuri as-Said. Criticism from those demanding political, economic, and social reforms, as well as from those who find the Board's planning too revolutionary or rapid will, however, undoubtedly continue.

The Development Program

The original (1950) law directed the Board

> [to construct a plan that would] define a general program of the projects to be undertaken . . . [and to] include in its scope but not be limited to projects in water conserving, flood control, irrigation,

> drainage, industry and mining as well as projects for the improvement of communications by river, land, and air.

The new law of 1953 paved the way for increased attention to small-scale projects (the first of which was initiated in 1955) designed to bring immediate benefits to the population:

> The Board's projects shall be divided into two categories. The first shall consist of capital development projects for which necessary provision shall be allotted under a specific chapter of the general program. The second shall cover small development projects and necessary funds provided for it under another chapter of the program. The Board shall entrust the second category projects to relative government departments for execution.

Selection of projects generally has involved compromise between technical and political considerations. On the whole, insufficient attention has been given to the relationship between programs and the society they are to serve and to the intricate adjustments which must be made before a program can be successfully completed and fully efficient, productive, and "economic" in operation.

The Board has been unable or unwilling to attack some of the most fundamental economic and social problems of the country. For the first five years it stressed engineering and technical matters, giving comparatively little attention to the country's human resources. Its plans until recently have been focused almost exclusively on large projects; there has been a decided preference for industrial rather than agricultural development, a tendency to employ centralized rather than decentralized forms of control, and a disposition to rely on unrealistic cost estimates (sometimes exaggerated, sometimes too low). The loan policies of the government banks have not reflected the needs of the small businessman, and it has been said of the Development Board program itself that it has been easier to obtain approval for the allocation of millions of dinars than of thousands. The centralization of both planning and operational supervision in Baghdad, lack of coordination in the timing of projects, and lack of cooperation among agencies have caused administrative bottlenecks, stifling of initiative at the local level, and ignorance of the real local needs. Thus dams which serve to halt the floods at Baghdad may at the same time diminish the flow of water on which the southern farmlands depend. Settlers—often poorly chosen—have been given land, then almost forgotten. Huge building projects in Baghdad have kept in the city construction contractors and workers needed in the rural areas.

Many of these shortcomings, however, are being remedied. Only lands with drainage facilities will be settled; social services, particularly housing, have received a much higher allocation. There has been added to the staff of the Board a technical section for rural development which will allow considerable autonomy to province and village. In the spring of 1957 a new Industrial Finance Corporation was planned to replace the old Industrial Bank and offer a revised credit policy more related to the needs of the national economy.

The most difficult problem confronting the Board, and one which it has not touched directly at all, is the social organization of agriculture which keeps the peasant impoverished and gives the landlord—usually an absentee owner—no motivation to improve methods or increase production. The government has made some effort to alleviate the situation by settling numbers of peasants on second-best state-owned land and providing them with irrigation facilities. Such steps are marginal; the problem of poverty and backward techniques will have to be coped with directly if the country's agricultural potential is to be realized.

At its inception the development program aimed at very long-range and little-advertised goals; today, as the government gives more attention both to immediate needs and to publicity, it is coming to the notice of larger numbers. The popular reaction has not been entirely favorable, for as people become more aware of the extraordinary magnitude of the funds available to the authorities many are correspondingly impatient with the rate of development. The Board's new information efforts have, however, resulted in more favorable popular attitudes. There is less grumbling and impatience in Baghdad as earlier expectations are tempered by a realization that change cannot be accomplished overnight.

"Development Week" has been one of the more successful means of publicizing the Board's accomplishments. The first such observance, held in April 1956, marked the opening of two large barrages, at Ar Ramadi and Samarra, and two important road bridges, at Hindiyah and Al Kufah. The second, held in March 1957, while less spectacular was still more successful and publicized a variety of projects costing some ID 40 million: in Baghdad, housing schemes, an Iraq Museum, and the Queen Aliyah Bridge; in the north, the start of the Dokan Dam and a modern textile factory at Mosul; and at Al Musayyib, just south of Baghdad, the distribution of land titles to several hundred fellahin. All these projects, as well as others, were covered by television, radio, and the press.

In carrying out the development program the government must contend not only with the indifference and increasing impatience of the majority, but with the suspicion and hostility of the well-to-do, particularly the absentee holders of agricultural land, who view the projects as a threat to their interests. The government has so far taken few effective measures to assuage such fears. Underlying the reluctance to take more positive steps toward social adjustments are not only conservative political groups but also the premise that the economic and social aspects of development can be allotted to different components. The application of this premise has been facilitated by the opportunity to use oil rather than tax revenues, and has been justified by the view that social and political dissatisfaction will be indefinitely allayed by increasing economic security.

Perhaps the most significant indication that a milestone in balanced development has been passed would be the adoption by parliament of legislation, pending in late 1957, permitting the government to tax the capital value of large estates to meet any future deficit in the national budget.

12

ORGANIZATION AND USE OF MANPOWER

IRAQ'S LABOR PROBLEM DIFFERS FROM THAT OF ITS NEIGHBORS in that the need for workers is greater than their availability. There is an abundance of unskilled labor in cities and towns, especially in Baghdad and Basra, but trained workers are in short supply. Often failing to consider the manpower factor in development plans, the government has been faced with a labor shortage, especially in specific locations and particular occupations. The labor force (persons from 12 years up) is estimated at 2.5 million. Existing occupations absorb about 1.8 million. About half the remainder are women who contribute labor seasonally and irregularly to agriculture and commerce. Since almost every source has been drawn upon, the demand for labor will have to be met eventually by more efficient use of the large numbers of underemployed workers. Perhaps half the labor force in Iraq—fellahin who work the fields for only part of the year, shop proprietors who sit for hours waiting for an occasional customer—either is seasonally employed or underemployed.

Labor statistics are poorly kept and inaccurate. Agriculture accounts for the greatest number of workers, followed by commerce, manufacturing, government and private services. Table 5 gives a very rough estimate of the distribution of the employed labor force between the various occupational groups.

The petroleum industry leads in industrial employment, followed by textiles and clothing, food products, metals, building materials, motor maintenance and construction (see chap. 15).

Although taking into account natural population increase and normal immigration, Iraq's economic potential is such that, if the present rate of development continues, employment possibilities will in time seriously exceed the available labor supply. The government has further intensified the problem by restricting certain occupations to Iraqis and encouraging industries to hire only Iraqi labor (see chap. 16).

Despite new occupational opportunities since World War II the occupational distribution of the labor force has not changed significantly because industries in which traditional forms of operation still persist have increased their demands and because Iraqi attitudes and social conditions work to prevent high labor mobility from one occupation and geographical area to another. Employer-employee relations and the organization of labor in Iraq are still for the most part based on concepts sanctioned by centuries of practice. Labor unions, relatively new to the Middle East, are discouraged by the Iraqi Government and play an insignificant part even in the new industries.

In general, the most important factor regulating an individual's place and type of work is his family or tribe: not only has the family and tribe provided significant economic security, but the individual's definition of his own interest has been developed in the context of traditional and highly developed family life. Sex and, to a certain extent, age are also important determinants. The employment of women is still frowned upon except in small family concerns and in agriculture. The employment of children is more common, particularly in some crafts industries where a special kind of manual dexterity is required. Children begin work at an early age, often as apprentices in small or family enterprises, and they are considered economic assets in agriculture and certain industries in which increases in production result largely from increases in the number of employees.

Certain jobs have acquired value mainly in terms of their location. A job permitting one to live and work in the city conveys additional prestige for the middle-income and small-landowning groups; the latter disparage the fellahin and refuse jobs, particularly in industry, in which they would have to work with their hands. In communities where tribal values are still strong, commerce may be looked upon with contempt.

Kinship ties and personal obligations between employer and worker are still of major significance in the small family and craft industries (which make up more than 95 percent of Iraq's manufacturing establishments). In larger industrial enterprises personal and kinship connections, though diminishing in importance, continue to inhibit labor-union organization by the way in which they influence recruitment and personnel management practices. Moreover, the upper levels of the Iraqi business community, closely allied with the governmental bureaucracy, enjoy special advantages in dealing with labor, whose right to strike and organize unions is legally restricted. Government and management have tended to equate labor unrest with political opposition, and there has been little tradition which would dispose the elite to tolerate opposition from those at the bottom of the social and political scale. Sensitivity to labor agitation is particularly strong in the oil industry, which is the main source of government revenue and the base of Iraq's current economic and social development program.

While the majority of workers have tended to cling to traditional ways, those employed in the newly created medium- and large-scale enterprises have been undergoing a process of adjustment to the new social and industrial patterns. Industrial reforms have given workers certain monetary benefits, but the physical and emotional security which the townsman, villager, and pastoralist of an earlier day found in a tight-knit web of occupational, kinship, and local groups has not been compensated for.

There is no rigid division of labor along ethnic lines. The Jews once dominated commerce. The Sabaeans, as always, prefer occupations located near water, such as boatbuilding and river navigation; they also are known as excellent silversmiths (see chap. 4). Some division along occupational lines still exists between Sunnites and Shiites: the Sunnite is generally better educated and more acquainted with modern as well as traditional technology. This contrast is being reduced, however, with the emergence of new job opportunities and the migration of many Shiite fellahin from the more backward south to other parts of the country.

Changing Labor Relations

The traditional pattern of labor relations in Iraq was largely shaped by Arab Moslem kinship and authority systems, and the Iraqi worker today, whatever his position, still expects his employer to supervise his work and give him paternalistic protection as well as guidance in personal affairs.

The traditional relationship of the landlord to the tenant, as exemplified by the power of the tribal sheikh over his followers, was one of mutual obligations. The sheikh exercised strong authority in his tribe, but strong demands were made of him; he was expected to perform extensive political, economic, and social functions on behalf of his people. To consolidate his position and create strong bonds of loyalty to his leadership, he found it expedient, and ultimately essential, to be generous in personal relations with his followers. To be well liked, he had to be lavish with gifts; he might act as go-between in the arrangement of marriages; he commonly mediated in family disputes, and he took an active interest in the problems and grievances of the members of the tribal group.

During the last century many of the tribal sheikhs acquired large tracts of agricultural land and became wealthy absentee landlords whose holdings were managed by overseers. While many of the benefits of the earlier pattern of reciprocal relationships were lost to those who worked the land (whether established peasants or former nomads), the authoritative attitudes persisted. The overseer, who generally had little personal interest in the tenants, took the initiative in establishing conditions of labor. The fellahin might resent his landlord or the overseer, but for the most part he remained apathetic because of inability to better his lot. The gap between landlord and peasant was further widened when in the latter days of Turkish rule many wealthy merchants and government officials invested a good share of their surplus wealth in agricultural land. They too were content to have their lands administered by overseers, and had even less knowledge and concern about the needs of their tenants.

In the handicraft industries and shops of the cities and towns the interests of the craftsmen or clerks and their masters tended to be regulated by kin ties, religion, and pride of workmanship. In these enterprises the owners had the right to determine working conditions, wages (when remuneration was given in this form), and standards of workmanship. Many of these concerns were family owned and operated, with the members of the family sharing the income under the authority of the head of the family. Apprentices learned their trade over a long period, and whether or not they were kinsmen of the master were thrown into a personal relationship which made the master an important figure in their personal lives as well as in their occupational activities.

The growth of new industries is altering the traditional pattern of labor relations. The larger modern enterprises must employ managers, technicians, and clerical workers. There is a shortage of trained Iraqi personnel for those positions, and the use of foreign managers and technicians has often complicated the problem of communication between management and employees. Whereas once the employer could set his own methods and pace of work, modern industry demands standardization of methods and minimum levels of performance. In such enterprise the old close relations between craftsman and employer are to one degree or another being altered toward more impersonal relationships. As more and more workers join the industrial labor force, they are faced with conditions of work which are new to them and to which they cannot readily adapt.

Although the exploitive position of the landlord has been little changed, the demand for workers in industry and on government projects is attracting a growing stream of unskilled workers from the farms. The central government, awakened to the urgent need for agricultural and land reform, has endeavored to enact legislation which would improve conditions of tenancy and reduce exploitation. Many of these reforms have been blocked or slowed by landowners, who fear that change will damage their interests.

Mobility

Mobility in Iraq is limited by the expense of traveling, the strong dependence of Iraqis upon family ties, their conservative response to social change, the landowners' opposition to removing fellahin from the land, and the debt laws (see chap. 14). Some workers migrate within a limited area to work in seasonal industries. There has been a large migration from the southern Euphrates provinces to the cities of Baghdad and Basra, where part-time work is available, but on the whole labor mobility is low. Not many jobs have enough prestige to overcome social obstacles and attract workers from a great distance. The few that do are in the city and their location is their most effective appeal. City dwellers in middle- or higher-income occupations are rarely willing to work in the country.

The head of the village, the landlord, or the sheikh also has stood between the worker and new job opportunities. The experience of labor contractors on road-building projects is typical: as a road progresses through the territories of various tribes, each sheikh may demand that the members of his tribe be employed on the stretch of road in his territory. Each time the contractors are forced to hire and train a new force. Oil companies operating in Iraq have found not only that they must draw on immediately surrounding villages and tribes for labor, but that they eventually have had to hire workers from particular communities for particular jobs; nearly all truck drivers come from one village, diggers from another, greasers from still another.

Recruitment of unskilled labor within a locality is not difficult. Word quickly spreads that an industry needs workers or that a project is about to hire labor. Applicants rapidly appear. Hiring is largely done by means of personal or family contacts or through labor contractors, often the heads of a village or tribe. Family or personal contact governs the selection of managerial and administrative personnel as well. Nepotism is a part of the culture and is accepted in both the economy and in politics (see chap. 18). Placement offices, established by law, are located in Baghdad, Basra, Mosul, and Kirkuk; but they have been little used for they have not yet gained the confidence of either workers or employers.

Skills and Training

Most of the small skilled labor force, moreover, is concentrated in the large cities, with almost 70 percent of the industrial force employed in Baghdad. With no skilled surplus on which to draw, industries and development projects hire unskilled workers and train them; occasionally, skilled workers are brought in from other countries. The textile industry, for example, has brought in Syrians, and the railroads have partly filled the shortage resulting from the Jewish exodus by hiring Pakistanis. Some 5,000 Palestinian Arab refugees have emigrated to Iraq but apparently their skills are not much more developed than those of the average Iraqi.

Iraqi workers respond well to training under good supervision, but the Iraqi economy has never emphasized efficiency or high productivity. The educational institutions have not offered training related to the modern economic requirements of the country (see chap. 19). Lacking technical training and not yet familiar with elementary factory procedures, the Iraqi worker can improvise repairs when a machine breaks down but tends to ignore the kind of maintenance that forestalls breakdowns.

There are at present only three technical schools in Iraq—in Baghdad, Basra, and Kirkuk. Even with the completion of a fourth in Mosul the supply of trained workers will be insufficient. It is also most likely that graduates of these schools as well as of the agricultural training schools will choose white-collar or industrial appointments. On-the-job training appears to be more successful. The oil companies, bound by concession terms to hire as many Iraqis as possible, have their own training programs as does the Port of Basra Authority.

The shortage of managerial personnel trained in modern production techniques and administration is perhaps even more acute than that of skilled workers. This is true not only in the higher ranks of business administration but at the foreman level, where literacy is usually necessary. Two methods of making up for the shortage have been devised. First, individual foreigners are hired to fill positions in the higher administrative levels; second, a "managing-agency" system has been instituted under which a complete force of foreign administrative, management, and accounting personnel is commissioned to run an establishment.

Information about the professional and white-collar occupational groups is incomplete. As in other Middle Eastern countries, the educational system provides many clerical and professional people for whom opportunities are becoming more and more limited and who generally refuse to work in rural areas (see chap. 19). The professional and white-collar elements constitute to a large degree Iraq's intelligentsia; the effect of frustrating them can be political unrest. The 1956 increases in civil service wages by one third for lower categories to two thirds for higher grades, at a time when the "saturation point" in government employment was apparently being reached, can be attributed in part to the government's realization of this potential source of trouble.

In certain fields, notably medicine and engineering, opportunities are increasing. Although doctors are in great demand, they tend to congregate in the cities at a time when the demand for medical care is highest in the rural districts (see chap. 17). The number of opportunities for engineers also exceeds the supply of engineering graduates.

Wage Rates and Working Conditions

Since 1921 several laws dealing with industrial workers and white-collar groups have been adopted although the agricultural labor force has been neglected.

The most important labor legislation is the labor code of 1936 and the labor laws of 1937 applying to workshops and factories. Establishments which do not use mechanical power, home industries, and enterprises employing fewer than four people or members of a single family are exempted.

The laws provide for a minimum wage of 250 *fils* (70 cents) per day for skilled and unskilled labor; weekly and annual holidays; maximum working hours (8 hours a day, 48 hours a week in some industries; 9 hours a day in others); severance pay; and compensation for injury, disease, and loss of life. A social security law was passed in 1956 (see chap. 17). The laws permit the employment—up to 20 percent of the workers in any particular establishment—of children over the age of 10 for apprenticeship or vocational training. Industrial establishments are required to keep a register of employed children between 10 and 12 years of age, and another for those between 12 and 15. The daily wage of children under 12 must not be less than 40 percent of the average pay for adults in the same establishment. The Ministry of Social Affairs is responsible for the enforcement of these laws and for the inspection of places of work.

So far it has been possible to inspect adequately only the larger urban factories; the more numerous workshops, where conditions are at their worst, have escaped government inspection. In these places child labor and night work are common and long hours the rule. Poor health standards are the norm except in the modern factories. In smaller industries—where manual labor is used more extensively than machinery and where increased production required hiring more workers—strict adherence to the legal requirements becomes prohibitively expensive.

Increased demand for labor has affected the level of wages outside agriculture. The legal minimum is exceeded almost everywhere. The over-all rate of wage increases during the last two years is estimated at between 10 and 20 percent; the cost of living has remained almost stationary over this period, and price rises are generally confined to the cities; the urban worker is probably slightly better off than he was a decade ago. Furthermore, 1956 income-tax reductions have benefited skilled and white-collar workers.

With the minimum wage as a base, the determination of wages as well as other conditions is made through contracts. Since the labor force is not organized, wage increases usually result from an unusual demand for labor of a certain type or in a limited local area, or from an increase in production. Thus while there has been a general increase in wages, marked wage differences exist between occupations and within similar occupations depending on the region. There has been a more extensive use of piecework wage incentives in the past few years, resulting in a noticeable increase in production. Straight wages are paid for overtime and double wages for work during holidays.

Modern industry pays much higher wages than the older and smaller-scale undertakings. In some handicraft industries workers may earn less than an ordinary unskilled laborer. Wages are somewhat depressed in industries which employ large numbers of women and children—cigarette manufacturing, tobacco processing, spinning and weaving; women and children usually receive lower wages than male workers in the same occupation.

Despite pay increases in 1956 wages of civil servants are generally lower than those prevailing in industry or in the professions. The government is able to get technicians and professional personnel by paying for their training and stipulating that they must work several years for the government; other factors: until recently the government provided the only social security system; civil servants received preference in public housing; the 35-hour government work week permits outside employment; government employment affords opportunities for graft and nepotism.

Within the agricultural sector, "wages" are paid mainly in kind as a percentage of the crop grown. The percentage varies from region to region. The fellah is constantly depressed and in debt. The few laws dealing with the agricultural worker are rarely enforced; any improvement in standard of living is effected through an enlightened landlord or sheikh, through moving to the city, or by applying for land in a government settlement.

Industrial Labor Organization

The government of Iraq has been willing to permit the growth of labor unions only under legal restrictions and close official supervision. Uneasy at the possibility of Communist penetration and control of the unions, the authorities are also apprehensive that organized labor might be used as an instrument of protest and a source of power for other political opponents. In 1945 the government dissolved the country's two largest labor unions, the Port Workers Union of Basra and the Railway Workers Union of Baghdad, charging them with harboring Communists. On similar grounds it refused to permit the oil-field workers of Kirkuk to form a union. In 1954 the union of cigarette workers was abolished, its leaders were tried and convicted of engaging in Communist activities.

The unions that have survived government intervention and surveillance have been severely restricted in their activities. The government has supervised union elections, organization, and membership, and in 1955 it strengthened its control by the appointment of a brigadier of police as the Director-General of Labor and Social Security.

Registered labor unions recognized by the Directorate of Labor in 1954 represented the following occupational categories: shoemakers, tailors, mechanics, drivers, construction workers, and carpenters. The total number of workers then registered in these unions was approximately 450. These organizations are numerically weak and suffer from inexperience and lack of knowledge of union work and from close official surveillance.

While the industrial worker has become more aware of his capacity to assert his rights in relations with his employer, many of the old attitudes persist. Often a worker views his grievances at work as personal matters rather than as issues to be settled by collective action and he may be suspicious of the latter because it runs counter to tradition. Accustomed to a strong kinship loyalty, workers find it difficult to achieve a sense of solidarity in a new type of institution based on quite different principles of association. And some also see labor unionism and collective bargaining as a western and therefore suspect innovation.

Iraq's feeble labor-union movement has suffered not only from official disapproval and most workers' unfamiliarity with this form of organization but also from the actions of union leaders. Often inexperienced and without any real accountability to a largely passive rank and file, they often have been incompetent or have viewed their office as a means of advancing personal ambitions and political interests.

The pattern of relations between management and labor varies considerably between the small family-owned enterprise and the large industrial establishment, though management consistently maintains a dominant position. In a small handicraft shop, for example, the relationship between the relatives and neighbors who make up the staff is highly personal, and all share a conscious and more or less direct interest in the success of the undertaking. Ultimate authority, of course, resides with the owner. In medium- and large-scale enterprises management sets wages and conditions of employment and is little restricted in this by existing labor legislation or government intervention. Formally the labor laws provide only a vague framework for employer-employee relations in medium-size industries; they establish minimum conditions in the larger industries.

Legal disputes between management and labor may be settled either by mutual consultation or by referral for conciliation to the Ministry of Social Affairs. It is within the authority of the Ministry to inquire into the causes of any dispute. When conciliation is resorted to, labor regulations require that a written agreement be drawn up and signed by both parties and that it be published by the Ministry with the approval of both parties to the agreement.

The use of the strike by unions is hedged by restrictive government regulations. Fourteen days before a strike is scheduled to begin, the union involved must give notice to the Ministry of Social Affairs. Another regulation, adopted in September 1954, authorizes the Council of Ministers, upon recommendation of the Minister of the Interior, to suspend or abolish associations, including labor unions, for any action defined as endangering public security or order. Between 1946 and 1953 the government suppressed four strikes in private industry: the 1953 strike against the tobacco monopoly, held to be Communist inspired, and three others which occurred in the oil industry at Kirkuk and Basra. Official intervention in these cases was so precipitate that management and labor, even had they been so disposed, had no time to come to agreement by collective bargaining.

Workers on government-sponsored projects are not permitted to organize unions. Wage controversies in the state-controlled railways and the Basra port, however, may be taken before a wage board for arbitration.

The petroleum enterprises, which are mainly controlled and operated by foreign interests, are by far the most advanced in providing amenities and training programs for their personnel. They began during the late 1940's to furnish medical services and housing, educational, recreational, and other facilities for their Iraqi employees.

In spite of the inducements offered by the oil companies, a high rate of labor turnover suggests that their policies have not been entirely successful. The percentage of Iraqi oil employees in all categories (clerical, supervisory, skilled, and unskilled) with over four years' continuous service has been very small. Moreover, the oil firms have found it necessary to secure order at their plants with sizable company police forces assisted by the government authorities. The oil companies have nevertheless set a pace for industry in providing training, increased wages, improved working conditions, and numerous fringe benefits.

Forced Labor

Forced labor in the sense of uncompensated work imposed on unwilling persons is specifically prohibited in Article 10 of the Constitution of Iraq. Paid compulsory labor may be resorted to in local and national emergencies, but in practice workmen have been recruited for such work without pay. Still other contradictions exist between law and usage, as in the compulsory nature of agricultural labor imposed under debt laws. Poverty, shortage of labor, and long tradition give only limited relevance to questions of "voluntariness," "involuntariness," "forced," or "free" in the daily work of Iraq's peasant majority. After little more than a generation of constitutional government which has only begun to affect the customary patterns of local authority in the countryside, it would occur to few peasants or tribesmen to ask whether their labor were voluntary or compulsory. This attitude is changing, however.

Detention camps for disciplinary purposes have been used but there are no forced-labor camps for political prisoners. Nationals arrested for subversive activity are normally isolated from other criminal prisoners in jails or are put under house arrest. Students and teachers detained for participation in the 1956 riots were inducted en masse into the military establishment and transported north to a camp on the Iranian border where they were subjected to rigorous military drill rather than to compulsory work.

Paid forced labor is legally permitted in such emergencies as flood, fire, or locust invasions. At such times the Ministry of the Interior may authorize senior administrative officials to call out labor at a rate of pay determined by the government. If the urgency is great the administrators may act without the prior approval of the Ministry. Workers who refuse to comply may be forcibly taken to the place of work and thereafter punished by imprisonment or a fine. The burden of such levies falls heaviest on the peasant.

Despite the constitutional prohibition, the government has in the past requisitioned labor for the ordinary maintenance and extension of irrigation systems, paying a wage to the workmen only in those localities where custom had established the liability of the government to do so. Even before World War II, however, it was recognized that such labor was inefficient and uneconomical as compared with trained and paid personnel. Since the war the government has carried at its own expense most of the work involved in the maintenance and construction of canals, relieving the cultivator of all but normal responsibility for minor repairs.

Convicts, normally employed within the prison, may also be employed by private organizations or persons, though not by government or quasi-governmental agencies. Such employment is permitted only with the approval of the Ministry of Social Affairs, and wages are established by law. Convict labor outside the prisons is also governed by certain regulations such as the prohibition against the use of prisoners to transport filthy refuse.

In late 1955 a trader was arrested for recruiting Iraqi girls to be sent to Saudi Arabia as slaves but there is no evidence that slavery is widely practiced within the boundaries of Iraq.

13

FINANCIAL SYSTEM

THE TRADITIONAL MOSLEM SYSTEM OF ADMINISTERING AND organizing public finance persisted in Iraq until roughly a hundred years ago. Before 1860 public bookkeeping had not been introduced, public funds could be disposed of without effective controls which would prevent abuse, and there were no comprehensively organized public welfare expenditures. Even when budgetary reforms were introduced in the late nineteenth and early twentieth centuries, many of their intended effects were nullified by widespread corruption.

Modern principles have now replaced the old, but the ingrained attitudes and conduct of most government officials and the people regarding public finance have not fundamentally changed. While the general attitude of the population may change with time and as visible improvements are produced by state expenditures to raise the standard of living and modernize the economy, much of the old mistrust of the government and easy acceptance of corruption continue. Tax evasion is as universally practiced and regarded legitimate by the elite, city dwellers, and rural population as it was in earlier times. The urban population, including absentee landlords, makes a common practice of falsifying account books, and the fellahin, having had centuries of unhappy experience with tax collectors, regard taxation as an evil to be avoided in every possible way.

The majority of the people have little or no understanding of the principles of banking and make no use of banking facilities. European banking practices were introduced only in the twentieth century, and the acceptance of transactions involving the taking and paying of interest comes hard to Iraqi traditionalists only partially satisfied by reassuring interpretations of Koranic prescriptions against usury.

A large part of the population is still wholly or mainly outside the "monetarized" sectors of the economy. Many persons live in a household or barter economy; the peasant produces most of what he con sumes, workmen may receive all or most of their wages in kind, and self-employed persons may exchange their products directly without resort to money. The subsistence standard of all these groups in any event leaves them with little or no surplus to deposit in a bank.

In the mainly urban sectors of the economy where money changes hands, both bank notes and coins are used; transfers by checks are rare outside the circle of the modern business community and even there are by no means the general rule. Practice in this sphere may be expected to accord more closely with modern business usage elsewhere as the country's economic life develops and expands.

Confidence in the domestic currency seems fairly well established but many observers believe that this would not be the case if the authorities were to discontinue their present policy of maintaining a full, or even excessive, note cover.

Among those who manage to accumulate cash surpluses, savings often take the form of hoarding valuables and bank notes. It was generally assumed in 1951 that virtually all of the 100 dinar notes and a considerable part of the 10 dinar notes in circulation were hoarded. The main reason, again, is probably the inconvenience of, unfamiliarity with, or distrust of other more profitable ways of using money. There are only a few bank offices scattered over the country, many persons are unaware of their existence or live too far from the nearest one to use it. Still others fear to part with their money in return for a receipt which they cannot read. Even the somewhat more familiar postal savings accounts have not escaped this kind of suspicion. Finally, opportunities for the investment of small amounts in bonds or shares are extremely limited and few persons have confidence in such transactions.

Even among the educated and in the business community there is a general preference for investment of capital in urban and rural real estate, which carries prestige and has considerable security, and in commerce, which yields a high return. Industry and agriculture have generally been starved for capital, although investments in these fields are mounting. In an effort to ameliorate the shortage of capital the government has established special public credit institutions in the fields of agriculture, industry, and building.

Islamic Concepts

The Islamic state derived its income from a number of sources, Moslem and non-Moslem. The taxes levied upon non-Moslems, which in earlier days provided a major contribution to the treasury, were the *jizyah* (poll tax) and the *kharaj* (land tax). The *jizyah* was an annual tax levied on men capable of bearing arms. Any man subject to this tax who volunteered for military service was exempted. Unbelievers who had had their lands confiscated by conquest were permitted to remain on their land if they paid the *kharaj,* which was based on the estimated income capacity of the land, the value of the crop, and the method of irrigation used. In addition, spoils captured from infidels during holy wars were in accordance with Koranic precept divided into five portions, one of which went to the state treasury to be used for helping the poor, the needy, and the wayfarer.

The largest contribution to the treasury was provided by the *zakat.* Levied upon the Moslem population, this tax was intended to benefit the poor by taxing the surpluses of the wealthy. The principle application was that income should be taxed in inverse proportion to the amount of capital and labor involved in generating it, that articles should be taxed in inverse proportion to their perishability and in direct proportion to their capacity for production, growth, and reproduction. Fruit or fresh garden produce would not be taxed; a mule would not be taxed as much as a mare. This concept of taxation was inextricably linked with religion; it was clothed with the sanctity of orthodoxy and was meant to apply in a relatively static social order. Change was decried, except for political and territorial expansion which would bring more persons into the Moslem fold. Within the faith all were supposed to enjoy the benefits of the leveling system of finance, which was directed at the goal of equality—the state in which all Moslems, theoretically, find themselves on the pilgrimage to Mecca.

This ideal was never realized. While the peasants appealed to Allah for protection from exploitation by the rulers, the privileged, often with the connivance of the government, became more wealthy and powerful. Though equality remained the ideal, a great gulf opened between the populace and the ruling class.

From earliest Islamic times the public finances of the Moslem state were reduced to chaos by unremitting warfare, which also reduced the taxable capacity of the people. Most revenue was appropriated for the maintenance of armies; most of the tax burden fell upon the peaceable settled populations and the conquered peoples. The bedouins evaded taxation by joining the conquering armies. In Iraq taxation fell most heavily upon the non-Moslems. The land tax levied upon them became the most important source of revenue.

In the tenth century the previous maladministration of the public finances led the Vizier Ali Ibn Isa to introduce reforms which would have improved the fiscal system. His reforms were nullified by the caliphs, who continued to divert a large proportion of the tax revenue into their private treasury.

Under Ottoman rule (1534–1917) the peasantry reached a state of destitution. Taxes on agricultural produce reached extraordinarily unrealistic heights. The methods of tax collection encouraged bribery and corruption, impoverished the fellahin while they enriched the wealthy landlords, and retarded agricultural development.

The Modern Fiscal State

During the British Mandate (1921–1932) a number of measures were introduced to establish uniform rates of taxation, to create a more equitable assessment of taxes, and to obtain better yields from government expenditure. These reforms were reduced in their effectiveness, however, by the desire of British Government officials in Iraq to retain the good will of the privileged classes. Tax evasion reached such proportions that assessments became meaningless; it became impossible for the government to balance its budget without floating loans.

The Iraqi Government has had control of the country's budget since establishment of the Mandate in 1921. Fiscal operations gradually expanded after the termination of the Mandate in 1932. During and after World War II expenditures continued to increase; by 1949–50 the ordinary budget had accumulated a total deficit of ID 8.8 million. This deficit would have been larger by ID 6.8 million had it not been for internal loans floated during that period. Since 1950 the situation has been changed by the sharp rise in oil revenues. Today, thanks to continued and increasing demand for its oil, Iraq is able not merely to balance the budget but to acquire an increasing surplus.

Fiscal operations are conducted through a number of separate budgets. The ordinary budget finances the regular activities of the central government. In 1953–54, the last year for which figures are available, 65 percent of the total public expenditures were allocated in the ordinary budget. Ordinarily, all oil royalties were assigned to the ordinary budget and between 1939 and 1950 they were spent on capital works. Since April 1, 1951, the beginning of the Iraqi fiscal year 1951–52, capital works have been eliminated from the ordinary budget and transferred to the budget of the Development Board, which receives 70 percent of the oil royalties, the remainder continuing to accrue to the ordinary budget. In 1953–54 the Development Board budget accounted for 16 percent of total expenditure.

Four other related budgets are separated from the ordinary budget; some of them, however, either receive a portion of their receipts from ordinary budget appropriations or contribute their surpluses to ordinary budget receipts. These are the budgets of the Iraqi State Railways, the Port Authority of Basra, the Al Faw Dredging Scheme, and the tobacco monopoly. They are presented to parliament at the same time as the ordinary budget and are enacted under the same law. In addition to these, there are individual municipal budgets, numbering 134 in 1955–56, which draw only a part of their receipts from the ordinary budget. The municipal budgets require governmental but not parliamentary approval. Fourteen other autonomous budgets of semi-independent government agencies only require approval from the Minister of Finance.

Table 6 shows consolidated budgets for the last seven fiscal years. Not included are the 14 autonomous budgets, many not published and some obtaining part or all of their receipts from ordinary budget appropriations. For these reasons and because of the modest amounts involved, omission of these autonomous budgets does not greatly affect the total receipts and expenditures shown in Table 6.

The public debt of Iraq is relatively small because expenditures have been kept as close as possible to revenues. After 1950 there was hardly any need for borrowing except when the government wished to absorb some of the money in circulation in order to check inflation.

Two domestic loans were floated in 1944, one for 20 years and the other for 3 years, totaling ID 2 million for development works including irrigation and railways. These were the first domestic loans floated by the Government of Iraq. In 1947 and again in 1948, ID 5 million of bond issues were floated, most of which were taken up by the Currency Board (assumed by the National Bank since 1949) and commercial banks. Aside from these debts the National Bank has made loans to some of the government administrations—the government-owned oil refineries and the state banks. A number of treasury bills amounting to about ID 1.1 million were taken up by commercial banks in 1950. Of these debts only about ID 300,000 were held by the public; the rest were mainly held by the National Bank and commercial banks.

In recent years Iraq has received several foreign loans. In 1939–40 the government obtained a loan of ID 1 million for the Iraqi State Railways. This loan was repaid during World War II. A loan of $12.5 million from the International Bank for Reconstruction and Development was received for the Wadi ath Tharthar project in 1951. Only $6.3 million of this loan was used and it was entirely repaid by the Development Board in 1955. A third loan was contracted by the Iraqi State Railways in 1950 for £3 million. This amount was never fully used and the National Bank has repaid most of the outstanding amount and has debited the Iraqi State Railways with it. During World War II the oil companies made several loans to the government; most of these have now been repaid. An internal loan of ID 4 million was floated by the government in 1955 for a 10-year period to build a lubricating-oil refinery.

Expenditure Patterns

The greatest increase in public expenditure in recent years has occurred in the budget of the Development Board. This expenditure increased from slightly more than ID 3 million in 1951–52 to approximately ID 62 million in 1955–56. During the same period the ordinary budget expenditures also increased rapidly from ID 30 million in 1949–50 to ID 54 million in 1954–55, an increase of over 90 percent.

The largest single category in ordinary budget expenditures is national security (controlled by the Ministry of Defense and the Directorate of Police), which accounted for 44 percent of the total ordinary budget expenditure in 1949–50 and for 37 percent in 1954–55. This expenditure, however, did not come near the percentage of the total expended by Egypt. Economic and social activities (ministries of Agriculture, Public Works and Communications, Economics, Education, Health, and Social Affairs) accounted for 33 percent of ordinary budget expenditures in 1949–50, compared with 31 percent in 1954–55.

The separate budgets of muncipalities and related budgets also show a marked increase in expenditures.

A regrouping of ordinary budget expenditures in 1955–56 on a functional basis presents this picture: national security (Defense and Police), 37.3 percent; economic and social activities, 27.0 percent; wages, salaries, and overhead in all other ministries, 33.2 percent; miscellaneous items, 2.5 percent.

"Economic and social activities" includes not only maintenance of public works but also a large number of developmental activities such as certain expenditures of the *miri sirf* program (see chap. 14), land survey, agricultural experimental stations, and the construction of many public buildings.

Ordinary budget expenditures continued to rise in most categories from 1946–47 until 1954–55. Percentage-wise the expenditures of the ordinary budget did not follow the same pattern. Though ordinary budget expenditures in Iraqi dinars had increased because of the larger revenues taken in by the state, the percentage of expenditures for the various ministries has fluctuated slightly from year to year; steady, though small, increases in the percentage of expenditure have occurred only for the ministries of Social Affairs and Health.

In 1949–50 the actual ordinary budget showed a deficit of ID 1.4 million. Six years later in 1955–56 the estimated ordinary budget expenditure showed only a ID 500,000 deficit over ordinary budget receipts. The deficits have fluctuated considerably from year to year as indicated by comparing Table 7 with Table 8. The larger expenditures have been met by revenue from improved tax collection and additional taxes, as well as from the expanding oil revenues and shares in the profits of companies other than oil companies.

Revenues

The annual receipts of the Iraqi Government in 1954–55 (excluding petroleum production) showed a fivefold increase over those for the period before World War II. In the 1930's annual receipts were approximately ID 6 million a year; this figure mushroomed to more than ID 30 million in 1954–55. While annual receipts increased five times during this period, however, the level of prices also increased between five and six times. In real terms, the burden of taxation today is probably much the same as before World War II.

Inadequate data makes it impossible to relate accurately the tax burden to the national income. Roughly speaking, however, annual per capita income in Iraq is a little over $100 while the total tax burden per capita in fiscal 1954–55 was approximately $15. Though this percentage appears high, the annual tax rate is much lower than in Great Britain, France, and the United States, where income tax absorbs between 20 and 30 percent of income. While the tax rates of Israel (20 percent) and Egypt (18 percent) are higher than that of Iraq, those of Syria, Lebanon, and Jordan have been about the same or slightly lower.

As in other underdeveloped countries, indirect taxation is predominant (see Table 7). The land tax, originally intended as a rent on government lands, is paid by the lessors of government land as well as those who farm government land without a lease. This land tax ranges from 2.5 percent to 10 percent of the value of the annual produce. Even though a large proportion of all cultivated land is *miri* (leased) land, collections from this tax are relatively low.

Agriculture is taxed very lightly. A large proportion of the agricultural produce consumed on the farm and in the village is not taxed at all. The *istihlak,* a tax on agricultural produce, is levied on marketed agricultural products and is collected at marketing points from wholesale merchants who buy produce directly from the farmers. The *istihlak* changed from 10 percent to 12.5 percent in 1948 to 11.5 percent in 1950; now it is 10 percent on cereals and dates, which are the most important products. In 1953 this tax was abolished for certain products (meat, fats, vegetables, fruit, wool, hides, cotton, etc.) when consumed in Iraq, but was raised to 20 percent on these products when exported. It has been discriminatory and regressive in nature, largely shifted to the producer on exported items such as barley.

There is much discrimination in favor of those who have obtained state lands in *lazimah* grants. Persons holding such grants, made on the basis of a rather tenuous proof of occupancy and cultivation, escape any tax or rent assessments on their land, while those farming regularly leased land from the state continue to be assessed rents.

Among direct taxes there is the property tax on dwellings, commercial buildings, and nonagricultural land. The rental value of these properties is taxed at a rate of 10 percent with a certain tax-free minimum. The income tax of 1939, amended by an income surtax law of 1943, established graduated income tax rates—on income from all sources except agriculture—ranging from 4 percent to 60 percent for individuals (highest group, over ID 9,500 annually) and from 15 percent to 40 percent for corporations. Receipts from the income tax have been declining somewhat since exemption limits were raised in 1952; these are now ID 350 for unmarried persons and ID 450 for married persons, plus an additional ID 30 for each child. There is no agricultural income tax nor are there any inheritance taxes. In recent years there has been considerable discussion of a proposal for an inheritance tax and a unified tax covering all sources of income. The parliament has not, however, enacted legislation to these ends.

Customs duties are in most cases not *ad valorem* but specific duties and often regressive in nature when imposed on imported necessities. They are calculated as a certain sum per ton, gallon, etc., and not as a percentage on the value of imports. During recent years imports have been growing and customs receipts have been increasing accordingly. In 1953–54 total duties collected amounted to ID 14.5 million, which was equivalent to 21 percent of the total value of imports in that year.

In recent years tariff rates have been raised on luxuries and some other products in an attempt to protect local industries. On the other hand, the government has at times temporarily exempted from duty various imported consumer goods, depending upon local prices and supplies available. Export duties of 5 percent were introduced temporarily in 1950 but were subsequently lowered to 1 percent and many products were exempted altogether. Excise duties accounted for 8.3 percent of total receipts of the ordinary budget in 1953–54.

Miscellaneous revenues such as receipts from the tobacco monopoly and from the Department of Post and Telegraphs and other public services show an increase between 1949 and 1956, although percentage of income from these sources relative to the total ordinary budget's receipts during the same period showed a slight decrease.

Currency and the Bank of Issue

With the dissolution of the Ottoman Empire after World War I, the Turkish pound was replaced in Iraq by Indian currency; Iraq remained a member of the Indian monetary area until 1931.

In 1931 the Iraqi Currency Board was established to control and maintain the country's currency. The board, which functioned in London, was composed of five members, two of whom were nominated by the Government of Iraq, two by the three private banks then operating in Iraq, and one by the governor of the Bank of England. The main functions of the board were to issue notes and coins in Iraq redeemable against prepayment in sterling in London and to buy Iraqi notes and coins for sterling payable in London. The new basic currency unit was the Iraqi dinar (ID), equivalent to one British pound sterling (now $2.80). The sterling acquired in exchange for notes and coins issued went into the Currency Reserve Fund, which was maintained wholly as a sterling reserve. The quantity of dinars in circulation in Iraq varied so closely with the balance of payments that there was no scope for a monetary policy aimed at influencing domestic economic activity by manipulating the volume of money in circulation. The foreign exchange situation, as it appeared to the Currency Board, solely and mechanically determined that volume.

In 1947 a law was enacted establishing the National Bank of Iraq (NBI) to take over from the Iraqi Currency Board the issue of currency. The new bank began operations in the middle of 1949 under a charter giving it the functions of a central bank. It is authorized to maintain a reserve of gold and foreign currencies at a ratio to the currency outstanding of not less than 70 percent and Iraqi Government securities at a ratio not exceeding 30 percent. So far the NBI has maintained a foreign exchange cover exceeding 100 percent of currency circulation and exceeding 90 percent of a total composed of currency circulation plus short-term liabilities.

Aside from its note-issuing functions, the NBI is charged with the administration of foreign exchange control and the supervision of the banking system in accordance with a bank control law which became effective at the beginning of 1950. This law requires banks to keep the equivalent of 15 percent of their time and demand deposits as a reserve with the National Bank and to keep 50 percent of these deposits in the form of cash and investments in Iraq. The National Bank is empowered to reduce the reserve requirement to 10 percent. It is also entitled to keep the accounts of the government and to undertake transactions relating to government and semigovernment loans of all kinds.

Authorized to operate as a genuine central bank, the NBI actually falls short of doing so, possibly because it has not had the time to organize itself adequately and to develop an experienced staff. The assets and liabilities of the Banking Department of the NBI have greatly increased, however, during the last four years. While the currency in circulation has also increased, its share in the National Bank's total liabilities has been considerably reduced.

Foreign assets of the NBI, which stood at ID 35 million in 1949, increased during the three years between the end of 1952 and the end of 1955 from ID 47 million to around ID 105 million, reflecting the recent increase in Iraq's income from oil. Of the total oil royalties paid to the Government of Iraq in sterling, 70 percent is transferred to the Development Board, which in turn sells sterling to the National Bank and is credited in the bank's books with a corresponding amount in dinars. To the extent that the Currency Board makes use of this deposit to buy foreign goods and services, it must repurchase foreign exchange from the National Bank. Since, however, the bank up to now has used only a relatively small part of its means and since, again, only a fraction of this has been spent on goods and services from abroad, a considerable amount of sterling is left at the disposal of the bank. While a part of this amount has been used to cover the deficit which developed in the balance of payments on goods and services apart from oil revenues, the foreign exchange reserve has nevertheless continued to increase.

Until recently the NBI possessed no gold reserve of its own and only limited amounts of foreign exchange other than sterling. Like the other members of the sterling area Iraq is under an obligation to surrender its gold and dollar earnings to the common pool, on which in turn it may draw according to its needs. But the NBI obtained the consent of the United Kingdom to maintain a modest working balance in American dollars, not exceeding the equivalent of ID 2 million ($5.6 million). During 1955 at the annual talks of the Anglo-Iraqi Economic-Financial Committee it was agreed that this working balance be increased by the equivalent of ID 1.5 million and that, in order to diversify the Iraqi currency cover, gold be purchased to the equivalent of ID 5 million.

In the execution of its statutory powers to influence the level of economic activity by expanding or contracting credit, the NBI is handicapped by the strong position of some of the other banks. Branches of foreign banks operating in Iraq can always obtain additional cash by drawing on their holdings elsewhere and by selling the foreign exchange to the NBI. The Rafidain Bank, owned by the government, holds the government accounts, including the 30 percent of the oil royalties not allocated to the Development Board. This situation also explains why loans and advances made by the NBI to different institutions are rather small in relation to its total assets. Since commercial banks have had no need to borrow from the NBI, its borrowers appear to be mainly specialized government agencies and state-owned banks other than the Rafidain Bank.

The management of the NBI is in the hands of a board of administration and a governor-general. The board consists of nine members, including the governor-general, all appointed by the Council of Ministers for four-year terms; board members cannot be removed during their term of appointment. One of the members must have practical experience in trade, another in agriculture, and another in banking—each to be appointed from a list of three nominated by the Chamber of Commerce, the Chamber of Agriculture, and the licensed banks respectively. The remaining five members are appointed in their personal capacity. At present, three members of the board are private bankers. As in the case of other governmental agencies, the NBI has been willing to invite and accept advice from foreign experts regarding both current operations and long-term planning.

State and Private Banks

Apart from the NBI, the state owns five other banks. Four of these —the Industrial Bank, the Agricultural Bank, the Mortgage Bank, and the Loan Bank (mortgage bank for movable properties)—were created to cover specific credit needs not sufficiently served by private banks and moneylenders; the fifth—the Rafidain Bank—is a commercial bank founded in 1941 (that is, before the establishment of the NBI) to act as the banker of the government and at the same time to compete with foreign banks.

The Industrial Bank was created in 1940 with an original capital of ID 500,000; later this was increased to ID 3 million, of which the government had supplied only ID 2.3 million in mid-1956. The Industrial Bank has also received minor loans from other sources and, like the Agricultural Bank, it receives money on current account.

The Industrial Bank can lend against the security of immovable property, plants and machinery, gold, silver, government bonds, stocks and shares, and negotiable instruments and goods in its custody. The maximum limit for individual loans is ID 20,000; the maximum period for loans to companies with a capital of ID 100,000 or more is 10 years, for smaller companies 5 years. The bank is authorized to participate in holding shares of companies, with a maximum limit of ID 250,000 per company. In recent years transactions have brought an average profit of ID 90,000 annually.

The Agricultural Bank was established as an independent bank in 1940 with a nominal capital of ID 2 million. By 1955 its capital had been increased to ID 3 million. Though having obtained loans from the NBI, the Agricultural Bank is barely holding its own: in 1951–52 and 1952–53 it had deficits totaling ID 45,000 and in 1953–54 made a profit of only about ID 19,000.

The Mortgage Bank for immovable properties was established in 1948; its primary purpose was to provide house owners with an opportunity to convert high-interest loans secured by mortgages on their properties into loans at a more reasonable rate. Its terms of reference were extended in 1952 and in 1953; today, in addition to taking over old high-interest loans at 5 percent, it encourages individual building activities by loans up to a maximum of ID 4,000 in any single case, secured by mortgages not exceeding 60 percent of the value of the property, for not longer than eight years; it builds houses, on its own account, for sale or rent to persons with limited income.

Originally the capital of the Mortgage Bank was set at ID 1 million (loaned by the Ministry of Finance without interest); in 1952 this amount was raised to ID 2 million and further increases are envisaged. The Mortgage Bank also has at its disposal 3 percent loans from the NBI. Since 1950–51, two years after its foundation, it has had regular profits averaging over ID 30,000 per year. Its activities could probably now be extended into providing more housing for the poorer sections of the population. For this purpose it may be necessary to raise the limit of loans for small and cheap houses and, perhaps, also to extend the period of repayment.

The Loan Bank (mortgage bank for movable properties), with a present capital of ID 1 million, was established in 1951 to provide small loans to government employees, officials, and pensioners, or to others against security. It also receives loans and deposits. During 1952–53 and 1953–54, loans totaled ID 1.3 million and modest profits were realized. The operations of the Loan Bank have had some importance in combating usury.

The Rafidain Bank, aside from its government business, operates as a commercial bank, extending credit facilities to wholesalers and retail merchants at the going rate of interest. With assets totaling (as of the end of March 1955) ID 46.5 million and showing a net profit, including income-tax provision of almost ID 600,000, it is the largest commercial bank in Iraq.

Private banks in Iraq operate under the Law for the Control of Banking, which requires them to have a license from the National Bank of Iraq. The National Bank exercises some control over other banks through the regulations which compel the latter to maintain liquidity and solvency by means of compulsory deposits with the National Bank.

All private banks in Iraq concentrate on commercial banking and all are branches of foreign banks having their origin in London (the Ottoman Bank, the Eastern Bank, and the British Bank of the Middle East) or in Arab countries (the Arab Bank of Jordan and the Intra Bank of Lebanon). The recently created Iraqi Commercial Bank is apparently also to be regarded mainly, if not entirely, as a branch of a Lebanese bank. Apart from banking institutions, a certain number of individuals, called sarrafs, are licensed to deal in banking. Traditional moneylenders of the area, the sarrafs have been greatly reduced in number both by their failure to meet the requirements of the bank control law and by the exodus of Jews following the Arab-Israeli war. At present, Iraq's total number of sarrafs and branches and offices of commercial banks seems to be slightly over 40; this compares with around 20 branches and offices of state-owned banks.

There has been a considerable growth in banking activities over the last few years. From December 1952 until 1955, private deposits increased from about ID 16 million to ID 28 million. During the same period the capital position (including certain reserve accounts) rose from ID 3.4 million to ID 7.4 million. This growth in deposits and capital has made possible a sizable expansion in credit extended to the private sector by the commercial banks.

Up to now the commercial banks operating in Iraq have generally followed a cautious policy, avoiding business ventures entailing dangers for the depositors. They have also maintained a high degree of liquidity. The ratio of cash (including deposits with the NBI) and foreign assets (deposits abroad and foreign investments) to current liabilities (deposits and debit balances abroad) has been declining but is still over 50 percent.

According to a law dating from 1936, the permissible maximum rate of interest on loans is 7 percent. Toward the end of 1953 commercial banks agreed to charge the following uniform rates: 4.5 percent on bills discounted (normally 3 months) and 5 percent on unsecured advances and overdrafts. In 1955, following a growing shortage of cash, interest rates for the two categories of loans were raised to 5 and 6 percent, respectively. At the same time, in order to encourage deposits, banks raised interest rates on fixed deposits from 2 to 2.5 percent and on savings accounts from 1.5 to 2.75 percent. On postal savings, 3 percent interest is paid but only up to a fixed amount of savings, above which no interest is paid. Persons who obtain credit outside the licensed institutions often have to pay interest charges above the legal limit, amounting to as much as 12 to 15 percent.

Inflationary Factors

The expansion in money in circulation and demand deposits from ID 43.4 million in 1952 to ID 65.1 million at the end of 1955 apparently reflects the higher demand for cash balances which is related to the higher level of economic activity. So far the increasing money supply has not had pronounced inflationary effects for a number of reasons: government surpluses, increases in savings, and adequate supplies of goods resulting partly from liberal import policies. Simultaneously with a growing money supply, prices followed a downward trend, the cost-of-living index decreasing from 115 in 1952 to 101 in 1955 (based on an index of 100 in 1953).

In the longer run, however, the danger of inflationary price rises is inherent in a country whose economy has large sums infused into it each year. While varying somewhat in the details of their recommendations, all foreign experts who have recently surveyed Iraq's economic position and prospects believe it essential that these potential inflationary dangers be taken into account in the distribution of the Development Board's expenditures and in the timing of different projects. It will be important to utilize efficiently available manpower and to maintain adequate supplies of certain materials and consumer goods for which increased incomes are likely to create an additional demand. If the need arises, corrective action will have to be taken to reduce excessive increases of spending power by fiscal, monetary, and credit policies. In the specific conditions prevailing in Iraq, no single factor such as the Treasury, the National Bank, other banks, or the Development Board is in a position to take effective measures by itself; cooperation among all of them will be required. A number of techniques to ensure such cooperation have been suggested by foreign consultants and are under study.

14

AGRICULTURAL DEVELOPMENT

IRAQ IS PREDOMINANTLY AN AGRICULTURAL COUNTRY, WITH about three fourths of the population deriving their income directly from cultivation and animal husbandry. Its resources in land and water (greater than those of any of its Arab neighbors), combined with a relatively small population, make agriculture a key factor in plans for economic expansion now and in the future.

The utilization of land and water, particularly river water, must be considerably improved, however, if Iraq's agriculture is to flourish as it did before invasion and internal disorder wrecked the superbly engineered irrigation system constructed in ancient times. For centuries the land has been abused by the shifting cultivation of semi-sedentarized nomads and impoverished peasants, and faulty irrigation and drainage practices have salinized large areas which can be recovered only through expensive and large-scale leaching processes. Farming output per unit of land is low, and any significant increase will require a major program of water control and scientific agricultural techniques. Other factors inhibit the development of Iraq's considerable agricultural productive power. These are primarily the scarcity of capital and labor and a system of land tenure which consigns the vast majority of cultivators to extreme poverty and provides them with no incentive to improve their lot.

Under the Ottoman Empire, from 1534 to 1917, political and economic power in Iraq was focused, not in settled villages, but in the towns and the nomadic tribes. The circumstances of that period, which witnessed the steady decline of Turkish authority, favored the evolution of the present system of land tenure—in which most cultivable land, and therefore agricultural wealth, is concentrated in the hands of the two strongest elements, the urban absentee landlord and the tribal sheikh. In 1953 it is estimated that only 7,732 proprietors held more than 240 acres, and they controlled a major portion of the total area in landholdings. The average size of all landholdings increases from north to south—from 122 acres in the four northern provinces to 250 acres in the central provinces and 1,243 acres in the four southern provinces.

Typically, the concern of the large absentee landlord has been with the revenue from his holdings rather than with their management, which is generally in the hands of a bailiff. The distance between landlord and village cultivator has been measured not only by wealth but by the contrast between the very different patterns of life, traditional in the Middle East, which have made town, village, and bedouin tribe literally separate segments of a heterogeneous society. For the town dweller the ownership of agricultural land has been a source of wealth and prestige. For the tribal sheikh it has been a means of augmenting income and of securing products which animal husbandry alone cannot supply; involvement in agricultural production also tends to transform the nomad; that is, the sheikhs are drawn to town to enjoy their new wealth and their lesser kinsmen are settled on the land as peasant cultivators. To both townsman and nomad, agricultural work itself is demeaning labor fit only for the lowly fellah, whose poverty is a natural concomitant of a contemptible existence.

A few peasants, largely confined to the northeastern part of country, own their own land, but they are only a little better off than the landless majority. Small holdings, lack of cheap credit, and primitive farming techniques keep the peasant owner poor and condemn him to a lifelong struggle to retain his land. Many, overwhelmed by debt, slip down into the landless group. In the course of a few generations even the more successful commonly find their holdings dissipated into minute parcels by the operation of the traditional inheritance practice under which land is divided equally among male heirs.

Most often the Iraqi peasant is a sharecropper, sometimes a renter or agricultural laborer. Extracting low yields by archaic methods from the abused soil, he is chronically in debt to the landlord and his intermediaries, who often receive half or more of his crop. He not only lacks incentive to raise his output but finds a kind of security in tying himself more closely to his creditors by allowing his debts to increase.

Government development programs, the expanding oil industry, and the growth of the towns are offering employment opportunities which are beginning to draw numbers of peasants off the land or settle them in new areas under more favorable conditions; but most continue to be pinned down by poverty, ignorance of the outside world, and reluctance to sever the kin ties which so tightly bind the Middle Eastern village community.

Land Tenure

The system of land tenure in Iraq has its roots in the traditional body of concept and usage common to the Moslem Arab world. Iraq's particular historical experience, however, has made for peculiarities in the pattern. Notable among these is the very large proportion of absentee ownership which has resulted from the manipulation of the Islamic land laws of the country. In Moslem law ultimate title to nearly all available land is regarded as residing with the state, and full private ownership is largely confined to urban property and orchards. Most agricultural land is held under various forms of usufructuary possession, some of which, however, are virtually indistinguishable from full private ownership since holdings may be sold, mortgaged, or willed to heirs.

In Iraq, with a relatively small population in relation to the amount of available land, this system has led to growth of absentee landlordism by enabling the urban entrepreneurs and the sheikhs of the more powerful nomadic tribes to acquire use title to huge tracts of territory. Initially, a number of intermediaries arose between the central authorities and those who were allowed to occupy the land against payment of taxes. These intermediaries—tax farmers responsible for the collection of government taxes in their respective districts—came in the course of time to regard themselves as the owners of the land. With the abolition of this method of tax collection, many tax farmers were compensated with land grants. Similarly, the urban investor, by payment of only token sums, could take up large holdings; so also could the tribal sheikhs, who were being encouraged to adopt a settled way of life by being given tracts of agricultural land on which they could place their tribesmen as sharecropping tenants. The land-grabbing process was accelerated in the last century by an Ottoman land-registration law which enabled various influential persons in collusion with corrupt officials to register in their names huge areas which in many cases the claimant had never seen. Often the peasant cultivator, fearing that registration would subject him to military conscription and additional taxation, renounced his opportunity to acquire title to the land he worked by registering it in the name of some well-to-do protector, thereafter being reduced to the status of tenant or even day laborer. In other cases the prevailing practice of shifting agriculture barred the cultivator from registering, since he could not meet the requirement of 15 years' occupancy on any single parcel of land.

New tenure laws were promulgated in 1932 and 1938, and by 1953 more than 16 million hectares (1 hectare = approximately 2.471 acres), or about 36 percent of the total area of Iraq, had been classified in the following categories: *mulk:* land held in full private ownership; *matrukah:* land reserved for public purposes; *wakf:* land administered in trust for the benefit of religious institutions or private persons; *miri:* government lands, of which there are three types: (a) *tapu*—permanent tenure amounting to full ownership of land long occupied and previously registered; (b) *lazimah*—title granted to land cultivated by the claimant for at least 15 years prior to registration, the government reserving the right under certain circumstances to veto the transfer of such holdings; (c) *sirf*—land belonging to the state with no previously established tenancy.

The allocation of land under these several categories in 1953 was as follows in thousands of hectares: *mulk,* 56; *matrukah,* 774; *wakf,* 178; *miri tapu,* 2,730; *miri lazimah,* 2,574; *miri sirf,* 9,814.

It is evident that the large proportion of *miri sirf* land provides the main reserve available to the Iraqi Government for carrying out its current policy of land resettlement based on the conversion of the landless peasant into a small farmer-owner. Meanwhile, except in scattered areas and in a few new settlements—such as Dujaylah, 25 miles south of the Al Kut Barrage—the peasant proprietor is almost absent from the Iraqi agricultural scene, a circumstance wryly reflected in the Arab saying, "Who tills the land does not own it, and who owns the land does not till it!"

The Cultivator

A small percentage of Iraq's cultivators are employed as wage laborers on the relatively few large holdings where plantation farming is practiced, and a somewhat larger number work land for which they pay a cash rental. A comparatively small number are peasant proprietors. The great majority, however, are sharecroppers who in return for the use of the land and certain materials and facilities surrender up to 50 percent of their crop to the landowner. Not all of the sharecropper's contribution goes to the landlord, for in addition to government taxes there are the demands of one or several intermediaries who stand between the tenant and the landlord as sublessors and bailiffs. A typical distribution of the crop in southern Iraq some years ago was given as 10 percent to the government, 7.5 percent to the principal tenant or sublessor, 2.5 percent to the sublessor's bailiff, and 40 percent to the landowner, with the remaining 40 percent going to the peasant cultivator.

The tenant's share varies with the contribution of the landlord—who in addition to land may provide pump irrigation water, seeds, and draft animals—and with local customs and circumstances. Cases are reported in southern Iraq in which the cultivator obtains only 20 to 40 percent of the crop, while in the northeastern areas having enough rain for some dry farming, where the peasant is relatively less dependent on materials and services provided by the landlord, the tenant's share may rise as high as 80 or 90 percent for nonirrigated winter crops, dipping to about 50 percent for the irrigated summer crops. This is by no means characteristic of the country as a whole, but it has permitted some peasants, particularly those in the hills of Kurdistan, to own their own oxen and plows and from year to year to supply their own seed.

The income of the fellah may be considerably increased in such areas of intensive cultivation as the Gharraf, where water from the Al Kut Barrage makes possible double-cropping with high yields per acre. Alternative forms of employment in the cities and on water-control and other government projects also work to the peasant's advantage: landlords offer more favorable terms of tenancy to retain their cultivators. In the absence of other employment opportunities and where average output is low, as around Al Amarah, the fellah still must live under the worst conditions.

From the standpoint of the landowner, sharecropping—much more widespread than cash rentals—has definite advantages. Whereas in a bad year he might not be able to collect any cash from a renter he is certain of a portion, however small, from the sharecropper. The system also gives the landlord or his agent the right to determine what crops shall be grown and a voice in field operations. Share tenancy has also not been without appeal to the peasant, who generally lacks the capital, implements, and animals necessary to operate a farm on his own, and who in any event usually cannot afford the risk of leasing land against cash, especially in nonirrigated areas where rainfall is uncertain and a dry year would spell disaster. Finally, the sharecropper is regarded as a more permanent member of the estate than the cash lessee, and, however poor he may be, he enjoys in his status some feeling of protection against a harsh environment. The mobility of the share tenant is reduced not only by his poverty but by legislation which forbids him to leave the land he cultivates if he is indebted to the landowner; few peasants escape debt—particularly in irrigated areas, where the landlord's contribution in water and equipment is appreciable. This factor, plus the dominant position of the landlord in the social system, has subjected the poorest sharecroppers to a kind of compulsory labor.

The Landowner

The growth of large-scale absentee land ownership was hastened after World War I by both economic and political factors. Economically Iraq was moving, however haltingly, from the subsistence production of the past to a market economy. Agriculture then as now was largely geared to production for local consumption and barter, but commercial farming and cash crops were making their appearance. This development at once provided new incentives and opportunities for the expansion of the landed holdings of the well-to-do and the politically influential, and increased the dependence of the peasants and the growing number of sedentarized nomads on the landowner, who alone had the money needed for commercial production.

With industrial development only beginning, the big landowners are the strongest economic group in the country. The position of the landlord derives not only from his material wealth but from the social prestige which traditionally has attached to the ownership of land in the Middle East. Recent decades have seen the ranks of the landholding minority augmented by new elements. Government officials, army officers, and urban professional men vie for the distinction of acquiring and owning rural estates. In this connection a *miri sirf* law passed in 1951 provides that up to 20 percent of new agricultural land opened up by the government shall be distributed to retired army and police officers and enlisted personnel, and that up to 25 percent of such land shall be given to retired civil servants who have had at least eight years of service and to unemployed graduates of elementary, secondary, and religious schools. The government's policy of sedentarizing the nomadic tribes and securing the loyalty of their leaders by grants of agricultural land has transformed many bedouin sheikhs into landed proprietors whose estates—in many cases once the property of the tribe as a whole—are worked by their poorer tribesmen or by landless villagers.

There are notable examples of enterprising landlords who have developed their domains to their own and their tenants' advantage by installing pumps for irrigation, introducing new and more remunerative crops, and investing in agricultural machinery, but the majority, viewing land as a prestige symbol and a source of income rather than a vocation, have shown little capacity to come to grips with the technical and human problems of Iraq's backward and depressed agriculture.

In the upper levels of the landowning group are many who, attracted by urban amenities, have gravitated to the towns. Here they are remote from the practical administration of their estates and cut off from the personal relationships which in some parts of the Middle East give landlord and peasant a sense of reciprocal responsibility, but they are physically and socially close to the centers of political power and able to influence government policy and legislation. The Chamber of Deputies in 1954 passed a bill requiring landowners to repay in installments the cost of drainage works affecting their property, but the bill was disapproved by the Senate and did not become law. A similar problem exists with respect to imposing adequate charges for irrigation water; owners are willing to receive the water but less willing to pay for it.

Tradition, wealth, and political advantage bolster the position of the Iraqi landlord; changing his motivations and attitudes on the one hand and educating and assisting the peasants to a more active role in the economic and political life of the country are as important to the ultimate success of the government's ambitious rural rehabilitation program as solving the financial and technical problems involved in the modernization of agricultural methods.

Rural Credit

One of the more serious problems in Iraqi agriculture is the absence of an adequate system of rural credit. The bare subsistence income of the average peasant forces him to borrow not just in the event of emergency but often to meet his minimum operating expenses for seed, draft animals, and equipment. Lacking security for low-interest institutional loans, he has no alternative but to obligate himself at usurious rates to his landlord or to the moneylender. Legislation provides that advances made by the landlord to his tenants shall be free of interest, but this regulation is easily circumvented when the advance is made in kind against a return in the form of a larger share of the crop. For the bulk of Iraq's peasants, increasing involvement in production for cash markets has meant, not greater access to the liquid capital required for commercial agriculture, but a mounting burden of debt.

Aside from the moneylender and the landlord, the principal source of rural credit in Iraq is the Agricultural Bank, established by the government to "assist agriculturists and to develop and improve agriculture" (see chap. 13). In addition to making loans the bank is authorized to engage in such activities as selling equipment and cattle on deferred payments, acting as agent for the sale of agricultural produce, and creating establishments which grade and clean crops. The bank has made mostly medium-term loans. Up to the end of March 1954 it had advanced ID 4 million to 12,212 borrowers, among whom large landowners predominated; but the number of persons indebted to the bank at any given time has rarely exceeded 2,000.

The accomplishments of the Agricultural Bank so far have not been impressive. Among the reasons for this, the most obvious is lack of resources. Little more than three fourths of the bank's nominal capital of ID 2 million, all of it subscribed by the government, has been paid up. Still another limitation to the bank's ability to bring its services to the neediest group is imposed by the strict requirements of its loans, which may not exceed 60 to 70 percent of the best security offered in gold, silver, bonds, shares, and agricultural produce. This regulation in effect restricts loans to the bigger landowners. Moreover, the bank seems to have suffered from a lack of administrative continuity in frequent changes of managers; it has been remarked that the bank lacks initiative in the pursuit of the broad goals for which it was founded.

Cooperatives are still in their infancy and the few that exist are mainly for consumers. There is, however, an active cooperative in Dujaylah which rents equipment to the new settlers, and it is possible that its example will be followed by other new settlements.

Land Utilization

Iraq enjoys certain advantages over much of the Fertile Crescent in possessing large areas of highly productive alluvial soils deposited by the Tigris and Euphrates rivers and their tributaries. Even so, deserts and semideserts comprise about one half of the country's total area of 171,000 square miles. Only one fourth of the remainder is under cultivation; of this, 48 percent is devoted to dry farming and 52 percent to various systems of irrigated production, the water being distributed by pump or flow techniques. Table 9 shows the pattern of land utilization in 1952–53, when the most recent national agricultural census was taken.

Climatically Iraq may be divided into a rainfall zone in the north and northeast and an irrigated zone in the center and south. In the rainfall zone the amount and reliability of precipitation and the character of soil and terrain largely determine the pattern of land use. The most important part of this zone is the rotation cropland area, where favorable conditions make possible the rotation of wheat and barley with fallow and allow, where there is irrigation, the cultivation of a summer crop. Iraqi Kurdistan (in the northeast) comprises a second subdivision, where soil depth and quality restrict cultivation to the valley floors and adjacent slopes; grass for summer grazing is found in the higher pastures. Scattered over the rainfall belt are small areas planted to apples and other orchard crops.

The irrigated zone farther south, drawing its water from the Tigris-Euphrates system, may be subdivided on the basis of irrigation techniques. Pump irrigation, necessary where the rivers lie below the level of the surrounding land, is characteristic of the middle Tigris region; it supports winter cereals, summer rice and cotton, and horticultural crops.

Flow irrigation is practiced along the lower reaches of the Tigris and Euphrates and in other areas where topography and river level make it possible. The same crops are irrigated by this method as by pump irrigation but rice becomes the major cereal crop in the southern part of this area. In areas of flow irrigation excessive use of water in combination with poor drainage has so heavily salinized the soil that large tracts have been rendered unfit for cultivation; they can be returned to production only with costly leaching measures. This problem lies behind the widespread practice in the flow-irrigated area of shifting agriculture, whereby the cultivator abandons the land as it becomes exhausted or salinized and moves to new fields. Marsh lands north of the confluence of the Tigris and Euphrates are devoted to the cultivation of rice and the breeding of water buffaloes.

Principal Crops and Yields

Table 10 gives production figures for Iraq's principal crops in various periods from 1934 to 1955. Barley, the country's major crop, and wheat are grown in both the rain-fed and the irrigated zones, with wheat dominating in the former. Barley's importance stems from its resistance to arid climate and saline soil, and its yield per acre averages about twice that of wheat. Scanty rainfall makes the summer crops dependent upon irrigation. Of these, rice—particularly in the lower Tigris-Euphrates valley—and cotton are the principal crops. Special laws obtain for rice cultivation, which can only be conducted under special license. A decree of 1944 defines the regions where rice may, or may not, be grown.

Other crops include tobacco, fruit, and nuts, which are grown mainly in the north; citrus fruit, much of which is produced in the Diyala valley; vegetables cultivated in the vicinity of the towns; small quantities of sesame, millet, corn, and sorghum grown in the south; and dates, also a southern crop, of which Iraq is the world's largest producer and exporter.

Livestock

Sheep and goats, which thrive despite poor pasture, are kept in large numbers in almost all parts of the country. Cattle predominate in the northern and central parts of the country, while the water buffalo is the principal farm animal in the riverine areas of the south. Many peasants have no livestock at all except perhaps one ox, donkey, or mule, which is essential to them as a draft animal. The bedouins who live a pastoral existence on the desert margins herd sheep, goats, and camels and may have numbers of horses—prestige animals in the desert; but the bedouins constitute only a small segment of the population and their ranks are being thinned by the process of sedentarization. Table 11 lists the livestock on holdings during the agricultural census of 1952–53 but does not include all of the livestock kept by the nomadic groups.

Fisheries

In spite of its rivers and considerable number of lakes, fresh-water fish are not plentiful in Iraq—apparently the result of overfishing in the past. The annual catch of fresh-water fish in 1953 was estimated at 8,000 to 10,000 tons. Domestic demand is high and in many local markets it exceeds the supply. A report of the United Nations Food and Agriculture Organization on the "Development of Inland Fisheries," submitted to the Iraqi Government in 1954, states that Iraq has a high potential for increased fish production provided that proper conservation measures are taken, but that in the absence of such measures further depletion can be expected.

Commercial sea fisheries of Iraq in the Persian Gulf are at the present time insignificant. They provide around 300 tons of fish annually to Iraqi markets, compared with about 3,000 tons produced in the Bahrein-Kuwait area. A company has recently been sponsored by Iranian and Japanese interests to undertake large-scale fishing operations in Persian Gulf waters. There is a remote possibility that, should Iraq either participate directly in this enterprise or become a market for its products, some seafish-processing industries might arise in the southern part of the country; these concerns would preserve fish, prepare fish meal, and perhaps also produce fish oil.

Forestry

Forests exist only in the four northern provinces of Irbil, Mosul, As Sulaymaniyah, and Kirkuk; they cover about 6,500 square miles, or less than 4 percent of the country's total area. They suffer from indiscriminate cutting for fuel and charcoal, from overgrazing by livestock, and from fires. The Forestry Division of the Ministry of

Agriculture at present lacks funds and personnel to give proper attention to the forests.

Production Problems

The productivity of Iraq's agriculture is low even by comparison with neighboring countries which contend with similar problems of natural environment and technology. In the nonirrigated areas some land is tilled where rainfall is not only irregular but frequently inadequate. During a ten-year period there will generally be five fallow years, two crop failures, two fair crops, and only one good crop. In the irrigated zone poor drainage and wasteful use of irrigation water combine to produce increasing salinization of the soil, reducing much of it to a submarginal state. Water-storage facilities are inadequate in many areas, and shortage of water during the critical months of the growing season impedes effective cultivation.

Most farmers—with such exceptions as the more successful small peasant proprietors in northern Iraq or certain farmers who practice double cropping in the irrigated zone—practice a haphazard and wasteful system of farming. They deplete the soil by failing to replace its plant food either with soil-building crops or with chemical fertilizer, which they cannot afford to buy, and by fallowing without clearing the ground of weeds, which are allowed to grow to provide grazing for animals. (Grazing animals do, however, provide some manure.) Plows and other equipment are generally antiquated, and methods of soil preparation are inadequate.

Under existing circumstances improvements with the best prospects are those which do not involve large capital expenditure and some which may be financed and supervised by the central government or a cooperative organization. These might include improved plows, proper fallowing with adequate tools to remove weeds during the fallow years, and over a long-range period the cultivation of soil-building and forage crops. The introduction of such measures in irrigated areas involves the assumption that the water-control projects completed on the Tigris and Euphrates in 1956 will make it possible and profitable to improve landholdings in the adjacent area, that the practice of shifting cultivation will be abandoned, that the fellah will receive state assistance in obtaining livestock, and that his dependence upon the landlord will be substantially reduced. Without these simultaneous developments, little over-all improvement in cultivation can be anticipated.

Improvement in both the quality and quantity of livestock production is likely to be of growing importance in the future, particularly since the general economic development of the country will create an expanding and more discriminating market for animal products. The types of livestock found in Iraq today represent rather hardy animals that have become fairly resistant to the rigors of climate and inadequate feed. Scientific breeding is almost unknown in the countryside, but steps for improvement could be taken—not only in this field but in other aspects of agricultural technique—by expanding agricultural extension services and experimental farms. Special measures need to be taken to assist the bedouin to improve their livestock. More widespread veterinary services are badly needed, particularly for the large flocks of sheep—most of which suffer from various pests and diseases easily controllable by relatively simple methods.

As in most of the neighboring countries, methods of grading and packing agricultural products are primitive and tend to lower the prices obtained, especially where export or further processing is involved. This applies in particular to fruit and nuts, of which Iraq grows a wide variety, and to tobacco. All the tobacco crop is sold to the government monopoly, but the unscientific methods used in picking, curing, and packing unfavorably affect the quality of the final product; in the absence of a policy of higher price offerings by the government monopoly for better grades, there is no incentive for improvement.

The quality of livestock products also leaves much to be desired. Hides and skins collected outside the abattoirs are frequently not properly prepared to prevent their deterioration before their arrival at the tannery. The wool collected from the various fat-tailed varieties of sheep makes good carpet materials and a valuable export product. Productivity, however, would be higher if better methods of shearing were introduced. This neglect may be partly due to the fact that milk rather than wool is considered the main product of the flocks.

There is no indication that the farming population at large would not accept better production methods if these were presented in a program which would begin to benefit the cultivator in ways concrete enough for him to see and modest enough to permit the social organism to adjust gradually and without serious disruption. The retarding factor in agricultural progress seems to be primarily the poverty of most farmers, who do not have sufficient land or money to make possible the purchase of new equipment or to give any incentive for the adoption of better techniques even if the knowledge of these were generally available. Moreover, under existing conditions, the cost of farm amortization, operation, and maintenance is high in relation to the cost of labor. Despite the difficulties, some progress is being made toward the use of modern agricultural methods, for which much of the terrain is admirably suited, and mechanization will no doubt become important.

Irrigation and Water Control

Present laws and regulations governing water use in Iraq have their foundation in the Ottoman civil code, though from time to time since 1923 amendments have been promulgated by the Iraqi Government. Noteworthy among these was a royal decree of 1932 which made the water laws, previously applied only in ten provinces, operative throughout the country.

Under the regulations now in force, the provincial governors are required to give assistance and facilities to cultivators and to ensure the distribution of water to their land; they are also responsible for the draining of pools and swamps and are empowered to include among the expenditures of the provincial administration the cost of constructing and maintaining irrigation works not directly undertaken by the central authorities. The "farm owner" must align his own watercourses and see to it that the water is properly distributed on his land.

In 1927 the Ministry of Communications and Works declared all rivers and waterways in the country to be "irrigation works," a term which covers all irrigation and flood protection installations; the Ministry reserved for the government the right to expropriate in the public interest private land for the construction of facilities. In practice, however, private owners may obtain licenses to construct small local installations if their projects are deemed worthwhile and they are able to make satisfactory agreements with neighboring proprietors.

All irrigation works of public importance, however, are constructed, maintained, and managed by an Irrigation Department. Government irrigation engineers determine the dimensions of canals and waterways, and the Department controls water distribution—interrupting supply when necessary. Labor may be requisitioned in cases of urgency when repair works for preventing loss of life or serious damage to land and property cannot be undertaken by the normal working force.

The death penalty may be imposed on any person who maliciously damages irrigation works in such a manner as to cause personal injury or damage to property. Obstruction of watercourses, fouling of water, damage to embankments, waste of water, obstruction of government officers, and refusal to supply labor under the requisitioning regulations are dealt with by fines, imprisonment, or both.

The Tigris and Euphrates have posed a challenge to the agricultural populations on their banks since earliest times. The ancient Mesopotamian empires were founded on the power and prosperity that came with the harnessing of the two rivers and the construction and management of an irrigation and drainage system which made possible a level of food production the country has not known since. The high technology and agricultural wealth of that day fluctuated with the fortunes of the various regimes and rose to new heights when Baghdad was the capital of the Moslem world; but they were almost obliterated by the onslaught of Mongol invaders in the thirteenth century. The population decimated, the canal system fallen into disrepair, and the old skills forgotten, Iraq became the victim rather than the beneficiary of its rivers. Seasonal floods made life along their banks precarious, and misuse of their waters salinized large areas of once fertile soil. Only in the last few generations has a new technology, borrowed from the West, begun to open the way to a reassertion of human control over these streams.

As recently as 1948 and 1954, devastating floods threw Iraq's economy into a state of acute emergency. Less spectacular, but no less serious in the long run, are the continuing problems of river use. These center on the development of adequate facilities for water supply, water storage, and drainage. In Turkey, as well as in Syria and in northern Iraq, both the Tigris and Euphrates, falling rapidly toward the sea, pick up a load of sediment (estimated to be five times that of the Nile) which endangers storage reservoirs by silting. Farther south in the Mesopotamian flatlands, where the river beds may be higher than the adjacent fields, high water brings the threat of floods, while poor drainage poses the problem of salinization. The annual sequence of high and low water is not well suited to the growing seasons, the first rise of the rivers coming too early for the summer crops.

In the absence of scientific irrigation procedure, which could alleviate these problems, the peasants are frequently forced to abandon poorly drained or salinized areas to marsh or desert and to engage in a form of shifting agriculture. Landlords are often reluctant to invest more than is absolutely necessary in their land. In the irrigated area only date cultivation has really thrived, and the poor yields of barley, wheat, cotton, and even rice—which frequently suffers from excessive flooding in the southern marshlands—reveal the pressing need for improved water management. Recent steps in this direction, together with parallel measures in other phases of agricultural technique and organization, hold promise for future advancement.

The Iraq Development Board, constituted in 1950, is now the main governmental instrument for Iraq's economic development. Work under its auspices is under way to restore the fertility of the central alluvial plain, and ambitious projects for flood control and water storage at Hawr al Habbaniyah on the Euphrates and Wadi ath Tharthar on the Tigris have been completed.

The total irrigation program of the Development Board would make available about 1.5 million hectares of new land (600,000 in the Euphrates basin and 900,000 in the Tigris basin); of this area 295,000 are to be developed over the next five years—at the rate of 59,000 per year.

The Euphrates

The harnessing of the Euphrates centers on the Hawr al Habbaniyah installation which serves for both flood protection and irrigation storage. The reservoir, completed in 1956, gives a substantial safety margin over the worst flood recorded. The waters of the Euphrates, according to the Development Board, are at present irrigating the following areas (in thousands of hectares). By gravity: Hindiyah Barrage system, 699; canals on the left bank, 210. By lift: upstream Hindiyah, 106; Ad Diwaniyah, 32; Ash Shinafiyah—An Nasiriyah, 109. Of this area, about 474,000 hectares are put annually to winter crops, utilizing about 270 cumecs (cubic meters of water per second) of the rivers's mean supply of 280 cumecs. The new storage provided at Hawr al Habbaniyah should increase the available supply to 440 cumecs, which will allow the development of some 600,000 hectares of new land in the Euphrates basin (see Map, Flood Control and Irrigation).

The Tigris

The Tigris lies close to the Zagros Mountains; along the whole length of its course from Asia Minor to the Persian Gulf it receives many tributaries. Within the river's wide catchment area local rainstorms, which in the north are quite frequent, can quickly affect the level of the river and produce destructive flash floods.

The most important flood prevention project on the Tigris is the diversion of excess water by the Samarra Barrage through an inlet channel to the Wadi ath Tharthar, a vast natural depression with its bottom at sea level and its rim rising to a height of 200 feet. The project, the cost of which was budgeted at near ID 10 million (an amount roughly equal to the damage which may be caused by one year's heavy flood), has been largely completed and since the spring of 1956 has been receiving water from the seasonal floods. Thus the

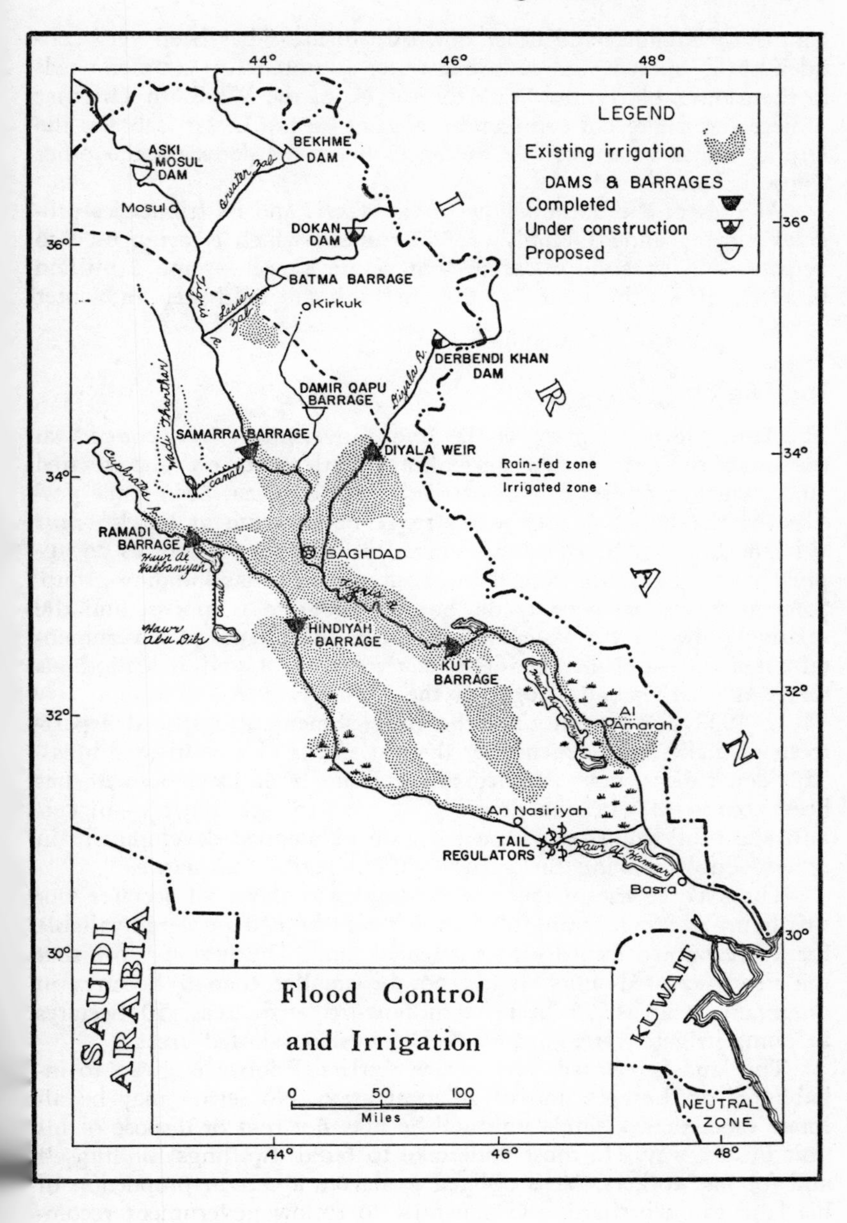

LEGEND
Existing irrigation
DAMS & BARRAGES
Completed
Under construction
Proposed
ASKI MOSUL DAM
BEKHME DAM
Greater Zab
Mosul
DOKAN DAM
BATMA BARRAGE
Kirkuk
Tigris R.
Lesser Zab
DERBENDI KHAN DAM
Diyala R.
DAMIR QAPU BARRAGE
SAMARRA BARRAGE
DIYALA WEIR
Rain-fed zone
Irrigated zone
Wadi Tharthar
canal
Euphrates R.
RAMADI BARRAGE
Hawr Al Habbaniyah
BAGHDAD
Hawr Abu Dibs
HINDIYAH BARRAGE
KUT BARRAGE
Al Amarah
An Nasiriyah
TAIL REGULATORS
Hawr Al Hammar
Basra
I R A N
SAUDI ARABIA
KUWAIT
NEUTRAL ZONE
44°
46°
48°
36°
34°
32°
30°
0 50 100
Miles

Flood Control and Irrigation

danger to Baghdad and other downstream areas has been very considerably decreased, and sufficient water is stored for summer needs in the foreseeable future. With the success of the Wadi ath Tharthar project and the recent completion of dams on the Lesser Zab and the Diyala, it has been possible to cancel plans for dams on the other Tigris tributaries.

At present the natural flow of the Tigris and its tributaries provides a mean annual supply of 350 cumecs, which is being used to irrigate—inadequately under present circumstances—some 2 million hectares, of which about 775,000 hectares are cultivated in winter crops.

Land Reform

The land-reform program of the Iraqi Government has centered on the establishment of new agricultural settlements on uncultivated land owned by the state. This particular emphasis has been made possible by the large uncultivated acreage in government hands (*miri sirf* land), and it has no doubt appealed to the authorities as an approach least likely to rouse the opposition of the landholding group. Some progress has been made, but the program is modest and the relatively low priority assigned to it and to other types of governmental assistance—outside the field of river control and irrigation—is reflected in the small budget of the Ministry of Agriculture.

In 1951 a law authorized the establishment of a special department to make arrangements for the settlement of uncultivated areas. This department, now attached to the Ministry of Development, has been concerned with the granting of land to new settlers—in certain areas following up with a program of planned development, in others simply making the grants without further assistance.

The average size of the new holdings was about 50 hectares, but this figure is less meaningful than it would be if data were available for a breakdown into dry and irrigated land. The law specifies that the newly created units should not be smaller than 5 hectares in mountainous areas, 25 hectares in flow-irrigated areas, 50 hectares in pump-irrigated areas, and 100 hectares in rain-fed areas.

The land is granted free to new settlers. Priority is given to inhabitants of the area and of adjacent areas. No settler may be allotted more than a single unit and he may not rent or dispose of his unit in any way. He must undertake to build dwellings for himself and for his workers; he is obliged to devote a certain proportion of his land to an orchard, and generally to follow government recommendations for cultivating the land. Ten years from the signing of the settlement contract the settler is given the freehold of the land (*tapu*). Thereafter he may leave the land to his heirs, provided that each share is not less than a quarter of the unit's acreage.

The best-known new settlement is Dujaylah, which was established in 1945 by special legislation. Situated 25 miles south of the Al Kut Barrage on the Tigris, an area which receives only six inches of rainfall annually, it consisted of some 70,000 hectares of semi-desert. When water was brought from the Tigris through the Dujaylah Canal, the sheikhs of five neighboring tribes claimed the area and were finally given about half of it against payments for the perpetual water rights to the canal; the rest of the land was to be divided into 25-hectare units.

The project at Dujaylah appears to have been quite successful, with the settlers, formerly poor sharecroppers, now more prosperous and contented. The number of applicants for such settlements greatly surpasses the available facilities in services and improvements. Particularly critical has been the failure to install drainage facilities, which has led to the salinization and abandonment of some tracts, and the lack of adequate guidance in improving agricultural and livestock practices among the new settlers.

15

INDUSTRIAL DEVELOPMENT

APART FROM THE EXPLOITATION OF OIL RESOURCES, INDUSTRY plays a minor role in Iraq's economy. Nevertheless, industrial activities grew between 1939 and 1956 at a rate probably exceeding that of the economy as a whole. The reason, apart from the expansion of petroleum production, was the increase in domestic manufacturing stimulated by the drastic reduction in imports during World War II. Woolen textiles and cigarettes were the only products manufactured in modern factories before 1939. Manufacture of cement, cotton textiles, distillery and tannery products, and vegetable oils was developed when the government was able to contribute part of the capital and when the end of hostilities made possible the importation of foreign machinery.

The total capital investment in industries other than petroleum increased from about ID 3 million in 1948 to about ID 20 million in 1954. The Iraq Development Board, established in 1950, has been responsible for the promotion and development of such major Iraqi industries as oil refining, cotton spinning and weaving, and cement production (see chap. 11).

The government has taken a very active interest in promoting the growth of industry. In 1956 laws to this end were further liberalized, industry received one of the highest priorities in the Iraq Development Program, and the Industrial Development Bank, a major financial support for modern enterprise, was provided with a substantial increase in authorized capital. The extent of these governmental measures to support industrial growth or to assume leadership in the promotion of industrial growth in Iraq reflects the demand for quicker industrialization. This demand is associated with the desire for higher income levels, fuller economic independence, greater military strength, and international prestige.

Experts who would emphasize agricultural development too

strongly become unpopular in government circles and were likely to be suspected of wishing to postpone the modernization of the economy. Yet practically all advisers who have been consulted on this subject during the last few years have cautioned against undue or over-rapid industrialization. The major reasons for this cautious approach were clearly set forth by Lord Salter (economic adviser to the Iraq Development Board in 1954–55) in his report of April 1955 on the development of Iraq's economy. The report emphasized that any substantial effort to create industries for which Iraq has no natural advantage would restrict the country's development, reduce its ability to finance imports, and would ultimately weaken rather than strengthen its military position. Iraq's economy, in Salter's opinion, is well suited to take an active part in international trade on a wide scale and has little to gain by becoming self-sufficient. The report also points out that Iraq is fortunate in having relatively abundant land resources and no population pressure and therefore that rapid industrialization is not such a necessity as it might be in underdeveloped areas where these conditions are reversed.

Realizing that it would not be too easy to reconcile all this advice with the ambitions of a young nation impatient of achievement, the government decided to have the problems of industrial development studied further and for this engaged an American firm of consultants, Arthur D. Little, Inc. Sponsored jointly by the International Cooperation Administration and the Iraq Development Board, the report drawn up by the company is of major interest since in 1957 it became the basis for the official plan for Iraq's industrial development. It offers, in effect, an outline for industrial expansion requiring an investment of approximately $120 million over a six-year period.

The Little report points out that growing foodstuffs for domestic and export markets is the only source of income for a great majority of the population and that this will remain so in the foreseeable future; it states, however, that Iraq at the moment is entirely neglecting or inadequately using some available resources which could enlarge industrial activity (such as sulfur, gypsum, salt, clay, calcite, sand and gravel). As a matter of principle the report does not recommend any industrial venture unless it can be anticipated to produce at a cost below the landed price of comparable imported goods or materials before import duty has been levied. In contrast to some other advisers, the report does not limit itself to industries designed to supply the domestic market, but in certain cases recommends plants that would produce mainly for export markets.

While the government has endeavored to carry out a substantial number of the projects recommended by the Little report, it was already apparent in 1956 that increased capacity resulting from previous plant expansion and new industrial enterprises exceeded the current market demand. Although the recommendations of the report present a very clear picture of the ultimate goals of industrial growth, it appears that at the present time the Iraqi economy has not achieved the basic foundation which is necessary for rapid industrial progress. Before industrialization can take place on a large scale the factors which impede Iraq's industrial potential must be overcome. The country's capacity for industrial growth is limited primarily by the shortage of skilled labor and technical and managerial personnel; the small domestic market; an inability to compete with foreign products; and the timidity of private initiative.

The illiteracy of large numbers of Iraqi workers makes it hard to train them for skilled or technical work, but those whose level of education has fitted them for the industrial apprenticeships provided by large companies have demonstrated an ability to develop a fair degree of skill. Skilled workers in especially short supply are machine operators, mechanics, construction workers, and English-language clerks and stenographers. The shortage of efficient managers is even more acute and the Iraqi Government is considering adopting the recommendations in the Little report that the Industrial Development Bank finance foreign managerial assistance until sufficient Iraqi personnel have been trained.

The small size of the internal market presents another difficulty, though the proportion of the population purchasing Iraqi-produced goods should increase as more and better paid jobs are provided by development projects.

One of the most important measures that might be taken for the improvement of the domestic market would be the development of rural handicraft industries, which would help to raise the low purchasing power of the rural population. This has been suggested in an excellent survey of handicrafts by the International Labour Office in 1952; very little action, however, has been taken in this direction. The principal hope is that beginning with the handicraft industry the improvement in quality of domestic raw materials (wool, leather, tobacco, cotton, jute) by better methods of sorting and grading and the development of technical skills by the labor force will eventually produce a situation in which an effective challenge may be presented to foreign imports. Iraq is handicapped in developing a foreign, especially European, market by the high cost of transportation from Basra via the Persian Gulf and the Red Sea, but the chief impediment is the poor quality of the goods produced.

Capital for private investment is lacking because large amounts accumulated from agriculture are invested primarily in urban or rural property, which offers security and social prestige, or in trade where the investor expects a high rate of return. Major investments by private entrepreneurs have been made only with the assurance of government financial assistance. The timidity of private initiative is an important factor in the government's increasing tendency since 1956 to assume leadership in promoting and developing major industries. Lack of adequate external capital equipment (such as power and transportation facilities), low productivity of labor, the narrow range of industrial raw materials of adequate quality (with the exception of petroleum), and the prohibitive cost of importing raw materials from distant sources—all combine to make the cost of establishing and running industries in Iraq very high. Nevertheless, several industries are now beginning to overcome these handicaps (including cement production, cotton spinning and weaving, sugar refining, and the manufacture of beer).

Composition of Industry

Of the more than 23,000 industrial establishments in Iraq in 1954, only 300, or a little over 1 percent, employed more than 20 persons each. At the same time, however, some 38,000 workers—close to 40 percent of the industrial labor force—were employed in this small group of large- and medium-size enterprises.

In Iraq, as elsewhere in the Middle East, various corporate forms are applied to what is in effect family ownership of businesses. At the present time there is still no developed capital market; there are nevertheless beginnings of a small market in stocks and shares traded mainly through the banks. While private capital is becoming increasingly available for modern industry, new enterprises still depend substantially on financial assistance from the government. It should be noted that public participation in business in Iraq often produces certain specific disadvantages. When the economic criteria of profit and loss are abandoned, the choice of industry and/or techniques to be utilized may be such that the industry will never become economically viable. There is a strong tendency to adopt overmechanized productive methods for prestige reasons. Much of the incentive for government participation may be opportunities for graft and nepotism.

Government attempts to promote industrialization began with the Law for the Encouragement of Industries in 1929, which exempted industrial machinery and certain raw materials from customs duties and also exempted new industries from certain taxes. This law was replaced in 1950 by new legislation which granted limited exemptions from income and surtaxes for four years; exemptions from property tax for 10 years; and use, rent-free, of government land not in excess of 25,000 square meters for a period of 10 years. Iraqi-owned industrial enterprises could qualify for these benefits so long as they primarily used raw materials available in Iraq or produced the types of goods which were being imported in considerable quantities.

These regulations were extended further in 1955 to provide exemptions from corporate profit taxes for five years and from taxation on income—up to 25 percent of annual profits—set aside to be reinvested in industry. To be eligible for these benefits the enterprise must use machinery valued at more than ID 5,000, must be at least 55 percent Iraqi-owned, must not employ more than 10 percent non-Iraqi personnel, and must use principally machinery rather than manual labor.

Financial assistance is rendered mainly through the government owned Industrial Bank. Up to the end of its operational year 1953–54 the Industrial Bank made 685 loans totaling ID 2.2 million and participated in the share capital of a number of companies.

The operations of the Industrial Bank are sometimes criticized as being too concentrated on large companies which would perhaps have no difficulty in obtaining private subscriptions to their capital. The Industrial Bank's participation in most of the above-mentioned companies represents between 20 to 30 percent of ownership; in no case does it exceed 50 percent.

Despite the growth of modern industrial installations, the large majority of Iraqi enterprises still consists of small concerns employing no more than five persons. In these establishments skills are not highly developed, the manufacturing process is rudimentary, and few or no improvements have been introduced since the project was inaugurated. This applies particularly to two industries: hand-loomed textiles, and mat making and basketry. Hand-made textiles are still produced at home in antiquated pit-looms or in workshops with flying shuttle pit-looms; mat makers and basket weavers, using traditional methods, produce goods which cannot compare in quality and price with imported reed products. Other handicraft industries such as ceramics, metalwork, iron and steel fabrication, leatherwork, and the processing of food, which provide many of the basic needs of the majority of the population, are characterized by low productivity; poor organization in processing, distribution, and marketing; crude methods of production; and mediocre quality.

Small family enterprises may also include services such as dyeing, tailoring, and carpentry, and artistic handicrafts such as jewelry and copperwork, embroidery, and rug making. Some of this work is of excellent quality, particularly the jewelry and copperwork of Baghdad and the very fine yarn spun by women in the villages. In most cases, however, the quality of handicraft work appears to have seriously deteriorated in recent years.

Traditional craft enterprises are increasingly being displaced by more modern enterprises. In many instances, however, the traditional artisan has sufficient basic skills to switch quickly to a trade—such as plumbing, bricklaying, mechanical work, electrical work, or foundry work—that fulfills the demands of a more advanced economy.

Modern Industries

Petroleum

Before 1951, Iraq's oil revenues were small, being used primarily to meet foreign exchange expenditures. Today these revenues are the cornerstone of the national economy. Not only are they used to balance the budget, they also stabilize the currency, help maintain a surplus balance of payments, and play a decisive role in financing the development of the economy through such bodies as the Development Board and the Industrial Bank.

Proved reserves of crude oil in Iraq as of 1954 were estimated at 1.9 billion metric tons, an amount which—at a rate of extraction of 30 million tons a year—should last for at least 63 years. While annual output is increasing beyond this volume, it seems most likely that actual reserves exceed proved reserves.

Petroleum exploitation in Iraq is predominantly in the hands of three companies which have equal amounts of capital invested: the Iraq Petroleum Company (IPC), the Mosul Petroleum Company (MPC), and the Basra Petroleum Company (BPC). In each of these companies, 95 percent of the ownership is shared equally by the Anglo-Iranian Oil Company, Royal Dutch Shell, the Compagnie Française des Petroles, and the Near East Development Corporation (owned jointly by Standard Oil of New Jersey and the Mobil Overseas Oil Company) and 5 percent is controlled by the Gulbenkian interests. In addition, the Khanaqin Oil Company, a subsidiary of the Anglo-Iranian Oil Company, has a small concession adjoining the Iranian border.

The growth of the petroleum industry since 1940 is shown in

Table 12. At first, efforts to develop production were concentrated mainly on the Iraq Petroleum Company's Kirkuk field, where oil is found as near the surface as 2,500 to 2,800 feet and drilling costs are consequently low. Production capacity has been increasing more rapidly than transport facilities. Until 1949 there were only two 12-inch pipelines, with an annual capacity of over 2 million tons each—one to Tripoli in Lebanon, the other to Haifa in Palestine. At the outbreak of war with Israel in 1947 the Haifa pipeline was shut down and work was halted on an additional 16-inch pipeline to Haifa, which was to have an annual capacity of 4 million tons. With the completion of another 16-inch pipeline to Tripoli in 1949, output in 1950 rose again to 6 million tons. Another large-diameter pipeline with an annual capacity of 13.5 million tons, linking the Kirkuk field to Baniyas in Syria, was completed in 1952. (In addition to the pipelines to the Mediterranean, a new one links the BPC-operated wells to Iraq's own oil terminal port of Al Faw.)

In the meantime, the activities of the Basra Petroleum Company and the Mosul Petroleum Company led to the discovery of the Ayn Zalah and Butmah oilfields in the Mosul area and the Az Zubayr and Rumaylah oilfields near Basra. A smaller oilfield has been discovered by the Khanaqin Oil Company at Naft Khaneh. A substantial increase in Iraq's petroleum export capacity resulted from the development of these fields and the installation of oil handling and transportation facilities.

Until lately, 70 percent of the domestic market for petroleum products was served by the small refinery of the Khanaqin Oil Company at Alwand (recently purchased by the government); the rest of the market was supplied by the Abadan refinery in Iran. A new, large oil refinery was completed near Baghdad in 1955 and the construction of a lubricating-oil plant was started in the same year by the Government Oil Refineries Administration. This brought the joint capacity of the existing refineries to 1.8 million tons per year, which at present exceeds domestic requirements.

The large increase in government revenues from oil operations has been accelerated by changes in the terms of payments agreed upon with the oil companies. An agreement of 1952 between the Iraqi Government and the companies provided for an equal sharing of profits, which were to be determined before the deduction of foreign taxes. A revision of this agreement in March 1955 increased the government's proportion of the receipts. This was accomplished by changing the method of computing profits. The IPC had been selling crude oil at a discount under posted prices and deducting the discount as a cost. By the new agreement, retroactive to 1954, the maximum discount allowed in the computation of profits was lowered from 17.5 to 2 shillings per ton of Kirkuk crude oil.

The 1952 agreement gave the Iraqi Government the right to demand higher royalties from the foreign-owned oil companies if neighboring Middle Eastern government increased their share of proceeds derived from oil production. The companies agreed to employ the maximum possible number of Iraqi workers consistent with efficiency and to appoint Iraqis to their boards of directors. The right of the Iraqi Government to obtain crude oil for its refineries at the low price of 77 cents per ton was also guaranteed.

The government also was able to ensure that oil would continue to provide an important source of public revenue regardless of unforeseen developments or of any changes that the foreign oil companies might make in their policies. The oil companies agreed to produce a minimum of 30 million tons of crude oil a year and to guarantee to the government a minimum payment of $14 million a year for two years if production had to be halted for any reason beyond their control. In agreeing to such terms, the oil companies were no doubt influenced by the nationalization of the oil industry in Iran, the 50/50 profitsharing arrangement with Saudi Arabia, and the declaration by Prime Minister Nuri as-Said that unless certain Iraqi demands to the oil industry were met the foreign oil concessions would be withdrawn.

As indicated in Table 13, most oil exports go to the European market. In 1954 almost 90 percent went to OEEC (Organization for European Economic Cooperation) countries, including the United Kingdom.

The relations of the petroleum companies with the government and with their labor force (over 16,000 employees) are relatively good. They have been well in advance of other industrial enterprises in providing housing and health services and in instituting labor-training schemes for their personnel (see chap. 12).

Other Modern Industries

Iraq has a good supply of certain agricultural raw materials: cotton (supplying fiber and cotton seed), wool, hides and skins, tobacco, and sesame oil. As irrigation is extended, agriculture will become increasingly important as a source of additional quantities of cotton and oil seeds, possibly also sugarbeets and cane, soy beans, and jute.

Preliminary geological surveys have indicated that Iraq may contain appreciable deposits of iron ore, copper, sulfur and sulfur compounds, gypsum, bitumen, dolomite, calcite, and different varieties of marble; up to the present, little use has been made of these minerals. A large and potentially valuable salt dome has been located near Basra, but so far salt is produced only by solar evaoporation, the major installation of this kind being at Al Faw.

Iraq has to import rayon yarn, timber, jute, copra, sheet aluminum, structural steel and chemicals.

The abundant supplies of petroleum and natural gas provide a cheap source of raw material and fuel for petrochemical industries. The first immediate use of natural gas will be for a new power plant at Dibs near Kirkuk.

Electricity for Baghdad is supplied by the recently nationalized Baghdad Light and Power Company, a thermoelectric fuel-oil installation previously owned by British-Belgian interests. The plant has an installed capacity of 41,000 kwh. This has been insufficient for the total requirements of the city, but a new plant, also using fuel oil, is being built.

In other parts of the country, power is generated by small municipal power stations. Large undertakings, such as the IPC at Kirkuk and the Port Authority of Basra, generate their own electricity and also supply the surrounding areas. Various new industries are also generating their own power because of the high cost of municipal supplies and in many cases lack of accessibility to them (see Table 14).

In 1954, Iraq's first industrial census, excluding petroleum mining and refining, was taken. It showed a total of 23,226 establishments employing 79,121 persons, a wage bill of ID 5.5 million, and total sales valued at ID 34.3 million. The industries described below represent the major industrial enterprises in 1956 (see Table 15).

The cotton textile industry consists of 1 firm established in Baghdad in 1948 (Iraq Spinning and Weaving Company) and a new mill under construction in Mosul. The first establishment has 40,000 spindles, 1,000 looms, and machinery for carding, combing, finishing, bleaching, and dyeing. The second mill is being built by the Development Board with 25,000 spindles and 630 looms. On its completion (scheduled for the last quarter of 1957) about two thirds of the country's requirements should be fulfilled.

While facilities for the production of cotton textiles are being expanded, it was reported in early 1957 that the industry was not operating at full capacity. The outlook for the cotton industry was improved in the last quarter of 1957 with a cotton crop of 30,000 tons, as compared to 25,000 in the previous year. It was further reported that the new cotton crop was of good quality.

Woolen textiles have been manufactured for many years. The 3 existing firms, all in Baghdad, produce about 1.2 million yards; a similar quantity is imported. These firms depended heavily upon army contracts until the army built its own textile establishment; they are now attempting to develop the civilian market, but are as yet unable to compete with high-grade imported products. The quality of domestic wool is very poor. In 1957 it deteriorated further due to disease among flocks and poor handling during the wet season.

Additional textile industries include artificial and natural silk weaving (6 establishments) and jute spinning and weaving (1 establishment).

Food-processing industries include many flour mills and bakeries, (one in Baghdad is highly mechanized), 3 sugar refineries, 3 *araq* distilleries (which use surplus dates as raw material), 1 brewery, about 30 date-packing factories, and many smaller establishments. Iraq's brewing, date-packing, and sugar refining industries are modern and maintain relatively high standards of quality.

The soap and vegetable oils industry, concentrated in Baghdad, consists of 2 major, 5 medium-size, and 16 small producers. The largest plant, owned by the Vegetable Oil Extraction Company, is capitalized at ID 600,000; its 1953 production was 2,000 tons. Although the total capacity of all these plants is now equal to domestic requirements, the public continues to buy the many imported brands of soap to which it has become accustomed.

There are 7 tanneries in Baghdad and 5 in Mosul. Production for 1954 was estimated at 5 million square feet of upper leather and about 500 tons of sole leather. The industry is handicapped by the poor quality of cattle skins, and high quality upper leather must be imported.

The mechanized tobacco industry consists of 6 factories in Baghdad; hand-made cigarettes are produced at a number of establishments in Baghdad and Mosul. The industry uses domestic tobacco, of which 8,816 metric tons were produced in 1954 for the government tobacco monopoly. In 1955 the government had under study a proposal to extend the tobacco monopoly's authority over manufacturing as well as growing. The proposals were opposed, however, by the three largest manufacturers and were shelved for the time being.

Bricks are made locally throughout Iraq. Many plants which use sun-drying methods could improve the quality of their output and increase it by as much as 50 percent by installing steam-heated drying equipment. The brick industry recently curtailed production after overexpansion.

The cement industry consisted in early 1957 of a single firm (Iraq Cement Company) near Baghdad which produced 198,000 tons of cement in 1954 but has increased its capacity since. Three other private plants, 2 in central Iraq and 1 in Mosul, were completed in 1956, and 2 additional plants were being built by the Development Board in the neighborhood of the Dokan and Derbendi Khan dams in the north.

Among metal products manufactured in the country are metal furniture and aluminum ware produced in Baghdad from imported sheet. An aluminum sheet-rolling mill that will use imported ingots has recently been established.

There is one modern shoe factory, with a productive capacity estimated at 30,000 pairs of shoes per year.

A petrochemical sulfur plant has recently been planned by the government. Ammonium sulfate, a fertilizer, will be its major product; by-products may include sulfur, carbon black, and cement.

16

DOMESTIC AND FOREIGN TRADE

DOMESTIC TRADE IN IRAQ DISPLAYS A DICHOTOMY WHICH, TO ONE degree or another, has characterized internal commerce throughout the Middle Eastern countries since the entry into the area of western mercantile patterns. To satisfy the demands of a western-influenced urban elite a lively import business in western luxury goods and other products has developed in Baghdad and Basra. But the bulk of trading in the towns and rural areas is done through the traditional bazaars and in ways that have altered very little over the past fifty years.

Efforts to develop the national economy are severely taxing the traditional methods of distribution. In general, the commercial community has shown itself reluctant to abandon old methods, and rationalization of commercial practice is in any event made difficult by deficiencies in transportation facilities, credit resources, and other requirements of modern trade. Nevertheless, new patterns of trade are coming in alongside the old ones, and they involve not only changes in the way goods are distributed but major shifts in the relationships between producer, merchant, and consumer.

A profound change has taken place recently in the complexion of the business community itself. Before World War II, domestic trade was dominated almost entirely by the Jewish minority; foreign commerce was divided between Jewish and British firms. Wartime opportunities for speculation and profit considerably enlarged the commercial community and the exodus of almost all Jews in 1949 and 1950 left a void in commercial, credit, and transport institutions which has had to be filled by Iraqis still inexperienced in trade and lacking the contacts possessed by their predecessors. A growing, if not yet dominant, element in this new group are the Shiites, who have seized the opportunity to assert themselves in commerce. In the countryside, with the disappearance of the Jewish moneylender, the role of creditor has shifted increasingly to the landlord and sheikh. And where once the collection and wholesale distribution of agricultural produce was the responsibility of the merchant, today the landowner or sheikh often ships produce directly to the market in his own motor launch or truck.

Trade has traditionally been a respected occupation in Islam, and only in communities where nomadic values are still strong are the "people of the market" looked upon with contempt. In conceding until recently the larger part of their domestic commerce to other hands Iraqi Moslems have by no means been averse to the profits of trade but rather appear to have been disadvantaged in competition with non-Moslems by a rigidly conservative pattern which discouraged the use of certain marketing techniques.

The merchant in the Middle East traditionally has functioned as more than the link between producer and consumer. When he actually traveled with his goods he was the conveyor of news between towns and villages, and was often moneylender as well as trader. Many Iraqi merchants still combine these activities, but the trend is toward greater specialization and the new businessman is less often both merchant and banker.

Foreign trade has assumed a position of major importance in the national economy. Iraq produces most of the food, fuel, and tobacco it needs, and some of the building materials, but most of its other needs must be imported. Almost all capital goods required for development are purchased abroad, and even local industries and handicrafts rely in part on imported raw materials. A considerable volume of agricultural products, such as dates and barley, is sent abroad and a fall in world prices affects domestic purchasing power almost as strongly as a poor harvest. Heavy dependence on the export of primary products has the effect of subjecting an important part of Iraq's economy to the vagaries of the world market and internal natural conditions, but this vulnerability will diminish as the country's industries multiply and as agricultural production is increased and diversified. In the meantime Iraq has the usual problems of the producer of primary products. Aside from its long-range development programs, the government is attempting to meet these problems by regulating foreign trade and by encouraging exports through special incentives and trade agreements.

A second feature of Iraq's foreign trade is the overriding significance of the oil industry. Oil exports offset a trade deficit which otherwise would drastically hinder, if not completely halt, the country's ambitious development schemes. These exports have likewise furnished revenues which have enabled the country to control strong inflationary pressures in its developing economy during the past seven years by easing import restrictions on consumer and capital goods.

A third factor affecting Iraq's foreign trade is the nature of its transportation arrangements. Oil is transported out of the country by pipeline to the Mediterranean, but, with no Iraqi port on the Mediterranean, ships carrying cargo from Iraq's only port at Basra on the Persian Gulf to markets in Europe and America must pass through the Suez Canal, and any stoppage in that waterway immediately and drastically affects Iraq. In addition to Iraqi exports and imports, some goods in transit through Iraq—most of them from the United Kingdom to the Orient or to and from Iran—may be similarly affected. Finally, almost all of this seaborne trade is carried in foreign ships—British, Dutch, Norwegian, German, and Japanese, in that order. The closure of the Suez Canal in late 1956 necessitated a painful, if temporary, readjustment of this whole system, and alternative routes were called into use; shortages arose, encouraging speculative hoarding of "scarce" goods. Ship detours around the Cape of Good Hope and increased utilization of land routes to Mediterranean ports increased transport charges by 10 percent. International air traffic, forced to avoid Syria, was rescheduled to Iraqi airports.

Determinants of Domestic Trade

Iraqi commercial operations are beset by a number of difficulties which slow the process of distribution: an inadequate transport system, lack of market information and credit, and a generally limited market. As a result, industrial enterprises habitually carry huge stocks to support production for long periods of time. Established merchants and wealthy consumers who recognize the inflexibility of the marketing structure seek to protect themselves by hoarding whenever any crisis seems imminent. A poor knowledge of the market encourages a rapid turnover and a small inventory. In such an environment, the newcomer and the small trader suffer heavy disabilities by comparison with the large and established merchant.

The domestic market is subject not only to the indirect influence of government development spending but to the direct effects of close official regulation of and actual participation in, business. Government control embraces most of the transportation system—railways, bus companies, airlines, shipping companies, and the Port of Basra. The government is a stockholder in commercial and development banks and in several important industries. While there is no direct control imposed on private enterprise, regulations concerning prices and profits, taxation, extensive state trading, and the limitation of certain commercial occupations to Iraqis have affected domestic trade.

The government also participates in commerce through its imports for economic development. Furthermore, during the Korean war a policy of state trading was initiated in order to stock goods which might come into short supply. Although such policies were temporary, the commercial community, contemplating the possibility of a depressed price, was reluctant to buy the items which the authorities were also accumulating. The government has further controlled the distribution and sale of a number of domestic goods such as petroleum by-products, asphalt, raw tobacco, and dates.

The government has responded to inflationary price rises in the cities by imposing price ceilings and lowering profit margins. Price regulations were established for imports of farm machinery, automobiles, and medicines; a maximum price was set for fruits, vegetables, and meat sold through retail shops; and the government has subsidized the price of bread. The price of cotton has been set below the world level to assist the domestic cotton industry. Price restrictions, however, have been only moderately successful since smuggling and illicit trade are carried on quite openly.

In Iraq's small domestic market the average merchant has little incentive to improve his stock or to introduce new merchandise, for price and the ability to deliver rather than quality and type of goods are primary considerations with his customers. The peasant receives most if not all of his income in the form of agricultural produce rather than cash, and his purchases consist mainly of a few staples; thus in 1954 estimates indicated that some 90 percent of the population had practically no impact on the commercial sector. In 1956 per capita purchases averaged a mere ID 15. For the rural majority, still more familiar with barter than cash transactions, changes in purchasing power derive only indirectly from changes in the value of money, while such natural factors as crop yields have a direct impact. A poor harvest or a drop in the world price for grain has a marked effect on the market and can bankrupt numbers of small retail merchants.

The market is, however, gradually expanding. Since 1951 the demand for consumer imports has increased considerably and there has been a substantial rise in credit sales. The impact of a growing middle-income group is reflected, for example, in the nature of automobile imports, which previously had been limited to large American cars; more recently they have included an increasing number of small, medium-priced European automobiles. This expanding market is still confined to the large towns and cities, such as Baghdad and Basra, where wages are relatively high. Moreover, much of the increased demand is confined to imported goods which have acquired higher prestige value than domestically produced articles.

16. *Determinants of Domestic Trade*

The recent urban-centered expansion of the domestic market is accompanied by some rationalization of commercial practice. Advertising through the use of showrooms, newspapers, and films is beginning to attract potential consumers. A developing wholesale apparatus is bridging the gap between producer and retailer, and the output of a small but growing domestic light industry may be expected further to stimulate consumer demand. Ultimately, however, any large expansion of Iraq's internal commerce hinges on the government's development program successfully increasing productivity and raising the buying power of the population.

Two essentials of modern commerce—adequate credit and systematic market information—have developed only slowly and with difficulty in Moslem countries. Traditionally the religious injunction against the taking of interest worked against the growth of credit institutions in Moslem society, and the Moslem merchant was forced to resort to devious and generally disapproved means of obtaining credit. A further handicap was present in the indifference of the old-style merchant to statistical information, which was no doubt related to his highly personal and informal way of doing business. Direct and indirect western influence, including the example of European and indigenous non-Moslem enterprises in the country, has produced a new generation of Iraqi Moslem businessmen who have adopted modern methods and deprecate the religious inhibitions and "backwardness" of their more conservative coreligionists.

The uneven spread of the new patterns is evident in the extreme sensitivity of Iraq's domestic commerce to rumor and in the tendency of the entrepreneur to buy or sell on a quick turnover basis with little regard to such long-range market information as might be available to him. This tendency is of course reinforced by objective factors such as inadequate storage and transport facilities, which make it difficult for dealers either to hold perishable goods or to adjust deliveries to changes in demand. The organization of credit also shows the conflict between the demands of large-scale modern enterprise and the needs of the small merchant. The banking system, constructed on the western model, provides credit at legally established rates; insurance is extended by both a national insurance company, established in 1950, and by branches of foreign firms, mainly British. The small trader has been accustomed to relying on the sarrafs, the traditional moneylenders of the area. The sarrafs charged high rates but did offer short-term money on conditions their clients could meet, and the reduction in the number of these small bankers has left a gap. Since the large commercial banks extend loans on the basis of collateral rather than the borrower's personal reputation for reliability and business acumen, the small businessman is at a serious disadvantage in comparison with the large and better-established firm. Moreover, Iraq has not yet developed an organized capital market. Operated within the larger banks, the market for stocks is still small and confined to industrial shares. The government has indicated its interest in extending credit on easier terms but has yet to take steps effectively to meet this need.

Commercial operations in most Middle Eastern countries suffer from a shortage of adequate storage facilities for merchandise, including customs sheds, bonded warehouses, and, particularly, grain silos. Iraq has made considerable progress in this respect but the lack is still great in rural areas. Still other problems are the varying standards of weights and measures, the lack of uniform grading and packing practices, and the number of intermediaries between producer and consumer. All of these deficiencies complete a pattern in which the marketing of goods is extremely costly and wasteful. The transportation system is both inefficient and expensive; it constitutes an effective limitation to the expansion of the country's domestic trade.

Marketing

Baghdad, the commercial as well as political capital of Iraq, dominates the wholesale and import trade and is the center from which the transportation arteries of the country radiate into the rural and desert areas. As a main distribution point the city directly serves the provinces of Baghdad, Al Hillah, Diyala, Ad Dulaym, Karbala, Al Kut, and Ad Diwaniyah. Its Chamber of Commerce exerts strong influence in national business life.

Mosul, the second most important distribution point and the third major wholesale center, serves Mosul province and the Jazirah desert and receives the agricultural produce of northern Iraq. Basra, Iraq's only seaport and second most important center in the wholesale and import trade, serves Al Amarah, Al Basra, and Al Muntafiq provinces. Kirkuk supplements Mosul as an agricultural distribution center in the north and is the commercial focus of the mountain provinces of Kirkuk, As Sulaymaniyah, and Irbil.

The 1956 census of distribution and trade (excluding purchases made by government agencies and contractors and by large enterprises such as the oil industry) reveals Baghdad's supremacy in wholesale trade. In that year there were some 1,600 wholesale businesses in Iraq employing 5,000 people; 600 of these were located in Baghdad and employed almost 2,200 people. The value in sales was ID 54 million in the country as a whole, while Baghdad wholesalers sold some ID 33.6 million of this amount. Most wholesalers tend to specialize in one commodity or in a line of similar products; only a few also engage in retail trade. In 1956 the largest group of wholesalers dealt in grains, the next largest in textiles, and the third in groceries and dates.

Wholesale goods, particularly agricultural produce, pass through many hands before reaching the major collection centers for distribution; and at each step the price increases. Because it is difficult to assess the size of his market the wholesale merchant feels compelled to pay the lowest possible price to the producer or cultivator and to attach the widest possible profit margin to the price before selling. The fellah, often in debt to the merchant, is usually bested in the transaction and the price he obtains is far below that charged the ultimate consumer.

Competition is keen in the wholesale sector, and because the market is not tightly organized it is difficult to construct effective monopolies. In the 1940's, however, when speculation, profiteering, and attempts to corner large volumes of essential goods and foodstuffs were widespread, the government initiated legislation to curb monopolistic practices and to ensure an adequate supply of goods to consumers. This legislation was not entirely successful nor did it extend to the operation of government monopolies. For example, tobacco cultivators and merchants, protected by a government monopoly, have been able to charge prices to the tobacco industry up to twice the original cost and force the industry to accept low-grade or deteriorated tobacco, thus encouraging illicit tobacco sales.

While established merchants have been able to expand their operations steadily, many new wholesalers and importers and those attempting to add new lines to their business have suffered in the past few years from miscalculations about the market. Encouraged by the rising volume of sales, wholesalers have overestimated the market and have found themselves with large inventories and a shortage of cash. Their difficulties have been intensified by the reduction of credit facilities and the growing practice of selling on terms. Unfamiliar with the aggressive sales techniques which might have enabled them to move their stock, they have tended to wait for customers to come to them and have done little to create a new demand.

Government policy has favored imports from hard currency countries by bona fide merchants who possess firmly established contacts and distribution facilities and who are experienced in dealing in such products. While it is fairly easy to obtain foreign exchange on the black market or to deal through the free-trade market in Beirut, it is the large dealer with ready capital rather than the small merchant with limited funds who can take advantage of this circumstance. Government attempts to instill confidence in the domestic market by easing certain import licensing and exchange restrictions apparently have only heightened the distress of the small traders, who inevitably demand that the government restrict imports so as to enable them to liquidate their inventories. The government has therefore reverted to a more rigid enforcement of its previous policy of granting licenses (particularly for luxury imports) only to a few well-established firms.

Retail activity in Iraq is less centralized than the wholesale trade, although Baghdad, with its large population, can boast of more retail shops than any other city in the country. The Holy Cities, An Najaf, Al Kufah, Karbala, and Al Kazimiyah, with their transient population of pilgrims, are likewise active consumer towns. In 1956, Iraq had approximately 36,000 retail establishments, employing some 47,000 persons (many of them women), with annual sales estimated at ID 82.6 million. Retail goods move through many channels: a few large department stores; smaller stores catering to the middle class in imported goods; the bazaars; the small town markets; cooperative stores; the peddlers covering established routes; and the traveling merchants visiting villages and tribes.

More than two thirds of the retail businesses are one-man shops specializing in a single or related group of commodities. These small dealers, operating in a highly saturated market served by hundreds of competitors, depend for their livelihood on a small volume of sales with a high margin of profit. It is difficult for such a dealer to increase his minute portion of the market; advertising is hardly feasible because the goods rarely carry a known brand and the customer must see the commodity with his own eyes and examine it carefully before he will purchase it.

It is only in direct negotiation between buyer and seller that supply and demand are finally accommodated and ultimate price determined. An extended process of bargaining normally ensues. The vendor proposes his highest price and the customer, who has made an active survey of the goods available—a housewife usually buys daily the exact quantities she needs and has as much knowledge of the market as the shopkeeper—makes a counteroffer; ultimately a mutually satisfactory price is agreed upon. The bargaining pattern, with its emphasis on personal and informal negotiation, extends into larger transactions; even in understandings involving sizable sums of money, Iraqis, like other Middle Easterners, tend to regard a verbal commitment as sufficient.

The bazaar is a characteristic commercial institution in Iraq. Situated in the older districts of the larger towns and cities, it is usually divided into sections dealing in particular goods: foodstuffs, clothing, metalware, leather goods, etc. The bazaars were once the commercial heart of the towns. Centers for the collection and distribution of all the retail goods available to the population, their wares were a reflection of the society's whole range of taste and their activities were an important part of the urban community's everyday life.

The organization of the bazaar and the activities of its merchants exhibit a number of differences according to the function and perishability of the many goods offered. The center of the bazaar is usually devoted to daily necessities for which there is a steady demand; it is most active in the morning. The peripheral areas cater more to special wants and to the luxury trade; here the activity is greatest in the afternoon when white-collar workers are leaving their offices.

The dealer in staple items, for which demand and price are subject to little variation, engages in a minimum of bargaining with his customers; that which does take place tends to be ritualized rather than earnest. The goods carried by such a merchant—or produced by him if he is a craftsman—are defined by his experience with a steady number of clients whom he usually knows.

By contrast, there are those speculative traders who must sell their complete stock the same day they acquire it. They deal in perishable goods—fruits, meats, vegetables—or any kind of goods which may prove profitable at the moment. Profits are relatively high but the market is not assured, and the dealer faces disaster if he fails to clear out his stock quickly. The prices asked by these dealers are apt to fall hourly, and hawking and bargaining become more vigorous by late afternoon. The merchant who deals in durable luxury goods faces a different but comparable situation. He is vulnerable, not because he must sell his complete stock daily, but because the demand for his goods is unpredictable and changes in taste threaten him if he holds his stock too long. He must at once operate with a high markup and strive to let no customer leave his premises without having made a purchase.

The country market is a smaller bazaar found in the larger rural centers. Peasants come to these markets from the surrounding villages, some of which may be a considerable distance. At the market the peasant may sell part of his crop and perhaps some chickens and eggs, and he buys such things as tea, sugar, cloth, salt, and cigarettes. The social aspect of the regular visit to the country market is perhaps as important as the economic one, and it provides as strong a motive for the fellah to go as do the meager necessities he will buy. Market day provides some relief from the rigors of workaday existence in the opportunity to exchange news and rumors and to wear a best jacket or dress.

Until comparatively recently Iraq's tribal nomads tended to satisfy part of their requirements for things they did not themselves produce by periodically raiding villages, towns, and caravans. Government police power has put an end to this practice. Today those nomads who still follow an extensive pastoral cycle visit the market seasonally to exchange meat, hides, and cheese for coffee, sugar, grain, tobacco, and such luxuries as they can afford. Tribes are also visited by traveling merchants.

In spite of ambitious legislation, there has been very limited progress in the establishment of rural cooperatives. Most of the existing cooperatives are consumer organizations stocking household goods, groceries, clothing, and even such commodities as radios. With limited membership, they have had only slight commercial impact. The Dujaylah settlement (see chap. 14) has operated a roadside farmers' cooperative with some success. Little has been done, however, to encourage the establishment of cooperatives in the rural districts.

Most large department stores of the western type are located in Baghdad, although a few are found in Mosul, Basra, and Kirkuk. These stores, some of which offer a delivery service, have been built in the newer sections of the cities. Catering to the westernized taste and the income of a relatively prosperous minority, they carry a wide range of goods imported from western countries.

Transportation

Fifty years ago the caravan was the principal means for moving agricultural produce between widely separated towns in Iraq. Supplementing this traffic on shorter hauls were river craft, donkeys, and porters. Along the caravan and water routes towns grew up whose major functions were to provide fuel for river craft and rest stops for caravans and river boats and to serve as collection and distribution centers for the surrounding areas. In the outlying districts nomadic tribes dominated communications, collecting protection money from merchants and sometimes looting caravans and river traffic.

The power of the central government has brought an end to these nomadic exactions on the movement of trade in Iraq, and the modern period has seen the introduction of new types of transport. Two characteristics of the historic transportation system remain, however. The first is the northeast-southwest orientation of the main axis of traffic, which parallels the Tigris and Euphrates rivers. Down this line come grain and other produce from northern Iraq for do-

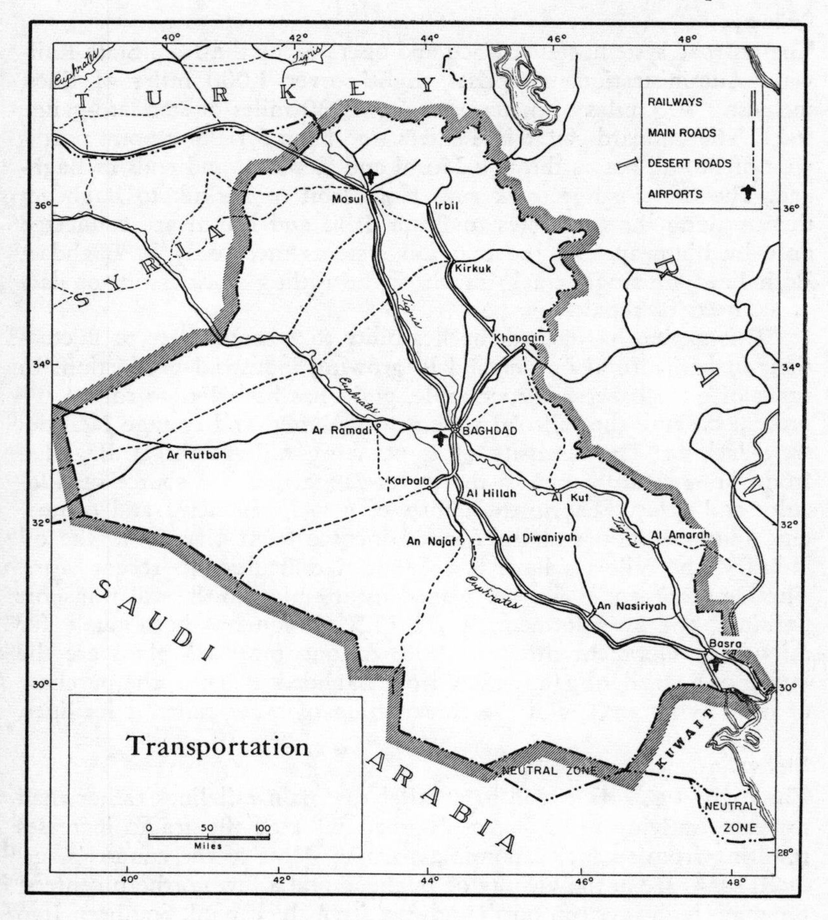

Transportation

mestic consumption or export. In the opposite direction move southern produce and sea-borne imports which come into the country through the Persian Gulf. The other characteristic is the concentration of transport facilities in the populated and cultivated eastern part of the country from Mosul in the north to Basra in the south, Iraq's only port; in between is Baghdad, the capital and largest city. Trains, buses, and trucks serve these centers and a few others, but improved roads and rail lines have not yet come to most of the rest of the country. River transport today plays a minor role (see Map, Transportation).

Railways

The railroad system, state-owned and operated by the Iraqi State Railways Administration, comprises slightly over 1,000 miles of lines, including 700 miles of meter-gauge and 330 miles of standard-gauge track. The standard-gauge line enters Iraq from Syria at a point northwest of Mosul, passes through Mosul and Samarra, and ends at Baghdad. The meter-gauge track runs from Irbil to Kirkuk to Baghdad, thence along the Euphrates to Basra. Irbil and Mosul are connected only by highway, and the two rail systems meet only in Baghdad. Both lines are single track; much of the rolling stock is out of date or in need of repair.

This system has lacked the flexibility to accommodate to fluctuations in agricultural output and to growing industrial production. In times of good harvest, for example, grain has been left to rot on the ground because the railroad system was glutted and storage facilities were lacking. The necessity of transferring rail freight at Baghdad from the standard-gauge to the meter-gauge line is a source of difficulty and delay. Despite the efforts of a well-organized and competent administration and the assured income from services to the oil industry, the railways have had financial difficulties in recent years. The Development Board has turned its attention to the rail transport problem, and an allotment of ID 15.5 million has been made for railway development through 1960. Among proposed plans are the laying of a standard-gauge track from Baghdad to Basra, the purchase of new locomotives, and the construction of other railroad facilities.

Highways

The highways, which tend to parallel the main rail lines rather than to serve outlying areas, have absorbed most of the traffic increases resulting from recent economic expansion. Most of the country's surfaced roads are in the vicinity of Baghdad and a few northern centers; the main highways run north and east from the capital. Southern Iraq is inadequately served by dirt roads, and the rural areas generally suffer from an absence of feeder roads connecting with the main highways.

Iraq's road system, controlled and maintained by the Public Works Department, except within the jurisdictions of the municipalities, consisted in 1956 of approximately 6,800 miles, of which 1,800 are hard surfaced and 5,000 miles are dirt and unimproved roads. The highway from Baghdad to Beirut has become increasingly important, since goods can be brought over it from the Mediterranean more rapidly than they can be carried by ship via the Suez Canal and the Persian Gulf.

The Development Board has undertaken a program of road and bridge construction involving the completion of several hundred miles of paved roads by 1960. Successful river-control measures have made it possible to build roads in areas which were once subject to periodic flooding, and although road construction is not proceeding as rapidly as planned, the work is going forward. When completed, major highways will run from Basra to Baghdad, from Baghdad to Mosul, and from Baghdad to Kirkuk, and will include a new highway from Baghdad to Jordan.

The Public Works Department, which is responsible for maintaining the national road system, has improved its efforts in recent years, but it continues to be handicapped by a shortage of trained technical personnel and it must cope with the results of years of neglect of the country's roads by both national and local authorities. Maintenance of the dirt roads in the south and those in the municipalities generally is poor. Iraq still has a relatively small number of motor vehicles, but the common practice of overloading trucks creates a special maintenance problem even for new paved highways.

Airports

Iraq has two international airports, one at Basra and the other at Baghdad. The latter is being expanded in keeping with the city's growing importance as a center of air transport. In addition, the Iraq Petroleum Company has its own extensive air transport facilities. The country's efficient airline, Iraqi Airways, is under the jurisdiction of the Iraqi State Railways, as are airport and summer resort hotel services. Iraq is served by the following foreign airlines: Air France, Alitalia, BOAC, KLM, Kuwait Airways, Middle Eastern Airlines, Misrair S.A.E., Pan American, Scandinavian Airlines, and TWA. Basra, closer to the main routes to the Far East, is served by more international airlines than is Baghdad.

Inland Water Transport

Inland water transport upstream from Basra has ceased to be important in Iraq's transport system. A decade ago the Tigris from above Badhdad south to Basra was navigable at all seasons; today it is navigable for only part of the year. Traffic consists mainly of motor-launch-propelled barges carrying bulky goods such as steel, petroleum products, and reed matting. Development plans do not contemplate any increase in river transportation, and it seems certain that, with the development of other forms of transport, traffic will continue to dwindle.

The Port of Basra

Basra, Iraq's one seaport, extends up the Shatt al Arab (the common outlet of the Tigris and the Euphrates) from the oil terminal at Al Faw to the wharves at Al Maqil. In addition to handling most of the goods of Iraq's vigorous import-export trade, the port is a transit point for goods being shipped overland to north Iran. The activities of the port are efficiently directed by the Port of Basra Authority, a semi-autonomous government agency which also performs municipal services—road maintenance, health facilities, airport and hotel services, and public utilities—for the city of Basra. The Authority is responsible for dredging the entrance to the Shatt al Arab through the Al Faw Bar, a service to the Iranian port of Abadan as well as to Basra. In spite of the efforts of the Authority, the port has become increasingly congested; in recent years wharf space has been at a premium, and goods are often unloaded in midstream by lighters. The government is studying the feasibility of establishing a second port at Umm Qasr.

Foreign Trade

Increasing imports, relatively stable exports, the offsetting revenues of the oil industry, and the comparatively minor role played by foreign remittances and donations are the outstanding features of the pattern revealed in Iraq's balance of payments (see Table 16). From 1951 to 1955 the value of exports remained relatively stable, save for the drop resulting from the floods in 1954. Statistics are lacking for the subsequent period (which included the brief economic disruption of the Suez crisis), but it appears that the basic level of exports has continued to hold up. The value of imports, on the other hand, has increased sharply over the same period, mainly as the result of capital purchases for the development programs, secondarily from some expansion of consumer purchasing power. The balance of trade deficit has been more than covered by the export earnings of petroleum, reflected in the accumulation of foreign exchange by the National Bank (see chap. 13).

Substantial changes in the destination of Iraq's exports other than oil have occurred since 1953. Agricultural exports to the United Kingdom and Japan have declined, whereas those to Holland, Germany, and Denmark have risen, mainly as a result of the increased demand in these countries for barley. The drop in exports to Japan reflects a temporary drop in Iraqi cotton production and the Japanese limitation of date imports (see Table 17).

In contrast, the relative importance of the sources of Iraq's imports has remained unchanged for a number of years; the United Kingdom and the United States are the principal suppliers. A slight temporary drop occurred with the completion of major pipelines and plant for the oil industry. A steady increase in imports from Germany reflects the general revival of German trade relations with the Middle East. Trade with the Communist bloc is insignificant, and Iraq prohibits the export of strategic materials to these countries. An attempt in early 1956 by the Soviet Union to revive a barter agreement for Iraqi dates (the arrangement had been canceled in 1955) met with no success, partly because the Iraqi Government demanded cash rather than merchandise. Following the Suez crisis, Iraq imposed a boycott on imports from France.

The import pattern reflects to some extent the increasing competition among foreign countries for the expanding Iraqi market. Germany, other western European countries, and Japan are attempting to establish new outlets in Iraq, while British traders are exerting themselves to keep and build upon their traditionally preferred market. By extending liberal credit terms and by assuring prompt delivery and precise specifications at set prices, Britain's competitors have had some success. The Iraqi importer—who may care less for the quality of the product than for a low price which will permit a high markup, and who sees in slow deliveries an attempt to take advantage of "escalator" prices—finds the trade terms now being offered highly favorable.

Iraq has been host to several trade missions and trade fairs in recent years. Furthermore, foreign contractors employed in Iraq's development programs normally buy equipment from their respective countries or advise the Iraqi Government to do so. Until recently British consulting engineers and contracting firms dominated the field, but Lebanese, French, German, and American companies have been competing successfully for these contracts, and Britain has been forced to increase its efforts in order to maintain its traditional position.

Import Trade

Iraq's imports, including those of the oil companies, are heavily weighted with capital and durable goods—machinery, vehicles and parts, iron and steel (see Table 18). These are purchased largely by the oil companies, particularly for pipeline equipment, and by the government. The bulk of consumer imports consist of sugar and tea (which are not produced in Iraq), textiles, and a growing volume of secondhand clothing, most of which comes from the United States.

Imports of tea and sugar have more than doubled since World War II, indicating, even with population increase, a higher per capita consumption.

The composition of Iraq's imports is governed by a licensing system which provides restrictive quotas for hard currency imports and classifies imports from other currency areas into prohibited, limited, and free lists. By and large, however, import policies have been liberal in recent years as large amounts of foreign exchange were accumulated in the banks and restrictions on the importation of luxury items were eased. The trend toward the protection of local industries would seem to indicate that an increasing share of Iraqi imports will consist of raw materials for domestic processing or manufacture.

Export Trade

Oil far overshadows all the rest of Iraq's exports combined. Its remarkable role is indicated by comparing the relative shares of petroleum, barley, and dates to the total value of exports. Even though only 50 percent of the profits from oil production accrues to Iraq's balance of trade, this contribution still far exceeds that of other exports.

On the other hand, while imports for the oil industry at one time made up almost one fifth the value of Iraq's total imports, these imports have fallen considerably with the completion of the major pipelines and oil installations; and, with the sharp increase of imports for other purposes, the percentage of imports destined for the oil companies is now small.

Iraq's share of the income from its fields is secured by the 1952 concession agreement with the oil companies (see chap. 15), but the amount of that income is dependent on oil sales in the major markets of western Europe—France, the United Kingdom, Italy, and West Germany—to which Iraqi oil must be transported via the Suez Canal or pipelines passing through neighboring countries to the Mediterranean. The vulnerability of these routes was dramatically illustrated during the closing of the Suez Canal and the destruction of pumping stations on the pipeline through Syria in 1956. The Iraqi Government lost three fourths of its revenues from oil during the last quarter of 1956 and the first quarter of 1957; by March 1957, Iraq was still exporting only half the September 1956 volume. For the first time since 1952, planned expenditures exceeded oil revenues and the government was forced to draw on the exchange reserves of the National Bank (see chap. 13).

The three principal groups of exports other than petroleum are cereals, dates, and animals and animal products (see Table 19). The volume of these exports—particularly cereals, the output of which may be drastically reduced by drought or flood—is subject to wide fluctuations. Nevertheless, the combined value of these three groups over the last 30 years has usually constituted at least 85 percent, and often more, of the total value of exports other than oil.

Barley is the most important cereal export today, and, with sharp fluctuations, exports of it have increased considerably over the years. Before World War II there was ordinarily a surplus of wheat for export, but population increase and a shift in rural consumption habits have in recent years made it necessary to import wheat.

Iraq is the world's foremost exporter of dates. The crop varies from year to year, however, and a particularly heavy yield may depress prices to a level that hardly justifies the cost of shipping. For quality varieties of dates—sold mainly in western Europe, Australia, and North America—marketing difficulties have been eased and prices somewhat stabilized by a series of contracts between British importers and the Date Association (an agency of the Ministry of Economics). Although the government has attempted through trade agreements to alleviate the marketing problems for inferior quality dates, which are sold to Middle Eastern and Far Eastern countries, prices have fallen steadily since 1950. In response to the situation a number of studies have been undertaken on the possibility of extracting sugar from dates or of using date waste for animal fodder.

Exports of animal products, derived mainly from sheep, have remained stationary for a number of years; the hazards of animal disease and natural conditions likewise affect these exports. The United States is a major importer of wool, casings, and skins, and these products are important dollar earners for Iraq.

Among other Iraqi exports are bricks, quantities of which are sold to Iran; various food products of relatively small value; and cotton, which may become a major export crop if high world prices continue to encourage Iraqi producers.

Regulation and Control

Although tariffs in the past were usually applied for revenue purposes, the government since about 1950 has employed them to protect Iraqi industries—particularly those which use domestic raw materials or those which, as in the case of textiles, may in time be able to free Iraq of dependence on foreign suppliers. The first general revision of the tariff system was not adopted, however, until 1956 and the new duties have not yet conspicuously affected the trade pattern. The tariff system has increased duties on luxury imports; has reduced rates on widely consumed but domestically unavailable articles such as agricultural and industrial equipment, certain raw materials, and foods; and has provided protection for domestic textile, leather, jute, and cement industries.

Another type of control is exercised through import licensing and the allocation of foreign exchange. Modeled after the United Kingdom import system, these procedures are aimed at ensuring sufficient imports for development and domestic consumption requirements. All imports from the dollar area must be licensed, while those from other areas are classified as prohibited, limited, or free. The prohibited list also includes some Iraqi export goods which are domestically in short supply. The principal purpose of the prohibited list, however, is to protect domestic industries, but it has to some extent operated against the shoe industry, which is forced to use domestic rather than higher-quality imported leather goods. On the other hand, a 25 percent export tax on cotton has directly favored the textile industry by keeping domestic prices below the world price; this export tax was reduced to 10 percent in 1956. The limited list, enumerating luxury imports, has been drastically cut to only about 60 commodities, and it now includes some export commodities normally reserved for domestic use but which may be exported if conditions warrant. Items on the free list do not require import license, and foreign exchange for their purchase is easily available.

With a few exceptions all foreign trade transactions are subject to exchange control and are conducted within the sterling area payments agreement to which Iraq adheres. Iraqi importers must generally obtain a license to acquire foreign exchange from authorized dealers. Iraqi exporters must declare the value of their shipments and surrender their foreign currency for dinars. Since Iraq is a member of the sterling area, dealers usually offer foreign currencies at London rates; the National Bank, however, quotes an Iraqi rate for United States dollars.

Allocations, made at the beginning of each year, establish the maximum amounts of foreign exchange to be made available for the importation of various items except those on the free list. In practice, however, the value of the licenses issued has always exceeded the annual allocation, and the government has recently begun to enforce more rigidly the regulations limiting to established and experienced merchants the licenses for hard currency and luxury imports. The value of licenses for scarce currency imports has almost doubled since 1953, and between 1953 and 1955 the number of registered importers rose from over 3,000 to over 4,000.

Payments for merchandise and "invisible" exports may be made in dinars, sterling, or any other foreign currency; but the sterling or foreign currency must be surrendered by the exporter. Date exporters to other Middle Eastern countries, however, have been exempted from this requirement as a measure of encouragement. Travelers and tourists may bring unlimited amounts of foreign currencies into Iraq but must declare them at customs.

In addition to the official procedures, there are alternative means of acquiring foreign exchange. Exporters and importers may legally transact their business in the free-trade market in Beirut or they may illicitly obtain foreign currencies at black market rates in Iraq. Although the Iraqi black market was fairly active before 1950, it is generally believed that the volume of these transactions has declined as exchange reserves have become more abundant and allocations more liberal. Authorized channels are still avoided, however, by smugglers carrying contraband across Iraq's frontiers. The undervaluation of exports and the overvaluation of imports on official invoices are other ways in which the law is violated. Such transactions, however, which involved probably ID 7 million in 1951, are estimated to have dropped to less than ID 1 million in 1955.

The oil companies operate under special exchange procedures, although these do not extend to oil-company employees. Under the current arrangement the companies are not required to surrender the proceeds of their exports and they may import free of customs duties and licensing requirements.

Trade Agreements

Iraq conducts its foreign financial transactions within the general terms of its membership in the sterling area. Its trade with most of its Arab neighbors—Egypt, Jordan, Lebanon, Syria, and Saudi Arabia—is governed by the Inter-Arab Trade and Transit Agreement ratified by Iraq in January 1955. The signatories are exempt from duty on certain agricultural items produced and traded among themselves; specified industrial goods of the participants also are favored by a 25 percent reduction in the prevailing tariff. The signatories assure one another of preferential treatment in the granting of import and export licenses. They further undertake to facilitate mutually in their customs procedures the transit of goods, personal effects, and animals. The agreement does not invalidate existing bilateral understandings nor does it preclude the conclusion of such agreements by any of the participants with other parties in the future. So far, the agreement does not seem to have established important new outlets for Iraqi exports, but it may have opened the door more widely for imports of certain industrial products from other Arab states.

In addition to these multilateral arrangements Iraq has concluded direct bilateral trade and payments agreements with Jordan, Lebanon, India, and Greece. Similar agreements with Italy and Germany facilitate the employment in Iraq of technicians from these countries. Iraq continues to blacklist ships and firms charged with violating the 1954 Arab League boycott against Israel; it also prohibits strategic exports to the Communist bloc. The country, unlike almost all others in the Middle East, has no trade agreements with the Soviet Union, its European satellites, or Communist China.

Iraq is represented on the Baghdad Pact Economic Committee, created in 1955 "to develop and strengthen the economic and financial resources of the region," and has received military, technical, and financial assistance from the United States and Great Britain. As the representative of the signatory powers, the committee can discuss regional questions with such international bodies as the World Health Organization and the International Bank for Reconstruction and Development. The committee promotes projects in trade, mutual assistance, and joint development—for example, the Atomic Energy Center for nuclear studies in Baghdad, plans for joint development of the Tigris and Euphrates rivers, and the regional coordination of charitable institutions such as the Red Crescent Society. In 1957 the United States, Great Britain, and Pakistan allocated technical assistance funds for communications development and a number of other regional projects to be undertaken by the committee.

Economic Assistance

Foreign aid has played a relatively minor role in Iraq's balance of payments since 1950. Moreover, a strong financial position—now being regained after the loss of oil revenues in 1956—has enabled Iraq to assume the functions of creditor to the neighboring state of Jordan. As a member of the Baghdad Pact, Iraq was among the beneficiaries of the $12.5 million in special aid granted in 1957 by the United States under the "Eisenhower Doctrine." This amount, together with $1.4 million from Britain, will be devoted to linking the member states through telecommunication, road, rail, and shipping projects drawn up by the Economic Committee of the Pact.

Iraq has lent Jordan, whose almost bankrupt economy is highly dependent on foreign assistance, $4 million, although payments were not made until the Jordanian political crisis of 1957 when a rift developed between Jordan and the Egyptian-Syrian camp. The Iraqi Government has reportedly reiterated its desire to extend further assistance to Jordan once oil revenues regain their normal level. While taking these steps, Iraq has sought to avoid any irreparable split in Arab unity. It has indicated its support of a regional development organization embracing not only Saudi Arabia, Jordan, and Lebanon, but Syria as well; and it has attempted by a generally conciliatory approach to relax the intra-Arab tensions which increased after the Suez crisis (see chap. 10).

Attitudes

Formally allied with the West, Iraq nevertheless has not been untouched by the wave of anti-western sentiment that has swept through the Arab world. Such feeling, however, is strongest in certain sectors of the urban population—notably students, some white-collar workers, and a proportion of skilled and semiskilled industrial workers. It is not characteristic of the ruling elite nor of the relatively indifferent rural mass (see chap. 22). The western business representative in Iraq moves in a generally friendly atmosphere, but he remains vulnerable to the hostile stereotypes which have gained strength in Arab countries as western power and influence in the area have declined. Whether a westerner or not, the foreigner in Iraq also meets some of the jealous quickness—characteristic in newly independent states—to suspect invasions of national prerogatives. Any negative factors, however, have been more than outweighed by Iraqi recognition of the importance of the role of foreign elements in the development of the country. The government, the Development Board, and private business do not hesitate to employ foreign advisers and consultants, and most of the country's large construction work is directed by foreign contractors, among whom Europeans and Lebanese predominate.

There is little foreign investment in Iraq outside the petroleum industry, but this is due more to the general difficulties in establishing a business in an underdeveloped country than to the lack of a favorable investment "climate." Legislation affecting investment has not been a deterrent to foreign entrepreneurs—other than Israelis—but it may be a retarding factor in that the set procedures for investment operations have not been clearly established. For example, while foreign capital invested in Iraq may be repatriated to its country of origin, there are no laws or regulations governing the repatriation of dollars or the dollar equivalent of dinars earned in Iraq. The decision in such cases is left to the discretion of the National Bank, which usually authorizes the export of dollars—whether obtained in the form of wages or profits—if the nature of the employment or enterprise involved is in the interest of the national economy.

Attempts to lessen Iraq's economic dependence on foreign skills and enterprise are evident in the restriction to Iraqi nationals of certain professions, specialized crafts, and trades. Also, certain foreign concerns are not allowed to benefit from tax rebates and other provisions of the Law for the Encouragement of Industrial Undertakings which apply to companies at least 55 percent Iraqi-owned.

Britain has long enjoyed a preferred position in Iraq's foreign commerce, first as the holder of the League of Nations Mandate over the country, subsequently as party to various bilateral treaties and understandings with independent Iraq. In the course of this association Iraqi and British businessmen have learned to work with each other in easy and mutually profitable ways. This established relationship, however, suffered some strain as a result of Britain's involvement with Israel and France in the attack on Egypt in 1956, and Britain is facing mounting competition from other countries for a share of Iraq's business.

Generally, Iraqis prefer to transact business directly with a foreign firm or its resident agent rather than through a regional representative. Personal contact and oral understandings are favored.

The oil industry, supplying by far the greater part of the income of the Iraqi Government, exerts stong influence on national policy. The oil companies, as foreign concerns, have generally avoided any direct involvement in Iraqi politics, but the exercise of their dual responsibility to their shareholders abroad and to the Government of Iraq as the "authorized providers of national wealth" inevitably has powerful indirect effects on the economic and political life of the country. The relationship between the oil companies and the Iraqi authorities has generally been one of mutual recognition of the ultimate requirements of each party. Within these limits there remains scope for compromise and a broad area of shared interest.

The impact on the national economy of the interruption of transportation channels during the Suez crisis drew attention to the dependence of the oil industry on the conduct of foreign relations in the Middle East. While the interests of the government and the Iraq Petroleum Company in this area are similar, the solutions proposed are influenced by different factors. The oil industry has proposed alternative routes to Mediterranean ports through Turkey in the north and Kuwait in the south, and it has deferred construction on another pipeline connection with Syria. The government, influenced by its concern for Iraq's relations with its Arab neighbors, is reluctant to cut off Syria and Lebanon from the transit fees they receive under existing arrangements.

Iraqi attitudes toward the oil companies range from the indifference of villagers and nomadic groups remote from oil operations to the strong convictions, for or against, of those who are directly affected by the industry or who see it in a political context. Politically, the industry has the approval of the conservative and moderate elements, who accept the government's political and economic program and agree that the arrangement with the oil companies is in the national interest. Another area of opinion centers in the urban intelligentsia, strongly affected by western influences but by no means pro-western. Some of the members of this group are communists, but most would regard themselves as moderate socialists, Arab nationalists, and Iraqi patriots. Their political views, reduced to slogans, are strongly echoed in the uneducated urban mass, and they tend to see the oil companies in the pejorative terms of "imperialism," "western capitalism," "exploitation," etc.

Differences of political orientation aside, those who are involved in the oil industry are apt to be more friendly to it than those who know it only by hearsay. In the northern cities and at Basra, where the complex operations and problems of the industry can be observed first-hand, relatively few regard it as a selfish giant. Merchants, contractors, trucking companies, and workmen in these areas have all benefited from oil and are conscious that they have done so. At the same time, other than economic factors bear on this group. Thus the tightly compartmentalized oil-company communities in which separation of Iraqi and foreign employees is institutionalized in housing, canteens, and recreational facilities is apt to leave the Iraqi with a bitter sense of being discriminated against.

Although the Iraqi Government has at times given the oil companies cause for concern in seeking to take over refining plants or in proposals to increase the number of Iraqis employed in the industry, in recent years there has been relatively little official intervention of this kind. On the contrary, in such areas as labor relations and import regulations the industry enjoys a privileged position. This can be attributed to increasing understanding in official circles of the problems of the industry; to some relaxation of the discriminatory arrangements in the oil community; to some disillusionment with the Iranian experience of oil nationalization; and to growing confidence that Iraq can best increase its benefits from its oil resources, not by fiat, but by the ability of its people to acquire the skills which will enable them in time to replace the foreign experts. With the volatile Middle East political situation and the large number of Iraqis who are beginning to have opinions about national issues, it is uncertain how long the oil companies can expect the currently favorable atmosphere to last. Meanwhile, the rise to prominence of Iraq's Development Board with its vast construction and rehabilitation programs is serving to draw attention from the oil industry to a new target of popular concern and criticism.

17

PUBLIC HEALTH AND WELFARE

THREE HUNDRED OUT OF EVERY THOUSAND PERSONS BORN IN Iraq die in infancy—a mortality rate more than six times that in western Europe or the United States. A large number of those who survive suffer throughout their lives from malnutrition, and their ranks continue to be thinned by preventable acute diseases and untreated chronic ones.

Poverty, ignorance, traditional attitudes, natural environment, and shortage of health facilities and trained personnel are the familiar main elements in this situation. The peasant majority and the bulk of tribal nomads and urban workmen are inadequately fed, housed, and clothed. The long inventory of diseases prevalent in the region includes those common in both temperate and tropical climates. Flies and dust contribute to eye infections, and sudden changes in temperature to respiratory ailments. The canals, drainage ditches, reservoirs, and marshes of the more densely populated areas are breeding places for malaria-carrying mosquitoes and various parasitic organisms. For the uneducated Iraqi these conditions are part of the natural order of things. The problems of disease and ill health are to be explained and coped with in terms of a body of traditional lore and prescription. These failing, he accepts what he cannot mend.

The Iraqi Government is attempting to improve the health of the population and medical and health services as they are constituted in the country today are almost entirely its creation. In the past the government program was directed mainly toward providing medical service to the ill and relatively little attention was given to the training of medical personnel and to preventive medicine and rural health measures. This emphasis is changing, however, partly as a result of suggestions by foreign missions and advisers, whose recommendations have generally been accepted and implemented by the government.

17. *Public Health and Welfare*

There is a growing realization among both doctors and laymen of the need, not only for a more extensive public health program and for the training of personnel to staff it, but for inducements which will make the doctor and other health workers more willing than in the past to leave the comforts of the city and go into the rural areas, where their skills are so greatly needed. Despite the difficulties, no part of the government's development program has met with more enthusiastic response than the effort to raise the health standards of the country.

As for the practice of public welfare in general there have been three almost distinct historical phases. Elements of all three systems persist, partly because they have remained relevant to continuing conditions, and partly as a result of the insistence of extreme Moslem traditionalists and the conservatism of a wealthy and influential minority. The causes of the changes that have taken place include both internal factors and influences from the West.

In the traditional society the practices of public welfare were based on a system of mutual rights and obligations between landlord and peasant, between master and man, and between kinsmen. Differentials in wealth and privilege in the community at large were mutually understood and accepted as part of the natural order of things but the wealthy were expected to assist the poor. This system, reflecting long social experience and a religious ideal, became less and less adequate in the onrush of change in the Middle East in the modern period.

The establishment of the British Mandate in 1921 brought a new approach to public welfare which culminated with the organization in 1950 of a national Development Board, generously financed and charged with carrying out a vast program of economic improvement. The new approach had been shaped by various factors: the advice of British and American experts, the belief of Iraqi leaders that the country might not be given recognition and independence unless it guaranteed social rights in a written constitution and provided for education, health services, and other needs which in modern times have come to be regarded as the responsibility of the state; there was also the sincere conviction that it was morally obligatory, as well as politically expedient, for the government to take steps to improve the depressed living conditions of the population. The basic assumption of the planners of the new program was that the central government should organize and execute sweeping, large-scale measures which would benefit indirectly the greatest number of people, rich and poor alike—such projects as the settlement of land titles throughout the country and the construction of dams and irrigation works and communications facilities. These expensive schemes, while providing a necessary framework for a viable economy, left great segments of the population untouched.

The third phase in the evolution of public welfare efforts in Iraq began after 1950 when the inadequacy of an overcentralized program devoted almost exclusively to large-scale works and very long-range benefits had become the object of general criticism. The massive engineering projects—many of which had been completed in the previous years—were not discontinued, but there began a gradual decentralization of welfare efforts. New emphasis was placed on the "human problems of development," and growing attention was turned to the immediate problems of the urban and rural poor. Labor and social legislation were enacted; in the sphere of health there was an increasing interest in preventive as well as curative measures; extensive housing schemes were formulated. The International Bank for Reconstruction and Development (IBRD) and, more specifically, Sir John Salter's report, *The Development of Iraq,* published in 1955, pointed to the economic and political implications of the gap between the water-control and land-reclamation projects undertaken by the Development Board and the living conditions of the people who were to maintain and build upon these works—and, hopefully, to benefit from them in the more or less distant future. Lord Salter argued that the Development Board must assume not only the responsibility for capital projects but also for direct, small-scale schemes hitherto undertaken solely by the various government departments. He believed too that the Board must take an increasing interest in those aspects of education and health which would prepare the nation to assume the burdens of development, and he spoke of the political advantages which would accrue from the immediate impact of small "publicity" projects. The completion of some of the major capital construction enabled the Development Board to turn its attention to these recommendations; it was further impelled to do so by internal conditions—such as the migration from rural to urban areas and the growing inflation in the cities—which called for special measures.

Iraq's present ambitious welfare measures are financed almost completely from oil revenues rather than from taxes; although a progressive tax structure is established by law, it does not yet operate in practice. The result is that, except for the contributions of the government welfare apparatus, the distribution of income and the existing socioeconomic pattern in the country do not change in proportion to improvements in the public welfare. By and large the wealthy merchants and landlords remain wealthy or become wealthier in their monopoly of the land or the pursuit of their businesses, while increases in the earnings of the middle-income groups and the agricultural and industrial workers are ultimately derived, not so much from a larger percentage of the output of the enterprises in which they are engaged, as from the direct or indirect contributions they receive from the government's development and welfare program. The government seems to have sought to strike a compromise between the resistance to taxation by the well-to-do—on whose support it so heavily relies—and the demands of the growing number of the politically articulate who propose to speak for the urban workers and rural peasants.

There is no doubt that the average Iraqi is much better off than he was ten or even five years ago—so short a space of time that he can recognize the change himself—but an increasing dissatisfaction with living conditions has been apparent. The rural standard of living is still very low, and the fellah, dimly but increasingly aware of the possibility of improvement, is beginning to grumble against the rapaciousness of his landlord or move to the city in hopes of a better life. The white-collar worker, benefiting by recent wage increases but frustrated by the distance between himself and the well-to-do, still clamors for political and economic reform. Not only does each improvement in public welfare stimulate demands for new advances, the government's programs are the object of often conflicting criticism from various sources; thus there are the strictures against the Development Board by politicians temporarily out of office, protests by the Shiites that most of the development programs have benefited the area north of Baghdad, and complaints that too little attention is being given to activities which will meet immediate rather than long-range needs. The government has been slow to publicize its efforts, with the result that the general public remains unaware of or unenthusiastic about what is being done; even in official circles, particularly those in the provinces, there is a tendency to deprecate the gains made thus far. Finally, the opposition of landed interests together with the indifference of most city dwellers to the conditions of the fellahin still hinders the adequate development of programs which would directly benefit the cultivator.

Iraq, nevertheless, has the resources of land, water, and mineral wealth necessary to raise the standard of living of its people far above the present level. The government has for a generation been committed to an ambitious capital construction program which continues to enhance the country's productive potential and increasingly to provide the material basis for those social adjustments which would weld the nation together by giving all sections of the population an equitable stake in the national economy.

Traditional Measures

The public-welfare programs of the Iraqi Government reflect the western influences of the modern period but alongside this activity a traditional appartus continues to function—though less and less adequately in recent generations. In this traditional system, common to the whole Middle East, the family or larger kinship group was the primary welfare agent. It was to his kinsmen that the individual turned for economic assistance and protection, and he was bound to them in a network of mutual obligation. The advent of Islam in the seventh century did not fundamentally alter this ancient pattern, but in the commandment to give alms there was superimposed a concept of the broader responsibility of the good Moslem within the community of the faithful. In accepting inequalities of talent and wealth—these were of God—Moslems also insisted on the obligation of the wealthy to assist the poor. Almsgiving, which represents the direct application of the religious ideal (see chap. 5), was originally viewed not as gratuitous generosity but as the duty of the donor and the right of the recipient. It has also furnished some precedent for modern tax systems and public welfare schemes. In time alms came to be collected by the authorities as *zakat,* an alms tax. Although almsgiving is purely voluntary today, for the most devout Moslem it is still a compulsory moral obligation.

Wakfs (pious, charitable, or family foundations) are another welfare device from an earlier day. Wakfs have been established for a wide variety of secular and religious purposes, but typically they have taken the form of endowments of land left by the donor in perpetuity to his descendants or to a religious beneficiary. In the course of time a considerable amount of land became tied up in the wakfs, and the abuses which developed in the management of their funds became so notorious that they were brought under government supervision during the British Mandate. Wakfs are today subject to the control of a Director-General of Wakfs.

The nature of the landlord's traditional responsibility for the welfare of his tenants is illustrated by the institution of the diwan, a weekly "court" or assembly. At this gathering, presided over by the landlord, the peasant could air his grievances, obtain judgment in minor disputes, and appeal for help in time of need. (The diwan was also the occasion for a meal provided by the landlord.) With the growth of absentee landlordism in Iraq, the rural diwan no longer occupies the important place it once did; it has become for many landowners, remote from the daily concerns of their estates, an exercise in prestige rather than a means of looking after the welfare of their tenants.

Family and kin solidarity and responsibility long antedate the coming of Islam in Iraq. The concept of mutual obligation within the family is taken for granted as both morally right and a self-evident necessity (see chap. 18). A large family becomes "social security" for the aged. The eldest male in the bedouin clan, in the village, and in conservative urban households receives the family income, sometimes including that earned by married sons, and disburses it for the benefit of the unit. In time of personal or economic crisis a father or uncle will give a young man financial assistance; the peasant kin group will assist in gathering the harvest and will come in times of sickness, death, or other adversity to offer help.

Such traditional forms of assistance, especially family self-help, have not been eclipsed by modern welfare programs and blueprints. They have not, however, sufficed to meet the problems of poverty under the changing conditions of the present day.

How far the old forms of mutual support and self-help have lost their relevance varies from region to region; the traditional patterns also vary among themselves in their strength and resistance. As between the family and the wakf, the former is undergoing change but the latter may well be disappearing. The forces of change are bearing hardest on the urban centers, and the need for new welfare mechanisms is most apparent, if not most pressing, there. The disintegration of the traditional structure is most readily seen in the relationships between the well-to-do and the poor. The gap between the two has always been wide, but generations of foreign rule and the impact of the West in this century have widened it still more. The growth of absentee landlordism in the latter days of Turkish control physically separated a large percentage of those who owned the land from those who worked it. Later, western education and western luxuries, the prerogative of wealth, drove a cultural wedge between the privileged few and the mass of the population. The rights of the wealthy were gradually emphasized at the expense of obligations to the needy. The absentee landlord or the sheikh who has moved to the city feels less responsibility for his tenants or tribesmen than when he lived among them; while the internal village and tribal ties continue to operate, the key benefactor is missing. It is possible to point to social security and progressive tax systems as modern adaptation of the traditional concept, but it is doubtful that many wealthy landlords or sheikhs recognize the relationship. In Iraq's larger industries a social security system is in operation, and the many small enterprises, almost invariably family owned and operated, care for their own; medium-size industries, however, fall between the two systems, since they are not covered by the state welfare program and the employer is apt to feel little responsibility for those employees who have no claims on him as kinsmen.

Absentee landlordism, urbanization, population growth, and the spread of a cash economy and wage work have tended to break down the small-group pattern and the highly personalized system of relationships through which Iraqi society once secured the welfare of its members. The family, in particular, is less able than it once was to function as a self-sufficient economic unit. The combined earnings of the peasant family which has moved to the city usually exceed its previous income, but as wage workers the individual members of the family no longer constitute a single close-knit economic unit and they lack the relative security they knew on the land. The single individual who leaves for the city can no longer rely on the family unit for security in times of economic difficulty unless a relative has preceded him, and for help he must look to such public and private assistance programs as exist. Nor can the rural family depend on contributions from the fellah who has "made good" in the city, because his earnings are generally too unreliable and too small for him to be able to bear his share of family responsibility (see chap. 18).

The Standard of Living

The economic potential of Iraq contrasts sharply with the widespread poverty generally prevalent in the country. Malnutrition, crowding, and lack of sanitation in village and city make disease and illness endemic in much of the population. Productivity is low in almost every sector of the national economy. Even though the annual average per capita income has risen from an estimated ID 30 (roughly $85; 1 Iraq dinar = $2.80) in 1952 to an estimated ID 50 (approximately $140) in 1956, the data upon which these estimates are based include a few considerable and some great personal fortunes but an overwhelming majority of incomes close to or at the subsistence level. Only in recent years has a potential bridge between rich and poor begun to appear with the emergence of a number of middle-income urban workers and professional people who constitute a developing "middle class." Fortunately, while the price level rose almost sixfold between 1940 and 1950, the prices of "necessary" commodities have remained fairly stable since then, and only in the large cities has there been a significant rise in the cost of living since that time.

Available statistics indicate that an Iraqi earning ID 20 per month spends more than half his income on food; 5 to 9 percent each on such necessities as clothing, household goods, and rent; and 15 percent on luxuries such as tobacco and recreation. For the average Iraqi, however, an income of ID 20 would be exceedingly high. His meager cash goes rather toward procuring the barest necessities. Attempts to determine general Iraqi preferences in the redistribution of expenditures as incomes increase are difficult in the absence of relevant statistics. It is not even possible yet to say whether Iraqis will be stimulated by larger incomes to increased economic activity or will show a tendency to work less and less as it becomes easier to maintain the accustomed level. Evidence for both possibilities exists. Wage incentives on the basis of piecework have contributed to higher production as ambitious workers exert themselves to achieve higher incomes. On the other hand, bedouins employed in the oil industry often work only long enough to buy a flock of sheep or cattle and return to the tribe. Generally, however, Iraqis respond to financial incentives.

Country and Desert

Almost two thirds of the population of Iraq live in the rural and desert areas in tribes, villages, or small towns. The impoverished and unsanitary conditions that surround them are rarely mitigated by the kind of amenities available to at least a portion of the urban population. The village in particular shows the marks of poverty and of customary ways reinforced by centuries of practice. The Iraqi peasant lives, not in scattered homesteads, but in tightly packed village clusters in which men and animals share their living quarters, foul the water supply, and wade in the summer dust and winter mud. A typical dwelling is a one-room hut constructed of mud reinforced with straw or cow dung (stone is often used in the north) with one door and possibly a small window. Furnishings usually consist of a few mats and a storage chest. Electricity is not available and lighting at night is provided by oil lamp or fire. Not the least problem in efforts to improve rural housing is the attitude of the peasant himself. The fellah does not assign great importance to his housing. But education, and the influences emanating from the towns, and new village housing schemes and settlement plans may be expected to whet his appetite for something better.

The fellah's average annual cash income (1952 figures) for a winter grain crop is roughly ID 10, and he earns perhaps another ID 10 for a summer crop such as sesame. He consumes a large portion of his share of the crop as food. Most cash income is spent for other food necessities, such as tea and sugar, and for clothing and some tobacco. Soap is an expensive luxury in the countryside. The commonest material for clothing is cheap cotton cloth, and men may possess a secondhand western-style jacket. Relatively few can afford to wear shoes save on special occasions. Tools and equipment are rudimentary, and modern implements in use on some of the larger estates are too expensive for the average peasant. Celebrations, such as weddings and circumcisions, are costly, but even the poorest fellah does not hesitate to go deeply into debt to meet the expense, for these occasions lend dignity and meaning to life and are among the few times that the peasant family enjoys a full meal and a respite from the round of toil.

The ordinary tribal nomad lives as frugally as the peasant cultivator, but his tent shelter, style of dress, and pastoral equipment reflect a different tradition and an adjustment to a highly specialized way of life in a harsh physical environment. Actual living conditions in this sector of the population vary from the threadbare poverty of splinter groups eking out an existence with a few sheep and seasonal wage labor to the wealth of certain camel tribes whose income from large agricultural holdings enables them to maintain lavish establishments in town and to spend only part of their time in the desert as managers of tribal affairs.

Iraq's pastoral nomads are rapidly being sedentarized—a process which has been hastened by the existence of a strong central political authority in the settled areas. This trend—encouraged by the government and favored by the wealthier sheikhs, whose land holdings yield a higher return under cultivation than as pasture land—is transforming increasing numbers of nomads, first into part-time farmers and finally into full peasant cultivators. The transition, involving as it does a new source of income, new ways of work, and new social values is not easy and it poses special welfare problems. Meanwhile, the pastoralist who still maintains his herd—forbidden by the government to engage in the raiding through which he once won property and prestige—must content himself with exchanging animals, hides, wool, dates, butter for coffee, and staples of sugar, flour, and rice. If he has some money to spare he may purchase a saddle, a rug for his tent, or something for his wife. Clinging to ideals of behavior deeply imbedded in the past he does not hesitate to put himself into debt in order to celebrate or entertain with an extravagantly bountiful table; and where two sheep might satisfy the appetites of the assembled guests, he will kill five—the uneaten meat is used at later meals.

The rural town can be distinguished from the large village (which may rival it in size) in that the town population comprises more specialized and wealthy groups: small landowners, merchants, and artisans, as well as the peasants and laborers who predominate in the village. Socially complex and with a wide range of status based on property, the town shows the marks of the varied influences which are reaching it from the city (see chap. 6). Both western and eastern styles of dress—and combinations of the two—are to be seen. Western-style clothes have prestige, but the conservative may retain traditional garb by preference.

Housing, too, ranges from the spacious and well-constructed homes of the wealthy to the one-room dwellings of the poor. Diet, in the village mainly dates, bread, and sour milk, is augmented among the more prosperous of the town with meat, vegetables, rice, and a variety of condiments and sweets. In the relative prosperity of some of its inhabitants the town reveals the contrast which is characteristic of the whole Middle East—that between the impoverished majority and the moderately well-to-do and wealthy minority.

Cities

City and town have in common a number of characteristics, but in the city complexity and contrast are magnified and changes in attitudes toward living standards are accelerated. The cities usually contain both old, congested sections centering around bazaar and mosque and newer, more spacious additions and developments. In the older sections houses are built tightly together along narrow streets. Stone or brick construction is common; typical features are a small interior courtyard, a flat roof or an open second story for sleeping in hot weather. In these old sections are found the multifamily units where related families live together, in part from economic necessity, but no less as an expression of family cohesiveness. The newer residential sections of the city, with their separate houses and gardens, have developed along broad avenues often lined with trees and flowers. Most population centers of over 6,000 have electricity and piped water, the former expensive and the latter not always pure. No Iraqi city has a modern sewage system, although Baghdad is installing one with the help of the Development Board.

The upper-income groups, composed of wealthy landowners, leading businessmen, high government officials, and the most successful members of the professions, have adopted western styles of housing and dress and western forms of recreation. The most modestly situated business and professional people and salaried white-collar workers, who comprise the small but growing middle class, emulate the upper group as closely as financial circumstances allow. Western influence, however, has not meant the same thing to the two groups. While the wealthiest have tended to favor the West politically as well as to borrow from it culturally, the middle group, struggling to assert itself, has ambivalently resented and at the same time sought to emulate the image it has of both its own elite and the West.

A recent urban phenomenon has been the growth of *sarifa* (hut) slums. *Sarifa*-dwellers have migrated mainly from the impoverished areas of the south and established themselves on the outskirts of such cities as Baghdad and Basra. There they try to eke out an existence amid pools of stagnant water dug for their buffaloes. The *sarifa* settlement in Baghdad was largely destroyed by floods in 1954, but despite new housing developments it has reappeared. These slums also exist at Basra and other places, however. The presence of the *sarifa*-dwellers in the cities is a source of friction since they compete for work with those displaced artisans who must seek employment as casual laborers (see chap. 12).

Government Health and Welfare Efforts

A number of philanthropic and charitable organizations dedicated to social welfare have appeared in the past decade. Notable among these are the Red Crescent Society (Moslem equivalent of the Red Cross), the Child Welfare Society, and the Women's Temperance and Social Welfare Society. The organizations have done constructive work, particularly distinguishing themselves in the 1954 flood. Privately supported, they have received some financial assistance from the government in connection with certain of their programs. Organized by the well-to-do and focused on the problem of poverty and misfortune, they are in some degree helping to establish new lines of communication across the gap between rich and poor which has widened so greatly in the modern period.

In addition to welfare groups of this type, several societies, many of them professional, have been organized by middle-class groups to render assistance to their own members and to promote general social reform.

The government, however, bears the main responsibility for public welfare in Iraq—its stated ambition is to double the nation's standard of living in ten years. If municipal leaders decry the centralized character of governmental activity they nevertheless turn to the government for assistance in time of need. In the rural and desert areas, where the central government is a more distant entity and there is even greater fear of official encroachment on local prerogatives, local leaders are less ready to call for or accept government assistance. This attitude is changing, however, and in the less remote villages the villagers are beginning to express interest in rural rehabilitation, education, and health programs.

Aside from the water-control and land-reclamation programs of the Development Board the authorities have tended to concentrate their welfare efforts in the urban areas. The emphasis is perhaps justified, for population growth in the cities has been rapid and inflation has constantly threatened the urban living standards. Furthermore, the concentration of the industrial and government working force in and around the larger centers has presented for the first time in the country's experience the need for labor legislation. In meeting the problem of inflation the government has pursued a policy which combines liberal import controls with direct government purchases of "necessary" commodities to regulate domestic prices; for example, the sharp increase in the price of wheat as a result of shortages and hoarding during World War II gave rise to a "bread subsidization scheme" under which the government purchased wheat domestically and abroad for resale on the home market at a price within the reach of the urban worker. This program remains in force, and as recently as 1956 the government employed it to prevent merchants from raising prices during a temporary grain shortage.

Government and white-collar workers in Iraq have long been greatly underpaid in relation to prices prevailing in the cities; in 1956 the government sought to alleviate this inequity by raising civil service salaries and by reducing the income tax for white-collar and skilled workers. The heavy demand for industrial labor has stimulated wage increases in that sphere, and both skilled and unskilled workers have also benefited from legislation (in 1953) providing a minimum daily wage of 250 *fils* (70 cents) and from the social security law of 1956 (see chap. 12). The latter legislation, applicable to undertakings employing 30 or more workers, provides benefits for disability, maternity, old age, unemployment, sickness, and funeral expenses; one fourth of the expense is paid by the employee, and three fourths is shared by the employer and the government. Government restaurants offer inexpensive meals to urban laborers. The Iraq Petroleum Company (IPC) has established a precedent with its own excellent welfare program, which has been followed to some extent by other large companies in the country.

The Development Board has increasingly undertaken various local welfare schemes or has assisted the regular ministries and the municipalities to initiate them. Aside from provisions for sanitation and pure drinking water, the most notable of these programs has been the construction of new housing. The housing problem in the cities has been acute; and although the IPC has instituted large-scale, successful housing projects for its employees, a 1947 law stipulating that large landowners and industries employing over 100 workers must provide housing benefits has not been enforced. A small city-planning division within the Department of Municipalities of the Ministry of the Interior was called upon only occassionally, and even then its responsibilities were not clear. The responsibility for housing shifted gradually to the Development Board, which undertook the construction of housing developments for industrial workers such as that at the Quayarah Bitumen Refinery. The self-help scheme initiated by the government in cooperation with the city of Baghdad to build homes for *sarifa*-dwellers was abandoned when effective local participation and financing proved to be lacking, and the Board assumed almost the entire burden of the program both in Baghdad and Basra. Until 1955, however, the Board's outlay for housing was relatively small. A growing appreciation of the need for better housing and community planning, including health and sanitation, has led to much higher allocation for these needs and for social services in general in the 1955–60 development budget. The funds for housing alone have increased more than fourfold.

The major part of the rural population has received far fewer benefits from these activities than have the urban groups, both because of the magnitude of the rural problem and the particular emphasis of government planning. A new trend is evident, however, in the attention which has been turned to the rural scene. An obvious obstacle in the way of large-scale measures to bring direct assistance to the fellah has been the difficulty in enacting any agrarian legislation unpopular with the landlords. The only over-all community development scheme carried out so far has been the Dujaylah project, and the establishment of rural welfare centers by the Ministry of Social Affairs has been uneven. Until 1957 no community planning had been undertaken for existing villages and towns; in a number of instances, however, town leaders themselves had launched programs, relying upon their personal ability to obtain financial assistance from the government.

Another obstacle to rural improvement in Iraq has been administrative: welfare officials have tended to be concentrated in Baghdad, remote from the local problems with which they are supposed to deal; and apparatus has been lacking for adequate coordination of work by the various agencies involved. In 1957 the Development Board established a new organ to coordinate the activities of the ministries concerned with health, education, agriculture, and social services, which had hitherto operated separately and not infrequently in conflict with one another. A further and promising departure from past practice is the provision for the village to play an active role in the planning for its welfare. Plans for a new road, a market, pure drinking water, sanitation, or housing are to be made at the request of the villagers, and although these plans will have to pass through the official hierarchy for approval in Baghdad, once the project is approved the money and experts will be sent directly to the village rather than, as formerly, back down through bureaucratic channels.

Vested interests, cultural conservatism, rural isolation, administrative difficulties, lack of trained personnel, and the indifference and contempt with which most townsmen still view the peasant are likely to complicate the welfare problems of Iraq's rural majority for a long time to come. But important steps have been taken which promise more rapid improvements than at any time in the past.

Nutrition and Diet

Malnutrition constitutes perhaps the major health problem in Iraq at the present time. Actual starvation is rare, but for the bulk of the population resistance to disease is lowered by a diet which is deficient in quantity, caloric content, and balance.

Diet, determined mainly by the character of the local food supply, consists largely of rice and fish in the marsh areas of the south; dates, fruits, and vegetables in the vicinity of Basra and along the Euphrates; and grain in the irrigated areas and in the north (see chap. 14). Cooking methods remove much of the vitamin content of the foods, as does the polishing of rice. The peasant consumes few fresh vegetables or fruits, items which he could raise to supplement his grain diet but tends to ignore. For both the fellah and nomad, vegetables and fruits are less "aristocratic" crops than wheat and barley. Iraqis generally enjoy dairy foods such as cheese or other fermented milk products—which possess a high nutritional value—but, except in certain areas, the fellah owns few livestock and the dairy yield is low. Flocks of ill-fed chickens are seen in most villages, but poultry and eggs are usually too valuable as a market commodity to be eaten by their peasant owners. Meat is an occasional luxury for most, usually reserved for feast days. The most commonly consumed meat is lamb (pork is forbidden to Moslems), and among nomads the meat of an old or sick camel may also be eaten. A relatively large proportion of expenditures on food is made for purchases of tea and sugar.

The principal beverages of the fellah are water and strong, syrupy tea. The nomad prefers strong coffee, and both tea and coffee are popular in the towns. There is a national alcoholic drink, *araq* (distilled from dates, it turns a milky white when diluted with water). Its consumption is, however, limited mainly to townsmen because the peasant can rarely afford it. Devout Moslems do not drink alcoholic beverages. Cola drinks have become popular in the last few years.

The monotonous fare of the fellah and the bedouin is rarely more than adequate for bare subsistence. The nomadic expression "eat like a camel" is applicable only to feast days and when guests are being entertained; then the table will be as bountiful as the supply permits. The diet is most ample in the north, where the system of land tenure gives the fellah a larger share of his crop (see chap. 14), and it is perhaps most meager in the congested southern areas, especially Al Amarah. The Dujaylah settlement offers a sharp contrast in the standard of living to the rest of rural Iraq (see chap. 14). Here the settlers have acquired animals and chickens and the government requires them to maintain small fruit gardens as a supplement to their main cereal crops. With no landlords to pay, they enjoy a higher income and better diet than does an ordinary tenant. The marsh dweller is on the whole better fed than his southern neighbors; milk, butter, and some cheese, fish, rice, and wild fowl are all available to him. He may go hungry, however, in the early summer when the rice crop has been consumed and the flooding waters curtail fishing.

For the wage earners in the towns and cities a more varied diet is possible. But for the unemployed or underemployed town laborer the high cost of bread and rice spells serious hardship. Wealthy urban dwellers, of course, can provide themselves with an adequate and varied diet.

Sanitation

Impure water poses a major health problem in Iraq and is the source of a number of diseases. A large percentage of the population lives in villages and towns which have sprung up along rivers and irrigation canals polluted with human and animal wastes. These rivers and canals, along with the stagnant pools of water that are the village reservoirs, continue to provide the major source of water for drinking as well as for bathing and laundering. Baghdad has filtration and chlorination facilities and roughly ninety cities and towns have water-purification plants in operation or under construction, but such protection is unknown in the average village. The belief, widespread in the Middle East, that unpurified water of certain rivers will enhance male fertility apparently has long been held in Iraq with regard to the Euphrates.

Except in the model settlements and in some sections of the cities, such sewage and sanitary facilities as exist are poor by modern western standards. The narrow streets are strewn with dirt, rubbish, and garbage; and dust clouds the air in summer. In the villages facilities for the disposal of garbage normally consist of ditches running along the rows of houses; pits dug near the houses or the banks of the irrigation canals serve as latrines. Contagion and sickness result also from the improper handling of perishable foods. Heat, dust, and flies contribute to food poisoning, as does irrigation with polluted water.

Incidence of Disease

The victim of one or more debilitating disease, the average Iraqi has been described as a "living pathological specimen," but medical treatment is being brought to more and more people. Progress has been made in curative medicine. The epidemic diseases of cholera, bubonic plague, and smallpox, which decimated the Iraqi population in the past, have been almost eradicated. Constant pilgrim travel, however, leaves open the possibility of the spreading of epidemics. The degenerative diseases are not a major factor in health, partly because most Iraqis do not live long enough to develop them—generally succumbing to diseases connected with poor sanitary conditions. While economic development may in time lower the incidence of these diseases, current conditions make it very difficult to apply modern remedies on a large scale.

Chief among the diseases common in the country are hookworm (ancylostomiasis), a result of poor sanitation; bilharziasis (schistosomiasis); malaria; and trachoma, a highly contagious eye infection.

Hookworm is largely a disease of the south. Prevention lies in proper sanitation measures. In recent years, cases of hookworm treated have diminished markedly, especially in Baghdad. In urban areas—such as Karbala—where sanitation is poor, the number of cases noted rose slightly. As city sewage systems improve and the wearing of shoes increases, the incidence of hookworm will in all probability decline.

Bilharziasis, a parasitic ailment, is also prevalent in the south, where it is estimated that as many as 30 percent of the total population are affected. The incidence is even higher in the provinces of Al Amarah, Al Muntafiq and Al Kut. Bilharziasis spreads primarily through the passing of human wastes into the irrigation canals, and the moist, flow-irrigation sections of the southern countryside favor the disease-producing organism. Like the hookworm, the bilharzia fluke is picked up through the skin of the foot; developing in the human liver, it reproduces, is passed through the urine into the water, goes through a stage of development in the body of a snail, and lives in stagnant water until it finds a human host. Typical symptoms of bilharziasis are lassitude, low vitality, and blood in the urine. The disease is very difficult to treat, but preventive measures are known. The host snail does not thrive in water flowing at a rate of as much as three miles an hour or in ditches of canals which are periodically drained. Footwear almost completely eliminates the chances of contact. Infected canals can be treated with copper sulfate. Unfortunately, irrigation projects have not so far been constructed in cooperation with health authorities, and there are indications that the incidence of bilharziasis has not declined with agricultural development.

Malaria, common throughout the watered areas of Iraq, is most prevalent in the north but has been spreading in the south with the expansion of irrigation facilities. The highest incidence has been in Mosul province, the lowest in Al Amarah. Transmitted by the mosquitoes thriving where there is stagnant water, the disease is normally endemic but sometimes breaks out in virulent form; recently it almost completely depopulated a resettlement area in the northern foothills. Malaria reportedly results in 50,000 deaths a year in Iraq, and in the areas of high incidence it contributes to an infant mortality rate as high as 500 per 1,000. As in the case of many other diseases, the means for preventing the spread of malaria are well known in Iraq, but preventive measures have not been developed in cooperation with agricultural programs. Useful work in drainage and DDT campaigns against both malaria and bilharziasis have, however, been undertaken by the Institute of Endemic Diseases, an agency within the Ministry of Health.

Almost half the cases of eye disease treated in Iraq involve trachoma, a common cause of blindness. This fly-borne ailment, which yields to treatment in its early stages, is another example of a disease which could be eradicated by improved sanitary conditions. In Baghdad the incidence of trachoma has declined; in the Dujaylah settlement, however, it has been estimated that about 80 percent of the population are afflicted with it.

Iraq's population suffers from numerous other ailments. Crowded housing conditions and improper diet contribute to a high incidence of tuberculosis. Typhoid and dysentery also are widespread. Many suffer from anemia (a result of poor diet) and intestinal parasites. Excessive childbearing tends to undermine the health of women, and complications in childbirth are a common cause of death among women, particularly in the nomadic tribes. Although circulatory disorders and the degenerative diseases of old age are not widespread in the population as a whole, ailments of this type do appear in the wealthy groups.

Medical Facilities and Personnel

Almost all medical facilities are controlled by the government, and most of the doctors in Iraq are officials of the Ministry of Health. In addition, under the 1955–60 five-year plan of the Iraq Development Board expenditures directly for public health have been estimated at $80 million. Many of the Development Board's other projects, such as the new sewage system for Baghdad and new water facilities, indirectly affect health conditions in many ways. Rural health services are developing, but the main effort is still concentrated in the towns. In the past there has been inadequate cooperation between the various government agencies concerned with public health. Recent reports, however, indicate that coordination is improving.

Each of the provinces and districts has a chief medical officer, who also has his own private practice to supplement his government salary. Even if rural medical officers devoted their whole attention to their public responsibilities, transportation difficulties and the necessity of obtaining permission from Baghdad to move from their headquarters would seriously curtail their activities. These officers are also burdened with administrative duties in hospitals, clinics, and the dispensaries which are rapidly increasing in number even in the smaller towns. Foreign advisers have strongly recommended an accelerated program of training for medical assistants, who could relieve the provincial and district medical officers of some of their responsibilities.

One of the most serious problems facing the Ministry of Health is the shortage of trained personnel. The needs of the rural areas, especially in the south, are not being met by the present number of doctors, nurses, and technicians. There is roughly 1 doctor for every 5,500 persons, and dentists are almost unheard of except in the cities. The shortage is accentuated by the fact that most medical personnel are concentrated in larger cities such as Baghdad and Basra. Doctors trained at state expense, and therefore bound to serve a term of years in public service, strongly resist appointments to posts outside the city and make every effort to remain in Baghdad. Some have been known to resign from government service in protest against rural appointments. The government, recognizing that the lack of amenities in country districts intensifies the preference of doctors for an urban practice, has recently started to build homes for doctors in the rural areas.

Medical training is given by the Medical College of the University of Baghdad. There has apparently been an overemphasis on training specialists rather than the general practitioners so badly needed. Moreover, the instruction is largely based on modern techniques and assumes the availability to the practitioner of up-to-date equipment. Thus many doctors when faced with rural conditions find themselves unable to apply what they have been taught. Since 1955, however, an attempt has been made to bring the orientation of medical courses more into conformity with the practical problems faced by the Iraqi doctor. Experiments which had previously been done in the laboratory are now carried into the field, and a course in industrial medicine has been included in the medical curriculum.

The Jewish exodus after the creation of Israel intensified the shortage of nurses and trained technicians—positions often filled previously by Jews. Moslem girls traditionally have not been attracted to a nursing career, but the recent use of the term "health visitor" instead of "nurse" to designate the position and the provision for their working in pairs seem to have had a favorable effect on enrollment. Recently the Red Crescent Society (the Moslem equivalent of the Red Cross) sponsored a nurses training program which may heighten the prestige of the profession.

The University of Baghdad has a School of Pharmacy and Chemistry in addition to the Medical College, but few pharmacists find the salaries paid by the government attractive enough to induce them to leave their private businesses. The dispensing of drugs is therefore often done by medical assistants with no specialized knowledge of pharmaceutics.

In addition to the cadre of medical personnel with formal training there are hospital orderlies and health inspectors who have generally had some practical hospital training.

Most hospitals, clinics, and dispensaries are run by the Ministry of Health. Medical facilities are also maintained by the army, railroads, police, Ministry of Education, the Port of Basra Authority, and the oil companies. Almost one third of all hospitals, however, are in the Baghdad area, and in general they are inaccessible to villagers and nomads.

Most of the hospitals offer general treatment. They are satisfactorily equipped, but some are in need of repair. All hospitals have suffered from a shortage of personnel and poor administration; in 1956 the Ministry of Health announced a postponement in the construction of new hospitals pending the training of adequate numbers of personnel to staff them.

More than 450 village dispensaries now offer treatment for minor injuries and inoculation against some diseases. They are staffed by local health officers, who usually adjust more readily to village life than doctors. While these dispensaries appear to be well supplied, they are rarely favored with visits from the district doctor.

Rural communities are also served by a number of small local health centers established by the Ministry of Social Affairs with the cooperation of the United Nations. These centers emphasize preventive measures as well as the treatment of sickness.

Two United Nations organizations have aided in the improvement of health standards as well as in the process of training medical personnel. The World Health Organization (WHO) has teams working on specific problems in districts where they are most acute; the United Nations Educational, Scientific, and Cultural Organization (UNESCO), has been engaged in a comprehensive effort in particular areas to raise community standards of health and sanitation. Both agencies have trainee programs designed to enable Iraqis to sustain these efforts unaided within a few years.

Attitudes toward Medical Treatment

Regarding illness as an inevitable and normal condition of life rather than as a temporary suspension of good health, the fellah is little disposed to seek medical advice and treatment while he still is able to follow a regular daily work routine. Hospital treatment is free but often unavailable. When he does have access to hospital treatment the peasant is usually reluctant to accept it, fearing to leave his wife and children and apprehensive about his ability to maintain them while away. Thus he continues to rely on folk practices.

Like other Middle Easterners, Iraqis have traditionally regarded illness as a manifestation of God's will or as the work of evil spirits. While the spirits and the "evil eye" could be warded off with charms, the Divine Will was unchangeable, for God had ordained all things, and sickness and other misfortunes were to be borne with resignation. Islam held out the promise of Paradise after life and taught that life is just a preparation for death, which is the end of pain, toil, and misery. In the towns these views are yielding to the spread of westernized education and modern medical techniques, but they still persist among the poor in general and are strongest in the relative isolation of the villages and the tribes.

One of the areas in which the traditional ways remain particularly strong is that of childbirth. For many, the midwife remains the proper—and the only—expert attendant in this crisis. Unseen dangers threaten both mother and child at this time and surround the infant during its first years of life. The mother is pampered and protected by all sorts of charms to ward off spirits. While pregnant she will not visit a childless woman or a woman with only female children lest she expose her unborn child to the "evil eye," and the young baby is thought to be vulnerable to the influence of spirits both good and evil. As the child grows older it moves further and further from this spirit world but may be snatched back to it at any time. As a measure of concealment the child may be kept dirty and disheveled, and sometimes a boy is dressed as a girl to trick the "evil eye." The infant mortality rate, highest during the first five years of life, lends support to these superstitions and to some well-meant but actually harmful measures. Thus the common practice of packing the infant's umbilical cord in manure to promote healing may cause tetanus.

There is a strong preference among both men and women for medical attendants of their own sex. Women doctors share in the respect generally accorded members of the medical profession, but they tend to be even more reluctant than their male colleagues to work in rural areas. The importance of the midwife, however, and the practical accessibility of her services to the villagers have been recognized by the government, and training clinics for midwives have been established.

An example of popular attitudes which have impeded the diagnosis and treatment of disease is the widespread feeling that tuberculosis is "shameful" and to be concealed if at all possible. The government is attempting to combat this attitude; it has plans to increase the number of beds available for treatment of the disease and also plans to construct a modern sanatorium. On the other hand, *bejel,* a disease resembling syphilis prevalent among the bedouins, does not seem to carry any stigma. World Health Organization teams have been working with some success to combat the disease.

There has been a certain amount of resistance to the mobile clinics, which are often the sole medical facilities available to villagers and nomads. These clinics do not seem as popular as fixed installations. In general it has been found that clinics which are integral parts of the communities they serve, staffed by familiar local personnel, are the most readily attended. The average Iraqi, given the opportunity, quickly turns to modern practitioners, and in the villages the news of new drugs and medical services is eagerly awaited. He usually submits willingly to treatment when its purpose is explained in terms he can understand and even feels "cheated" if he leaves the hospital or clinic without having had an injection, pill, or medicine of some kind.

In the fields of sanitation and preventive medicine, however, widespread ignorance and apathy persist. Patients often return to the clinic or hospital with a recurrence of a disease cured previously. Popular ignorance of the causes of disease is responsible for the high incidence of many easily preventable ailments. The problem is intensified when preventive measures must be carried out on a broad scale. A successful example of concerted action to improve health conditions, however, was the "Health Week" in Ad Diwaniyah in 1952, to which the inhabitants responded enthusiastically. Their pride in the hygienic measures they learned at that time and in the subsequently improved health of the community have encouraged government advisers to suggest more of these projects.

18

FAMILY

THE TRADITIONAL FAMILY IN IRAQ, AS ELSEWHERE IN THE Middle East, in addition to providing its members with support and social orientation in childhood, remains throughout their lives a primary agency for economic cooperation, social control, and mutual protection. The first loyalty of an individual is to his family—on whose wealth, welfare, and reputation his own are to a considerable degree dependent. Prescriptions relating to family honor are binding, and there is a strong tradition of kin solidarity, reinforced by Islam but long antedating its advent. Relatives may quarrel but in the face of outside threat the family displays its fundamental cohesiveness.

Deeply ingrained family loyalty manifests itself in business and public life no less than in domestic matters and personal relationships. The mutually protective attitude of relatives is taken as a matter of course and kinsmen are expected to render one another special favors and services. Taken for granted, the widespread practice of securing employment and favored treatment for relatives bears no stigma of nepotism and relatives tend to be preferred business partners since they are likely to be more "reliable" than persons over whom one does not have the hold of kinship ties.

The impact of western influences and technological and social change is modifying family patterns as well as other aspects of Iraqi life, especially in the cities. New forms of economic activity are tending to break down the old self-sufficiency of the family and to lessen its cohesiveness. Increased educational opportunities are broadening the once highly circumscribed role of women to include many activities outside the home, and new political loyalties are beginning to compete with the once almost exclusive ties of kin and local groups. In the remoter rural areas of Iraq, however, among Arabs and Kurds—both nomadic and settled—the family essentially has preserved its traditional character.

Structure and Dynamics

The basic principle determining membership in the Iraqi family is kinship reckoned in the male line. The separate terms for paternal and maternal relatives reflect the importance placed on keeping the two lines distinct and differentiating between their roles.

A typical household in the traditional urban and village pattern consists of an extended family: a man and his wife and their unmarried children along with the married sons and their wives and children. Often it also includes the father's widowed sister, his aged parents, a paternal orphaned nephew or niece, or a paternal cousin. The essential bond in this extended family is relationship to the father, and in the event of a quarrel between the families of the father and mother a son is expected to stand by his father against his mother's father or brothers. Upon marriage a girl leaves her family and becomes a member of her husband's. She is supposed to relinquish loyalty to her own father and brothers and to identify herself completely with the extended family of her husband. In practice, however, the wife often retains ties and contact with her own blood relatives and in the event of a marital dispute she can return to her father's house.

Traditionally the various branches of the large family living under the same roof or close together cooperated in economic activity. Although not so commonly found as in the past this pattern survives among many Iraqi peasants—particularly in areas where it is economically advantageous for several branches of the family to work the land jointly and in areas where alternative means of livelihood are scarce. The economic role of the extended family is no longer as great as it once was, however, and in the larger towns and cities, under the impact of western influences and new economic opportunities, there is a growing tendency for married sons to set up separate residences and to strike out on their own. For instance, where the oil companies offer relatively attractive employment an alternative to family enterprise is provided and individuals feel less dependent on family connections.

Among the bedouins, the household unit typically consists only of a man and his wife and their unmarried children, but close relatives tend to be clustered in nearby tents and the extended family still functions as an economic unit. This residence pattern is also found in those villages where tribal traditions remain strong, as in the marsh area of southern Iraq.

Among the Kurds, too, the households tend to be small. As among the bedouins, most consist of a man and his wife and their unmarried children; married sons set up separate households. Although the members of the Kurdish household function as an independent economic unit they recognize an obligation to come to the support of a wider circle in times of bereavement or need.

Beyond the extended family, kinship ties reach into the lineage, the group of extended families related to each other through descent from a common male ancestor. In small villages everyone is likely to belong to the same lineage, but in larger villages there may be two or more lineages. In such places, rivalry between lineages is common but is tempered by economic cooperation, intermarriage, and the political authority of the village headman and elders.

This pattern of kinship organization is most pronounced among the bedouins and those Kurds who are still tribally organized. It involves allegiance to a hierarchy of units ranging from the family through the sublineage and lineage to the tribe.

Elsewhere, awareness of these larger kin ties varies. It is fading among long-sedentarized groups in the larger villages and towns. Among the tribally organized marsh people, however, it is not uncommon for a villager to know the names of every relative on both his mother's and father's side for five or six generations. Individuals have certain obligations to other members of their lineage, and in general family ties are traced back different distances for different purposes. For example, whereas one's near kinsmen within the extended family may suffice for economic cooperation, it may be necessary to seek the help of more distant kin in order to avenge a murder.

Authority and Children

For Moslems the rules of personal and group conduct are laid down in the Koran and sanctioned by associated religious tradition. The small minority of Christians in Iraq have their own codes of behavior, but among Moslems and Christians alike the family is the paramount social unit and family authority is vested in the father. Paternal authority is particularly emphasized among Moslems, who regard the master of the household as theoretically exercising absolute control over the wife and children. In practice, however, here as elsewhere a strong-willed wife can, and generally does, dominate a weaker husband. Moreover, the wife in her later role of mother-in-law exerts considerable authority and influence over her sons' wives and children.

Ultimate authority in the extended family generally rests with the oldest male, but personality, ability, or wealth may bring about the selection of a younger man. Matters of family policy, honor, relations with other families, and so forth, traditionally are determined by the head of the family in consultation with other ranking male kin. Within the lineage the authority of the senior member dwindles to an advisory power.

Koranic injunction, economic motivation, and considerations of prestige and family strength all contribute to the traditional high value placed on large families. The greater the number of children, especially sons, the greater the prestige of the father, and through him that of the family as a whole. Among the poor, children are regarded as economic assets; the cost of their maintenance is small and they begin to contribute to the family income at an early age. The subordinate position of the daughter-in-law in the household of her husband's family provides an additional motive for having many offspring, since the young wife, unless she is from a more important family than her husband, gains prestige and position only with the birth of children. A childless woman—often said to be cursed by God—is regarded with commiseration mixed with contempt. Failure to bear children may frequently result in divorce or in the husband's taking a second wife.

In the rearing of the Iraqi child, strong emphasis is placed on teaching him to conform to the patterns laid down by his elders and to be an obedient member of the family group. Family solidarity is stressed and the child learns early that his wishes are subordinate to the interests of the family. Corporal punishment is employed, but more commonly among urban dwellers than in rural families.

Children know much greater intimacy with their mothers than with their fathers (who tend in public to avoid overt expressions of affection toward their offspring), and maternal influence may be very great. Moreover, the mother, in her role as the compassionate figure in the family, may temper through discreet intervention any undue severity on the part of the father.

Responsibility for the training of boys is in the hands of the father, who starts preparing them for the economic tasks of adulthood at an early age. In rural areas the *amm* (paternal uncle) also plays an important role in a boy's upbringing and figures prominently in the circumcision ceremony and on other occasions. Should the father die, the *amm* takes the boy as his own son, supporting and training him for his role in later life.

At the age of four or five a girl has already been given some simple household duties, and she now begins to help tend the younger children. From this time on the mother prepares the child for her eventual role in her husband's household, explaining that she will serve not only husband but mother-in-law as well.

In rural families sons even after marriage are expected to give obedience to their fathers. A son may accompany his father to work in the fields or to deliberations of the village council, but he should remain in the background and listen quietly to his elders. Only when he himself becomes a father does he begin to gain any prestige or authority, and he is still expected to consult his father and respect his decisions.

In the towns and cities, particularly in relatively westernized middle-class families, the pattern of paternal authority is being considerably modified. Sons of this growing group (and unmarried daughters as well among Christians) tend more and more to leave the family household and often to move to other parts of the country, sometimes deliberately relinquishing family ties in the interests of moving up the social scale unburdened by responsibilities toward relatives.

Marriage and Divorce

Marriages in Iraq, as in other parts of the Moslem world, in the past were customarily arranged by the parents of the young people. This practice persists in conservative circles—both rural and urban—but it is very rare nowadays for the prospective partners not to be acquainted at least by sight, and the girl's consent is becoming increasingly important.

Marriages contracted within the large extended family traditionally have been preferred and those between the children of brothers are still considered ideal. Such marriages within the family are favored for a number of reasons: a girl married to her father's brother's son remains in the same extended family as her parents and thus conflicts of loyalty are less likely to arise; both sets of parents are likely to be satisfied that the match is socially suitable since the young couple are of the same descent; the bride's father acquires the support of a son-in-law who already has a close relationship with him as his nephew; and, finally, a girl's inheritance from her father remains in the family. In return for these advantages and in the interests of the political solidarity of the family the dowry paid by the groom is generally reduced for a paternal cousin.

Among the bedouins, Kurdish tribesmen, and some settled villagers, marriage with a paternal uncle's daughter came to be regarded as a man's right, and a father was expected not to give his daughter to anyone else without the consent of the girl's cousin. The Kurds and tribally organized marsh Arabs still enforce this right and there have been cases in which girls refusing their cousins have been murdered. In the majority of the population, however, marriage between cousins, although still regarded as ideal, occurs less frequently than in the past. No statistics are available on its actual incidence but in parts of Kurdistan it has been estimated to range as high as 50 percent. Next to a relative, a girl from the same village is considered the most desirable partner and marriage within the village is more common among all groups than marriage with outsiders.

Marriage choices in the towns and cities tend to have a far wider range than do those in the countryside. Only in the upper segment of urban society is the preference for intrafamily alliances strongly emphasized. Anxious to limit its ranks and to preserve its special status, the small, wealthy elite maintains a tightly knit family organization; its members tend either to marry relatives or to link themselves with other prominent families through marriage ties.

Young men of the emerging middle class are tending to take the initiative in seeking brides and their choice is more apt to be influenced by personal preference than by considerations of family. To such persons the advantages of a union with an old-fashioned cousin are less compelling than the attraction of an educated wife able to help in the climb up the social and professional ladder.

Statistics are not available on the average age of men and women at marriage. In the countryside early marriages are still the rule; in the towns and cities increased educational opportunities and western influences are bringing about later marriages.

Marriage Ceremonies

Among the Moslem majority marriage is concluded as a civil contract between the families of the bride and groom after negotiation—often through an intermediary—of the dowry to be paid. Weddings provide an occasion for celebration and the reaffirmation of kinship ties. In the villages and in conservative urban circles two ceremonies precede Moslem marriages: the *khutbah,* or engagement, and the *katb al-kitab,* or signing of the contract. For the *khutbah* a few relatives and friends are invited to the prospective bride's house, where the parents of the couple announce the forthcoming marriage. Held sometime later the ceremony of *katb al-kitab* is attended by an official of a sharia (Moslem religious) court and a large gathering of friends.

An essential part of the contract is the specification of the amount of dowry to be paid by the bridegroom. Generally a portion of the dowry is held back and is payable only in the event of divorce or death; among the marsh Arabs the amount withheld is seldom stipulated. The father of the bride customarily spends at least some of the dowry on clothes, jewelry, or land for his daughter. The actual marriage, accompanied by feasting and dancing, may take place immediately or it may occur several months or a year or more after the signing of the contract. Among the nomadic tribes the wedding ceremony is likely to be a simpler affair, the principal formality being the escorting of the bride into the groom's tent.

Among Christians a formal marriage contract is not required but there is sometimes an informal agreement to pay a bride price. Prohibited by Islam, marriages between Moslem women and Christians are extremely rare in Iraq. Intermarriage of members of the Sunnite and Shiite sects of Islam, while not forbidden by religious doctrine, is generally frowned upon.

Polygamy

Polygamy in Islam is regulated by tradition and Koranic prescription. A man is allowed a maximum of four wives and he is enjoined to treat them equally and to provide each with a separate domicile. He must also pay a bride price for each and must support the children. Only the relatively well-to-do are able to meet these costs, and it has been estimated that fewer than 8 percent of Iraqis have more than one wife, while those having more than two are extremely rare. Repeated divorce and remarriage, however, is fairly common among certain groups.

Polygamy is most prevalent among small landowners, to whom plural marriage is a symbol of wealth and status; the wives serve too as a means of gaining increased influence in the village through the acquisition of a large number of kin who can provide economic and political support. Among the marsh Arabs there are cases of sheikhs taking five or six or even more wives, although only the first four are legally recognized. Polygamy is becoming increasingly rare in the towns and tends to be deprecated by educated Iraqis.

Divorce

Under Moslem law a man can divorce his wife at will by pronouncing three times the traditional formula "I divorce you" in the presence of two witnesses. The wife does not have the right to oppose this action; and, in practice, a Moslem wife will almost never initiate a divorce unless a special provision granting her the liberty is included in the marriage contract. She does, however, have the formal right to appeal for a divorce, or have a male kinsman appeal for her, to the shariah court. Dissatisfaction with the law has been increasing in recent years, and among westernized townspeople unilateral divorces are becoming less common.

A divorced woman usually returns to her father's or brother's household, and she can claim that portion of the dowry reserved for divorce. If, however, a religious official judges her to be at fault because of sterility, bad temper, impropriety, or other reasons, she forfeits this part of the dowry. After a divorce a man may remarry at once, but a woman must wait for three months to make sure that she is not pregnant; meanwhile the man is entitled to revoke his decision. Should the wife be pregnant she may not remarry until she has borne and weaned the child. During this time her former husband must support her and the baby. Under Moslem law the children of divorced parents belong to the father, but they generally remain with the mother until the age of seven in the case of boys and nine in the case of girls.

19

FORMAL EDUCATION

UNTIL THE ADVENT OF WESTERN INFLUENCE IN THE NINEteenth century, education in Iraq as elsewhere in the Middle East was dominated by the Islamic tradition of religious and classical learning. The curriculum of elementary schools was based on memorization of the Koran; reading and writing received secondary emphasis. Higher education, available only to a small minority, was concerned largely with Islamic theology and mastery of classical Arabic. The Christian and Jewish minorities (see chap. 4) maintained their own schools with a comparable emphasis on religious training. The prestige attached to religious learning was reflected in the strong pressure put upon even the poorest villager or urban dweller to see that his sons acquired at least some formal knowledge of the Koran.

It was not until the reforms of the mid-nineteenth century that a secular system of public education was established throughout the Ottoman Empire, of which Iraq was a part. Extremely limited in extent, this public system did not displace the network of village kuttabs, the traditional religious schools. With the establishment of the Mandate in 1921, the public school system organized under Turkish rule began slowly to expand under British supervision. American influence also began to make itself felt in Iraqi education—directly through mission schools in Baghdad and Basra, and indirectly through the impact, on the educational system as a whole, of teachers trained at the American University of Beirut.

Education in Iraq today represents an amalgam of the religiously oriented Islamic traditions on the one hand and a western-inspired secular system on the other. While the kuttab is disappearing, the old pattern of rote learning persists in secular education, and it frequently conflicts with teaching methods and texts borrowed from the West. Similarly, the traditional value placed on facility of verbal expression has left a deep imprint upon education. Eloquence and the ability to quote from the Koran or to marshal proverbs in argument are still the marks of an educated man.

Although the government has waged an active campaign for a number of years, it is still far from its goal of universal literacy. According to the census of 1947, about 15 percent of the male population (excluding nomads) and less than 5 percent of the females were literate. The Christian minority has always shown a higher rate of literacy. Among the Moslems, members of the Shia sect are often less literate than the Sunnis.

The enrollment in private schools represents only about one sixth of that in educational institutions as a whole. Most private schools are traditionalist village kuttabs, which are gradually disappearing as government schools begin to reach the smaller villages.

Other private institutions, including a small number of foreign schools, are concentrated in the cities and among the religious minorities. Resented by nationalist elements, they are subject to the close control and inspection of the Ministry of Education and their curricula and texts are required to conform to government specifications.

Primary and Secondary Schools

Public education is centralized under the Ministry of Education, which has responsibility for the organization of the school system, the setting of examinations and curricula, and the appointment of teachers. Provincial councils retain administrative control over primary schools in their respective areas of jurisdiction. Education is free for both primary and secondary school pupils, and is compulsory at the primary level. The latter provision, however, is enforced only in specific areas—designated by the Ministry of Education—where the necessary facilities exist.

Despite a steady increase in government spending on education and a sizable expansion of the school system in recent decades, it was estimated in 1954 that educational facilities were accessible to less than one third of Iraq's children of primary school age. The number of primary schools increased from 88 in 1920 to 1,307 in 1951, and with the added impetus of the educational program of the Iraq Development Board, to 1,748 in 1957. This expansion, however, has not kept pace with the increase in the number of children eligible for primary education, now estimated at more than a million. Considerable improvement in the ratio of educational facilities to children is expected to take place as a result of the government's 1955–1960 five-year plan, which envisages the expenditure of some $25 million for the building of schools and the recruitment and training of teachers. In providing additional educational facilities, however, the government faces a chronic shortage of personnel. All teachers in the public schools are civil servants and are inclined to prefer administrative posts in the Ministry of Education, where the chances of promotion are better than in teaching. The difficulty of recruiting teachers of high caliber is especially acute since few are willing to accept the privations accompanying rural teaching.

In addition to increasing the number of regular primary schools, the government has established special night schools and "Fighting Illiteracy" schools for adults, and enlisted men in the army are taught to read and write. Through these efforts and additional educational projects of the 1955–1960 development plan, the over-all literacy rate may soon be expected to show an increase over the 1947 estimates.

Curriculum

Primary schooling provides a six-year course leading to a public examination which, if passed, qualifies the pupil to enter secondary school.

Although based largely on western secular models, the curriculum also provides for the study of religion. Conservative Moslems nevertheless resent the fact that religion no longer occupies the preeminent position it once held in basic education. An attempt is being made to give the curriculum of rural schools a more practical focus by the introduction of such innovations as agricultural training. By and large, however, the elementary program remains highly academic in orientation and much importance is attached to the mastery of classical Arabic. The relatively large proportion of time devoted to the study of Arabic not only reflects this emphasis but is in part necessitated by the substantial difference between the classical written and the colloquial spoken languages (see chap. 4).

In northeastern Iraq, where Kurds are in the majority, primary instruction in the first years is conducted in Kurdish. (Similarly, the small Turkoman communities may have their children taught in Turkish, but this practice is dying out with the gradual assimilation of the Turkoman minority.) It has been suggested that the use of Kurdish in public education is apt to perpetuate the separatist tendencies of the Kurds. The curriculum, however, is strictly controlled by the Ministry of Education, which is attempting to instill among all groups loyalty to the Iraqi nation.

Secondary schooling is divided into a three-year intermediate course and a two-year course which prepares students for higher education. The latter stage is followed by national examinations designed to determine whether the candidates are qualified to proceed further. In the intermediate course the same subjects are studied as in primary school, with the addition of physical sciences. The program of the final two-year course is divided into branches which focus on science, literature, and commercial training. (Girls also have the option of a child welfare course.) Few students choose to specialize in science, partly because the qualifying examinations for this course are more difficult. The emphasis in secondary education continues, as in the past, to be literary, with a majority of students preparing for a university education and a future in government or one of the professions. The academic orientation of secondary schools of course does little to alleviate the serious shortage of technicians needed to carry out Iraq's ambitious economic development program. The government is aware of the problem and has indicated that it does not favor the umlimited extension of secondary education on its present academic basis.

School Attendance

Attendance at public schools is restricted not only by the inadequacy of educational facilities but also by the attitudes and extreme poverty of many of the peasants, who comprise the bulk of the population. There is a widespread view among villagers that the aims and methods of government schools are neither relevant to practical life nor suitable on religious grounds. An even more compelling factor limiting rural school attendance is the paramount importance of children as members of the agricultural labor force. The peasant child becomes an economic asset to his family at an early age, and the impoverished farmer cannot readily dispense with his children's services in the fields. Moreover, many also fear that primary schooling may make children discontented with agriculture as a way of life without equipping them for any occupation other than unskilled labor in the towns. Secondary schooling, with all its attendant expenses remains beyond the reach of the great majority.

Still another obstacle to universal education is the distance of most public schools from the average villager. They are seldom located in any but the largest villages, and the cost of boarding children away from home is prohibitive to the fellah. A recently inaugurated free-lunch program, however, has considerably increased school enrollment.

Among those children who do enter school there is an extremely high rate of "drop-outs" at both the primary and secondary levels. Thus enrollment figures show that a disproportionately large number of children attend the first years of both courses, and only about one in ten reaches secondary school. This situation cannot be attributed only to economic factors; it stems in part from the system of rigid government examinations, which has the effect of presenting education as a series of hurdles dissuading or barring many children from continuing to the higher levels.

Education of girls in Iraq has always lagged far behind that of boys, and secondary schooling for girls dates only from 1929. Although the proportion of girls in the student population has been increasing steadily, they still account for only about 26 percent of the total enrollment in primary and secondary schools. Until recently coeducation was not sanctioned by public opinion and did not exist where school facilities permitted segregation of the sexes. As a result of western influence, however, model primary schools have been established on a coeducational basis, and the trend is expected to spread.

Education for the bedouins has been the subject of much experimentation on the part of the government but no over-all program to deal with the problem has yet been developed. Except for the sons of sayyids (persons claiming descent from the Prophet Mohammed who often function as religious leaders) and the sons of tribal chiefs, nomads have traditionally had no formal education. A few mobile schools have recently been established to accompany tribes on their migration. The extent to which bedouin children are given educational opportunities, however, will probably for some time to come depend largely on the attitude of individual tribal leaders. The Shammar tribes of the north, for example, are anxious to have their youth educated, and they cooperate closely with government educational authorities.

Higher Education

Higher education in Iraq, dating from the 1920's, is offered in ten institutions, incorporated in 1956 as the University of Baghdad. All are coeducational except the College of Agriculture (for men only) and Queen Aliyah College (for women). Tuition is free in all but the colleges of law and commerce, where modest fees are charged. The government may, however, require a student's services for a specified number of years after graduation.

Enormous prestige attaches to a college diploma in Iraq. It serves as a passport to the professions and government positions, and it may compensate for humble origins in an individual's efforts to gain social position.

Since the establishment of the Mandate, many Iraqis have been sent abroad for higher education. In recent years their number has increased, and in 1954 it was estimated that 3,000 Iraqis were studying abroad on scholarships provided by the government, by international organizations, or by private foundations. The majority of these students were in the United States, Great Britain, and Lebanon, but there were appreciable numbers in France and Egypt.

Education abroad has had various social effects. It has made available to Iraq a body of educated young people who could not have been trained at home in so short a time. It is giving impetus to the growth of a new middle class and, in general, is contributing to greater social and economic mobility. Dissatisfactions with the program, however, have been numerous. Students sometimes choose fields of study of doubtful use to themselves or to the country. Moreover, exposure to ways of life differing widely from that familiar in Iraq and a higher standard of living often make the student upon his return an unhappy misfit in revolt against the traditional patterns to which he is expected to conform.

Technical Training

Apart from the training provided by the Iraq Petroleum Company, the facilities for technical instruction are limited to three technical schools at Baghdad, Basra, and Kirkuk (which were graduating a total of only about fifty students a year between 1945 and 1955) and an agricultural school at the Abu Ghurayb experimental farm near Baghdad. These facilities are inadequate for the country's needs in terms of quality as well as quantity. The on-the-job training offered by the oil company, on the other hand, is excellent, and many trainees enter other industries, thereby affecting the level of technical efficiency in the labor force as a whole. The government's efforts to expand its own technical training program in line with its development goals must overcome resistance engendered by popular notions of the objectives of education. Despite the country's pressing economic needs for technical skills, education in the eyes of most Iraqis is still primarily a path to urban life, to white-collar jobs, and to government positions in particular. Like other Middle Easterners, they traditionally have looked upon manual work with disdain and aversion, and those who receive technical training tend to regard themselves as supervisors no longer obliged to work with their hands.

20

ART AND INTELLECTUAL EXPRESSION

BY THE CLOSE OF THE NINETEENTH CENTURY, THE POLITICAL and social disintegration of hundreds of years had left its mark on almost every aspect of art and intellectual expression in Iraq. Nonetheless, the country's contributions to the artistic and intellectual achievements of the whole Middle East had been one of the most significant elements in its long history. Throughout its pre-Islamic past the Tigris-Euphrates area witnessed the rise and decline of great civilizations which left magnificent architecture, irrigation systems, sculpture, textiles, pottery, and work in precious metals. Excavations at ancient Babylonian and Assyrian sites have uncovered vast collections of clay tablets containing writings on history and philosophy, law (such as the famous legal code of Hammurabi), advances in mathematics, and experiments in chemistry.

The advent of Islam in the seventh century stimulated a new outpouring which continued for more than four hundred years. Baghdad came to rival Constaninople as a seat of learning and art. Scholars from all over the Middle East gathered there, intermingling Greek, Indian, Persian, and Judaic thought and talent. In time these diverse elements were submerged and transformed into an all-embracing Islamic synthesis in which a compelling monotheistic religion defined man's place and duties in a supernatural order and constituted the inspiration and guide in art and scholarship as well as in the ordinary affairs of daily life.

The golden age under the Abbasside caliphs (749–1258 A.D.) began to decline and was completely destroyed by the catastrophic Mongol invasion. In the following centuries a devastated Iraq was repeatedly torn by internal strife and foreign conquest. In the general ruin the Islamic religion—which had earlier provided a broad framework within which intellectual life flourished—fell back on a defensively rigid orthodoxy. Originality of thought was sacrificed to the cautious exposition of dogma, and both artistic and intellectual expression were characterized by sterile uniformity until the twentieth century. Little has been written about the cultural influence on Iraq of the Ottoman Turks, who ruled the country from the sixteenth century until the end of World War I; the common Arab view is that the Turkish period was repressive and stultifying.

In the present century western influence has tended to undermine the religious orientation of creative activity in Iraq: new forms have appeared in art and literature, and contact with the West has initiated a period of re-evaluation of traditional values and of the religion itself (see chap. 5). In its initial response to the new influences the urban elite tended toward either uncritical imitation or categorical rejection. In one degree or another the old forms have been weakened or modified. Attempts to reconcile the traditional and the modern, or even to delineate the elements of a discrete culture, are very recent.

Today western influence is reviving and reinforcing the cultural dominance of the urban centers, among which Baghdad is foremost. In general the flow of cultural influence is from the towns to the countryside; because this process is gradual and not easily discernible many aspects of urban culture do not penetrate the rural districts at all. Western influence is introducing forms of artistic and intellectual expression that are alien and unintelligible to the ordinary peasant and nomad. It remains to be seen whether these innovations can gain a wider acceptance, blending to one degree or another with the indigenous patterns, or whether they will remain the province of the few and a source of confusion and often of resentment for the majority.

Ethnic and religious differences also mark artistic and intellectual expression in Iraq but nationalism is providing an important leavening influence.

Intellectual Expression

The importance assigned to intellectual activity in Iraq was long ago reflected in the saying: "Seek knowledge though it be in China." Under the Abbasside caliphs Baghdad witnessed a great intellectual flowering: a time marked by the translation of Greek and other foreign works was soon followed by a period of innovation. In the sciences the foundations for algebra, astronomy, and alchemy were laid, and the system of Arabic numerals became a tool for mathematicians all over the world.

Early in the Abbasside dynasty Iraq came under strong Persian influences which contributed new concepts useful to the exposition of religious and philosophical ideas. Persian questioning of the values and forms brought to them by the Arabs supported indirectly the existing atmosphere of intellectual freedom and inquiry in Baghdad. The tenth century Iraqi theologian al-Ashari (d. 935) encouraged the use of the dialectic in religious argument, and Syrian and Coptic Christian scholars helped to introduce Greek logic and metaphysics into Iraqi philosophy, although the Greek concept of man's ability to participate in a perfect, universal knowledge through the systematic use of mind was never fully assimilated. While the central motif of Islamic intellectual life in Iraq was always Arab, this Semitic-Persian-Greek combination contributed greatly to the elaboration of the theories upon which Islam as a religion and as a body politic came to be based.

Greek concepts and terminology also contributed to the clarification of Sufism, or Moslem mysticism, which until that time had been confined to an orthodox vocabulary in its attempts to describe essentially intuitive religious experience. Sufism, which took form in the Shiite holy city of Al Kufah in the eighth century, was apparently derived from a pre-Islamic tradition of mysticism, itself reaching back to still more ancient antecedents in the area. It took on a specific character through its use of intense meditation and rhythmical recitations from the Koran. The practice of Sufism in its various forms gradually became embellished with and systematized under external influences—Indian, Christian, Greek, and Persian. Originally associated most strongly with the Shiites, it spread to Basra and to its eventual center in Baghdad; Sufism in time came to denote the entire body of Moslem mysticism.

Generally, the ultimate goal of the Sufi is to draw near to God in a mystical union through prayer or through a defined series of steps. Such ecstasy is possible by definition: "the existence of created things is nothing but the very essence of the existence of the Creator," and since man pre-exists as an idea in the mind of God, it is inversely possible that the soul can again unite with God.

This doctrine had important effects on the Moslem community in which it emerged and on the intellectual life of that community. Aside from the positive influence of such great thinkers as al-Ghazali 1058–1111) and Ibn Sina (980–1037), who were adherents of mysticism, these Sufi convictions presented a real challenge to the dogma of orthodox Islam. Sufism constituted a rebellion of the individual conscience against the rigidly defined collective practices and exclusive preoccupation with public behavior that characterized the orthodox. Furthermore, Sufis had a generally disinterested view of politics and the spread of Sufism coincided with the weakening of

Islam as a political force. In spite of the adverse response of conservative theologians, the Sunnites never wholly rejected Sufism and even incorporated some of its more moderate beliefs.

After the thirteenth century the speculative trend in theology and philosophy gradually gave way to a hardening dogmatism in religion; Hellenism disappeared as an active influence. Bound within the limits of a rigid and pervasive religious code, intellectual expression was thereafter characterized by emotion rather than reason; its language became connotative rather than denotative, and the intellect served to embroider rather than test the verities laid down by religion. Overshadowed by the preoccupation with religion, the earlier interest in natural sciences diminished; mathematics, physics, and biology became "foreign" fields, and as such second best. Medicine, for example, reverted to folk remedies and magic until its revival in 1872 with the construction of a hospital in Baghdad by Midhat Pasha. Arid discussion of established propositions and the rejection of original thought marked the intellectual climate of Islam for nearly six hundred years before its exposure to the modern West. The process of change set in motion by western contact in the nineteenth century was hastened by the very inflexibility of the traditional outlook, which was no more capable than the political and economic order of adapting to or competing effectively with the new dynamic forces which were entering the country.

Iraq felt the full impact of the West later than many other Middle Eastern countries. As late as the twentieth century formal intellectual activity in Iraq was confined to a small number of scholars in the Moslem, Christian and Jewish communities and to the few families, those who could afford their own libraries, who concerned themselves with the writing of their genealogies. Sunni Moslems regarded religious dogma as the most legitimate field of study; for the Shiites, whose intellectual life was isolated within the traditional schools of the holy cities, religious scholarship was almost equivalent to virtue. Even among literate groups there was little comprehension of the foreign thought which was so strongly at work in some other parts of the Middle East. Among the illiterate nomads and village agriculturalists the world outside Iraq remained dim and unknown. In the past fifteen years, however, the publication of books and other printed matter has increased more than fivefold; academic standards in modern fields of study have been established and improved. The press has attracted many able men. During the political crisis in the decade after World War I out of which the country achieved independence, the Shiite intellectual center at An Najaf helped to infuse in its students a feeling of nationalism and the importance of the "Arab heritage" (see chap. 5). Poetry, too, has been used as a vehicle to express new currents of thought in Iraq.

Iraq's growing modern intelligentsia is still relatively small in numbers and many of its members continue to devote much time to the defense of Moslem traditionalism against the inroads of innovation. It is significant, however, that more and more persons of the educated urban class are looking to secular rather than religious leadership for guidance in the definition of social aims.

The Oral and Literary Tradition

Poetry and formal prose and speech have long been esteemed as the highest of the arts in Iraq and elsewhere in the Arab world. In this tradition language was more than a means of communication: its skillful use was an end in itself. Where logic failed, the apt employment of a quotation from the Koran, a proverb, or a bit of verse might succeed. Each element of a literary product was regarded as an individual experience: a line in a poem need have no evident relation with the whole, and sometimes even the words themselves seemed to lose all but an esthetic significance. Within the limits of conventionally approved subject matter the appreciation of sheer rhetoric transcended any concern for internal coherence and logic as these canons have come to be applied in western literature. The old poetry, recited or sung, is still popular in Iraq and the storyteller has not lost his ability to draw an audience on feast days and festive occasions.

The traditional models in poetry and prose, defended and preserved by the literate few educated in the old way, long resisted any change. Set content and formal style so reinforced each other that literature, like the other forms of artistic expression, had little scope for originality. Nevertheless, it was in literature that the beginnings of a new creative effort were first manifested in the last century; and the new directions, which are still being pursued, have involved changes in both style and content. Whereas philosophy and rhetoric, religion and history, biography and geography dominated the literary scene a century ago, today politics and foreign affairs, social and economic concern are the major interests. The press, a medium borrowed from the West, has become a major vehicle for literary expression.

Poetry

Poetry continues to be held in highest esteem by all levels of society in Iraq. Here as elsewhere in the Middle East it is a popular art and its enjoyment is limited neither by education nor by sex. A wealth of traditional verse has been maintained by the nomads, while formal poetic composition has centered in the towns.

Early Iraqi poetry shows strong pre-Islamic influences in its use of old bedouin themes. With the advent of Islam and the elaboration of town life under the Abbassides a poetry developed which reflected the narrowly urban preoccupations of the court. Persia contributed the romantic and heroic epic as well as a poetry which permitted full elaboration of mystical themes. Later, with the decline of Abbasside power, a reaction set in and poets again began to glorify the bedouin ideals of simplicity, courage, and independence. (The peasant cultivator, despised by townsman and nomad alike, was never regarded as a suitable subject for poetic treatment.)

Sufism also had a profound influence on Iraqi poetic achievement, stimulating poetry written for the express purpose of inciting a state of ecstasy in the listener; though monotonous in its use of repetitive allegories and expressions, its essential elements were soon absorbed into the whole body of Islamic poetry. In the past fifty years, however, this kind of poetry has been increasingly rejected by modern Moslems, and the number of professed Sufi poets in Iraq today is small.

Poetry produced around the turn of the twentieth century was still traditional in form and spirit. The typical diwan, or collection of odes, of that time was devoted to involved puzzles in verse, commemorative poems for wedding ceremonies, and poems in praise of the Prophet and religious leaders, the governors and their associates. The work of such famous nineteenth-century poets as Abd al-Baqi al-Umari and Abd al-Ghaffar al-Akhras—and of their younger contemporaries Haidar al-Hilli and Mohammed Said al-Habbubi—all falls within this tradition.

The intellectual and political crisis of the first quarter of the twentieth century, however, was reflected in the emergence of a new approach, associated with two of Iraq's greatest modern poets, ar-Rasafi (1875–1945) and az-Zahawi (1863–1936). The movement they initiated is characterized by the shift from an almost exclusive preoccupation with style for its own sake to the use of language to inform; social and political topics replace the idealized bedouin themes; modern Arabic is employed and new poetic forms make their appearance. This trend is being continued today by a number of younger poets who are attempting to popularize a language which lies between the traditional classical form and the modern classical medium of newspapers and school books. The attention of these contemporary poets has shifted from the doings of a small elite to those of the ordinary people—to whom they dedicate their work. This change of focus has not attracted any large audience, however, and the new poetry is scanty and is frequently marred by an overenthusiastic imitation of western masters. Even so, there are signs that the work of these writers may have a lasting influence in helping to make Iraqi poetry something more than a repository for obsolete words and outdated subjects.

Ar-Rasafi, of Kurdish descent, is still read with great admiration in Iraq, and his poems have been included in school texts. His language, although far removed from the colloquial, is clearly of the ornate style which prevailed in the classical period. Knowledge of Turkish enabled him to read the works of European thinkers and he was the first poet in Iraq to come to grips with the social problems of his age.

Az-Zahawi has been called the "philosopher of the poets." Viewing science as the greatest development of modern times and employing it as a major theme in his poetry, he appears more an intellectual philosopher than a poet. Like ar-Rasafi, he was sensitive to the social and political evils of his day, but he went further than ar-Rasafi in the quest for simplicity of style and language. His poetry, however, gained general appreciation only after Iraq had attained independence. Az-Zahawi's impact on the country is beyond dispute—particularly his support of the emancipation of women and his efforts to popularize science and invention. Both az-Zahawi and ar-Rasafi lapsed into comparative silence after World War I, and new poets appeared whose works differed in technique and subject.

During and immediately after World War I, the traditional schools at An Najaf, the Shiite intellectual and religious center, inspired a new group of poets with the idea of nationalism and the revival of the "Arab heritage." This neo-Arab school produced a poetry highly charged with patriotic emotion. Arab culture and history were uppermost in their minds; they rarely turned from these resources or attempted to employ new forms in developing their own themes and ideas. However clearly the public understood this rather esoteric poetry, it was taken very seriously and was widely memorized.

During World War II and after, poetry in Iraq entered another phase. The older literary movements at An Najaf and Baghdad no longer appealed to the younger writers and poets. More than ever before the educated community was exposed to new terms and ideas from Europe and America, both directly and indirectly through a flood of books and pamphlets coming into the country from Egypt and Lebanon, where western influence had already been felt. Much of the poetic output of this recent period is characterized by imitation of western forms; objection and dissent are its keynotes. While the new generation of poets recognizes the contribution of the pioneers of modern poetry, it has critically rejected much of the work of its predecessors; for example the traditionally approved *Qasidah* (which was written according to certain rigid rules, including the use—throughout a whole poem—of a single rhyme sound and one of several approved meters). Among the new group are Nazik al-Malaikah, a woman; Buland al-Haidari, a Kurd; Abd al-Wahab al-Bayati; and al-Jawahiri, one of the most prominent contemporary poets in the Arab world.

Prose

Before the twentieth century nearly every author of Arabic prose employed the traditional pattern of rhymed prose, or *saj*. History, biography, theology, philosophy, and other branches of knowledge were written in this manner, as were stories and tales, called *maqamah*. Prose literature in the forms known to Europe was, strictly speaking, nonexistent, and the novel and essay are recent borrowings. Thus modern Iraqi prose, unlike modern poetry, has few roots in the past; its techniques, derived from Europe, came to Iraq indirectly through Egypt, which had come into contact with the West considerably earlier.

The lack of publishers, the smallness of the literate public, and the tendency of intellectuals to be drawn into politics rather than literature—all have helped to postpone the development of creative prose writing in Iraq.

In the field of letters poetry has dominated the twentieth century in Iraq, but creative prose is assuming a more conspicuous place as writers gain greater control over their medium.

Aside from journalists (see chap. 9), there have been such pioneers in prose as the late Rafail Butti (himself a prominent newspaper editor); Mahumd Ahmad as-Sayyid and his greater successor, Dhu an-Nun Ayyub, both of whom show a familiarity with the Russian novel; Anwar Shaul, who specialized in the colloquial short story; Abd al-Majid Lufti, who popularized the short story form; and Abd al-Malik Nuri, who, next to Ayyub, is generally regarded as Iraq's most distinguished modern writer.

Music

A tradition of folk music enters intimately into the life of the people in Iraq. Despite the ban on the use of music in Moslem religious services, song has even penetrated here in the chanted recitations from the Koran in the mosque and the call to prayer. Music is also inextricably meshed with the poetic tradition in Iraq; traditional Arab music, which resembles the ballad more closely than it does any other western lyrical form, is remembered by association with the verse for which it has provided a vehicle.

Unlike western music, most of which is composed according to fairly explicit formal rules, music in the Arab world is commonly improvised by the performer, working within an informal tradition rather than any clear-cut theory of composition. Unable to write down what he sings or plays, the musician learns his art by ear and transmits it through his performances. The life of a song is marked by changes introducted by succeeding generations, and the ability to improvise and embellish a melody still constitutes one of the standards by which a performer is judged. Just before World War II, the Institute of Fine Arts initiated a program to revive interest in classical Arab music and the traditional instruments upon which it is played.

Like other aspects of Iraqi art, music has come to include western forms. In urban circles appreciation for western music is growing, encouraged by the phonograph and the radio. A modest army band was reorganized and improved; students were sent abroad to study music, and performers were trained in new instruments. By 1941 these efforts culminated in an Iraqi Symphony Orchestra performing in a newly completed concert hall.

Theater and Dance

Notwithstanding the Greek influence early in Iraqi history, the theater has been unknown in Iraq except for the Shiite passion play commemorating the death of Husein, son of Ali and grandson of Mohammed. This almost violent religious performance, reminiscent of the morality plays of Europe's Middle Ages, has a set pattern which varies slightly in dialogue and costume depending upon the region and the wealth of the particular Shiite community.

Egyptians were among the first to try to write plays in Arabic, but, while their work is known in Iraq, no first-ranking Iraqi writer has paid attention to this form. Iraq has few professional actors and no regularly established legitimate theater. Such plays as have been written locally show structural defects which make staging difficult if not impossible. Unlike the novel and other prose forms, their content has not been deeply influenced by foreign material; most draw their subject matter from Arab history and literature, although some have been concerned with social and political problems.

In these feeble beginnings Iraqi drama has tended to be quite serious in tone, and only recently have comedies such as those of Yusif al-Ani came to the stage.

Dramatic training is offered at the Institute of Fine Arts at Baghdad. Some drama criticism appears in the newspapers; but limited by the few performances presented in the country, it is devoted mainly to encouraging public interest in the theater—now confined to a very small urban elite. Some of the modern writers have also found an outlet in Radio Baghdad.

Iraq shares with other Middle Eastern countries a number of traditional folk dances which are performed during holidays and feast days in the rural areas. The Coffee Dance, known widely throughout the Arab world, seems to have had its origin in Iraq. The tribes have traditional dances which are performed for the entertainment of guests and on feast days. Another popular form of entertainment is the "belly dance," known to westerners in Middle Eastern cabarets and urban clubs; the "belly dance" is widely performed at feasts and weddings in villages and towns, and on these occasions guests often bring their own dancers. Western social dancing is generally confined to clubs and cabarets.

Motion Pictures

Motion pictures are popular in Iraq, but attendance is largely confined to persons living in or near the towns. The sizable number of European- and American-made films exhibited in the country draw large audiences despite the language problem which, in view of the general illiteracy, is only partly solved by the use of classical Arabic subtitles and the murmured translations by the linguistically more accomplished members of the audience. Iraq's own small production of films is supplemented by imports mainly from Egypt.

There are 137 movie houses in Iraq, the first having been opened in 1911. Iraqi newspapers and magazines carry criticism and reviews of Arabic-language and foreign films.

Film production in Iraq is still in its infancy. The movie industry consists of one fully equipped studio, begun with the aid of foreign technicians and actors (mainly Egyptian), which by 1956 had produced two feature films. The Institute of Fine Arts has graduated at least one motion picture actress. Although the prospects of the relatively high salaries offered by the film industry are undoubtedly attractive, motion-picture acting is widely regarded as a highly direputable profession, and for women the role of performer or "artiste" is held synonymous with that of prostitute.

Iraqi audiences tend to appreciate singing even more than acting, and music is an important element in most Arabic films. Educated Iraqis prefer American and European films, but there is a general taste for the extremes of tragedy, excitement, and spectacle. Movie audiences often exhibit a high degree of emotional participation: scenes are punctuated by sighs, cheers, and other vocal manifestations by the onlookers, and an occasional clamor breaks out at such screen episodes as a woman slapping a man—conduct which is extremely improper to the Iraqis.

The Visual Arts

Scholars disagree on the extent to which forms of graphic art were "invented" to meet the prohibitions in the Hadith (the traditions and sayings of Mohammed) against the portrayal of human and animal figures. Certainly the Moslem proscription was preceded by earlier notions of magical attributes attaching to living forms. In any event, throughout the Middle East with the coming of Islam certain media of artistic expression hitherto used were disqualified, others were emphasized, and the distinctive style known as "arabesque" was developed. Characterized by floral and geometric design and the decorative use of calligraphy, this abstract and fanciful style in Iraq is less elaborate and colorful in the north than in the south and at Baghdad. The country has also been strongly influenced by Persian Shiism, which was less bound by the prohibition against the representation of living forms. In this connection it is noteworthy that historically the artisan and craft guilds in Iraq were controlled almost exclusively by the Shiites. Other influences are also apparent in Iraqi art: the work of the Christian textile weavers and the Armenian craftsmen, and Chinese influences in ceramics, architecture, painting, and textiles.

As religious orthodoxy hardened and as Baghdad in time became an isolated eastern outpost of the Ottoman Empire, the finer techniques of miniature and fresco painting and glassware and pottery manufacture were lost. In the face of economic vicissitudes and the loss of social incentive and opportunity, even the most firmly established art forms deteriorated. By the twentieth century, geometrical brickwork in architecture and a few primitive handicrafts constituted the visual arts of Iraq. Esthetic appreciation had reached a low ebb among the well-to-do, while in the villages and tribes the graphic and plastic arts continued, as always, to be confined to a few handicrafts.

In modern times the visual arts in Iraq have been strongly affected by western influences. Whereas the old art forms found their highest expression in textiles, intricate tile mosaics, calligraphy, and mosque architecture, new and revived forms of painting and sculpture are now making their appearance. Painting in particular is attracting the attention of the urban public.

Contemporary art in Iraq has not been entirely divorced from the religious tradition, but contemporary painters are finding inspiration in designs which go back to Sumer and Babylon. Their greatest debt, however, is to modern Europe, where a number of them have studied. The painting of Picasso and the French Impressionists are closer to these artists than the tradition of miniature painting which their ancestors shared with the Persians. In 1955 a group of Iraqi artists held their first exhibition in India, sponsored jointly by the governments of Iraq and India and organized by the All-India Fine Arts and Crafts Society. On this occasion one observer wrote: "The School of Paris has completely reduced the young painters and sculptors. The walls are full of little Bonnards, Matisses, Van Goghs, Cezannes and Gaugins."

Turkish influence in early Iraqi modern art is reflected in the romantic landscapes enlivened with small figures (suggestive of Henri Rousseau) painted by Abd al-Kadir ar-Rassam (1872–1951), the "father" of modern art in Iraq. The Impressionist style in contemporary work was introduced by those students who had studied abroad. Art critics in Iraq have lately been gratified to find indications of a developing local style which is neither bound to the past nor mechanically imitative of western schools.

The best-known Iraqi painter is Jawad Salim (1920–). One of a group sent to study in Paris, Rome, and London, he returned to Baghdad to teach sculpture at the Institute of Fine Arts and painting at Queen Aliyah College. He helped found the "Friends of Art," Iraq's modern art group, and had his own exhibition in New York in 1954. Salim has turned to Babylonian and Sumerian themes as well as to Islamic and western traditions in developing his personal style.

The first uncritical phase of imitating western models has passed, and Iraqi artists are in the process of formulating their own distinctive idioms. Faiq Hassan, who has studied abroad, has looked for inspiration to the customs and scenes of his own people and homeland. Other artists whose work has been exhibited in Baghdad are the painter Sayid Mahumud Sabri and the sculptor Khalid ar-Rahal.

In the modern period the development of architecture has followed a course similar to that of painting and sculpture. A concert hall and the city hall in Baghdad, completed in 1941, show a conscious attempt to blend the functional character of modern architecture with traditional Arab design, although other recent construction is completely western in conception.

The Institute of Fine Arts and the "Friends of Art" have done much to encourage the development of an art-conscious public in Baghdad through discovering significant talent and popularizing the works of the famous artists. They also attempt to create a favorable climate for creative work by awarding honors and prizes and selling the works of the artists. An exhibit held by the Iraqi Artists Society, whose honorary president is King Faisal, was held in Baghdad in May 1957. The works of some sixty painters and five sculptors were displayed, and the exhibit attracted thousands of visitors from all social and economic levels.

Status of the Artist and Intellectual

Throughout much of the Islamic period, artists and writers in Iraq enjoyed high prestige as illuminators and glorifiers of the word of God. The scholar too has been esteemed as the interpreter and keeper of Allah's word. The artist and intellectual are still highly regarded, but with the drift away from the religious framework they are finding themselves in need of new sanctions for their specialized role in society. Esthetic appreciation, particularly in educated urban circles, is not lacking (the King himself is an amateur painter and possesses a private collection), but the mass of the population, economically impoverished and confronted with new patterns which it has not had time to assimilate, is not yet in a position either to appreciate or to patronize the modern artist.

Many educated Iraqis are aware of the decline of cultural expression in the country and of the problems posed by the attempts to find new and meaningful forms of expression. Among the motives for extending education in Iraq in the early 1920's were the awareness among Iraqi and British leaders that Syria and Lebanon (see chap. 2) had assumed cultural leadership in the Middle East and the desire to reassert Iraq's once high place in this field. The government is acting to assist this revival mainly through its Ministry of Education, which was the first government agency to be removed from direct British supervision.

In 1941 the Institute of Fine Arts—with faculties in painting, sculpture, music, and dramatic art—was opened in Baghdad, and the results, though modest, have been promising. The government is also sending music and art students abroad for study. In 1943 a national modern art gallery, attached to the Museum of National Costumes, exhibited the paintings of about a hundred Iraqi painters and several foreign artists who had resided in Baghdad. Some of these paintings, chosen for the way in which they portrayed the country and its people, were specially commissioned by the government. Although this exhibit was later closed there have been demands that a national gallery be established. The government has also encouraged new buildings in Baghdad; in 1957 it commissioned the American architect Frank Lloyd Wright to design, in consultation with Iraqi architects, a cultural center for the city.

Despite financial and other assistance by the government, it is difficult for intellectuals, artists, and writers to achieve recognition or financial security. Many are forced to find jobs with schools, museums, or newspapers. Despite the increase of such printed matter as newspapers, periodicals, and government publications, relatively little original work is published, and printing is generally at the author's expense. Writers are discouraged by government censorship, and both writers and artists are deterred by the reluctance of the wealthy to support or patronize arts and letters.

Meanwhile, the process of social change is presenting the Iraqi intellectual with new opportunities no less than with new problems. Sometimes with considerable success, women are beginning to enter fields of intellectual endeavor which were once almost exclusively the province of men. The traditional modes of expression continue to have a following, but new patterns show both strength and vitality.

21

VALUES AND PATTERNS OF LIVING

IRAQ IS A COUNTRY OF SHARP GEOGRAPHICAL CONTRASTS AND diverse ethnic and religious groups. Important differences in outlook and ways of living distinguish various segments of the population. Moreover, the largely tradition-bound rural population as a whole is on many levels cut off from meaningful communication with the towns and cities, where a whole new way of life is taking shape under the impact of influences from the modern world. The peasants of the countryside, the desert nomads, and the tribesmen of the remote Kurdistan mountains might almost be said to be living in another, an earlier, time than the educated urban elite. The world of the peasant still revolves around the land he works, his family, and his village. Although the nomad is accustomed to considerable freedom of movement, his interests are similarly restricted to family, clan, and tribe and the unremitting struggle for subsistence.

In the face of this heterogeneity there are forces making for unity, forces which stem from the Arab and Islamic heritage of the vast majority of the population. No longer as powerful a unifying force as in the past Islam has been eroded by secular trends which even antedate the western influences felt so strongly from the nineteenth century onward. Western ideas and values have considerably affected many aspects of Iraqi life and have contributed to an increasing difference in outlook between the upper classes, who have had access to the new knowledge, and the mass of the people, who have not. At the present time educated Iraqis are reappraising traditional values; for them this is a period of transition and frequently of intellectual and emotional conflict, of rejection of the old and uneasiness with the new.

Traditional Values

Man and the Universe

From the time of the coming of Islam to Iraq, the Koran and the Hadith together with their interpretation by religious leaders, formed a comprehensive guide for life which defined man's place and duties and injected an element of shared value into the different settings of nomadic tribe, village, and town. Islam not only introduced new practices and beliefs, it also provided a framework within which many old ones, such as belief in spirits, went through a process of unconscious reinterpretation and came to be regarded as native to the Moslem tradition.

Islam presents man as inherently good but weak and subject to the temptations of Satan. A major function of Islamic society was to protect its members from their frailty, teaching them to submit to the will of God. In traditional Islam, as understood by both the Shiite and Sunnite sects, social life was so minutely regulated by religious precepts that social values came to be largely indistinguishable from religious values, just as law and education were inseparable from religion. Moreover, in the settled population strict observance of religious obligations early became a means for the attainment of social prestige as well as a religious duty. Similarly, the nomadic virtues of generosity and courage acquired sanction in the Koran and value in the eyes of the people as a whole.

An important consequence of the traditional Islamic regulation of virtually all aspects of life was the tendency of Iraqis, like other Moslems, to adjust to and accept life rather than attempt to manipulate it. This attitude was reinforced during the decline from the golden age as Moslem thinkers increasingly subordinated speculation to exposition of revealed religious truths with an emphasis on rigid dogmatism and a consequent stifling of original thought and experimentation. The commonly quoted Koranic phrases "it is written" and "it was willed by Allah" symbolize attitudes toward the value of human effort which many Moslems have held for centuries. Man exercises no ultimate control over events in a world in which all things are ordained by God. Success is the manifestation of God's benevolence; failure is simply God's withholding of benevolence. Among the peasants of the plain this outlook has been reinforced by generations of subservience to landlords and government officials which have conditioned them to a degree of submission not found among bedouins, highland Kurds, or marsh dwellers.

Religion and religious observances loom large in village life, and rural recreation focuses on religious feasts or ceremonies occasioned by circumcisions, weddings, or funerals. Traditionally, recreation patterns in the towns were similarly oriented.

Among the nomads specific Koranic prescriptions and rituals occupy a much less important place. Sedulous in affirming their faith, they pay scant attention to the other four Pillars of Islam. Many nomadic social values, however, such as that assigned to hospitality, closely parallel virtues enjoined upon all Moslems by the Koran.

The Kurds, for the most part nominally Sunnite Moslems, also tend to be lax in their observance of ritual obligations. While quick to profess their Moslem faith they are said often secretly to derogate Islam as an alien religion of the desert and hence inappropriate to their way of life. The Kurdish warrior tradition and deep admiration for courage, power, and enterprise conceivably might render difficult any deep-rooted acceptance of the Islamic ideal of humility before God. A Kurdish proverb runs: "Lion, put your confidence in your paw; the saints will not come to help you."

Iraqis hold certain traditional conceptions of the ideal person, although the stereotype varies from group to group. Such a person is not a citizen in the western sense but rather a member of society, with traits mainly relevant to a social order in which until recently formal government played but a small part. In this traditional setting the socially and politically effective ideal individual is male—although ideal female qualities are well defined. Above all, it is important for the person in full manhood to have been sexually potent, for without such potency other virtues lose significance. These virtues, as exemplified in numerous historical or legendary figures, are: shrewdness, intelligence, generosity, hospitality; high qualities as poets, warriors, husbandmen, etc. Temperamentally, the characterization is of a man dynamic, warrior-like, and nonsedentary by preference, contrasting with another widely-held Middle Eastern view of the long-settled townsman and villager exemplified by the Egyptian and the Lebanese.

Symbolic figures have emerged to represent the various groups. For the Arab majority the fictitious Abu Jassim (Qassim) Ler, bearing one of the most common Arab nicknames, symbolizes the average man. He is unwesternized, not to say anti-western in attitude, and modifies his Arab-type dress only with a western jacket (often bedraggled) and, occasionally, western shoes. He is quick to anger, sensitive in matters of honor, courageous before his enemies, and generous to his friends. Questions of his honor revolve obsessively around the actions or reputations of his womenfolk. He is honest, likewise in Arabic terms, although he will exaggerate accounts of his own accomplishments, virility, and powers. His politics rarely rise above the level of coffeehouse rumor and scandal, but he invariably takes the side of strident nationalism. His economic activities and attitudes in relation to government are individualistic—in the context of the family, collectivist. Gleanings of Communist propaganda come to him by way of students but he is distrustful not only of the students themselves but of what he hears from them in general. He is not a religious fanatic in the western sense; he has been able to live for generations in peace side by side with peoples of other, sometimes completely divergent, religions. He often does not observe the obligations of Islam but sacrilege or expressions of doubt about the divine inspiration of the Koran move him to emotion and violence. He is opposed to westernization and is filled with confidence that the West will meet its just deserts on the Day of Judgment, if not before. This conviction is related to a complete sense of superiority concerning himself in the world. He leaves to Arab intellectuals any self-questioning concerning the Arab order of things. This gives his nationalism a quality of disdain and rectitude that leaves to Allah the chastisement of those who doubt his values.

Abu Jassim exists as the abstract embodiment of attitudes that the dominant Iraqi Arab presumes to find in himself. The caricature does reflect a psychological reality. Even the elite and the most westernized Iraqis partake of Abu's qualities in some respects, though they may overtly deny them—just as they will express contempt for the bedouins yet vigorously claim bedouin descent.

Man and Society

The pre-eminent role of the Iraqi family in the lives of its members places it at the center of some of the most deeply felt values and loyalties. Traditionally, the type of occupation to which a man could aspire, his standing in the community, and his range of choice in selecting a wife were all determined by the relative wealth, power, and prestige of his family. The individual in dealing with other groups did so from the vantage of his security as a member of a close family group. Today—both as a matter of expediency and as a moral duty—the reciprocal obligations between relatives still loom large in the life of the Iraqi. Strong family loyalties also enable the Iraqi, like other Middle Easterners, to adhere to separate standards of conduct and morality in dealing with relatives and outsiders. Within the family certain norms of obedience and industry are required; outside the family different standards of behavior and honesty may prevail.

Closely related to the concept of family solidarity is the emphasis placed on honor among all segments of the population. Shame or dishonor, which causes one's "face to become blackened," is a major disaster, and violation of an individual's honor, until avenged, brings discredit upon his entire family. Many blood feuds mark Iraqi tribal and village life, and crimes of violence committed in defense of honor are common, particularly in the remoter rural areas. Violations of sexual prohibitions are generally regarded as bringing the most serious dishonor to a family.

Another traditional value shared by all groups of Iraqis—Arab and Kurd, rich and poor alike—is that placed on generosity. In the past, the wealthy, as those having received the blessing of God, were expected to be generous in almsgiving and also to distribute food to the poor. However much practical force this tradition may have lost in the course of the centuries, one of the severest criticisms a tenant can level against his landlord is that of lack of generosity—an offense against both God and man. The peasant too is under strong social pressure to extend hospitality and the honor of his family requires that the entertainment of guests be as lavish as possible. Over the years elaborate prescriptions for behavior connected with the extending and receiving of hospitality have developed and among the nomads numerous customary rules govern the protection as well as the reception of guests.

Wisdom and knowledge have traditionally been respected in Iraq as elsewhere in the Moslem world. The prestige attached to learning was enhanced by the fact that the learned man, as a person trained in Islamic theology, often functioned as a religious leader, teacher, or judge. Religious knowledge coupled with a mastery of classical Arabic was considered the highest achievement of learning, and despite the increasing prestige of the secular-trained intellectual in this century, the religious figure is still widely esteemed by conservative groups for learning and piety. The prestige attached to religious learning has perhaps been equally strong among the small Christian and Jewish minorities.

Courage and prowess have traditionally been admired by the bedouins and the Kurds. Through the historic process of sedentarization of the nomads and the interaction which to one degree or another has always taken place among the various segments of Iraqi society, these qualities have come to represent values held by the people as a whole, and heroic themes pervade folklore and popular poetry and songs. Although the settled population through the centuries has despised the nomads as predatory raiders a somewhat romantic stereotype of the desert Arab—brave and independent—has persisted, and townsmen and villagers are quick to claim ancestry in one of the noble bedouin tribes. Similarly, settled Kurds cherish stories of their former glory under great tribal warrior leaders. With the gradual extension of the central government's control into the areas inhabited by both these groups, raiding for plunder and tribal warfare have largely receded into the past. Nevertheless, something of the outlook associated with these activities still colors the attitudes of Kurdish and bedouin leaders and their relations with officials of the government.

Man and Man

It would be difficult to exaggerate the importance traditionally, and to a great extent actually, placed on personal relationships by all segments of Iraqi society. The individual tends to be identified and rated not so much in terms of his own qualities and attainments as in terms of his place in a network of personal and kin relations. A man is important if he has powerful relatives and friends and his relationship with them is one of mutual obligation. The essentially impersonal patterns which in the West are regarded as appropriate in business and governmental affairs are only beginning to find acceptance among Iraqis, who are conditioned to feel that security and success are to be obtained largely through personal relations and the claims of personal acquaintance.

This preference for highly personalized relationships is nowhere more evident than in the traditional bargaining process. Except in the cities, where there are western-style *prix fixe* stores, bargaining is the dominant way in which goods are bought and sold in Iraq as elsewhere in the Middle East. The bargaining pattern is also applied to a wide variety of noncommercial situations. An Iraqi finds it natural to bargain in almost any situation calling for agreement between two parties and he derives satisfaction from the give and take of the process. Bargaining provides an opportunity for the persons concerned to demonstrate their virtuosity and to exchange gossip and opinions as well as to conclude a transaction.

In the interest of maintaining harmonious personal relations, great care is taken to avoid serious conflict between individuals. Men may argue and expostulate but seldom harbor a grudge after an argument; in the event of impending conflict recourse is frequently had to an intermediary.

The emphasis placed on the personal relationship is also reflected in the tendency, stemming from the bedouin tradition, to rely on oral rather than written commitments. The Kurds likewise pride themselves on the integrity of their word. Written agreements are of course common in westernized business circles, but in the community at large, insistence on a written contract in many situations tends to be regarded not only as implying distrust of the individual's word but also as potentially prejudicial to the kind of personal adjustments that agreements in the Middle East have traditionally been subject to.

The Sexes

Although the social segregation of the sexes is part of the Islamic tradition, the veiling and seclusion of women has in practice been confined to a small segment of Iraqi society centering in the upper classes. Nomad and peasant women customarily are not veiled although they are taught from early childhood to be circumspect in their behavior toward males other than their brothers and are generally kept segregated from boys from the time of puberty until marriage. While their sphere of activity is largely confined to the family circle, they help their husbands outside the home and move freely about the community. On the other hand, the wives of upper-class rural dwellers—sheikhs and landowners—traditionally have been veiled and secluded.

Until recently a mark of social status, a sign of belonging to the coveted upper reaches of society, the seclusion of women in the towns and cities is now becoming restricted to the most conservative well-to-do families and to certain less prosperous urban elements among whom women are likely to be veiled in imitation of the upper classes. Under the impact of western influence, veils have almost disappeared among middle- and upper-class groups in Baghdad, but in provincial towns they tend to remain the rule rather than the exception. In Basra and Mosul, for instance, even educated wives of government officials are expected to lead rather circumscribed lives. The seclusion of women is particularly rigid in the Shiite holy cities of An Najaf and Karbala, where few women go unveiled.

Kurdish women have never been veiled. They participate in economic activities and public festivities, and in the course of history individual Kurdish women have achieved positions of political leadership among their people.

Traditional Islamic codes governing sexual behavior were rigid, and among villagers, nomads, and conservative elements in the towns they remain so. Premarital sexual relations and adultery are regarded with violent disapproval, usually focusing on the female offender. Among the nomads a woman guilty of adultery may be severely punished, even put to death, by her father or brothers, who are responsible for her moral conduct. In the villages, especially where tribal traditions are strong (as in the marsh area) the attitude toward sexual laxity in women may be almost as severe. Actually, in rural areas the opportunities for sexual relations outside of marriage are severely limited by the kinship system; every woman is enmeshed in a network of kinship ties which is interposed between her and the community at large. The wronging of a girl dishonors her household and lineage, thereby calling for vengeance. Similarly, improper conduct involving a married woman may bring about retaliation against the offenders by both her husband's and father's families.

Although sexual relations outside of marriage are also frowned upon in the cities, there are indications of some slackening in observance of the traditional sexual code. Young women of the middle and upper classes, however, despite their increasing educational and professional opportunities, still tend to be subject to traditional restrictions in their social life and are generally chaperoned by brothers or other relatives.

Prostitution is common in the cities, although in the Shiite holy places it is perhaps to be distinguished from the Shiite tradition of "temporary marriage." This arrangement involves a contract which must specify the duration of the arrangement and a reward for the woman. Thus a "wife" may be offered to pilgrims by a mullah for the period of their stay.

Westernization

Since the early nineteenth century, Iraq has been exposed to a variety of western influences through missionary activity, exploration, business interests, and educational endeavors. The impact of the West was directly felt during the British Mandate, and in recent years it has been considerably broadened by the activities of the oil companies and by the government's ambitious education and economic development programs constructed on western models.

Western thought and technology have affected different segments of the Iraqi population in varying degrees and ways. The strongest impact has been felt in the cities and the most vocal reactions have been those of the educated urban groups. While some conservative Iraqis—religious leaders in particular—have persisted in a fundamental opposition to western values and institutions, most upper- and middle-class townspeople not only have accepted western technology and educational methods but have also tended to espouse much of western, especially secular, thinking. Consciously imitating western social patterns, these groups are tending to reject much of their heritage of traditional culture without acquiring any real comprehension of the western forms. Thus in education, western curricula, teaching methods, and texts notwithstanding, Middle Eastern patterns persist—in particular the practice of rote learning with its repressive effect on initiative and original thinking, and the tendency for eloquence and diction to take precedence over substance. Moreover, western notions of academic honesty are apt to have little relevance for the Iraqi student, whose tradition tells him that cheating is a clever and justifiable means to a desirable end rather than a morally reprehensible act.

Exposure to the West has not necessarily induced pro-western sentiments. Those who have been quickest to adopt the outward trappings of western culture and to identify themselves with the West—often as a means of enhancing their social prestige—have frequently harbored feelings of inferiority and envy in the face of western power and achievements. While practical techniques imported from the West may be admired, western "materialism" is often deprecated. Some Iraqi traditionalists, going further, advocate rejection of the West and an assertion of the moral leadership of the East through the revival of a purified Islam. Many modernists, on the other hand, impatient with the pace of economic and social reform, tend to advocate a wholesale adoption of western solutions to Iraqi problems.

Western influence in the towns and cities has affected business, industry, and professions, as well as general patterns of social life. The highly personalized business dealings of the past show signs of yielding to the more impersonal methods familiar in the West, and individual accomplishment vies increasingly with wealth and family affiliation as an avenue to success and social prestige.

Similarly, the traditional means of recreation centering on family activities and religious ceremonies are gradually being replaced by new, mass-produced media of entertainment modeled on western prototypes. Urban recreation revolves around coffeehouses, clubs, societies, and films, and in the larger cities it increasingly includes mixed social life.

While many traditional patterns have remained intact among lower-class urban dwellers, the growing middle-class groups have been quick to adopt western prestige symbols in imitation of the upper classes. Western clothes and automobiles, western-style clubs, and modern housing are the marks of the ambitious middle-class man. He will also tend to marry an educated, emancipated woman and attempt to dissociate himself from traditional roots and conservative relatives. Having discarded the surface symbols of the old society, superficially he is westernized. While verbally rejecting the old patterns of family loyalty and religious conformity he is, however, still governed by them to some extent and suffers considerable ambivalence in his values and attitudes.

In the countryside, traditional patterns strongly persist but there too they are being affected. The influence of the towns radiates into surrounding areas and the old isolation of the village is breaking down. Growing numbers of peasants are drawn to the towns as visitors or for education and temporary or permanent employment. Through this increased mobility and the impact of the government's development program, which is beginning to be felt in rural areas, the villager's horizon is broadening and his attitudes toward his environment are changing. Economic hardships, which a few years ago were accepted as God's will and hence inevitable, are beginning to be regarded as inequities as the peasants come to see that with the government's assistance they can improve their lot.

Although still relatively untouched by the influence of modern education or western ideas, Iraq's Arab nomads of the western desert and Kurdish tribesmen of the remote northeast mountains have not been immune to the new forces at work in the country. The coming of the airplane, the oil pipeline, and modern motor transport has altered their vistas and set in motion far-reaching changes in their customary living patterns and attitudes. Moreover, they are gradually becoming an integral part of Iraqi society as a whole. The bedouin sheikh, who in the past thought reading and writing "unmanly" accomplishments, now wants a city education for his sons—even at the risk of their becoming townsmen, whom he once despised. Similarly, barred from some of their historic activities, more and more Kurds are finding their way into oil-field work, government positions, and city life.

22

NATIONAL ATTITUDES

AT THE TOP OF THE COUNTRY'S CONTEMPORARY STRUCTURE OF political and social power are members of the twenty or thirty families who actually rule Iraq and who are closely allied with one another through intermarriage and shared interests. Their limited number makes it possible for them to act with greater unity of purpose than is found in most Middle Eastern elites. Most of the elder politicians representing these families came to maturity under the influences of the latter days of Ottoman rule. With the Turks they saw in western ideas and techniques a means of reviving Middle Eastern power and they were particularly impressed with the legal systems which were so important a component of the European political order. They acquired a conception of the state as embodying a structure of legal norms. This orientation has also made possible a detachment from the strictly Arab nationalism that characterizes in greater or less degree the stated goals of political leaders in most other Arab countries. In Iraq the elder politicians have held together more effectively than elsewhere—a fact that explains at least in part why the controls continue to rest with them, although they have also produced men who have turned against the basic social and political order. The political techniques of the elder group have often been harsh but not purely repressive or negative. They have for instance given their approval and leadership to the ambitious national reconstruction and welfare programs of the Development Board (see chap. 11).

Another segment of society increasingly important in Iraq and representing dynamic forces of transition in the country are the emerging middle groups who by virtue of more education and improved economic status are growingly alive to political and social issues (see chap. 6). They more and more fill the gap between the older ruling elite and the mass of the people. They still do not constitute so much a channel of communication between the two as a source of intellectual and social restiveness and discontent influencing those below. Many members of this middle group suffer from a kind of ambivalence—their western egalitarian social concepts do not prevent them from patronizing the fellah and bedouin and allowing the fellah to perform menial services as a kind of obligation owed to higher station. They often represent a third generation of quasi-western education which has brought no significant loss of Arab-Moslem patterns. This attitudinal ambivalence makes for individual emotional discomfort, and in its more violent forms produces a sense of resentment against the West for providing a mirror in which Arab deficiencies, in western terms, may be seen. This whole group is affected by the sense that there is something "wrong" in Arab and Iraqi society. The stress under which it labors becomes more acute because it is felt in a religious milieu that very sharply sets off the faithful from the infidel; even for the more secular minded religion becomes a source of credo in a broad sense to be employed against enemies of Iraq and the Arab world.

From a different standpoint, a segment of the population whose attitudes and reactions are dynamically important are city and town dwellers in general. Their political views are amorphous and yet analyzable in terms of their Arab origins and Islamic or other religious backgrounds. Their attitudes toward political issues are not well articulated and tend to be mercurial. Given to sporadic outbursts of temper on particular issues they can move quickly from optimism about particular political programs and confidence that an improvement in their lot is about to occur to deeply skeptical conviction that no reform will touch their misery. They are becoming aware that their lot need not be what it has been; but their deep suspicions of government make it difficult for them to collaborate for long with the authorities for the accomplishment of reform. These are the people who are and have been most easily manipulated in civil disturbances and riots, often to the point of causing the downfall of governments (see chap. 7).

In contrast with all the above groups the fellahin and the bedouins are little aware of the larger society or of themselves within it and are not clear participants in the political processes of the country. Their attitudes and reactions have a much more limited relevance to politics than those of other groups, although they—especially the bedouins—may be used by their leaders to exert various types of political pressure. Their attitudes and reactions have been of minimal significance to the leaders of the community as a whole, and they rather lend weight to those above them who are closer to the seats of power. They may supply the rank and file of the armed forces but their social and political passiveness is their most important characteristic.

Iraqi Nationalism

Iraq's dominant Arab majority does not have a conception of the Iraqi nation, or even the Arab nation, in a strictly western sense. It does not possess an organic view of state or nation as an entity which has a reality apart from the individuals who make it up. Nevertheless, there is an indestructible Arab and Iraqi identity which a person born into this community cannot escape. Thus an Iraqi Arab who acquires other citizenship will still be viewed by his fellows as an Iraqi Arab.

A key word in the thought of Iraqis, as well as other Arabs, is *watan*—coming from a root meaning to settle in a place but referring in the form used here to the land upon which the people are settled. To the more self-consciously intellectual and educated, the land unit is at the same time a political unit based on common language and culture. For those who are primarily Iraqi in their loyalties, it is *al-Watan al-Iraqi;* for others, larger concepts may be involved so as to include the land upon which are settled all Arabs, *al-Watan al-Arabi.* In each case the binding factors are a combination of language, history, cultural tradition, and territory. The uneducated generally receive their views indirectly from the elite but think more simply of the land unit along with people settled upon it.

A second word of importance is *ummah,* meaning people. There are people who belong and those who do not. Effectively, the definition is made by the dominant Arabs, but the *ummah* includes others than Arabs. In Iraq the Christian Arabs are part of the *ummah.* The indigenous Jews, until the growth of the hostility produced the Zionism and the establishment of Israel, were on the borderline of the *ummah.* The placement of the other minorities by the dominant Arabs varies with time, situation, and the background of the Arab making the assignment. Those minorities not speaking the Arabic language are generally not accepted (although the Kurds are included by many despite this disability). Other groups may be rejected because their religious practices or political behavior put them quite obviously apart. The Yezidis and the Assyrians, despite long residence in Iraq, remain essentially outsiders for the Arabs. The Shiite Arabs, separated by sectarian difference from the dominant Sunnite Arab group, are nevertheless part of the *ummah* and they place strong emphasis not only upon their Arabism but on their membership in the *ummah.* The *ummah,* therefore, is not a homogeneous entity but an aggregation of peoples drawn together first and fundamentally by language, then religion, and finally by residence or birth in a particular place.

No single Arabic word seems clearly to connote the modern western concept of "nation" in itself meaning people and land. It is necessary to combine the concepts *watan* and *ummah* in order to arrive at an approximation of the western idea, although either may be used as a rough synonym of nation. They are, of course, constantly used by Iraqi Arabs, but only among the educated does *watan,* for example, begin to acquire a political connotation paralleling "nation." The Arab words for nationalism are *wataniyah* and *qawmiyah.* The meaning of the first has been suggested, and this enjoins the caution with which Arab concepts related to nationalism—as understood generally in the West—should be viewed. The second derives from a word meaning an aggregate of people. The connotation of these terms varies among Iraqis, depending on whether they are traditional nationalists or neo-nationalists, Pan-Arab nationalists or Iraqi nationalists, or some variant (see chap. 7). The traditionalists tend to be found among the elder Iraqi elite. Most were Pan-Arab in their views before independence; today they are more strictly Iraqi nationalists. The neo-nationalists differ among themselves in the nature of their nationalism; they have been strongly influenced by the Pan-Arabism of the Egyptian leader, Nasser, although some may have reservations about Egyptian presumptions of leadership.

Iraqis often refer to their country as *al-bilad al-Iraqiyah. Bilad* is the plural of *balad*—town or locality—and in connoting an aggregation of settled places the term reveals the essentially local orientation of Iraqi social life. Whatever his awareness of the larger entities of which he may be a part, the average Iraqi thinks of himself, first of all, as coming from Baghdad, Basra, An Najaf, or Mosul, etc. There is implied a hierarchy of loyalties in which the Baghdadi, for example, may proceed from loyalty to his home city to loyalty to Iraq and to a larger Arab world and, for some, to a still larger Islam. The broad Islamic ideal is most consciously held by the elite and the growing middle groups. In these circles a term approaching the western "Fatherland"—*Bilad al-Aba,* "the home place of the fathers"— is often heard. In emphasizing common Arab antecedents, the term adds a unifying social dimension to the geographical emphasis of *al-bilad al-Iraqiyah.*

The symbols of statehood and political sovereignty reflect some inarticulated expectation that a stable political framework will be preserved within which orderly, evolutionary change may occur. Yet they do not possess the significance such symbols have in the West.

Among them are Iraq's flag, described in Article 4 of the Constitution as follows:

> Its length shall be double its breadth and it shall be divided horizontally into three parallel and equal strips, the uppermost being black, the next white, and the next green. Next to the staff it shall bear a red truncated cone, of which the greater base shall be equal to the breadth of the flag, the smaller base equal to the breadth of the white strip and the height equal to one fourth of the length of the flag. In the middle of the cone shall be two white stars of seven points placed in a perpendicular line parallel to the staff.

A state emblem appears on official state publications. An approximation of a national anthem exists in "*as-Salaam al-Malaki*" (Salute to the King), which is without words and but eight bars in length. Iraqis give little attention to it. Four main holidays mark the King's birthday, the King's succession, the revolt against the Ottoman Empire (Renaissance Day), and the gaining of independence, but it is quite likely than even an educated Iraqi long removed from the country might forget these dates.

The institutions of government in Iraq, constructed on western models and staffed by a large bureaucracy, provide an occupational framework within which people are acquiring new interests and loyalties. In the army, for example, a corps of career officers has developed for whose members pride of professional proficiency and notions of duty to the state are overlaying the narrower allegiances of the past. Within both the civil and military service the highly personal relationships of the Middle Eastern tradition are yielding, however slowly, to the more objectively defined administrative and operational criteria of modern bureaucracy. The Iraqi civil servant still may often owe his job to whom rather than to what he knows and his personal connections may influence many of his official actions; but he cannot escape awareness of another standard of performance, and the very terms of his work draw him toward it. As the government service draws into its ranks members of the minority groups, these too find themselves propelled into the larger national community where, in their new status, they begin to see themselves as Iraqis with responsibilities to state and nation. In the community at large the developing educational system is reinforcing the trend toward national and civic consciousness.

Loyalty

The inhabitant of Iraq has not been a citizen in the western sense, although the premises underlying the western-inspired Constitution and recent political experience are moving him in this direction. He does not easily envision himself as participating in a system of rights and obligations existing between himself and the government under which he lives. He has been for centuries acquainted with the more or less distant operation of a central authority and has been immersed in a tradition in which government has been considered inimical to the individual's interest. The system of reciprocal rights and obligations of which he is fundamentally a part have not primarily involved government which has traditionally and for the most part acted through the social units, rather than directly upon the individual, in exercising its fiat. The individual did not escape the effect of government actions, but family, tribe, village, and unit leaders acted as intermediaries on behalf of their followers in gaining for them privilege or opportunity or in cushioning for them the worst effects of governmental authority.

New loyalties to Iraq and attachments to a concept of the Arab nation have developed in recent years, but the old ties remain very important. Loyalty to religion for most Iraqis requires not so much the observation of its practices as its defense against infidels and those who would attack the Islamic community. These loyalties require opposition, first and foremost, against Israel; for many, against Turkey, despite the Baghdad Pact (see chap. 10); and generally against the British and French and others who may be denoted "colonialists" or "imperialists."

Within this frame of reference loyalty to government is not basically relevant. No stigma attaches to one who leads a riot or in other ways attacks government. The person who does so may the next day be in the government or in the government's good graces. Traitorous conduct, despite the broad official definition of subversion (see chap. 7), which covers almost all opposition, has in the minds of the people a most limited meaning. The government's denotation of subversion is largely a political device with few moral overtones. The real traitor to society in the public mind today is the person who sympathizes with Israel, and, at particular times, Britain and France.

Nuri as-Said, the Iraqi strongman, as well as many of those about him, might fail the popular test of the good Iraqi. The government and constitutional order represent a great deal that is novel in the life of the country. Most of the leaders represent new influences and imported ideas, many of which are inimical to the old institutions, and are viewed by many Iraqis as the real subverters of the proper order —as the creators of *al-Wad ash Shadh* ("the unnatural political order").

Aspirations

Iraqi politicians, placing a high value on survival, respect flexibility and durability. In recent years they have been taking political and economic steps toward the reconstruction of Iraq; by these methods the country will be made stronger and they will also be better able to perpetuate their own rule. The development of this new kind of civic virtue is by no means complete. There remains a strong urge to enhance one's own glory at all costs and, despite notable exceptions the general proposition still holds that the average politician believes what is good for him is good for Iraq. This reflects the popular attitude that one's future, along with family interests, is one's most important consideration. Political parties and their programs are largely projections of personalities; they rise and fall with their leaders (see chap. 7). Politicians in their determination to identify themselves with popular programs claim to favor multitudes of often contradictory projects, thus becoming identified with alternating waves of confidence and skepticism concerning the prospect of community, party, or national undertakings. Economic change on a vast scale is planned and strongly supported, but the same leaders often resist social changes demanded by technological innovation. Tension between westernization and tradition poses the greatest threat to evolutionary, as opposed to revolutionary, change.

TABLES

TABLES

Table 1. IRAQ'S AREA AND POPULATION BY PROVINCE

Province	*Approximate Area in Square Miles* [(a)]	*Population in 1947*
Al Amarah	7,178	307,021
Baghdad	4,981	817,205
Al Basra	4,802	368,799
Ad Diwaniyah	5,889	378,118
Diyala	6,297	272,413
Ad Dulaym	15,935	192,983
Al Hillah	2,123	261,206
Irbil	7,024	239,776
Karbala	2,367	274,264
Kirkuk	7,951	286,005
Al Kut	6,427	224,938
Mosul	1,155	595,190
Al Muntafiq	5,781	371,867
As Sulaymaniyah	3,728	226,400
Total	81,638	4,816,185

(a) Figures converted from square kilometers; 1 sq. km. equals 0.386 sq. mi.

Source: Adapted from Salter, Sir James Arthur, *The Development of Iraq,* p. 143; and Steinberg, S. H. (ed.), *Statesman's Yearbook, 1956,* p. 1121.

Table 2. IRAQI TOWNS WITH OVER 10,000 POPULATION

Town	Population	Town	Population
Baghdad (& suburbs, including Kadhimain)	730,549(1956)	An Nasiriyah	20,713
Mosul	133,625	Ad Diwaniyah	20,015
Basra	159,355(1956)	Az Zubayr	17,884
Kirkuk	89,917(1956)	Al Kut	16,237
An Najaf	74,089(1956)	Zakhu	14,249
Karbala	44,150	Al Kufah	13,700
Al Amarah	36,907	Al Hindiyah	11,077
Al Hillah	36,577	Al Fallujah	10,981
As Sulaymaniyah	33,510	Baqubah	10,511
Irbil	27,036	Al Hayy	10,199
		Khanaqin	10,091

Source: Adapted from working papers prepared under contract with the Human Relations Area Files at Johns Hopkins University under the direction of Majid Khadduri.

Table 3. **MAJOR DAILY NEWSPAPERS IN IRAQ**

Newspapers	*Place of Publication*	*Circulation*	*Key Personnel*	*Political Orientation*
Al Akhbar	Baghdad	3,000	Jubrail Malkon, proprietor and editor.	Progovernment regardless of the prime minister in office.
Al Bilad	Baghdad	---- [a]	The late Rafail Butti, former proprietor and editor (until April 1956, when one of his sons assumed control).	Considered the best edited and most reliable of all Iraqi Arabic-language papers, its future is in doubt since it was largely Butti's personal vehicle. Has been nationalist but not violently so, and since Butti's death increasingly anti-American.
Ad Dustur	Basra	---- [a]	Mahmoud al Amer, editor.	---- [a]
Fata al Iraq	Mosul	2,500	Ibrahim al Chalabi, editor.	---- [a]
Al Hawadith	Baghdad	3,500	Adil al Awni, editor.	Progovernment.
Al Hurriyah	Baghdad		Qasim Hammudi, chief editor; Faiq as Samarrai, former editor of *Liwa al Istiqlal*, editorial writer.	Extremely nationalistic and anti-Western; in 1957 as Samarrai was believed to be in jail or in exile for criticism of the government in November 1956.
Iraq Times	Baghdad and Basra	4,000	G. Reid Anderson, managing editor.	Formerly the voice of British influence in Iraq and still influential; read by many educated Iraqis; extensive coverage of British and international news. Most cautious in its comment on Iraqi politics, the paper indirectly supports the government in power and depends largely on official press releases for its local news.
Liwa al Istiqlal [b]	---- [a]	---- [a]	Faiq as Samarrai, former editor.	Organ of the Istiqlal party, this paper had tremendous influence and was in constant opposition to the group now in power.

Table 3. (continued)

Newspapers	*Place of Publication*	*Circulation*	*Key Personnel*	*Political Orientation*
Al Manar	Basra	---- (a)	Abdul Aziz Barakat, editor.	---- (a)
Al Mawsil	Mosul	---- (a)	---- (a)	---- (a)
An Nas	Basra	3,500	Abdel Qadar as Sayyab, editor.	---- (a)
Sada al Ahali (b)	---- (a)	---- (a)	Kamil Chadirchi, former editor.	Very influential organ of the National Democratic Party; followed Chadirchi's antigovernment and leftist policies; some tendency to be sympathetic to the USSR.
Sawt al Ummah	Mosul	2,000	Michael Dawoud Haddad	---- (a)
Ash Shab	Baghdad	4,000	Yahya Qasim, editor.	Has tended to represent the views of Salih Jabr, former prime minister, who was opposed to many government policies.
Ath Thaghr	Basra	---- (a)	Shalsir an Naamah	---- (a)
Al Ummah (b)	Baghdad	---- (a)	Rafiq Sayyid Aisa, former editor.	---- (a)
Al Yaqazah	Baghdad	---- (a)	Salman as Safwani, proprietor and editor.	Nationalist; reported to be one of the most anti-American and anti-Western papers currently published.
Az Zaman	Baghdad	7,000	Tawfiq as Samani, proprietor and editor.	Highly respected; has in the past played neutral role; progovernment now.

(a) Not available.
(b) Suspended 1954.

Source: *ibid.*; and *Editor and Publisher*, International Yearbook Number, 1957, p. 414.

Table 4. **RADIO STATIONS IN IRAQ**

Station Name	*Power in Watts*	*Wave Length*	*Frequency*
Radio Baghdad (Abu Ghurayb)	20,000	392.60	764
	16,000	91.05	3295
Radio Baghdad	16,000	48.90	6135 [a]
" "	16,000	42.48	7062 [a]
" "	16,000	42.16	7115 [a]
" "	50,000	25.57	11735

(a) Alternate frequency.

Table 5. **OCCUPATIONAL DISTRIBUTION IN IRAQ 1953–54**

Agricultural Workers	1,400,200
Commerce	120,000
Manufacturing	90,300
Petroleum Industry	11,900
Government and Private Service	97,500
Railroads	14,300
Port of Basra Authority	7,800
Public Utilities	3,500

Source: Adapted from *The Middle East—1957*, p. 167; and Iraq Ministry of Economics, Principal Bureau of Statistics, *Statistical Abstract, 1955*, passim.

Table 6. CONSOLIDATED STATEMENT OF IRAQ'S BUDGETS

(in thousands of Iraqi dinars)

	1949–50	*1950–51*	*1951–52*	*1952–53*	*1953–54*	*1954–55* (a)	*1955–56* (a)
Receipts (eliminating known duplications (b)							
Ordinary budget	28,633	33,494	37,534	50,543	47,721	52,179 (c)	50,973
Related budgets	6,562	6,382	7,319	7,237	10,643	10,998	12,208
Development Board	----	----	7,467	23,999	35,257	43,660	43,155 (d)
Municipalities	3,465	3,598	6,398	7,045	9,192	10,521 (d)	16,102
Total Receipts	38,111	42,605	57,751	87,857	99,830	113,508	119,792
Expenditures (eliminating known duplications) (b)							
Ordinary budget	30,006	29,319	30,820	44,480	50,157	53,798 (c)	51,546
Related budgets	7,250	7,271	6,834	7,274	9,869	10,977	12,285
Development Board (e)	----	----	3,128	8,308	12,187	20,332	61,772
Municipalities	3,443	3,936	5,001	5,781	8,437	9,875 (c)	16,030
Total Expenditures	40,150	39,657	44,816	64,876	77,667	91,132	138,987

(a) Estimated.

(b) The figures shown in this table under the individual budgets are as reported by those individual budgets. The figures eliminated from the totals, to avoid double counting, cover transfers from the related budgets to the ordinary budget and transfers from the ordinary budget to the municipalities amounting to the following (in thousands of Iraqi dinars): 1949–50, 549; 1950–51, 869; 1951–52, 967; 1952–53, 967; 1953–54, 2,983; 1954–55, 3,850; 1955–56, 2,646.

(c) Actual.

(d) Plus ID 37 million estimated carry-over from previous years.

(e) Excludes loans of the Development Board, which totaled ID 15,363,000; most of these loans went to the municipalities and are believed to be included here with receipts of municipalities.

Source: Adapted from working papers prepared under contract with the Human Relations Area Files at Johns Hopkins University under the direction of Majid Khadduri; and Iraq Ministry of Economics, principal Bureau of Statistics, *Statistical Abstract*, 1955, p. 317.

Table 7. **IRAQ'S ORDINARY BUDGET RECEIPTS IN RECENT YEARS**

(in millions of Iraqi dinars)

Source of Revenue	*1949–50*	*1950–51*	*1951–52*	*1952–53*	*1953–54*	*1954–55* [a]	*1955–56* [a]
Indirect taxes							
Land tax and agricultural produce tax	4.0	5.0	4.6	3.9	3.5	3.3	3.0
Customs and excise receipts	10.4	13.2	15.4	15.2	18.6	19.0	20.0
Total indirect taxes	14.4	18.2	20.0	19.1	22.1	22.3	23.0
Direct taxes	3.7	3.8	3.4	3.6	3.4	3.1	3.0
Registration fees	0.5	0.5	0.5	0.5	0.6	0.6	0.7
Income from government property	0.1	0.1	0.1	0.1	0.1	0.1	0.1
Miscellaneous revenues from public services	3.8	4.3	3.5	4.8	4.8	4.6	4.8
Government share in profits of the National Bank of Iraq	0.5	1.1	3.0	0.7	0.7	1.0	1.0
Government share in profits from other companies	(b)	(b)	0.1	(b)	0.1	0.2	0.3
Extraordinary revenue	2.3	0.1	(b)	(b)	0.7	---	---
Revenue from oil royalties	3.2	5.3	6.6	21.5 (c)	15.0	16.6	18.1
Total Revenue [d]	28.6	33.5	37.5	50.5	47.7	48.5	51.0

(a) Estimated.

(b) Includes a reported ID 9.5 million of income tax from oil companies plus a reported ID 12 million of oil royalties. The latter figure includes not only royalties due during the year but also a lump sum of compensations by the oil companies for differences between the exchange rate at which royalties were actually paid and the rate finally agreed upon between the companies and the government.

(c) Negligible amount.

(d) Because individual items have been rounded, the columns may not add to the totals given.

Source: Adapted from working papers prepared under contract with the Human Relations Area Files at Johns Hopkins University under the direction of Majid Khadduri.

Table 8. **IRAQ: ORDINARY BUDGET EXPENDITURES IN RECENT YEARS**

(in millions of Iraqi dinars)

	1949–50	*1950–51*	*1951–52*	*1952–53*	*1953–54*	*1954–55*	*1955–56* (a)
Ministry of Defense	6.6	7.2	7.9	13.8	15.9	15.6	14.9
Ministry of the Interior	4.2	5.7	5.4	8.8	10.4	12.8	12.6
Ministry of Finance	1.6	1.4	3.3	4.5	5.2	5.2	4.2
Ministry of Education	2.6	3.6	4.0	2.2	2.7	3.3	4.8
Ministry of Social Affairs	0.1	0.2	0.2	0.4	0.4	0.8	0.9
Ministry of Health	1.3	1.8	2.3	2.8	3.0	3.8	4.0
Ministry of Justice	0.5	0.7	0.8	0.9	1.0	1.0	1.2
Ministry of Communications and Public Works	1.1	1.3	1.4	2.1	3.0	2.5	2.5
Ministry of Agriculture	1.0	0.9	1.0	1.3	1.5	2.1	2.1
Ministry of Economics	0.2	0.2	0.3	0.4	0.2	0.3	0.4
Capital Works (b)	3.4	3.6	n.a.	n.a.	n.a.	n.a.	n.a.
Emergency Expenditure (c)	5.9	0.2	0.1	n.a.	n.a.	n.a.	n.a.
Other	1.2	1.8	3.9	7.3	6.8	6.4	3.7
Total (d)	30.0	29.3	30.8	44.5	50.2	53.8	51.5

(a) Estimated.
(b) Capital Works expenditures transferred to Development Board beginning in 1951–52.
(c) Includes special expenditures in the Department of Supply and high cost-of-living allowances paid to government employees.
(d) Totals do not add to the totals given due to rounding.

Source: Adapted from working papers prepared under contract with the Human Relations Area Files at Johns Hopkins University under the direction of Majid Khadduri; and Iraq Ministry of Economics, Principal Bureau of Statistics, *Statistical Abstract*, 1955, p. 318.

Table 9. **LAND UTILIZATION IN IRAQ**

Area planted during the year (winter or summer crops; double cropping in a few areas)	6,241,600 acres
Area lying fallow during the year	6,903,700
Fruit trees and vines	316,200
Pasture	570,500
Woodlands	128,400
Total	14,160,400

Source: Adapted from working papers prepared under contract with the Human Relations Area Files at Johns Hopkins University under the direction of Majid Khadduri.

Table 10. **PRODUCTION OF PRINCIPAL CROPS IN IRAQ**

(in thousands of metric tons)

Year	*Wheat*	*Barley*	*Rice*	*Cotton*	*Dates*
1934–38	478	575	205	2	260
1945	400	650	245	1	---
1948	301	570	350	2	301 (a)
1950	545	851	242	8	305
1951	487	839	190	6	350
1952	480	800	250	3	370
1953	762	1,111	200	4	350
1954	1,160	1,239	180	2.3	365
1955	483	768	---	2 (b)	421

(a) 1947.
(b) Estimated.
Source: ibid.

Table 11. **LIVESTOCK ON AGRICULTURAL HOLDINGS IN IRAQ, 1952–53**

Horses	137 (a
Cattle	712
Buffaloes	47
Sheep	4,484
Goats	1,618
Donkeys	399
Camels	38
Mules	57

(a) Figures are for thousands of head.
Source: ibid

Table 12. **CRUDE OIL PRODUCTION AND PAYMENTS BY IRAQI OIL COMPANIES IN SELECTED YEARS**

	Payments by Oil Companies [a] (in millions of Iraqi dinars) [b]	*Crude Oil Production* (in millions of metric tons)
1940	2.8	3.2
1950	5.3	6.4
1951	13.2	8.3
1952	37.4 [c]	18.8
1953	49.8	28.2
1954	68.3 [d]	29.5
1955	73.7	32.9

(a) In fiscal years, beginning April 1 of the year stated.
(b) ID 1 = $2.80.
(c) Including ID 5 million for settlement of previous claims.
(d) Calendar year; after readjustment for a retroactive 1954 settlement pursuant to the March 1955 agreement.

Source: ibid.

Table 13. **IRAQI OIL EXPORTS, 1951–54** [a]

	1951		*1952*		*1953*		*1954*	
	Value	*Quan.*	*Value*	*Quan.*	*Value*	*Quan.*	*Value*	*Quan.*
United Kingdom	5.9	1.3	13.1	2.9	19.8	4.4	22.2	4.5
Other OEEC countries	26.1	5.8	58.2	12.9	87.7	19.4	98.4	19.8
United States	----	----	0.2	----	0.3	0.1	0.3	0.1
Other	3.6	0.9	8.1	1.9	12.3	2.9	13.7	2.9
Total	35.6	8.0	79.6	17.7	120.1	26.8	134.6	27.3

(a) Value in millions of ID; quantity in millions of long tons.

Source: ibid.

Table 14. **CONSUMPTION OF ELECTRICITY IN IRAQ, 1952–54**

(in millions of kwh.)

	Total	*Lighting*	*Manufacturing*	*Other Purposes*
1952	207.2	77.0	119.7	10.5
1953	271.6	98.5	159.1	14.0
1954	390.0	116.2	260.9	12.9

Source: ibid.

Table 15. **IRAQI INDUSTRIAL CENSUS, 1954** [a]

	Number of Establishments [b]	*Number of Workers*	*Wages Paid* [c]	*Sales* [c]	*Machinery* [c]	*Buildings* [c]
Textile Manufacturing	2,847	11,828	742	4,279	1,720	917
Tailoring	4,236	7,385	166	1,628	209	92
Brickmaking	203	6,840	486	1,411	709	359
Metal Products	2,346	5,375	170	1,452	290	143
Food Provisioning	5,701	13,416	487	3,528	121	185
Construction	39	4,679	547	4,963	1,842	81
Auto Repairs	1,239	4,046	220	547	268	222
Cigarettes and Tobacco	1,057	3,988	267	3,867	138	64
Grain Milling	954	3,783	273	2,013	1,273	931
Carpentry	1,914	3,337	71	815	62	43
Shoe Manufacturing	1,239	3,186	166	1,413	105	149
Cement and Gypsum	266	2,558	216	1,663	716	479
Railway Workshops	8	2,506	435	12	701	9
Water Supply	22	1,384	250	1,137	2,231	713
Shipbuilding and Repairs	5	442	435	476	253	32
Electric Power	49	1,359	250	1,067	2,229	266
Tanneries	291	646	69	819	112	98
Soap and Chemicals	319	1,100	113	1,510	760	327
Spirits and Brewing	211	304	51	713	404	219
Printing	280	959	118	1,025	265	84
Total	23,226	79,121	5,532	34,338	14,408	5,413

(a) Excluding petroleum.
(b) Including operations in homes if product is for sale.
(c) Value in thousands of Iraqi dinars.
Source: ibid.

Table 16. **BALANCE OF PAYMENTS IN IRAQ**[a]

(in millions of Iraqi dinars)

	1951	*1952*	*1953*	*1954*	*1955*
Goods and Services					
Exports and Imports					
Oil exports f.o.b. and local sales	37.45	79.81	120.24	156.09	169.18
Imports for oil companies c.i.f.	−8.77	−14.42	−13.19	−5.78	−6.27
Balance	28.68	65.39	107.05	150.31	162.91
Other exports f.o.b.	34.77	23.51	23.67	20.68	16.18
Other imports c.i.f.	−43.24	−48.61	−56.58	−68.70	−90.89
Balance	−8.47	−25.10	−32.91	−48.02	−74.71
Other Oil Transactions					
Investment income	−14.05	−32.73	−51.34	−68.49	−73.74
Salaries remitted abroad	−.33	−.50	−.45	−.41	−.40
Capital movements, etc.	3.35	15.30	.04	−14.67	5.61
Total Other Oil Transactions	−11.03	−17.93	−51.75	−83.57	−68.53
Other (net)	.27	−.72	−.18	.37	−1.34
Balance of all Goods and Services	9.45	21.64	22.57	19.09	18.33
Other Private Donations	−.09	−.15	−.08	.01	.01
Other Private Capital	−.14	1.34	.97	1.05	1.44
Official Donations	.01	.17	.10	.56	2.43
Official and Bank Capital	−.40	−10.04	−23.30	−23.28	−22.43
Long-Term					
Repayment of loans	−.06	−.75	−1.97	---	−2.29
Drawing on loans	.26	1.70	.43	.14	.04
Security holdings	−1.10	.08	−2.12	−3.71	−2.98
Short-Term					
Liabilities	−.16	.06	.03	−.07	.33
Foreign assets (increase −)	.66	−11.13	−19.67	−19.64	−14.53
Monetary gold	---	---	---	---	−3.00
Net Errors and Omissions	−8.83	−12.96	−.26	2.57	.22

(a) These statistics do not include military assistance under MDAP and purchases of military supplies and equipment.

Source: **Adapted from International Monetary Fund, *International Financial Statistics,* October 1957, p. 254.**

Table 17. **DIRECTION OF IRAQ'S FOREIGN TRADE** [a]

(in millions of U. S. dollars)

	1938	*1952*	*1953*	*1954*	*1955*
Imports from					
North America	4.1	33.0	30.0	29.4	42.0
United States	4.1	31.7	29.5	28.9	41.0
Northwestern Europe	21.4	88.1	105.1	107.9	137.7
United Kingdom	13.7	64.6	72.3	63.6	76.7
Belgium-Luxembourg	1.8	5.7	6.4	6.8	9.3
France	.5	3.2	5.7	5.3	10.5
Germany	3.6	3.7	9.3	16.7	21.2
Southern Europe	2.1	11.1	9.2	7.1	8.1
Italy	1.8	10.0	8.4	6.0	6.3
Eastern Europe	1.4	4.4	3.5	4.9	7.0
Middle East	3.6	6.9	7.0	9.7	10.1
Other Asia	12.1	27.3	36.0	45.6	61.4
Ceylon	.2	9.2	11.2	14.9	21.3
India	2.9	6.8	6.5	6.5	7.1
Japan	6.7	8.7	12.2	16.6	22.9
Other Countries	1.0	2.6	1.6	3.0	5.7
Total Imports	45.7	173.3	192.4	207.6	272.0
Exports to					
North America	2.9	3.0	4.8	5.1	12.0
United States	2.7	2.9	4.4	4.8	11.2
Northwestern Europe	51.4	191.4	260.8	312.7	252.3
United Kingdom	10.8	75.5	95.0	80.1	60.1
France	38.1	78.6	116.2	152.9	120.3
Germany	.8	16.2	19.1	30.6	33.6
Belgium-Luxembourg	1.3	10.5	13.8	16.5	20.9
Southern Europe	2.3	39.2	78.5	109.0	114.3
Italy	2.3	31.7	71.3	94.6	99.8
Eastern Europe	--	4.5	6.7	6.0	2.8
Middle East	4.0	26.7	25.3	21.8	23.9
Egypt	.2	1.4	1.5	.7	.7
Saudi Arabia	.2	1.0	1.4	1.4	1.7
British Areas	.4	3.7	5.1	5.1	2.7
Syria	1.3 (Syria and Lebanon combined)	15.7	12.8	11.8	3.6
Lebanon		2.9	1.9	1.6	11.9

Table 17 (continued)

	1938	*1952*	*1953*	*1954*	*1955*
Other Asia	3.3	13.3	14.2	32.5	41.3
India	1.4	3.4	4.3	3.0	2.5
Indonesia	--	.5	3.3	6.1	34.9
Japan	1.7	6.5	.5	1.3	2.4
Other Countries	3.7	.7	1.6	1.6	81.2
Total Exports	67.6	278.9	391.9	488.7	517.8

(a) Including oil.

Source: Adapted from International Monetary Fund, *et. al.*, *Direction of International* .r*ade.* (Statistical Papers, Series T) 1956, pp. 214–215.

Table 18. **COMPOSITION OF IRAQ'S IMPORTS** [a, b]

(percentage of total value [c])

	1950	*1951*	*1952*	*1953*	*1954*	*1955* [d]	*1956* [d]
Sugar	12.8	11.4	10.2	7.4	8.0	5.8	7.4
Tea	7.7	8.0	5.7	6.9	9.5	8.9	6.8
Cotton, Artificial Silk, and Woolen Piece Goods	19.2	21.2	14.3	12.6	14.4	10.9	7.9
Soap	1.3	1.2	1.1	0.7	0.8	n.a.	n.a.
Iron and Steel	9.8	12.4	14.1	17.1	11.3	12.4	12.1
Boilers and Machinery	9.6	7.6	10.8	14.7	12.3	12.2	15.1
Vehicles and Parts	4.8	3.5	6.2	6.9	8.5	10.0	9.0
Electrical Machinery	4.8	3.5	3.9	4.8	4.5	4.9	6.6
Chemicals and Pharmaceuticals	2.1	2.5	2.6	2.3	2.8	n.a.	n.a.
Paper and Cardboard	1.1	1.8	1.9	1.2	1.6	n.a.	n.a.
Timber	0.5	1.4	1.6	1.7	2.1	n.a.	n.a.
Other	26.3	25.5	27.7	25.0	24.9	n.a.	n.a.

(a) Including imports by oil companies.

(b) Note that figures in Table 4, as in Table 3, are given as percentages of total value. The absolute value of sugar, for example, has increased steadily, while its percentage shows a decrease.

(c) Figures may not total 100 percent because of rounding.

(d) Figures are for first half of year only.

Source: Adapted from working papers prepared under contract with the Human Relations Area Files at Johns Hopkins University under the direction of Majid Khadduri; and *Three-Monthly Economic Review of Iraq and the Arabian Peninsula,* Annual Supplement: *Iraq* (1957), p. 13.

Table 19. **COMPOSITION OF IRAQ'S EXPORTS**[a]

(percentage of total value [b])

	1950	*1951*	*1952*	*1953*	*1954*	*1955* [c]	*1956* [c]
Cereals (barley, wheat, other grains, flour, pulses, etc.)	58.4	56.8	50.5	50.8 [d]	55.5 [e]	54.3	51.7
Raw Cotton	5.5	6.6	5.9	2.1	1.6	4.1	6.4
Raw Wool	6.9	6.2	5.9	5.2	5.2	9.1	8.7
Dates	21.3	20.5	25.0	22.0	19.6	17.9	15.9
Live Animals	2.5	1.8	4.8	8.4	8.7	2.6	3.8
Seeds	.5	2.2	1.6	3.1	1.7	n.a.	n.a.
Hides and Skins	1.5	1.1	1.0	1.6	1.7	n.a.	n.a.
Other	3.1	4.8	5.3	6.8	6.1	n.a.	n.a.

(a) Excluding oil.
(b) Figures may not total 100 percent because of rounding.
(c) Figures are for first half of year only.
(d) Figures not available for wheat.
(e) Figures available for barley, wheat, and flour only.
Source: ibid.

RECOMMENDED READING

RECOMMENDED READING

The following are recommended as additional reading on the basis of quality and general availability.

Atyeo, Henry C. "Reform through Riot," *Middle Eastern Affairs,* IV, No. 3 (March 1953), 90–95.

Barth, Fredrik. *Principles of Social Organization in Southern Kurdistan.* (University Ethnographic Museum Bulletin, No. 7.) Oslo: Brodrene Jorgensen, 1953.

Bonne, Alfred. *State and Economics in the Middle East: A Society in Transition.* London: Kegan Paul, Trench, Trubner, 1948.

Boveri, Margret. *Minaret and Pipeline: Yesterday and Today in the Near East.* Translated by Louisa Marie Sieveking. New York: Oxford University Press, 1939.

British Colonial Office. *Reports to the Council of the League of Nations on the Administration of Iraq, 1920–1931.* London: His Majesty's Stationery Office, 1930–32.

Coke, Richard. *The Heart of the Middle East.* London: Thornton Butterworth, 1925.

Coon, Carleton. *Caravan.* New York: Henry Holt & Co., 1951.

al-Dalli, Abdul G. "Problems of Industrial Enterprise in Iraq." Pages 37–54 in *Middle East Economic Papers.* Beirut: American University of Beirut, Economic Research Institute, 1954.

"Development in Iraq," *The Economist,* Vol. CLXXXIII, No. 5939 (June 22, 1957).

Drower, Lady Ethel S. "Arabs of the Hor Al Hawiza." Chap. 5 in Henry Field (ed.), *The Anthropology of Iraq, the Lower Euphrates-Tigris Region,* Part I (Anthropological Series, Vol. XXX, No. 2 [July 1949]). Chicago: Field Museum of Natural History, 1949.

———. *The Mandaeans of Iraq and Iran.* Oxford, England: Clarendon Press, 1937.

Edmonds, C. J. "The Kurds of Iraq," *Middle East Journal,* XI, No. 1 (Winter 1957), 52–62.

Empson, R. H. W. *The Cult of the Peacock Angel.* London: Witherby, 1928.

Fisher, Sydney N. (ed.). *Social Forces in the Middle East.* Ithaca, N. Y.: Cornell University Press, 1955.

Foster, Henry A. *The Making of Modern Iraq: A Product of World Forces.* Norman: University of Oklahoma Press, 1935.

Franck, Peter G. "Economic Nationalism in the Middle East," *Middle East Journal,* VI, No. 4 (Autumn 1952), 429–454.

Gibb, H. A. R. *Mohammedanism.* New York: Mentor Books, 1955.

Grunebaum, Gustave E. von. *Medieval Islam.* Chicago: University of Chicago Press, 1946.

al-Habib, Mahmud M. "The Labor Movement in Iraq," *Middle Eastern Affairs,* VII (April 1956), 137–143.

Hitti, Philip K. *History of the Arabs.* London: Macmillan Co., 1956.

Hooper, C. H. *The Constitutional Law of Iraq.* Baghdad: Mackenzie & Mackenzie, 1928.

International Bank for Reconstruction and Development. *The Economic Development of Iraq: Report of a Mission.* Washington, D. C., 1952.

International Cooperation Administration and Iraq Development Board. *A Plan for the Industrial Development of Iraq.* Cambridge, Mass.: Arthur Little, 1956.

Ionides, M. G. *The Regime of the Rivers Euphrates and Tigris.* London: Spon, 1937.

Iraq Ministry of the Interior: Director-General of Propaganda. *Iraq Today.* Lewisham, England: T. J. Hunt, 1953.

Ireland, Philip W. *Iraq: A Study in Political Development.* London: Jonathan Cape, 1937.

Jurji, Edward J. *The Middle East, Its Religion and Culture.* Philadelphia: The Westminster Press, 1946.

Khadduri, Majid. "The Coup d'Etat of 1936, A Study in Iraqi Politics," *Middle East Journal,* II, No. 3 (July 1948), 270–292.

———. *Independent Iraq: A Study in Iraqi Politics Since 1932.* New York: Oxford University Press (for Royal Institute of International Affairs), 1951.

———. *The Government of Iraq.* (Facts and Prospects in Iraq Series, No. 1.) Jerusalem: New Publishers Iraq, 1944.

———. "Governments of the Arab East," *Journal of International Affairs,* VI (1952), 37–50.

———. *Independent Iraq: A Study in Iraqi Politics Since 1932.* New York: Oxford University Press (for Royal Institute of International Affairs), 1951.

———. "The Role of the Military in Middle East Politics," *American Political Science Review,* XLVII, No. 2 (June 1953), 511–524.

Kirk, George. *The Middle East in the War.* New York: Oxford University Press, 1952.

Laqueur, Walter Z. *Communism and Nationalism in the Middle East.* New York: Frederick A. Praeger, Inc., 1956.

Lenczowski, George. *The Middle East in World Affairs.* Ithaca, N. Y.: Cornell University Press, 1956.

Lloyd, Seton. *Foundations in the Dust.* New York: Oxford University Press, 1947.
———. *Iraq.* New York: Oxford University Press, 1944.
———. *Twin Rivers: A Brief History of Iraq from the Earliest Times to the Present Day.* New York: Oxford University Press, 1945.
Longrigg, Stephen H. *Iraq, 1900 to 1950: A Political, Social, and Economic History.* New York: Oxford University Press, 1953.
———. *Oil in the Middle East: Its Discovery and Development.* New York: Oxford University Press, 1954.
McFadden, Tom J. *Daily Journalism in the Arab States.* (Journalism Series, No. 15.) Columbus: Ohio State University Press, 1953.
Main, Ernest. *Iraq from Mandate to Independence.* London: Allen & Unwin, 1935.
"Oil and Social Change in the Middle East," Supplement to *The Economist,* Vol. CLXXVI, No. 5836 (July 2, 1955).
Royal Institute of International Affairs. *The Middle East: A Political and Economic Survey.* (2d ed.). New York: Oxford University Press, 1954.
Salter, Sir James Arthur. *The Development of Iraq: A Plan of Action.* Baghdad: Iraq Development Board, 1955.
Siddiqi, S. A. *Public Finance in Islam.* Lahore, India: Muhammed Ashrof, 1948.
Smith, Wilfred Cantwell. *Islam in Modern History.* Princeton, N. J.: Princeton University Press, 1957.
Stafford, R. S. *The Tragedy of the Assyrians.* London: Allen & Unwin, 1935.
Stewart, Desmond, and Haylock, John. *New Babylon: A Portrait of Iraq.* London: Collins, 1956.
Tannous, Afif I. "Land Reform: Key to the Development and Stability of the Arab World," *Middle East Journal,* V, No. 1 (Winter 1951), 1–20.
Warriner, Doreen. *Land and Poverty in the Middle East.* New York: Oxford University Press (for Royal Institute of International Affairs), 1948.
———. *Land Reform and Development in the Middle East: A Study of Egypt, Syria, and Iraq.* New York: Oxford University Press (for Royal Institute of International Affairs), 1957.
Weulersse, Jacques. *Paysans de Syrie et du Proche-Orient.* Paris: Gallimard, 1946.
Wigram, W. A. *The Assyrians and Their Neighbors.* London: Bell, 1929.
Wilson, Sir Arnold T. *Loyalties: Mesopotamia, 1914–1917.* London: Oxford University Press, 1930.
———. *Mesopotamia 1917–1920: A Clash of Loyalties.* London: Oxford University Press, 1931.
W. K. "Political Trends in the Fertile Crescent," *World Today,* XII, No. 4 (April 1956), 215–222.

OTHER USEFUL SOURCES

Adams, Doris G. "Current Population Trends in Iraq," *Middle East Journal,* X, No. 2 (Spring 1956), 151–164.
American University of Beirut: Economic Research Institute. *Middle East Economic Papers.* Beirut, 1954.

Anshen, Ruth N. (ed.). *Mid-East: World Center, Yesterday, Today and Tomorrow.* New York: Harper & Brothers, 1956.

Antonius, George. *The Arab Awakening: The Story of the Arab National Movement.* London: Hamish Hamilton, 1945.

Barth, Fredrik. "Father's Brother's Daughter Marriage in Kurdistan," *Southwestern Journal of Anthropology,* X, No. 2 (Summer 1954), 164–171.

Bedr Khan, Emir Dr. Kamuran 'Ali. "The Kurdish Problem," *Journal of the Royal Central Asian Society,* XXXVI (July–October 1949), 237–248.

British Board of Trade: Commercial Relations and Export Department. *Iraq: Review of Economic Conditions.* London: His Majesty's Stationery Office, 1945.

———. *Markets in the Middle East: Report of the United Kingdom Trade Mission to Iraq, Kuwait, the Lebanon, Syria, and Saudi Arabia.* (November–December, 1953). London: Her Majesty's Stationery Office, 1954.

British Broadcasting Corporation: Monitoring Service. *Summary of World Broadcasts. Part IV. The Arab World, Israel, Greece, Turkey, Persia.* May–July, 1957, *passim.*

British Colonial Office. *Report by His Majesty's Government in the United Kingdom of Great Britain and Northern Ireland to the Council of the League of Nations on the Administration of Iraq for the Year 1930.* London: His Majesty's Stationery Office, 1931.

———. *Report on Iraq Administration.* 10 vols. London: His Majesty's Stationery Office, 1920–31.

Burne, Alfred H. *Mesopotamia: The Last Phase.* Aldershot, England: Gale and Polden, 1936.

Burns, Norman. "Development Projects in Iraq: the Dujaylah Land Settlement," *Middle East Journal,* V, No. 3 (Summer 1951), 362–366.

Burr, Malcolm. "A Note on the Kurds," *Journal of the Royal Central Asian Society,* XLIII (July 1956), 289–292.

Cleland, W. Wendell. "Social Conditions and Social Change," *Journal of International Affairs,* VI, No. 2 (1952), 7–20.

Cragg, Kenneth. *The Call of the Minaret.* New York: Oxford University Press, 1956.

———. "The Intellectual Impact of Communism upon Contemporary Islam," *Middle East Journal,* VIII, No. 2 (Spring 1954), 127–138.

Creswell, K. A. C. "The Lawfulness of Painting in Early Islam," *Islamic Culture,* XXIV (July 1950), 218–225.

Critchley, A. Michael. "The Health of the Industrial Worker in Iraq," *British Journal of Industrial Medicine,* XII, No. 1 (January 1955), 73–75.

el-Daghestani, Kazem. "The Evolution of the Moslem Family in the Middle Eastern Countries," *International Social Science Bulletin,* Vol. V, No. 4 (Winter 1953).

Davies, D. Hywek. "Observations on Land Use in Iraq," *Economic Geography,* Vol. XXXIII, No. 2 (April 1957). Worcester, Mass.: Clark University, 1957.

Dimand, M. S. *A Handbook of Muhammadan Art.* (2d ed.) New York: The Metropolitan Museum of Art, 1944.

Drower, Lady Ethel S. "Marsh People of South Iraq," *Journal of the Royal Central Asian Society,* XXXIV, No. 1 (January 1947), 83–90.

Elphinston, W. G. "Kurds and the Kurdish Question," *Journal of the Royal Central Asian Society,* XXXV (January 1948), 38–51.

Evans, F. Bowen. *Worldwide Communist Propaganda Activities.* New York: Macmillan Co., 1955.

Faris, Nabih Amin (ed.). *The Arab Heritage.* Princeton, N. J.: Princeton University Press, 1944.

Faris, Nabih Amin, and Husayn, Mohammed Tawfik. *The Crescent in Crisis: An Interpretive Study of the Modern Arab World.* Lawrence: University of Kansas Press, 1955.

Gamble, F. H. *Iraq: Economic and Commercial Conditions in Iraq.* (British Board of Trade, "Overseas Economic Surveys.") London: His Majesty's Stationery Office, 1949.

al-Ghita, Ahmad Kashif. *Outline of Modern Iraq.* (International Studies Series.) London: Diplomatic Press and Publishing Co., 1949.

Gianni, A. "La Constituzione dell' Iraq," *Oriente Moderno,* X (1930), 525–546.

Gibb, H. A. R. *Arabic Literature: An Introduction.* London: Oxford University Press, 1926.

———. *Modern Trends in Islam.* Chicago: University of Chicago Press, 1945.

Gibb, H. A. R., and Kramers, J. H. *Shorter Encyclopaedia of Islam.* Ithaca, N. Y.: Cornell University Press, 1953.

Greenridge, C. W. W. "Slavery in the Middle East," *Middle Eastern Affairs,* VII (November 1956), 435–440.

Grunebaum, Gustav E. von. *Islam: Essays in the Nature and Growth of a Cultural Tradition.* (Comparative Studies of Culture and Civilizations, No. 4. *American Anthropologist,* Memoir No. 81, Vol. LVII, No. 2, Part 2. Menasha, Wis.: The American Anthropological Association, 1955.

Habermann, Stanley J. "The Iraq Development Board: Administration and Program," *Middle East Journal,* IX, No. 2 (Spring 1955), 179–186.

Haldane, Sir Aylmer L. *The Insurrection in Mesopotamia, 1920.* London: Blackwood, 1922.

Hallsworth, J. A. "Freedom of Association and Industrial Relations in the Countries of the Near and Middle East," Parts I and II, *International Labor Review,* LXX, No. 5 (November 1954), 363–384; and No. 6 (December 1954), 526–541.

Harrison, Paul W. *The Arab at Home.* New York: Thomas Y. Crowell Co., 1924.

"Helping Iraq's Villagers," *The Economist,* CLXXXIV, No. 5952 (September 21, 1957), 950.

Institute of International Education. *News Bulletin,* Vol. XXI, No. 8 (May 1956).

International Labour Conference (Twelfth Session). *Forced Labour, Report and Draft Questionnaire.* Geneva: International Labour Office, 1929.

International Labour Organisation. *Manpower Problems.* (Report I of the ILO Regional Conference for the Near and Middle East, Tehran, April 1951.) Geneva: International Labour Office, 1951.

———. *Report of the Ad Hoc Committee on Forced Labour.* Geneva, 1953.

———. *Social Security.* (Report III of the ILO Regional Conference for the

Near and Middle East, Tehran, April 1951.) Geneva: International Labour Office, 1951.

International Monetary Fund. *Eighth Annual Report on Exchange Restrictions, 1957.* Washington, D. C., 1957.

———. *International Financial Statistics,* X, No. 10 (October 1957), 140–141.

International Monetary Fund, United Nations Statistical Office, and International Bank for Reconstruction and Development. *Direction of International Trade* (Statistical Papers, Series T), VII, No. 6 (Annual Issue, October 1956), 214–215.

Iraq Committee of Officials. *An Introduction to the Past and Present of the Kingdom of Iraq.* Baltimore: Lord Baltimore Press, 1946.

"Iraq," *Encyclopaedia Britannica* (1956 ed.), XII, 587–590D.

Iraq Ministry of Economics: Principal Bureau of Statistics. *Statistical Abstract, 1955.* Baghdad: Zahra' Press, 1956.

"Iraq: Pasha," *Time,* LXIX, No. 24 (June 17, 1957), 23–27.

"Iraq: Summer Shareout," *The Economist,* CLXXXIII, No. 5938 (June 15, 1957), 962.

Iraq Times, May 18 and May 22, 1957; 1957, *passim.*

"Iraqi Development," *Middle East Journal,* X, No. 3 (Summer 1956), 271–273.

Izzeddin, Nejla. *The Arab World: Past, Present, and Future.* Chicago: Henry Regnery Co., 1953.

Jewish Agency for Palestine: Research Department. *The Jews of Iraq: A Prosperous, Well-Organized Community; the Anti-Jewish Regime since 1933; the Catastrophe after May 15, 1948.* New York, 1948.

Johns Hopkins University. *Area Handbook on Iraq.* Human Relations Area Files Subcontractor's Monograph, 1956.

Katabi, Adnan A. "Some Economic Aspects of Oil Investment in Iraq." Unpublished Ph.D. dissertation, American University, 1955.

"Kurdistan," *New Statesman and Nation,* XXXIX, No. 998 (April 22, 1950), 452.

Landau, Jacob M. "The Arab Cinema," *Middle Eastern Affairs,* IV (November 1953), 349–358.

Leach, Edmund R. *Social and Economic Organization of the Rowanduz Kurds.* (Monographs on Social Anthropology, No. 3.) London: Percy Lund, Humphries, 1940.

Leatherdale, D. "The Material Background of Life in Northern Iraq," *Journal of the Royal Central Asian Society,* XXXV (January 1948), 66–73.

Lloyd, Seton. "Iraq," *Journal of the Royal Central Asian Society,* XXXI (July–October 1944), 308–414.

MacDonald, Alan D. *Euphrates Exile.* London: Bell, 1936.

al-Masumi, M. Saghir Hasan. "Rusafi—A Modern Poet of Iraq," *Islamic Culture,* XXIV (January 1950), 50–59.

"The Medical College at Baghdad," *The Lancet,* CCLVII, No. 6576 (September 10, 1949), 475.

The Middle East—1957. London: Europa Publications, 1957.

Morris, James. *Islam Inflamed.* New York: Pantheon Books, Inc., 1957.

Nicholson, Reynold A. *A Literary History of the Arabs.* Cambridge, England: Cambridge University Press, 1956.

"On Reading Arab Omens," *The Economist,* CLXXXV, No. 5954 (October 5, 1957), 19–20.

Patai, Raphael. "The Dynamics of Westernization in the Middle East," *Middle East Journal,* IX, No. 4 (Autumn 1955), 1–16.

———. "The Middle East as a Culture Area," *Middle East Journal,* VI, No. 1 (Winter 1952), 1–21.

Peaslee, Amos J. *Constitutions of Nations.* (2d ed.) Vol. II, 412–432. The Hague: Martinus Nijhoff, 1956.

Perowne, Stewart. "Life in Baghdad," *Journal of the Royal Central Asian Society,* XXXIV (July–October 1947), 251–261.

Polk, W. R. "Perspective of the Arab World," *Atlantic Monthly* (Special Supplement), Vol. CXCVIII (October 1956).

Safrastian, Arshak. *Kurds and Kurdistan.* London: Harvill Press, 1948.

Shwadran, Benjamin. *The Middle East: Oil and the Great Powers.* New York: Frederick A. Praeger, Inc., 1955.

Simmonds, S. *Iraq: Economic and Commercial Conditions in Iraq.* (British Board of Trade, "Overseas Economic Surveys.") London: Her Majesty's Stationery Office, 1953.

Sinderson, Harry. "Some Health Problems of the Middle East," *Journal of the Royal Central Asian Society,* XXXIV (July–October 1947), 131–143.

Stark, Freya. *Baghdad Sketches.* New York: E. P. Dutton & Co., Inc., 1938.

Steinberg, S. H. (ed.). *Statesman's Yearbook, 1956.* New York: St. Martin's Press, 1956.

Thesiger, Wilfred. "The Ma'dan or Marsh Dwellers of Southern Iraq," *Journal of the Royal Central Asian Society,* XLI, No. 1 (January 1954), 4–25.

Three-Monthly Economic Review of Iraq and the Arabian Peninsula. (*Iraq* [Annual Supplement], August 1957.) London: Economist Intelligence Unit, 1957.

United Nations: Department of Economic and Social Affairs. *Economic Developments in the Middle East, 1955–1956.* (Supplement to *World Economic Survey, 1956.*) New York, 1957.

United Nations: Department of Social Affairs. "Social Conditions in the Middle East." Pages 148–163 in *Preliminary Report on the World Social Situation.* New York, 1952.

———. Economic and Social Council, *Ad Hoc* Committee on Forced Labour. *Replies from Governments to the Questionnaire on Forced Labour.* Geneva, 1953.

United Nations Educational, Scientific, and Cultural Organization. *Compulsory Education in the Arab States: With Special Reference to the Cairo Conference, December 1954.* Vol. XVI in *UNESCO Studies on Compulsory Education.* Paris, 1956.

———. *World Communications. Press, Radio, Film, Television.* (3d ed.) New York, 1956.

———. *World Survey of Education: Handbook of Educational Organization and Statistics.* Paris, 1955.

United Nations: Food and Agriculture Organization. *Problems of Food and Agricultural Expansion in the Near East.* Rome, 1955.

———. *Problems of Production and Trade in the Near East.* Rome, 1956.

United States Department of Commerce: Bureau of Foreign Commerce. *Economic Developments in Iraq, 1954.* (World Trade Information Service: "Economic Reports," Pt. 1, No. 55–28.) Washington, D. C., March 1955.

———. *Economic Developments in Iraq, 1955.* (World Trade Information Service: "Economic Reports," Pt. 1, No. 56–27.) Washington, D. C., March 1956.

———. *Establishing a Business in Iraq.* (World Trade Information Service: "Economic Reports," Pt. 1, No. 57–45.) Washington, D. C., April 1957.

———. *Foreign Trade of Iraq, 1953–1954.* (World Trade Information Service: "Statistical Reports," Pt. 3, No. 55–43.) Washington, D. C., November 1955.

———. *Licensing and Exchange Controls . . . Iraq.* (World Trade Information Service: "Operations Reports," Pt. 2, No. 55–122.) Washington, D. C., December 1955.

———. *Marketing in Iraq.* (World Trade Information Service: "Economic Reports," Pt. 1, No. 56–71.) Washington, D. C., September 1956.

———. *Preparing Shipments to Iraq.* (World Trade Information Service: "Operations Reports," Pt. 2, No. 55–112.) Washington, D. C., November 1955.

———. Office of International Trade. *Iraq—Economic Review, 1951.* (Business Information Service: "World Trade Series," No. 232.) Washington, D. C., June 1952.

———. *Iraq—Economic Review, 1952.* (Business Information Service: "World Trade Series," No. 397.) Washington, D. C., June 1953.

———. *Iraq—Economic Review, 1953.* (Business Information Service: "World Trade Series," No. 588.) Washington, D. C., June 1954.

United States Department of State: United States Embassy, Baghdad. *Economic Review, Iraq, 1956.* (Department of State Dispatch No. 621, March 27, 1957.)

Wellek, René, and Warren, Austin. *Theory of Literature.* New York: Harcourt, Brace & Co., 1956.

Winslow, Hall. "Homes within Reach," *Middle East Forum,* XXXI, No. 4 (April 1956), 12–16.

W. L. E. "Iraqi Kurdistan, A Little-Known Region," *World Today,* XII, No. 4 (April 1956), 417–432.

Woodsmall, Ruth F. (ed.). *Study of the Role of Women: Their Activities and Organizations in Lebanon, Egypt, Iraq, Jordan, and Syria, October 1954–August 1955.* New York: International Federation of Business and Professional Women, 1956.

Wright, Quincy. "The Government of Iraq," *American Political Science Review,* XX, No. 4 (November 1926), 743–769.

Young, T. Cuyler (ed.). *Near Eastern Culture and Society.* Princeton, N. J.: Princeton University Press, 1952.

Zeki, Memdouk (ed.). *Iraq Yearbook, 1953.* Baghdad: Baghdad Printing Press, 1953.

INDEX

INDEX

D0955624

FIRST EDITIONS OF TO-DAY
AND HOW TO TELL THEM

REVISED AND ENLARGED

FIRST EDITIONS OF TO-DAY AND HOW TO TELL THEM

UNITED STATES AND ENGLAND

BY

H. S. BOUTELL

SECOND EDITION

REVISED AND MUCH ENLARGED

BY

ROGER BOUTELL

PHILADELPHIA

J. B. LIPPINCOTT COMPANY

LONDON

1937

EXPLANATORY NOTE TO THE REVISED EDITION

The number of new publishing houses established since 1928 in the United States and England, and the changes since that time in the methods of identifying first impressions used by the houses already in existence when this book was published, have made necessary a complete revision. This revision like the original edition is made up of the publishers' own statements. In addition, wherever possible, publishers have supplied the dates when they first adopted their present methods. It is hoped that this feature will make the book more useful to both collectors and dealers.

In cases of publishers in existence prior to 1928, only one statement is given if the method has remained unchanged, or if the publisher wished an entirely new statement substituted, or if the publisher wished merely to make minor changes.

When two statements of one publisher are given, the first is the statement in the 1928 edition of this book, and the second statement is the one made for this revision, appended to show a definite change of method, or to clarify the original statement.

In one case a publisher who was included in the first edition has not complied with the reviser's request, and this publisher's 1928 statement is repeated, but in this case the statement is headed 1928.

The reviser wishes to thank the contributing publishers for their courtesy and promptness in answering his inquiries, which made the preparation of the present edition possible.

R. B.

PUBLISHER'S NOTE TO THE ORIGINAL EDITION

As Messrs. Arrowsmith observe, the correct term is not First Edition but First Impression or Issue. Unfortunately this error of terminology is almost universal; and it was felt that to use any but the usual phrase in the title of the book would be to invite misapprehension. One hopes that a better state of things will one day prevail.

In the case of firms having both English and American houses there are cross-references, and the replies received from each side of the Atlantic have been given, except in one case where the replies were identical. It would hardly, however, be safe to assume that these invariably represent divergences of practice.

INTRODUCTORY NOTE TO THE ORIGINAL EDITION

Generally speaking, the collector of first editions is really a collector of first impressions, a first impression being a book from the first lot struck off the presses, and a first edition comprising all books which remain the same in content and in format as the first impression. A second impression is a second printing. A second edition postulates some alteration of text or format. But these terms are, unfortunately, not strictly adhered to.

It is hoped that this book will serve to guide the collector amidst these intricacies.

The publishing houses of Great Britain and the United States are listed in alphabetical order, and in every case the information is quoted directly from letters, material, or information received from the publishers themselves.

Every attempt has been made to make this book as complete as possible, but some of the compiler's letters were not answered. And if any of the publishing houses whose books are being collected have been overlooked by the compiler, he would like to express his regret both to them and to his readers.

H. S. B.

AMERICAN HOUSES

THE ABINGDON PRESS

First editions of Abingdon Press publications can be identified by examining the copyright page. There does not appear on the bottom of the copyright page of first editions a statement as to the number of the edition and when printed. This statement does not appear until the second edition and thereafter.

D. APPLETON & CO.

(*Merged with Century Co. to form D. Appleton-Century Co., Inc., on May 31, 1933.*)

Our first editions are designated by a small numeral one in parentheses (1) at the foot of the last page. Later as we reprint the book this numeral is changed according to the number of the reprinting, that is, (2), (3), etc.

∴ *See D. Appleton-Century Co., Inc.*

∴ *See also English section.*

D. APPLETON-CENTURY COMPANY, INC.

Our first editions are designated by a small numeral one in parentheses (1) at the foot of the last page. Later as we reprint the book, this numeral is changed according to the number of the printing, that is, (2), (3), etc. This numbering was inaugurated by D. Appleton and Company in 1902.

ARCADIA HOUSE

∴ *See Hillman-Curl, Inc.*

THE ARGUS BOOK SHOP, INC.

Later printings are indicated on the verso of the title page in all our publications. We have used this method since 1926.

THE ATLANTIC MONTHLY PRESS, INC.

On first editions of Atlantic Monthly Press titles beginning with the fall of 1925 (when they appeared under the Little, Brown and Company imprint) the date at the bottom of the title page coincides with the date of publication printed on the copyright page immediately beneath the copyright notice. Later printings are likewise listed on the copyright page, so that reprints are easily distinguishable.

Prior to the fall of 1925, however, it is not an easy matter to distinguish first editions of our books. In many instances it has been necessary for us to check back on text corrections to be quite sure, as at that time our title pages carried no dates and our copyright pages did not consistently list reprints of our titles. There is therefore no definite ruling one can give, although in general it is safe to say that such copies containing simply the copyright line on the copyright page are first editions.

∴ *See Little, Brown & Co.*

ROBERT O. BALLOU, PUBLISHER

(*Out of business.*)

∴ *See Jonathan Cape and Robert Ballou, Inc.*

THE BOBBS-MERRILL COMPANY

1928 Statement

We are not entirely consistent in our first edition attitude. Whenever we do mark a first edition the distinguishing mark is a bow and arrow at the bottom of the page on which appears the copyright line.

However, not all of our first editions are marked.

1936 Statement

We are consistent in our first edition attitude. We print the words "First Edition" on the copyright page. All of our first editions are so marked.

ALBERT & CHARLES BONI, INC.

We run a note on the copyright page of all our books indicating all subsequent printings after the first.

BONI & LIVERIGHT
(*Became Horace Liveright, Inc.*)

∴ *See Liveright Publishing Corporation.*

BRENTANO'S
(*Now out of business.*)

Up to the end of 1927 all books published by this company had no edition printed on them unless they reached a second edition. This information would be printed on the back of the title. From January 1st, 1928, the words "First Printed 1928" were substituted and if the book reached a second edition the words "second impression April 1928 (or . . .)"

∴ *See also English Section.*

BREWER & WARREN

(Succeeded Payson & Clarke, Ltd., q.v., on Jan. 1, 1930. Became Brewer, Warren & Putnam, Inc., in autumn of 1931. Now out of business.)

We do not put the actual words "first edition" on the reverse of the title page for the first edition but when we go into the second printing we say "first printing such and such a date," "second printing such and such a date," therefore, all copies of a book which do not carry such designation may be taken as being "firsts."

BREWER, WARREN & PUTNAM, INC.

(Succeeded Brewer & Warren, q.v., in autumn of 1931. Firm was dissolved on December 8, 1932, and publications taken over by Harcourt, Brace & Co., Inc.)

We do not put the actual words "first edition" on the reverse of the title page for the first edition but when we go into the second printing we say "first printing such and such a date," "second printing such and such a date," therefore, all copies of a book which do not carry such designation may be taken as being "firsts."

BRUCE PUBLISHING COMPANY
(*Milwaukee, Wis.*)

We follow no regular rule to indicate first editions of books. In the case of trade books, we usually indicate the second and subsequent printings by an appropriate line on the copyright page.

BRUCE PUBLISHING COMPANY
(*St. Paul, Minn.*)

The words First printing, Second printing, etcetera, together with notation of the date of printing—7-21-36—are imprinted in 6 point type on the last page of the book in the lower left hand corner. This method has been in use in our printing plant since 1928.

UNIVERSITY OF CALIFORNIA PRESS

The few books that have gone into a second edition have had printed on the verso of the title page "Second Edition" or "Third Edition." Such a notice will be printed on all editions after the first.

JONATHAN CAPE & ROBERT BALLOU, INC.

(Organized in May 1932. Out of business. Succeeded by Robert O. Ballou, Publisher, q.v.)

Both Jonathan Cape and Robert Ballou, Inc., and my own firm Robert O. Ballou, Publisher, made no particular attempt to distinguish first editions. The first edition usually bore a statement on the reverse of the title page, just under the copyright line which read "First published 19—." But I find, on checking back through some of my own publications, that this was omitted as often as used. When it was used the year only was mentioned. On subsequent editions there was usually (or always if my memory is right) a statement of the month and year in which each edition was printed. This was also directly under the copyright notice. Thus the second printing of the trade edition of "Roll Jordan Roll" has this statement under the copyright notice:

First Printing December, 1933
Second Printing January, 1934

I have no copy of the first edition of this book so I cannot tell you how it is marked, but it is probably not marked at all, having simply the copyright notice. As a matter of fact the only two books under my own name (Robert O. Ballou, Publisher) which I ever reprinted were Julia Peterkin's "Roll Jordan Roll," and Henry Roth's "Call It Sleep." Each of these had two editions and any copies which are not marked as second printings are firsts. Of course a number of my publications were made up of sheets imported from England and I have no way of knowing, in most cases, whether these were sheets from the first edition there or not.

JONATHAN CAPE & HARRISON SMITH, INC.

(Out of business. This firm divided and was succeeded by the two following: Harrison Smith, Inc., organized in Nov. 1931, q.v., and Jonathan Cape and Robert Ballou, Inc., organized in May 1932, q.v.)

Although no strict rule was followed, in general it will be found that unless books are marked "Second printing," they are first editions.

THE CAXTON PRINTERS, LTD.

We do not as a rule designate our first editions by printing the words "First Printing" or "First Edition" on the back of the title page, but when we make a reprint, we give the date of the first printing and the date of each subsequent printing, on the back of the title page.

The purchaser of a Caxton book will know, then, that he is getting a first printing, unless there is information indicating that we have made more than one printing, on the back of the title page.

In the case of books such as Fisher's works, published jointly with Doubleday, Doran, the first edition may be ascertained by examining the bottom of the title page. If our name appears before the name of the cooperating publisher, at the bottom of the title page, the edition is a Caxton first.

This procedure has been followed since the first book was published by The Caxton Printers.

CENTURY COMPANY

(*Merged with D. Appleton & Co. to form D. Appleton-Century Co., Inc., on May 31, 1933.*)

We have no special mark showing first editions of our publications, except in the case of a few special books. We are planning, however, in the future to put each printing as made on the back of the title pages of all of our publications.

∵ *See D. Appleton-Century Co., Inc.*

CHELSEA HOUSE

So far as the cloth-bound book publication goes so few of the books that we have published have run into more than one edition, that we have not been faced with the necessity of marking first editions in any way.

UNIVERSITY OF CHICAGO PRESS

You will notice that the publication date, and record of each new impression and new edition, is entered on the copyright page. Unless notice happens to be made in an occasional new preface, no other record is made in the book. This method has been used for at least twenty-one years.

EDWARD J. CLODE, INC.

There is no way in which it is possible to distinguish any of our first editions from later ones.

COKESBURY PRESS

Most Cokesbury books carry an edition symbol at the bottom of the copyright page. The first edition carries a symbol "C"; second editions, the symbol "O," and subsequent editions according to the following scheme:

1 2 3 4 5 6 7 8 9 0
C O K E S B U R Y P

A few books in certain classifications carry no edition marks at all. Occasionally a first edition carries the words "First edition" on the copyright page.

COLUMBIA UNIVERSITY PRESS

1928 Statement

No distinction exists in regard to first and other editions except that there is printed on the title page the date of first printing for the first editions. On succeeding editions the date is removed from the title page and the second or third printing is noted on the copyright page.

1936 Statement

The first printing of any edition is indicated by the presence of a date with the imprint on the title page. On subsequent printings the date is removed from the title page, and the information is given on the copyright page. Revised editions are so noted on the title page, and first or subsequent printings of such editions are indicated in the same way as they are indicated for the first editions.

COSMOPOLITAN BOOK CO.
(*Out of Business*)

Up to the present time we have published only large editions of popular authors and there has been no cause to designate the first edition. We are changing our policy slightly now and it is possible that we may find it necessary to mark the editions. In this case we will probably print the words "First Edition" under the copyright notice and remove it on any later printings.

PASCAL COVICI

(*Became Covici, Friede, q.v.*)

Sometimes we print "first edition" on the reverse of the title page, and sometimes not, but invariably we print, "second printing" on the second issue.

COVICI, FRIEDE, INC.

We do not identify our first editions in any way. However, when a book goes into a second printing we record on the copyright page the date of the first printing and the date of the second printing, etc. In other words, a first edition of Covici, Friede is generally identified by the fact that the copyright page does not designate anything regarding the edition.

COWARD-McCANN, INC.

When we first began to publish in 1928, we used to print our colophon on the copyright page of all first editions:

On second and subsequent editions we omitted the torch part of the colophon and used only the lower half.

However, we did not continue with this arrangement, so that it is impossible to be certain of our first editions. What is certain though, is that any edition appearing with the colophon without the torch is not a first.

At present our first editions bear no distinguishing marks. If a book goes into a second or third printing, a note to this effect appears on the copyright page.

THOMAS Y. CROWELL COMPANY

Our present practice is not to indicate in any way the first edition. Subsequent printings are so indicated.

In the absence of the words, "Second Printing," "Third Printing," etc., it can be safely assumed that without such an inscription the book is a copy of the first edition.

We began using this method about ten years ago.

JOHN DAY & CO.

1928 Statement

This company has adopted the method of designating first editions on the copyright page with a line reading: First published, month, year. Subsequent printings are designated by a line below this reading: second printing, date, third printing, date, etc.

Now called the John Day Company.

∴ *See Reynal and Hitchcock, Inc.*

STEPHEN DAYE PRESS

We mark second editions and second and subsequent printings on the copyright page. We do not print the words "First Edition."

THE DERRYDALE PRESS, INC.

All of our publications are limited editions. This is so stated, together with the number of copies in the edition, either at the end of the book or on the back of the title page. If a second edition of one of our books is issued, it is so noted in the limit notice.

∴ *See Windward House.*

DIAL PRESS, INC.

(*Formerly Lincoln MacVeagh, The Dial Press*)

We wish to state that our system is to carry on the title page the year in which the edition is published and on the back of this page, merely a note as to when it was reprinted, such as is done by most publishers.

DODD, MEAD & CO., INC.

We have never made a practice of labelling our books as first editions or second editions, etc., in fact, to our mind an edition is not the same thing as a printing. The first seems to us to denote some change in the contents of a book while the second is simply the number of times the book has been put to press. While we do not label our books First Edition or First Printing, we do, as soon as a second printing is ordered, add a notice on the copyright page giving the date of the publication of the book and the date of the second printing. If other printings follow, a third, etc., up to sometimes as many as fifteen, we add the date of each subsequent printing as it is ordered. This has been our practice up to the present time, and has been in use at least since 1925.

DODGE PUBLISHING COMPANY

First editions of our books carry the line:

FIRST EDITION

on the copyright page. On subsequent editions this line is eliminated and the month and year of publication is substituted; the number of subsequent printings is listed below that:

PUBLISHED, JANUARY, 1936
THIRD PRINTING, MARCH, 1936

GEORGE H. DORAN & CO.

(*Merged with Doubleday, Page, as Doubleday, Doran & Co., q.v., on December 30th, 1927*)

The sign of a first edition of a Doran book is a small round colophon in which the initials "G H D" appear and which is always placed directly beneath the copyright line.

Occasionally, the colophon is omitted, in which case the words "*First Printing*" always appear.

DORRANCE & CO., INC.

As a usual thing, First editions are not indicated as such other than by a line giving copyright and year, but when other Editions are got out, full information is given. Take for example, the volume "Record

Flights." On the Second Edition we had "Copyright 1928. First printing March—Second printing March." In a special Limited Edition of this book there was printed "In a limited Edition of five hundred copies, of which this is No.—" In the future, in the case of unusual books and rare books, we expect to print "First Edition" on the First edition. This method has been in use since 1920.

DOUBLEDAY, DORAN & CO., INC.

Our method of indicating first editions is the printing of the words "first edition" beneath the copyright notice which backs up the title page.

Unfortunately there is no record of the date on which we began to follow this plan. It was many years ago.

DOUBLEDAY, PAGE & CO.

(*Merged with George H. Doran & Co. as Doubleday, Doran & Co., Inc., q.v., on December 30th, 1927.*)

Our method of indicating first editions is the printing of the words "first edition" beneath the copyright notice which backs up the title page.

DUFFIELD & CO.

(Became Duffield & Green, now out of business. Publications purchased by Dodd, Mead & Co., in April, 1934.)

We designate our first editions by printing the copyright date on the reverse of title page. Occasionally we insert the phrase "First edition printed such and such a date," in cases where the first edition is assumed to be important.

DUNSTER HOUSE BOOKSHOP

1928 Statement

Our own publications have always had the date in the First edition on the title page. This is the same method as that used by Messrs. Houghton Mifflin Company.

E. P. DUTTON & CO., INC.

1928 Statement

Unfortunately we have no definite scheme for identifying First Editions. Recently a copyright notice behind a title-page, on which nothing occurs but that, is an indication it is a first, because when we begin the second printing we mark it on the back.

1936 Statement

Since 1929 we use the words "first edition" immediately below our copyright notice for all such books. If the book is reprinted a notice is substituted on the copyright that this is the second or third printing as the case may be.

EQUINOX COOPERATIVE PRESS, INC.

Most of our previous books have been limited editions, and there was therefore only one printing. The only book on which we have had a second printing is our last, "Imperial Hearst," by Ferdinand Lundberg. All subsequent editions carry a line to that effect on the copyright page.

THE ESSEX INSTITUTE

It is very unusual for our publications to run to more than one edition and we have not designated the first in any case except by the date. We have designated second editions as such on the title page.

FARRAR & RINEHART, INC.

Farrar & Rinehart first editions can be identified by the small oval colophon, forming the letters *F* and

R, which appears immediately above the copyright line in all first editions of our books.

FOUR SEAS COMPANY

(*Out of business, see Bruce Humphries, Inc.*)

FUNK & WAGNALLS COMPANY

In February 1929 we published the first book in which we used the following line, under the copyright notice, to designate a first edition:

"First published—February, 1929."

A reprint of the same edition would be distinguished by a line beneath the above line such as:

"Reprinted—March, 1929."

A new edition would be designated by a line such as:

"Second Edition—April, 1930."

A book might then bear under the copyright notice,

"First published—February, 1929"
"Reprinted—March, 1929"
"Second Edition—April, 1930"

LEE FURMAN, INC.

We make no particular attempt to distinguish first editions from subsequent printings.

WILLIAM GODWIN

∴ *See Hillman-Curl, Inc.*

GREENBERG, PUBLISHER, INC.

We do not designate first editions in any special way. But all later editions bear a notice to that effect.

HALE, CUSHMAN & FLINT, INC.

In books published by us we give on the copyright page the information as to the edition or printing.

HARCOURT, BRACE & CO., INC.

1928 Statement

We have not been following any fast rule for indicating first editions. On all books for which we think there may be some demand, we indicate the first edition by placing a small figure 1 on the copyright page under our copyright notice, or by putting on a line "Published" and then the date. Subsequent editions have either a number 2 on them or a line "Second Printing," and then the date.

1936 Statement

In general it is the practice of Harcourt, Brace & Company to indicate the first impression of their general trade books by the words "first edition" on the copyright page underneath the copyright notice. In cases where the book has been first published in another country, the words "first American edition" or "first printing" are substituted. Previous to about 1930, first editions were generally indicated by placing a small figure 1 underneath the copyright notice, or by putting on a line "Published" and then the date.

HARPER & BROTHERS

It is our custom to print on the copyright page of all first editions the two words "First Edition." These are removed from the plate on all subsequent printings.

In addition to these you will find on our copyright pages two key letters beneath the copyright. These give the month and year when the edition was printed. The key letters can be read by the following chart:

Key to Editions on Copyright Page

A—January	M—1912
	N—1913

B—February	O — 1914
	P — 1915
C—March	Q — 1916
	R — 1917
D—April	S — 1918
	T — 1919
E—May	U — 1920
	V — 1921
F—June	W — 1922
	X — 1923
G—July	Y — 1924
	Z — 1925
H—August	A — 1926
	B — 1927
I—September	C — 1928
	D — 1929
K—October	E — 1930
	F — 1931
L—November	G — 1932
	H — 1933
M—December	I — 1934
	K — 1935
	L — 1936
	M — 1937

The use of the key letters on copyright pages began in 1912. The use of the words "First Edition" began a number of years later, so that there are early copies of books by Harpers in the area between 1912 and perhaps 1920 or thereabouts (unfortunately the date is not a matter of record) which have the key letters but which do not have the words "First Edition." This is, of course, important.

∴ *See also English section.*

HARVARD UNIVERSITY PRESS

We have no distinguishing mark which signifies that a book is a first edition. As a general thing, we put second, third, fourth impression, etc., on the reverse of the title page whenever we make new printings.

RAE D. HENKLE CO., INC.

∴ *See the Henkle-Yewdale House, Inc.*

THE HENKLE-YEWDALE HOUSE, INC.

As to our method of marking first editions, we omit any edition reference on the first printing and on the reverse of the title page note the first, second and other printings in subsequent editions. It has been in continuous use since 1928.

HILLMAN-CURL, INC.
(*Including Arcadia House and William Godwin*)

First editions of our publications are distinguished by the lack of any printing notice on the copyright page. Following editions bear the date of the first printing, together with date of new printing, and which printing it is.

HENRY HOLT & CO., INC.

We have never had a definite method of indicating a first edition in our books. Ordinarily, under the copyright line, we insert the dates of the printings so that any book which bears a single date is probably a first edition. In some cases, however, where we know there is to be only one printing, no date is inserted. Also, when sheets are imported from Europe, no special notation is made.

HOUGHTON MIFFLIN COMPANY

We endeavor to make a clear distinction between "edition" and "printing."

It is our general custom to place the date on the title page of the first printing of all of our books and to drop this date on all subsequent printings. There have been cases when for special reasons this rule has not been followed, but the custom so far as this House is concerned is almost invariable.

When a new edition—meaning a revision on which new copyright is taken—is printed, the same procedure is followed: that is, the date appears on the first printing of the new edition and is omitted from the second and subsequent printings.

The copyright page after the first printing sometimes bears the legend "second impression," "third impression," "fourth impression," etc. This, however, is not the general practice.

There are very likely instances where the date has not been removed from the title, after the first printing, and therefore it would not be an infallible rule to look for a date on the title page, but you may be sure that if the date is omitted, it is not a first edition.

We are sorry that we can't tell you just when the custom of omitting the date from the title page of later impressions of the book was instituted. It was a good many years ago. Our best impression is that it was about 1891.

B. W. HUEBSCH

(*Out of business, see The Viking Press Inc.*)

BRUCE HUMPHRIES, INC.

Books published by Bruce Humphries, Inc., if limited editions, contain a colophon giving the details of the edition, and when these books are reissued the colophon is dropped. Other books generally contain no special marking in the first edition, but second printings are almost invariably so marked on the copyright page.

Bruce Humphries, Inc., took over many, but not all, of the publications of the Four Seas Company in 1930. In books published by the Four Seas Company there was apparently no uniform system for indicating first editions, but generally first editions were not marked, but second printings were so marked on the copyright page.

THE JOHNS HOPKINS PRESS

We seldom publish but one edition of the work, endeavoring to estimate the number of copies that will be required for some time in the future. There have been, however, several instances in which another edition was published and these are indicated as a second edition or a second impression. The latter reference is used if no change is made from the original edition.

MARSHALL JONES COMPANY

1928 Statement

It is our custom to print on the copyright page the date of printing, *i.e.*, Printed April 1927, but we do not always do this. When we reprint we usually put on the date just below the other.

1936 Statement

Since our practice has changed somewhat since the first edition of your book appeared, I think it would be best to substitute the following:

We make a practice of giving the date of the second and subsequent printings or editions on the copyright page. In nearly all cases, if the copyright date alone appears, the book is of the first printing. The words FIRST EDITION on the copyright page, although we do not always use them, invariably designate the first printing.

CLAUDE KENDALL, INC.

It is our custom to identify first editions by printing the legend "First Printing" on the copyright page.

CLAUDE KENDALL & WILLOUGHBY SHARP, INC.

∴ *See Claude Kendall, Inc.*

H. C. KINSEY & COMPANY, INC.

Our system is very simple—if there is no printing date under the copyright notice then that is the first edition. The second printing is always indicated by a line giving the date and all subsequent editions in the same way:

First Edition—November 1935
Second Edition—December, etc.

The Mary Pickford books were the only exception to this rule and we included "First Edition" on the copyright page of the small first order for "Why Not Try God."

ALFRED A. KNOPF, INC.

1928 Statement

It is our practice to indicate on the copyright page with a line thus: "Second Printing, Third Printing," etc. This note does not appear on the first edition.

1936 Statement

Up until 2½ or 3 years ago, the first editions of our books bore no note on the copyright page. When a book was reprinted, however, a notice of the printing was added to the copyright page. If a book was reprinted before publication date a note reading, "First and second printings before publication" was added to the copyright page and this indicated that the particular book belonged to the second printing.

About 2½ or 3 years ago, however, we changed our practice only in the matter of first printings. On the copyright page of any one of our books issued since then we carry the note "First Edition" or "First American Edition." The latter term is used only where the English edition precedes or is simultaneously published with ours.

∵ *See also English section.*

J. B. LIPPINCOTT COMPANY

Since about 1925 we have been putting First Edition on the copyright page of our important books. Before that, and at present on general works, including fiction, we have not indicated the first edition, but we indicate all *subsequent* printings by placing on the bastard title or the copyright page the words "Second Impression" and so on.

Twenty years or so ago it used to be the habit, we think, of most publishers to date the first edition of Fall books the following year, so that for instance a book might bear the date 1901 when it was copyrighted and first published in the Fall of 1900.

∵ *See also English section.*

LITTLE, BROWN & COMPANY

1928 Statement

With few exceptions we make no attempt to designate first editions.

Where we have brought out limited editions as well as trade editions of the same book we have sometimes indicated the first trade edition.

1936 Statement

A Little, Brown or Atlantic Monthly Press first edition can for the most part be identified by a single line on the copyright page giving the month and year of first publication. Each new printing of a book carries an additional line on the title page also giving the month and year.

∴ *See Atlantic Monthly Press, Inc.*

LIVERIGHT PUBLISHING CORP.

As a general rule we have no marking on the copyright page of our publications to show our first edition although on subsequent editions we print Second, Third, Fourth, Fifth, Sixth edition, etc. We have had one or two books with first edition marked on the copyright page but this is not our general practice.

HORACE LIVERIGHT, INC.

(*Became Liveright Publishing Corporation*)

∴ *See Liveright Publishing Corporation.*

LONGMANS, GREEN & CO.

1928 Statement

With regard to the identification of our first editions, we would say that at the present time we are printing "First Edition" on the reverse of the title page of our general literary works.

To distinguish between first editions and others of those books printed previous to the adoption of the present method, one may compare the date used on the title page with that of the copyright date to appear. If the date appearing at the foot of the title page and that of the copyright are the same, the volume is a first edition.

1936 Statement

We are identifying "First Editions" by printing the words "First Edition" on the reverse of the title page of all works printed in the U. S. A.

In the case of a reprint, we give a notation of the month and year in which the first edition was published and the month and year of each reprint.

In case of a "Revised Edition" (where there have been major changes made in the text of a new printing) we indicate that it is a new edition and not merely a reprint.

∴ *See also English section.*

LORING & MUSSEY, INC.

We have not followed a consistent practice in regard to first printings. One or two of our books contain the words "First Edition" with the printer's colophon. In general we would probably print "Second printing" on the copyright page when reprinting a book.

The name of this firm will very shortly be changed to Barrows Mussey, Inc.

JOHN W. LUCE & COMPANY

We have never made a practice of specifically designating the different editions of the works of our authors. Had we done so with the books of Mencken, Lord Dunsany, Synge and certain of Wilde's work which we published for the first time, it would have been a distinct convenience. In the case of "George Bernard Shaw; his Plays" by Mencken, which was his first published book, we made but one printing. His other books ran into a number of editions which we can identify but which would not be easily recognized by a casual collector. The same holds true of other authors, though there was but one printing in separate form of the complete "A Florentine Tragedy" by Wilde and one printing of "Pan and Desespoir," previously unpublished poems by the same author.

THE MACAULAY COMPANY

We wish to state that we have not been marking our first editions in any particular way. Usually, when second and further editions are issued of the same title, they are so marked.

THE MACMILLAN COMPANY

On the reverse of the title page of our books, just below the copyright notice, always appears a notice to the following effect "Set up and electrotyped. Published ...." or "Set up and printed. Published ...." Usually any reprintings or new editions are listed below. If there are no such reprintings or new editions listed and if the date above our imprint on the title page and the publishing date as given above coincide, the book is a first edition. In cases where the reprintings are listed on the back of the title page, a comparison of this imprint date and the publishing date is usually sufficient to identify the book.

From now on (April 24, 1936), however, we propose to place the words "First Printing" under the copyright of all trade books which we print here in America, these words to be deleted with the second printing.

We are unable to tell you just when we used our present method of identifying first printings. In checking up renewal of copyright notices, we find that books reprinted since 1894 as a rule have had their imprint date corrected with each printing, but the words "Reprinted," etc., do not always appear.

∴ *See also English section.*

MACRAE SMITH COMPANY

Prior to 1930, the copyright page of our books contained only the copyright notice. Subsequent printings were identified with the number of the printing and occasionally the date. Since 1930 the copyright page has contained either of the following to indicate a first edition: "First Edition" or "First Printing."

MACY-MASIUS
(*Combined with Vanguard Press, q.v.*)

On the page backing the title page, we place invariably this legend on the first editions of our books:

Published (with the date of publication).

We don't refer to further printings as editions, since they obviously aren't in the true sense of the word. But we list the date of each further printing within the first edition. We call a printing a second edition only if there is something different in it from the first.

ROBERT M. MCBRIDE & CO.

Our designation of the first edition is usually the line reading either First Published April 1927 or Published April 1927. This line is retained in all subsequent editions but the number of the printing is added below it in the second line such as Second Printing, June 1927, changed on the next printing to Third Printing, etc.

Our practice, of course, in the past has not been uniformly thus, but we are among the few houses which have consistently printed the number of the edition on the back of the title page.

DAVID MCKAY CO.

There isn't any way you could identify the first editions of our books.

JULIAN MESSNER, INC.

We have, up to now, made no differentiation between our first and subsequent editions of books other than the conventional copyright page revision.

UNIVERSITY OF MINNESOTA PRESS

University Press books, as you know, are usually published in small editions and, with no exception that I can think of, the *absence* of the words "Second Edition" is enough identification for a first edition of our books. We do, however, make a distinction between a second edition and a second printing of the first edition, and almost invariably add the line "Second Printing," "Third Printing," etc., under the copyright notice.

MINTON, BALCH & CO.

All first editions of our books contain the date on the title page and the copyright date following. Subsequent printings are indicated by the words (under the copyright notice) "second printing" with the month and year in which this printing is made.

WILLIAM MORROW AND CO., INC.

The first printing of our books either carry on the page following the title page the line

First Printing..........

or in some cases merely the copyright notice without anything further.

Subsequent printings are always designated as "Second Printing" or "Third Printing" as the case may be.

A new edition of the book is also clearly marked.

You will note that we distinguish between editions and printing. An edition with us is where some material change has been made in the copy or the make up of the book.

BARROWS MUSSEY, INC.

∴ *See Loring & Mussey, Inc.*

THE UNIVERSITY OF NORTH CAROLINA PRESS

We do not have any general rule by which a first edition of one of our books may be distinguished from a later edition.

We sometimes reprint from type within a few weeks after the first printing, without distinguishing in any way the second from the first printing. We may indicate on the back of the title page, after the first printing, the dates of various subsequent printings, but we do not always do this.

Whenever we publish a new edition of a work, we usually secure a copyright to cover the new matter.

Both the new and the old dates will appear on the back of the title page.

W. W. NORTON & COMPANY, INC.

On books when first published by us, we run a legend on the copyright page reading "First edition." On subsequent printings this legend is deleted, but we do not indicate second, third, etc., printings in the books.

UNIVERSITY OF OKLAHOMA PRESS

All of our books contain on the copyright page a statement of the day, month, and year of first publication. This usually takes the following form: "Set up and printed at Norman, Oklahoma, by the University of Oklahoma Press, Publishing Division of the University. First edition May 18, 1936." If a second printing is issued, this information is always added to the material on the copyright page, though the day of second printing is usually not given. Notice of second printing is almost uniformly carried on our jackets as well. We have employed this method of differentiating first from subsequent printings since the founding of the Press in 1928.

OXFORD UNIVERSITY PRESS NEW YORK

In regard to the indicating of First and subsequent printings of books we use in general the system followed by our home office.

∴ *See also English section.*

L. C. PAGE & CO.

We print "first impressions" with the month and the year on the reverse of the title page. We do not, however, add the date on the title page.

PAYSON & CLARKE, LTD.

(Became Brewer & Warren on Jan. 1, 1930, which later became Brewer, Warren & Putnam, Inc.; all three firms are now out of business.)

We do not put the actual words "first edition" on the reverse of the title page for the first edition but when we go into the second printing we say "first printing such and such a date," "second printing such and such a date," therefore, all copies of a book which do not carry such designation may be taken as being "firsts."

THE PENN PUBLISHING COMPANY

1928 Statement

As we indicate first editions in none of our books, we are unable to give you any information regarding the subject about which you inquire.

1936 Statement

The only way they can be distinguished from subsequent editions is by the fact that in later editions the words second, third, or fourth printing, with the date, will be found on the copyright page.

UNIVERSITY OF PENNSYLVANIA PRESS

All titles published by us are first printings unless otherwise noted on the copyright page. In the case of second and subsequent printings, we give the date of publication and the dates of further printings.

THE PRIMAVERA PRESS, INC.

Please be advised that printings of our books following the first editions are so marked, i.e., "Second Printing," etc. This is true with one exception—the second printing of "Who Loves a Garden" is distinguished by the date on the title-page "1935" being one year later than the date of copyright "1934."

PRINCETON UNIVERSITY PRESS

Our only way of designating first editions is by negative implication. In other words, our first editions bear no special designation. If, however, a title is reprinted or reissued that fact is set forth on the copyright page.

We have apparently always used our present method of designating first printings from subsequent ones. "Always" in this case means for the approximate quarter of a century that we have been publishing.

G. P. PUTNAM'S SONS

Our system as to new publications does not usually include printing any entry on the back of the title page or otherwise indicating first edition.

When a book is printed a second time, as a rule we print under the copyright notice the words "First printed March 1927. Second printing April 1927, etc." Where there is no note of this kind it may be assumed that the work is the first printing.

It is always our intention not to use the word "second edition" unless there is some distinct addition or change from the first edition. When that is the case, usually on the title page is the line "second edition revised, or second edition corrected, or second edition revised, corrected and enlarged" or some such expression. A similar entry is often printed under the copyright notice.

As to the date on the title page, this is supposed to be the date when the particular copy was printed. Reprints without change would generally have that title page, and when such reprint is made it would be the copyright entry which would tell by comparison that it was not a first edition.

For staple items that had been reprinted from year to year, as a rule the date is omitted from the title-page.

∴ *See also English section.*

RAND MCNALLY & COMPANY

We are sorry to tell you that the first editions of our publications have no marks to distinguish them from later editions, except in a few cases you will find the letters "MA" in the lower right-hand corner of the copyright page. The "M" before the "A" has no connection with the edition, but the "A" does signify that the book is a first edition. Sometimes this "A" is omitted on the first edition, but "B" appears on the second edition, "C" on the third edition, etc.

RANDOM HOUSE, INC.

1928 Statement

Since Random House only publishes limited editions, all of the necessary information that you require is contained in the colophon, i.e., as far as we are concerned, there is only one edition, the first.

1936 Statement

As far as Random House first editions are concerned, with the exception of limited editions where all the necessary information is contained in the colophon, all books are plainly marked "first edition" on the copyright page.

THE REILLY & LEE CO., INC.

In the future we intend to put "First Printing" on the copyright page and when that edition is exhausted the "First Printing" will be removed and no other mark will be put in its place.

REYNAL AND HITCHCOCK, INC.

For some time now The John Day Company has adopted the following method of distinguishing first editions: On the first printing copyright page appears only the copyright notice: Copyright, 1936, by John

Doe, and the usual printer's imprint: Printed in the United States of America by The John Smith Printing Company. Lately we have included a paragraph: All rights reserved, including the right to reproduce this book or portions thereof in any form. However, all other printings of the same book may be distinguished by: Second printing, Jan. 1936. Third printing, February, 1936, et cetera, with the proper month inserted.

You will notice that "John Day & Co." is no longer used; when the book is wholly owned by The John Day Company "The John Day Company, New York" appears on the title page.

The same method applies to Reynal and Hitchcock; that is, no notice of first printing appears on the first edition, but notices of second, third, and fourth printings being added as is the case. In 1935, The John Day Company was associated with Reynal and Hitchcock, and on the title page of books published under this new association you will find the imprint: "a John Day Book, Reynal and Hitchcock, New York." This method of imprinting our books is similar to The Atlantic Monthly Press and Little, Brown & Co., with which you may be familiar. On the copyright page of books put out under the joint imprint you will find on both first printing and subsequent printings the words: Published by John Day in association with Reynal and Hitchcock. However, this has no bearing on the edition printings.

RUSSELL SAGE FOUNDATION

The Russell Sage Foundation has been issuing books and pamphlets in the general social field since 1908. In general our practice has been to indicate on the copyright page the year of first publication and the copyright. If nothing else appears on this page the volume concerned is a first printing of a first edition. Subsequent printings and subsequent editions are all entered on this page in clear form with the inclusion of the date of the first edition or printing. We distinguish between printings and editions on the basis of textual changes. If they are very numerous, the edition is called a new edition. If they are slight, or if no changes are made, the new issue is called a new printing.

WILLIAM R. SCOTT

Our policy will be to mark seconds, thirds, etc., clearly on the copyright page; marking firsts or not as the spirit moves us.

CHARLES SCRIBNER'S SONS

There is no sure way of telling in most cases what is a first edition of a book printed previously to 1930 except that in most cases in the front matter a second printing or any later printing is usually so indicated in the front matter. On books published since 1930 first editions are indicated with a capital "A" on the copyright page.

∴ *See also English section.*

SHEED AND WARD

Whenever we reprint a book we note this fact on the reverse of the title page. If this is not indicated, the reader is generally safe in assuming that the book is a first edition. Occasionally we explicitly state the fact that the book is a first edition, but more often we do not indicate it.

∴ *See also English section.*

SIMMONS-BOARDMAN PUBLISHING CO.

We print on the copyright page the date of each revised edition of our books.

Each revised edition is copyrighted as to its new material.

SIMON AND SCHUSTER, INC.

Our first editions are marked by the fact that the copyright page bears *no* printing or edition notice, whereas in subsequent editions the dates, and sometimes even the quantity of the printings, appear, as

First Printing, April 1936
Second Printing, May 1936, etc.

The date is not always used nor is the phrase "First Printing" but second and subsequent editions are always marked.

HARRISON SMITH, INC.

(*Out of business. Became Harrison Smith & Robert Haas, Inc., in March, 1932, q.v.*)

Although no strict rule was followed, in general it will be found that unless books are marked "Second printing," they are first editions.

HARRISON SMITH & ROBERT HAAS, INC.

(*Organized in March, 1932. Out of business. Merged with Random House, Inc., on April 1, 1936, q.v.*)

Although no strict rule was followed, in general it will be found that unless books are marked "Second printing," they are first editions.

PETER SMITH, INC.

Date of edition is always indicated on title page.

SOUTHWEST PRESS
(*Succeeded by Turner Company, q.v., in 1935*)

ROBERT SPELLER PUBLISHING CORPORATION

Each book published by us carries, on the copyright page, the words FIRST EDITION. Subsequent editions are marked thus: Second Printing, Third Printing, etc.

STACKPOLE SONS

TELEGRAPH PRESS

The lack of notice of additional printings shows a Stackpole Sons first edition. There is one exception—"Caleb Catlum's America." The first printing of this book is marked "First Edition" at the bottom of the verso of the title page.

The Telegraph Press has adhered to no strict policy in the past, though usually its first printings have been marked "First Edition"; but hereafter it will follow the same method as that used by Stackpole Sons, and its first printings will be identified by the lack of notice of subsequent reprintings.

STANFORD UNIVERSITY PRESS

Our method of indicating our first editions is the negative one of not mentioning reprinting or revision. Editions or printings subsequent to the first edition or printing carry on the copyright page both

"First published, 19—"
and
"Second Printing, 19—"
or
"Second (Revised) Edition"

We believe we have followed this practice since we issued our first books in 1925.

FREDERICK A. STOKES CO.

To date we have omitted putting any special mark or distinction upon first printings of any of our books, but in general these can very readily be distinguished from succeeding printings by the fact that on the Copyright Page (reverse of Title) no printing notice appears. After first printings we generally put the date of publication and the words "Second Printing" and date of such printing.

SUTTONHOUSE LTD.

Please note that all first printings of SUTTONHOUSE LTD., in the past have been identified by the appearance of the same date on both the title and the copyright page, unless "second printing" appeared on the copyright page.

In the future, however, "first edition" will appear on the copyright page, so that there will be no confusion whatsoever. This means that all books published after May 1, 1936, will carry this marking. The second printings will have no such marking.

TELEGRAPH PRESS

(*See Stackpole Sons.*)

TURNER COMPANY

We purchased the assets of the Southwest Press in 1935 and continue to publish all titles formerly published by that concern.

Since 1935 we use the following plan to differentiate first from subsequent printings of our books: On all editions except the first we run a line on the copyright page stating the number of printing, second printing, third printing, etc., as the case may be.

THE VANGUARD PRESS

The Vanguard Press uses no special mark or wording to indicate its first editions, but states on the copyright page when a book is in any but the first printing.

THE VIKING PRESS INC.

Our first editions can be distinguished by the fact that there is no indication to the contrary on the copyright page. That is, we indicate the date and number of each reprinting.

This has always been our method and we shall continue it until further notice.

The Viking Press and B. W. Huebsch, Inc., merged in August, 1925, to be known as The Viking Press Inc.

The policy of B. W. Huebsch, regarding first editions, was the same as the present policy of The Viking Press.

FREDERICK WARNE & CO., LTD.

∴ *See English section.*

IVES WASHBURN, INC.

We print the date of publication on the title page and on the reverse run a copyright date line but do not print "first edition" or "first printing" beneath it. When we make a second printing, we change the date on the title page, provided it is done in a subsequent year; otherwise, it remains the same.

In making a second printing, whether new material is added to the book or not, we always print beneath the copyright date line on the reverse of the title page in italics the words "first printing" followed by the month and year, and below "second printing" with month and year, and so on for subsequent printings. In other words, unless we give this information on the reverse of the title page the buyer may know that he has bought the first editions of our books.

We have used this method since 1927.

G. HOWARD WATT

On second printings we always mention the fact that it is the second edition. That is our only distinguishing mark.

WHITTLESEY HOUSE

The first printing of the first edition of Whittlesey House books has the words "first edition" under the statement of copyright, which, of course, includes the year of publication. Subsequent printings have "second printing," "third printing," etc. Considerably revised editions are designated "second edition," "third edition," etc. This statement is run on the verso of the title page of all Whittlesey House books.

WILLETT, CLARK & COLBY

(*Became Willett, Clark & Co. on Oct. 22, 1930.*)

∴ *See Willett, Clark & Co.*

WILLETT, CLARK & COMPANY

Any book published by Willett, Clark & Company that goes into a second edition has the designation "second edition" under the copyright notice or at least on that page. The first edition is never given any distinctive marking of any kind, therefore, any book not designated as second, third, or fourth edition is a first edition.

WINDWARD HOUSE

All books published under this imprint are trade editions. Unless they are new editions of Derrydale Press books, they are first editions of the text, though this is not stated in the book. In the case of a second edition this is so stated on the back of the title page.

∴ *See Derrydale Press.*

THE JOHN C. WINSTON COMPANY

We publish books in a number of different classes and have private marks on some of our editions, notably on our text-books, which give us the date of each edition for our own information.

We have not, however, made a practice of marking the first editions of our trade publications and should we decide to do so we will probably adopt a symbol which would not mean anything to the public, as I can think of at least one good reason why it might not be desirable to have first editions indicated.

I must confess that this is undesirable from a book collector's standpoint but other considerations unfortunately outweigh this to such an extent that we are not as yet prepared to establish a permanent system of marking our first editions.

YALE UNIVERSITY PRESS

1928 Statement

We do not print the words "First Edition" in any of our books, but on the reverse of the title-page, under the copyright notice, we indicate the subsequent printings as follows:

First Published, 1915.
Second Printing, 1916.

Third Printing, 1919.
Second and Enlarged Edition, 1922.
Third Edition with Many New Chapters, 1924.

It is therefore safe to assume that any of our publications which have no designation below the copyright notice are first editions.

1936 Statement

The statement of method as used by us is correct as far as it goes. In the case of some of our earlier books, we ran a line under the copyright line reading, "First published January 1921." In most cases, and on all books which we are now publishing, the first edition simply carries the copyright line, but some first editions carry a second line as indicated above.

ENGLISH HOUSES

PHILIP ALLAN & CO., LTD.

It is our practice to put the date of publication of any book either on the title page or on the back of the title page. If the book is reprinted, the date of the reprint appears on the back of the title page beneath the date of the first printing. Subsequent editions and reprints are similarly printed on the back of the title page.

GEORGE ALLEN & UNWIN, LTD.

It is our practice in the first edition to print the words "First Published in ——" (the year of issue) and in subsequent impressions or editions to add the additional dates. With translations we give the original title, date and place of publication.

We began using our present method of identifying first printings about 1914.

D. APPLETON & CO.

(*Became D. Appleton-Century Co., Inc., on May 31, 1933, q.v.*)

D. APPLETON-CENTURY COMPANY, INC.

The practice of our New York house is to print the figure 1 within brackets at the end of the last printed page on any book issued by them. When a second printing takes place this figure is, of course, changed to the figure 2, etc., etc.

In addition our New York house invariably dates the title page and the American copyright law requires the year of first publication to be on the back of the title page, in order to preserve the copyright. This numbering was inaugurated by D. Appleton & Company in 1902.

∴ *See also American section.*

DENIS ARCHER

(*See John Long Ltd.*
See Andrew Melrose Ltd.)

We find that our affiliated Company, Messrs. John Long Ltd., wrote to you on the 3rd of June 1936. The same procedure also applies to this Company and to Andrew Melrose Ltd.

EDWARD ARNOLD & CO.

We do not designate our first editions of books in any special way. If the book reaches a second edition or second impression we designate it as such on the title page or on the reverse of the title.

J. W. ARROWSMITH, LTD. (LONDON)

Our custom is to put on the back of the title page "First published in 1928," or whatever the year may be. Reprints are marked "First published in 1928—Second Impression 1928—" and so on.

May we take this opportunity of pointing out that the words "First Edition" are invariably misused. What is meant is "First Impression" as a First Edition may include 20 or 30 impressions and presumably it is only the first which is of value.

ARTHUR BARKER LTD.

It is our general practice to print the number of impressions and editions of our books on the reverse side of the title page.

The first edition of a book merely has "first published 1936" or whatever the year happens to be. If the book is reprinted we run a line

"2nd impression June 1936
3rd impression July 1936," etc.

If the author makes any changes between the first printing or second printing, we usually replace "2nd impression" by the words "revised edition" followed by the date.

We started this method in 1933.

B. T. BATSFORD, LTD.

In all our publications the date appears either on the verso or recto of title-page, or where this is not included on this leaf it is to be found as preface date. Reprints or revised editions are always clearly shown on the recto of title.

G. BELL & SONS, LTD.

1928 Statement

The title page of the first edition carries the year of publication at the foot, and when it is reprinted the month and year are indicated on the reverse of the title page, e.g.:

First Published (say) February 1928.
Reprinted (say) July 1928.

1936 Statement

We only indicate the months when a book is reprinted twice in a year. We have used this method of identifying first printings since the Great War.

ERNEST BENN LIMITED

We have two forms of designating first editions, (1) a bibliography printed on the back of the title page stating first published in —— and then the year.

We use this form mostly. (2) is to have no bibliography on the first edition but to put the year of publication on the front of the title page with our imprint.

We have used this formula since we first started book publishing in 1923.

A. & C. BLACK, LTD.

First Editions of our publications have the date on the title-page only; Second and Reprints have the date of reprint on the title-page and particulars of all printings in a bibliography on the verso.

The same particulars would apply to the principal books which we publish over the imprint of S. W. Partridge & Co. Prior to our taking over the business, however, Messrs. Partridge had seldom printed a date on the title-pages of their Juveniles, and as some of these have now been selling for a number of years we are not always giving a bibliography on the reverse of title-pages.

BLACKIE & SON, LIMITED

It is not possible to give a general rule for the detecting of our first editions.

In the first editions of our more recent educational works and general publications (exclusive of Reward or Story Books) the date appears on the title-page, and if it is a new edition, it is so stated. The dates of subsequent reprints are noted on the back of the title-page.

We are afraid it is impossible to say just what date we started using this present method.

BASIL BLACKWELL

Our first editions are published without any reference on the title page whatever; all subsequent editions bear the fact on the back of the title page.

WM. BLACKWOOD & SONS, LTD.

Although we have no hard and fast rule, our general practice is to omit the notification of the first edition on the first issue of a book, the date of publication appearing below the imprint. Subsequent editions are notified accordingly.

GEOFFREY BLES, LTD.

Our practice is to give the date of the first edition of the book on the title page verso. Subsequent reprints and editions are noted under that, e.g.

FIRST PUBLISHED FEBRUARY 1933
REPRINTED MARCH 1933
REPRINTED APRIL 1933

BRENTANO'S, LTD.
(Now out of business.)

Up to the end of 1927 all books published by this Company had no edition printed on them unless they reached a second edition. This information would be printed on the back of the title. From January 1st, 1928 the words "First Printed 1928" were substituted and if the book reached a second edition the words "Second Impression April 1928 (or . . .)"

∴ *See also American section.*

BURNS, OATES & WASHBOURNE, LTD.

We print on the back of the title page of each of our new books:

Made and Printed in Gt. Britain 19. .

All new editions or new impressions of a work state First Edition (or impression) 19. . with the added information about subsequent editions.

THORNTON BUTTERWORTH, LTD.

It is our habit to place on the back of the title page of all our books the date of first publication, thus:

"First Published . . . 1928." If the book should be reprinted we add below indented "Second Impression" and give the date, further reprints are added immediately under. Should another *edition* of the work be issued we add "Second Edition" with the date not indented ranging with the first line, e.g.

First Published May 1928
  Second Impression July 1928
  Third Impression Sept. 1928
Second Edition Jan. 1929
  Fifth Impression Aug. 1929

CAMBRIDGE UNIVERSITY PRESS

It is our practice to put the date of the publication of any book on the title-page itself. If the book is reprinted, the date of the reprint appears on the title-page and a bibliographical description on the back of the title, e.g.

First Edition 1922
Reprinted 1923
Second Edition 1924

JONATHAN CAPE LTD.

Our practice is to print on the back of the title page "First published 1928" or whatever the year may be. When the book is reprinted without revision or alteration, we add to this "second impression," again giving the year. Each printing is thus recorded in like manner in the same place. It follows then that a book published by us which has on the back of the title page "First published 1928" and no other information with regard to further printings, is, *ipso facto,* a first edition.

CASSELL & COMPANY, LTD.

The date of publication of each book issued by this firm appears on the back of the title page; the publication dates of subsequent editions are added as they occur.

W. & R. CHAMBERS, LTD.

1928 Statement

It is our intention to adopt the plan in future of marking the first impression of our general books "original edition." We do not intend to do this in the case of school books.

1936 Statement

We mark the first impression of all books published by us, including school books, "Original Edition."

CHAPMAN & HALL, LTD.

We do not specify either on the title page or on the back of the title that a first edition is a first edition but all our publications are now dated, technical books bearing the date on the title page and general books carrying the date on the verso. It may therefore be taken that a book carrying dates on the title page is a first edition, as well as books carrying the words "First published 1936." Any subsequent reprints or editions are shown in the bibliographical note.

CHATTO AND WINDUS

We use no particular distinguishing sign to mark our first editions.

CHRISTOPHERS

We always put the date of first publication on the back of the title, thus—

First published 1923

When the book is reprinted we alter this to—

First published June 1923
Reprinted September 1923
" October 1928

R. COBDEN-SANDERSON, LTD.
(*Formerly R. Cobden-Sanderson.*)

We do not follow any rule in regard to the designation of our first editions. We can only give you examples such as the following:

First published 1926

Copyright 1926

First published 1925
Second impression May 1925
Third impression October 1925
Fourth impression (cheap edition) September 1927

First published October 1927
Second impression November 1927

First published 1920
Second edition 1920
New and revised edition 1926

All the above appear on the back of the title page, but sometimes we have the year of publication printed on the title page only.

W. COLLINS SONS & CO., LTD.

We do not adopt any special method of designating first editions or first impressions. All our books bear on the reverse of the title page the date of publication and the word "copyright."

In case of subsequent publication of a cheaper edition, the date of the original edition and that of the cheap edition are inserted on the back of the title-page.

We have always used this method of identifying first editions.

CONSTABLE AND COMPANY, LTD.

We have no standardised method of designating our first editions, but, generally speaking, we put "First published (date)" on the back of the title-page, and if this appears without any other detail, the book on which it appears is a first edition. Reprints are noted also on the back of the title-page, under the original legend. Please observe that this is merely our usual practice and not a standardised or official method.

COUNTRY LIFE, LTD.

It is our practice not to put the date of publication on the title page but on the back of the title. In subsequent editions the Bibliographical description is added. Thus:

First Published 1934
Second Impression 1935
Second Edition 1936.

THE C. W. DANIEL COMPANY, LTD.

(*Formerly C. W. Daniel Co.*)

Our method of designating first editions of our books is to put "First published, etc." on the back of each title page, and to add to that the dates of all further editions as they are issued.

PETER DAVIES, LTD.

I have no hard and fast method of designating a first edition.

More often than not a bibliographical note is printed on the verso of the title-page of my publications. It reads: "First printed in (e.g.) May, 1928." In case a further edition or impression is issued, there will be an addition to the note, e.g. "Reprinted, June 1928." In the absence of any such addition, the book will be a first edition.

If there is no bibliographical note at all, in which case the date, that is the year, will almost certainly appear on the title-page, then also the book may be taken to be a first edition.

J. M. DENT & SONS, LTD.

1928 Statement

Our usual practice is to print a date on the title-page of a first edition; if a book is reprinted we put a new date on the title page and print on the reverse—"First published so-and-so. Reprinted so-and-so." Thus you will be able to identify first editions by the absence of any such note on the reverse of the title-page.

1936 Statement

The procedure which we follow for identifying first editions is now slightly different from that of 1928, and I think the following paragraph states the present position.

Our usual practice is to print on the back of the title page a biblio. note giving the date of publication of the edition. If a book reprints the date of the reprint is added. Thus it may be assumed that if the following line "First published......" only appears it is a first edition. If it is a reprint of our own first edition the line "Reprinted......" will be added underneath. If it is the first time that we have published it and it is the reprint of some earlier edition, we print "First published in this edition......" This applies particularly to reprints of old and established books. This has been our practice since 1929.

LOVAT DICKSON LIMITED

It is our practice to print bibliographical data on the reverse of the title page of all our books, in which the date of first publication and subsequent reprints is stated, as follows:

First Published 1934
Second Impression 1935
Third Impression 1936

Lovat Dickson Ltd. 38 Bedford Street London
and St. Martin's House Bond Street Toronto
set and printed in Great Britain
by Billing & Sons Limited Guildford and Esher
Paper made by John Dickson and Company Limited
Bound by G. & J. Kitcat Limited
Set in Monotype Baskerville

NOEL DOUGLAS, LTD.

We designate our first editions by printing the date of publication on the reverse of the title page, as, "published 1928." Subsequent editions or reprints are added below, as,

"published 1928
reprinted 1929
second edition 1930"

This method was adopted about 1926 or 1927.

GERALD DUCKWORTH & CO., LTD.

Our usual custom is to put on the reverse of the title page "First published, 1928." In some cases instead of this we put the date at the foot of the title page. In either case a second edition has a definite statement that it is a New Impression or a New Edition on the reverse of the title page.

We are sorry it is not possible for us to give the date when we first began using this method of identifying first printings.

ELDON PRESS LTD.

First Editions are marked on the back of the title page

Published by
Eldon Press Ltd.
1934

For reprints the month of publication is added together with the date of the reprint, e.g.

Published by
Eldon Press Ltd.
December 1934
Second Impression January 1935

EPWORTH PRESS

It is our practice to put the date of the publication of any book on the back of the title-page. If the book is reprinted, the date of the reprint appears on the back of the title-page, e.g.:

First Edition 1922
Reprinted 1923

EYRE & SPOTTISWOODE (PUBLISHERS) LIMITED

First Edition. Year of publication printed under our name at the foot of title page.

Second and subsequent editions are shown as follows:

Upon the reverse side of the title page:

First published ......19......
Reprinted...........19......
Reprinted...........19......

Where two editions have been printed in the same year, the month is added, i.e.,

First published June....19......
Reprinted October......19......

FABER & FABER, LTD.

When, in 1929, the firm became Faber and Faber, we started our present method of wording the note on the back of the title page of all our books.

FIRST PUBLISHED MAY MCMXXXIV
BY FABER AND FABER LIMITED
24 RUSSELL SQUARE LONDON W.C.I
SECOND IMPRESSION JULY MCMXXXIV
PRINTED IN GREAT BRITAIN BY
THE CURWEN PRESS, PLAISTOW
ALL RIGHTS RESERVED

This is a typical example, and we now adhere rigidly to this form.

FABER & GWYER, LTD.

(*Reorganized as Faber & Faber, Ltd. in 1929.*)

Our practice—and I cannot say that we have adhered to it absolutely rigidly up to the present, has been to print on the back of the title page "First published by Faber & Gwyer, Ltd. in so and so" and with subsequent editions, or impressions, "Second Impression . . ." etc. We do not as a rule print the date of publication on the title page itself.

∴ *See Faber & Faber.*

THE FENLAND PRESS, LTD.

It is our practice to print the year of publication on the reverse of the title page, e.g.

FIRST PUBLISHED 1934

When the book is reprinted we then insert the month and year when it was first published and the date of the 2nd impression, e.g.

FIRST PUBLISHED MARCH 1934
SECOND IMPRESSION APRIL 1934
THIRD IMPRESSION AUGUST 1934 and so on

THE FOREST PRESS

It is our practice to put the date of publication of any book on the title-page itself. If the book is reprinted, the date of the reprint appears on the title-page and a bibliographical description on the back of the title.

T. N. FOULIS, LTD.
(*Out of business.*)

My usual plan with regard to title pages is to print the date of publication on the back thereof, e.g.

"First published January the fifteenth 1928
Reprinted February 1928.
Reprinted March 1928."

WELLS GARDNER, DARTON & CO., LTD.

We have followed no strict principle in designating our first editions or first impressions. The nature of our publications, which include fiction, children's books, religious books and some poetry, as well as miscellaneous works, has been so varied, and the trade conditions in regard to format, price, re-prints, and other details have changed so frequently during the past quarter of a century, our methods have depended very much on circumstances of the particular time, and, of course, to a certain extent also on the personal discretion of the author and the member of the firm concerned with a particular book. We are, therefore, unable to give you any definite information in general. If there is any particular book which we publish, about which you wish to make enquiry, we can probably give you the accurate facts whether they are printed in the book or not.

GAY & HANCOCK, LTD.

(*Purchased by A. & C. Black, Ltd., April, 1929, who continued to issue a few volumes under Gay & Hancock, Ltd. imprint at least as late as 1935.*)

First Editions of our publications have the date on the title-page only; Second and Reprints have the date of reprint on the title-page and particulars of all printings in a bibliography on the verso.

THE GOLDEN COCKEREL PRESS

With a few exceptions all our books have been issued in a first edition only limited to between 150 and 750 copies, often signed by the author and the artist, for collectors of finely produced and illustrated books of literary worth.

The exceptions are:

1921, ADAM & EVE & PINCH ME by A. E. Coppard
(of which there were three editions)

1921, TERPSICHORE & OTHER POEMS by H. T. Wade-Gery
(of which there were two editions)

1922, THE PUPPET SHOW by Martin Armstrong
(of which there were two editions)

1932, RUNNING by A. E. Coppard
(of which there were two editions)

1932, CONSEQUENCES
(of which there were two editions)

The Press will be pleased to answer any questions which may arise about any of their books.

VICTOR GOLLANCZ, LTD.

Our first editions are distinguished by the fact that they contain no information on them as to what edition they are. All editions other than first editions bear, at the back of the title-page, the words "First Published —— second impression (date)" and so on.

GRAYSON & GRAYSON, LIMITED
(Formerly Eveleigh Nash and Grayson Ltd., q.v.)

In all books published by us we insert bibliographical details on the *back* of the title page as follows:

For first editions

First published by
Grayson & Grayson Ltd.
1935

For reprints

First published by
Grayson & Grayson Ltd.
May 1935
Second Impression May 1935

ROBERT HALE AND COMPANY

This Company was formed in February 1936, and we have not yet published any books—the first lot of titles will be issued next month (September).

Our books may be divided into two categories—NON-FICTION and FICTION. The title-pages of the former will bear the year of issue in roman numerals beneath our imprint at the foot; and where they are first editions the title-page itself will bear no date. When the book is reprinted the bibliography will be placed at back of title.

In the case of FICTION, the title-page will bear no date of issue, but at back of title-page will be given the month and the year when the book was first published. Any subsequent reprints will be added to that bibliography.

HAMISH HAMILTON, LTD.

When a book is first published, we print a notice at the top of the reverse of the title page reading 'First Published, 1934, 1935 or 1936," as the case may be. When we come to a second impression, we alter this notice by inserting in the top line the month upon which the book was published, January, February, etc., and beneath it we insert a second line reading. Second Impression....(Month) 1934, 1935, 1936, as the case may be, and so on for subsequent reprints.

JOHN HAMILTON, LTD.

It is our practice to have no date shown on our first edition. If the book is reprinted then the date of the first edition appears together with the reprint date underneath.

e.g. First Edition 1922.
Reprinted 1923.

HARPER & BROTHERS

(London house discontinued. Hamish Hamilton, Ltd. now are the agents for Harper & Brothers New York publications.)

Our first editions are designated by printing at the back of the title page the following words: First Edition.

∴ *See also American section.*

GEORGE G. HARRAP & CO., LTD.

Our first editions are distinguishable by the date of publication appearing on the reverse of the title-page. We print a notice in that place, running, for example:

First published 1928
By ———

followed by the name of the firm and the address. Should the book reprint the notice is added to as follows:

Reprinted March 1928

and the month of first publication is added to the original notice (the month is not put in at the outset because when a book goes to press the date of publication cannot conveniently be determined to a nicety). The notice in the case of a reprint, therefore, would be, for example:

First published June 1916
By ———
Reprinted March 1928

Succeeding reprints are entered thus:

Reprinted: July 1925; *January* 1927
February 1928

When a book has previously been printed in America or elsewhere abroad we nevertheless include "First" in the notice, implying that publication under our imprint was first made at the time referred to.

We began using our present method at some date prior to 1924.

HEATH CRANTON, LTD.

In the first edition of books published by us, the year of publication will be found on the Title page or on the back thereof. In the case of a reissue or further edition, we insert on the back of the Title page the year of the original publication with a note of the year when the reissue or further edition first appears.

W. HEFFER & SONS, LTD.

1928 Statement

It is our custom to put the date on the title page as part of our imprint. Only in the case of later impressions or editions do we put bibliographical data on the verso of the title page. May we say that although this is our invariable practice now, we have not been strictly consistent in the past.

1936 Statement

Our present custom is to put the date of the book and other bibliographical details on the verso of the title page. This is our invariable practice now, although we were not consistent in books published by us before 1930.

WILLIAM HEINEMANN, LTD.

During the early years of the history of this firm there was, I believe, no attempt made specially to designate first editions. The date of publication of a book was usually placed underneath the imprint on the title page. In some cases when further editions or further impressions were issued, the words "second edition," "third edition," etc., appeared either on the title page or on the fly overleaf, and the absence of such a notice was the only indication of the fact that the book was a first edition. In recent years, however, we have instituted the practice of printing on the back of the title page, or on a fly, a bibliographical note in all the books we publish. That is to say, on the first edition we print "First published such and such a date" and as each new impression or new edition is called for we add the note "second impression such and such a date" and so on. We take great pains to get these bibliographical notes accurate and to discriminate carefully between new impressions and new editions. In the event of a book being reprinted without any alterations in the text as it originally appeared, we call the re-issue a new impression. If the text is changed in any way we call it a New Edition.

We do not follow the American practice of printing the words "First Edition" anywhere in our books. This I believe is quite a recent idea inspired by the interest taken by the modern American in first editions of modern books.

I am afraid I cannot tell you the date at which we first began using this present method, but it was certainly soon after 1920.

JOHN HERITAGE, PUBLISHER
(*Incorporated with Unicorn Press, Ltd.*)

∴ *See Unicorn Press.*

HODDER & STOUGHTON, LTD.

We are unable to help you with regard to our First Editions, as our methods vary with every book.

THE HOGARTH PRESS

In first editions our custom is to have the year of publication on the title page and no other indication. In case of a second impression or edition we print "Second Impression (or edition)" on the title page with the year of publication and on the back the dates of first and second editions.

The method as set out has been our method since the beginning of the Press.

MARTIN HOPKINSON, LTD.

Our practice is to put the date of publication on the title page. When a reprint takes place we place on the back of the title page the usual bibliographical information "First Printed" with date—and date of reprint.

If material alterations are made in the text or format we should call the reprint a new edition.

We have followed our present practice since 1928.

GERALD HOWE, LTD.

In our first editions the top of the title-page verso either contains the statement "first published" with the date or is left blank, and in subsequent printings the dates of the first edition and of reprints and new editions are given in this place. This has been our practice since 1926 when we began business.

HURST & BLACKETT

∴ *See Hutchinson & Co., Ltd.*

HUTCHINSON & CO., LTD. (PUBLISHERS)

We do not mark First Editions in any way.

This may be taken to apply also to those firms which have amalgamated with Messrs. Hutchinson.

JARROLDS PUBLISHERS (LONDON), LTD.

In the case of first editions of all our non-fiction books, the year of issue is placed in roman numerals below our imprint on the title page. There is no reference anywhere else in the book to the fact that it is the first edition. In the event of further reprint(s) being called for, the bibliography is set up on back of title, thus, for example:

First Published May 1934
Second Impression June 1934
Third Impression August 1934

In the case of fiction, the month and year of first publication in this country are set up at back of title page, thus, for example:

First Published in Great Britain May 1934

In the event of subsequent reprint(s) the dates are set forth as in the example for non-fiction given above.

HERBERT JENKINS, LTD.

It is now our custom to put the date of our publications on the back of the title page, and if a reprint is called for we show the date of the reprint also on the back of the title page. If, however, we produce a cheap edition of the work we omit the date therefrom.

We began using our present method about 1924.

MICHAEL JOSEPH, LTD.

It is our custom to print the year of publication of our books on the reverse of the title page.

If the book is reprinted the arrangement indicated below is followed:

First published May, 1936
Second Impression June, 1936

The word "edition" is only used in the event of a cheaper reprint or when textual alterations have been effected.

ALFRED A. KNOPF, INC.

(*English house discontinued December 1930.*)

Our practice of designating our first editions is to place on the verso of the title page the legend "first published" followed by the month and year. The further impressions are designated by the number of the impression, and further editions by the number of the edition. In both cases the dates are shown.

∴ *See also American section.*

JOHN LANE THE BODLEY HEAD LIMITED

With regard to first editions, the practice here has varied in the course of time. Originally first editions had simply the date on the title page; further printings had the words "Second" or "Third Edition" as the case might be, and also the date, though there may have been cases in which the practice was varied slightly. Nowadays we print on the back of the title page the words "First Published in" followed by either the date of the year or the month and the year. In event of reprints the words are added "Second Impression" with the month and the year. In no case have we ever printed the words "First edition" on a book.

T. WERNER LAURIE, LTD.

We follow the custom laid down by the Publishers' Association; namely, we print on the *back of the title,* the words:

First Published	in	1926
Second Impression	—	1926
Third Edition	—	1928

An impression is an exact reprint of a former edition. An edition is where some alterations have been made.

We cannot tell you the exact date we first issued the form but we believe it was some time in 1925.

J. B. LIPPINCOTT COMPANY

Our books are usually designated as follows:

Copyright notice followed by the date and the name of author or this Company on the back of the title, followed by the words "First Edition" on important books. The date also sometimes appears on the front. In any case subsequent impressions are so noted on the copyright page or the bastard.

With regard to limited editions, we usually state the words "Limited edition printed from type and type distributed." This information appears as a rule on the half title; copyright notice, name of author, date, or our name also appearing on the back of the title.

We began using our present method many years ago.

∴ *See also American section.*

JOHN LONG, LIMITED

1928 Statement

New books published by us are printed with year date of Copyright on back of Title Page in the first edition and subsequent editions are marked 2nd Edition, etc., on title page. This applies to novels published at 7s.6d., the cheaper editions being issued later.

1935 Statement

Actually, though we put the date in our General Books, this practice does not apply to novels. In cases, however, where 7/6 novels are reprinted at the same price, we put Second or Third Impression, as the case may be.

We would also mention that the same procedure also applies to our affiliated company, Messrs. Andrew Melrose, Ltd.

LONGMANS, GREEN & CO., LTD.

1928 Statement

We always date the title page of our books, and unless the book is marked "—— Impression" or "—— Edition" it is a first edition.

1936 Statement

In reply to your letter we regret to say that since 1928 we have modified our practice, in that we do not now put the bibliographical information regarding edition, impression or date on the title page. It is all, however, given on the back of the title.

∴ *See also American section.*

SAMPSON LOW, MARSTON & CO., LTD.

We beg to say we have no settled rule with regard to stating on the title page or elsewhere, the date of first publication or reprints.

ALEXANDER MACLEHOSE & CO.

It is our general practice to put the date of the publication of any book on the title page itself.

If the book is reprinted, the date of the reprint appears on the title page and a bibliographical description on the back of the title.

MACMILLAN & CO., LTD.

Our first editions carry the date of publication on the title page. If the book is reprinted a statement is put on the back of the title page, saying: "First edition (say) 1900 Reprinted 1902." Any subsequent reprints are indicated in the same way. We do not call a book "second edition" unless (1) the type has been reset, or (2) very substantial alterations have been made. In that case instead of "Reprinted," "Second Edition" would be printed on the back of the title page and occasionally on the title page itself, though there is no special rule about this. The date appearing on the title page itself is the date of printing in every case.

To give a concrete example, a book that was first published in 1900 and then reprinted without much alteration in 1902, and of which a second edition appeared in 1908, would be designated as follows: On the title page the date 1908 would appear, and on the back of the title page the words:

First Edition 1900
Reprinted 1902
Second Edition 1908

We are sorry to say that it is impossible for us to give the date when we first adopted this practice.

∴ *See also American section.*

ELKIN MATHEWS & MARROT, LTD.

(*Succeeded by Ivor Nicholson & Watson, Ltd., q.v.*)

In the case of a first impression we make no special mention; subsequent printings are noted on verso of title-page. In the case of Limited Editions we insert an explanatory note. All our books without exception we date on the title-page. Such has in former years been the usual practice: it is now invariable.

Since 1933, when the policy of the firm changed and only educational text books have been issued, no indication whatsoever of a first edition or subsequent edition is given.

MEDICI SOCIETY, LTD.

As you are probably aware, we are publishers of both the Riccardi Press books, which are set by hand, and also books produced in the normal manner from machine set type. All the Riccardi Press books are published in limited editions and not reprinted, the editions being limited to the number stated on the certificate which faces the half-title. Date on title page. With our ordinary books it is usual to put the publication date:

1. On the foot of the title page, or
2. On the reverse of the title page below the line "Printed in Great Britain."

On reprints we do not usually put the date on the title page, but on the reverse, printing a bibliographical note as—

> FIRST PUBLISHED (or FIRST PRINTED) 1930
> REPRINTED (or 2d. EDITION) 1931

the difference being that if the book is printed from standing type we state REPRINTED or if the book is revised to any extent then we use the words 2d. EDITION.

ANDREW MELROSE, LTD.

∴ *See John Long, Ltd.*

METHUEN & CO., LTD.

Since 1905 all first editions of books we have published have had on the back of the title page "First

Published in ——." As and when the book is reprinted so a further note is added.

In the case of books first published in the U. S. A. the words "First published in Great Britain in ——" are used.

Limited Editions bear on the back of the title page a note to the effect that "This Edition is Limited to — copies of which this is No. —."

Translations of foreign books published by us bear on the back of the title page "First published in (French) under the title of "——————." This translation first published in Great Britain in ——."

MILLS & BOON, LTD.

We place on the back of the title page the month and the year that we publish our books; as for instance one published in January of this year would be as follows:

Published January 1936

We have used this method since we first started publishing in 1909.

FREDERICK MULLER, LTD.

On the back of the title pages of our books is a bibliographical note which reads:

"First published by Frederick Muller Ltd. (here

follows the year in which the book was published)."

When a second edition is published we add the words:

"Second Edition," and the year. We then also add the month when the first edition was published.

JOHN MURRAY

The practice we have followed for many years is to omit the date from the title page and to insert at the back of the title page the words "First Edition" together with the year of issue.

In the case of certain books, chiefly those printed for private circulation, the date appears at the foot of the title page with no biblio. on the reverse.

EVELEIGH NASH AND GRAYSON, LTD.

(*Now Grayson & Grayson, Ltd., q.v.*)

THOMAS NELSON & SONS, LTD.

1928 Statement

We have used the following three phrases on the reverse of the title page in a number of our General and Fiction publications:

First Printed ———
First Published ———
First Impression ———

When a second impression or a reprint is issued, we usually put the following in the same position:

First Impression ———
Second Impression ———

———

First Published ———
Reprinted ———

1936 Statement

We may say that the method we now use on the title page of our books is as follows:

First Published ....
Reprinted ....

GEORGE NEWNES, LTD.

We have no fixed rule. The greater part of our Book publishing work is concerned with the re-issue of books that have already appeared in library editions.

In cases where we do publish original work ourselves, we usually print the word "Copyright" and the date of issue on the back of the title page of the first edition of a book. On our second and subsequent editions or impressions we generally state under this the number of editions that have been published with the date of their publication, thus: "First Impression May, 1936, Second Impression July, 1936" and so on.

IVOR NICHOLSON & WATSON, LTD.

(*Successors to Elkin Mathews & Marrot, Ltd.*)

Our first editions are indicated by the words "First published in 1936" on the title page verso. Subsequent issues and impressions are added below and the month of original publication is also included, i.e.:

First Edition	. . .	May 1936
Reprinted	. . .	May 1936
Reprinted	. . .	June 1936

This is now our invariable practice, although since the firm started in 1931 various methods have been used.

JAMES NISBET & CO., LTD.

It is our practice to insert the date of our First and subsequent Editions of general books on the reverse of the title page.

We much regret that we cannot tell you when this practice commenced, but we have dated our editions over a considerable period.

THE NONESUCH PRESS, LTD.

Our practice is to date our books, whether they be first or subsequent editions, upon the title page; and to record upon the back of the title page or elsewhere the particular impression to which the copy belongs.

This has been our practice since the publication of our first book in 1923.

OLIVER & BOYD, LTD. (EDINBURGH)

It is our practice to put the date of the publication of any book on the title-page itself. If the book is reprinted, the date of the reprint appears on the title-page and a bibliographical description on the back of the title, e.g.

First Edition 1922
Reprinted 1923
Second Edition 1924

GEORGE OVER (RUGBY), LTD.

Our practice is to print date of publication only, and in case of later editions to state which.

THE OXFORD UNIVERSITY PRESS

We never, I think, print *first edition* on any first edition. All our title pages of first editions are dated, and so are the title pages of the first printing of editions which we distinguish as "second," "third," etc. For the information of the public we distinguish "second edition," i.e., an issue embodying substantial alterations (whether reset or not) from "second impression," i.e., an issue substantially (though not always identically) the same as the first. I know that this is not quite sound from a bibliographical point of view; but I think publishers in our position are bound to put the convenience of the public first. It is often important for a student to be sure he has the latest edition of a book; but it would be unfair to cause him to buy a mere reprint by calling it "nth edition" simply.

It is probably unnecessary to explain in this note our regular practice, when we produce an unaltered or corrected "impression," of taking the date off the title page and giving the necessary bibliographical information opposite the title page: with us, the absence of the date from the title page is a sign that the issue is not the first printing of an "edition" in our sense of the term.

We are afraid we cannot give you the date when we began using our present method of identifying first editions, but it was a good many years ago.

CECIL PALMER
(*Out of business*)

The plan we have always adopted is to print on the back of the title page "First Edition" and then the year of publication. In the event of further editions, we add to this information the following example:

First Edition	June 1927
Second Edition	September 1927
Third Edition	January 1928

ERIC PARTRIDGE, LTD.
(SCHOLARTIS PRESS)

It is our practice to put the date of the publication of any book on the title-page itself. If the book is reprinted, the date of the reprint appears on the title-page and a bibliographical description on the back of the title, e.g.

First Edition	1922
Reprinted	1923
Second Edition	1924

S. W. PARTRIDGE & CO.

∴ *See A. & C. Black, Ltd.*

POETRY BOOKSHOP

The First Editions of the Poetry Bookshop are generally designated by the words *on the back of title-page:* Published: month: year:

For second and subsequent editions the words Reprinted or 2nd Impression, etc., are *added.*

We would mention that this has only been a general rule heretofore, but it is certainly one we should be prepared to adopt in the case of future publications.

THE PORPOISE PRESS

The first impressions of our ordinary issues bear on the back of the title, to which all bibliographical matter is relegated: "First published in (date of year) by The Porpoise Press, 133a George Street, Edinburgh." On the second and subsequent impressions, there is stated "First impression (month and year); Second impression (month and year)," etc.

Where special editions have also been issued, this fact is stated on the ordinary edition, and on the special edition itself there appears a statement as to the size of the edition, etc.: e.g., "This edition, on hand-made paper, is limited to fifty signed and numbered copies. This copy is Number —"

PUTNAM & COMPANY, LTD.
(*Formerly G. P. Putnam's Sons, Ltd.*)

Our English procedure for indicating first editions is as follows:

On the reverse of the title page, we print the line

First published........

followed by the month and year.

When the book is reprinted, we retain this line, adding underneath it:

Reprinted............

followed by the month and year.

Further impressions are indicated in the same way. If, however, there is any definite alteration in matter or style, we indicate this by the words

Second edition........

followed by the month and year.

The same procedure would apply for subsequent editions.

∵ *See also American section.*

QUOTA PRESS (BELFAST)

In case of first edition the date is usually put on title page or the book is described:

First Published ....

In the case of a new impression or edition this is stated below, e.g.

First Published ....November 1930
Second Impression....December 1930

RICCARDI PRESS

∴ *See Medici Society, Ltd.*

RICH & COWAN, LIMITED

It is our custom now to put "first printing 1936" "second printing—such and such a date." In special occasions, as with H. V. Morton, we put the number printed of the first edition.

Our early system was to include the month of publication.

THE RICHARDS PRESS, LTD.

It may be taken that any book published by us is the first edition unless there appears a note on the back of the title page indicating more than one printing. It is possible that in a few cases the fact that the book is not a first edition may be indicated by the words "cheap edition" or "new edition" on the title page itself.

GEORGE ROUTLEDGE & SONS, LTD., KEGAN PAUL, TRENCH, TRUBNER & CO., LTD.

If there is no statement at all as to a second or later edition or impression, the assumption, of course, is that the book is a first edition. In the case of reprints, or new editions, we state this on the reverse of the title page.

We regret we cannot tell you the date on which this method was started but it has been going on now for a very long period.

SCHOLARTIS PRESS

∴ *See Eric Partridge, Ltd.*

CHARLES SCRIBNER'S SONS, LTD.

1928 Statement

In response to your inquiry as to the method followed by my firm distinguishing first editions, I do not think that there is any absolute hard and fast rule laid down which would apply in every case. The rule generally followed is to note on the reverse of the title page under the copyright notice the dates when the book has been reprinted. The words "First Edition" or "First Printing" do not usually appear on first editions, but if the copyright date and the date on the title page are in agreement, and there is no further note, the assumption is that the copy is a first edition. Taking half a dozen books at random I note the following details:

Edward Bok. "The Americanization of Edward Bok."

New York
Charles Scribner's Sons
1927

on the reverse—Copyright 1920, 1922 by Charles Scribner's Sons. First Edition September 1920, Second Edition November 1920, Third Edition December 1920, and so on down to 24th Edition August 1923, 25th Edition (Popular Edition) August 1923, and so on down to 34th Edition (Popular Edition) March 1924. In the meantime a different edition known as the Library Edition was published in February 1924 which goes down to the 40th Edition March 1927.

Will James. "Smoky"

Charles Scribner's Sons
New York—London
1927

Copyright 1926 by Charles Scribner's Sons. Published September 1926. Reprinted September, October, twice in November, five times in December, 1926, once in February 1927; August 1927. Popular Edition published August 1927.

Pupin. "From Immigrant to Inventor"

Charles Scribner's Sons
New York—London
1924

Copyright 1922, 1923 by Charles Scribner's Sons. Published September 1923, Reprinted November 1923, January, March, July, October 1924. In this case the copyright notice of 1922 indicates prior publication of part of the book in the Magazine, but here the actual publication date is mentioned.

The assumption is that unless otherwise stated on the reverse of the title page the book may be considered as a first edition. Of course it does not take into account such questions as issues. A mistake might be discovered while the presses were running and an alteration made in later copies. There would naturally be nothing on the book to indicate such a change.

1936 Statement

Charles Scribner's Sons, Ltd., are associated, as you doubtless understand, with Charles Scribner's Sons, New York. As far as editions which we import from America are concerned, the rule for distinguishing first editions is naturally the same as that adopted by the New York house of Charles Scribner's Sons. In future any books published separately here will bear on the title page "First Published in —," and if this coincides with the date on the title page, and there is no reprint notice, the book may be assumed to be a first edition.

∴ *See also American section.*

MARTIN SECKER & WARBURG, LTD.

(*Formerly Martin Secker, Ltd.*)

Bibliographical entry on the reverse of the title page.

Above is the new style of the firm. No alteration in policy of differentiating reprints, which has been in existence since the business began.

SEELEY, SERVICE & CO., LTD.

The following has been and is our present practice: We used to put the date on the title page of the first edition, and generally altered it, in the same position, to the date of any reprint which might follow.

Now we sometimes follow the above practice and if not, we insert the date of printing after the printer's name at the end of the book.

SELWYN & BLOUNT, LTD.

1928 Statement

We always show our first editions by the words "First Printed............" and the date. On all further editions the words "Reprinted............" and the date, are added. These words are printed on the back of the half title page.

1936 Statement

The system as originally stated has not been adhered to during the past two or three years.

SHEED AND WARD

Our usual method of indicating first editions from subsequent printings, is to add to the bibliographical note on the reverse of the title-page, the number and date of the impression. For instance the bibliographical note of the first edition will have the name and address of the printer, our name and address, and "first published September 1936," and reprints will have "2nd impression September 1936" added beneath "first published." In the case of a new *edition* "2nd edition, October 1936."

This method applies only to books published by us in England.

∴ *See also American section.*

SHELDON PRESS

∴ *See Society for Promoting Christian Knowledge, of which it is an offshoot.*

SIDGWICK AND JACKSON, LTD.

1928 Statement

We do not designate our first editions at all, except by the negative method of there being no second or later edition or impression indicated on the back of the title page. Occasionally we state "Second Impression" or so on, on the front of the title page.

1935 Statement

If there is no indication, either on the front or the back of the title-page of any of our publications, that the issue is a second or later edition or impression, it must be taken to be the only, and therefore the first, edition or impression.

We have employed this method from the start of this business in 1909.

SKEFFINGTON & SON, LTD.

It is not our practice to insert the date of publication on the title page of our new books. In cases where they are reprinted, second, third, or fourth impressions, are printed on the title page and where new editions are issued, the words "New Edition" are also printed.

Our First Editions are therefore quite easy to identify as the title page appears without date and no reference to any edition.

SOCIETY FOR PROMOTING CHRISTIAN KNOWLEDGE
and
THE SHELDON PRESS

It is our practice to put the date of the publication of any book on the title-page itself. If the book is reprinted, the date of the reprint appears on the title-page and a bibliographical description on the back of the title-page, e.g. First Edition 1922

Reprinted 1923
Second Edition 1924

If only slight corrections are made we put Second Impression: and Second Edition when changes in the text are important.

ELLIOT STOCK

The first editions of our publications are marked with the date thereof upon the title page. All later editions carry the record, i.e., the date of the first edition, and of the subsequent editions or reprints as the case may be.

STREET & MASSEY, LTD.

It is our rule to place on the title page of each book the year in which the book is last printed. On the back of the title page we clearly state:

First published in January, 1936

This indicates the initial printing. After this:

Second Impression March, 1936
Third Impression June, 1936
Second Edition (Revision) January, 1937
Fifth Impression June, 1937

We have adopted the use of the word revision in brackets after every new edition. Collectors are quite aware that a new edition is (or should be) a revision, but the general public is not so sure and we prefer to emphasise the fact.

UNICORN PRESS, LTD.
(*Incorporating John Heritage, Publisher*)

It is our practice to put the date of the publication of any book on the verso of the title-page. If the book is reprinted, the date of the reprint appears on the verso of the title-page under the original insertion.

It should read so:

First printed February 1935

In the case of a reprint, as above, but with the following appended:

Reprinted May 1935

WARD, LOCK & CO. LIMITED

1928 Statement

We have no fixed method of designating our first editions.

1935 Statement

Generally speaking, at the present time we are placing on the back of the title page:

First published in ....

FREDERICK WARNE & CO., LTD.

We did at one time mark first editions of our publications with a private mark, but we are afraid the habit has been discontinued over a number of years now, and we have even lost trace of the private marks.

WILLIAMS & NORGATE LTD.

Our usual practice, adopted a good many years ago, is to put the date of original publication and particulars of any reprint on the back of the title page. Thus:

> First printed in Great Britain in 1934
> Second impression (or) Reprinted
> Third (revised) edition, 1935

Very occasionally the date appears on the title page itself.

WISHART & CO., LTD.

1928 Statement

The title page carries the date of the edition. On the back of the title page there are the words "First published in . . . . . ." The date of the second and subsequent editions and impressions is printed below this. First editions are therefore not specifically marked as such.

1935 Statement

We do not print any bibliographical information on the back of the title page, unless the book goes into a second impression, in which case we give details as to date. The absence of such information implies therefore that the copy is a first edition.

H. F. & G. WITHERBY, LTD.

Our usual practice is always to give a full biblio. on the reverse of the title page. In certain cases the date appears in the title page, but more usually the date of publication appears on the biblio.

NOTES